The Old Testament in Eastern Orthodox Tradition

EUGEN J. PENTIUC

OXFORD
UNIVERSITY PRESS

OXFORD
UNIVERSITY PRESS

Oxford University Press is a department of the University of Oxford.
It furthers the University's objective of excellence in research, scholarship,
and education by publishing worldwide.

Oxford New York

Auckland Cape Town Dar es Salaam Hong Kong Karachi
Kuala Lumpur Madrid Melbourne Mexico City Nairobi
New Delhi Shanghai Taipei Toronto

With offices in

Argentina Austria Brazil Chile Czech Republic France Greece
Guatemala Hungary Italy Japan Poland Portugal Singapore
South Korea Switzerland Thailand Turkey Ukraine Vietnam

Oxford is a registered trade mark of Oxford University Press
in the UK and certain other countries.

Published in the United States of America by
Oxford University Press
198 Madison Avenue, New York, NY 10016

© Oxford University Press 2014

Library of Congress Cataloging-in-Publication Data
Pentiuc, Eugen J., 1955–
The Old Testament in Eastern Orthodox tradition / Eugen J. Pentiuc.
p. cm.
Includes bibliographical references.
ISBN 978–0–19–533123–3 (paperback) — ISBN 978–0–19–533122–6 (cloth)
1. Bible. Old Testament—Canon. 2. Bible—Study and teaching—Eastern churches.
3. Orthodox Eastern Church—Doctrines. I. Title.
BS465.P467 2014
221.088'2819—dc23
2013028095
9780195331226
9780195331233 (pbk.)

To Flora, Daniel, and Cristina

If the faithful are keeping vigil in the church,
David is first, middle, and last.
If at dawn anyone wishes to sing hymns,
David is first, middle, and last.
In the holy monasteries, among the ranks of the heavenly warriors,
David is first, middle, and last.
In the convents of virgins, who are imitators of Mary,
David is first, middle, and last.
In the deserts, where men hold converse with God,
David is first, middle, and last.

PSEUDO-CHRYSOSTOM, *De poenitentia*

Contents

Preface and Acknowledgments

Unless the Lord builds the house, those who build it
labor in vain.
Ps 126[127]:1

THE PURPOSE OF this book is to provide a general overview and a succinct analysis of the primary modes in which the Old Testament has been received, interpreted and conveyed within Eastern Orthodox tradition.

There exists a common assumption, not only among non-Orthodox, that the Eastern Orthodox use the Septuagint text exclusively, following closely the patristic interpretations of the Scripture as the only abiding authority, leaving almost no room for other text-witnesses and hermeneutical ventures. This faulty assumption arises from the dearth of Eastern Orthodox literature regarding the topic of this book.

Among the few works on this topic authored or edited by Orthodox scholars, one may mention first Georges Florovsky's *Bible, Church, Tradition: An Eastern Orthodox View* (Nordland Press, 1972). In this collection, consisting of seven of Florovsky's previously printed articles, the Russian theologian argues for a return to the Gospels, Chalcedon, and church fathers, a common Christian desideratum going beyond the great schism between East and West. In *The New Testament: An Orthodox Perspective* (Holy Cross Orthodox Press, 1977), Theodore G. Stylianopoulos offers a synthesis of traditional Orthodox biblical exegesis as represented by church fathers and modern biblical scholarship, reassessing the need for a balanced use of ancient and modern modes of interpretation. A special contribution of this work is the treatment of biblical hermeneutics as a multilevel endeavor (exegetical, interpretive and transformative) within today's ecumenical context. Stylianopoulos also edited a collection of essays authored by Orthodox biblical scholars, *Sacred Text*

and Interpretation: Perspectives in Orthodox Biblical Studies (Holy Cross
Orthodox Press, 2006), on a broad array of topics from text-critical analysis to biblical theology and hermeneutics pertaining to the Old and New
Testaments. This collection and the international Orthodox biblical studies conference, held on the campus of Holy Cross Greek Orthodox School
of Theology (Brookline, MA) in the fall of 2003, demonstrate the need for
a more articulate and critical examination of the Old Testament's place
in Eastern Orthodox tradition. This topic finds a thorough and in-depth
analysis in John Breck's *Scripture in Tradition: The Bible and Its Interpretation in the Orthodox Church* (St. Vladimir's Seminary Press, 2001), which
surveys the patristic views on Scripture as compartment of Tradition. The
first part of the book—the only section which pertains substantively to
Scripture—offers a fresh look at the way Eastern patristic writers used
Scripture in elaborating what would become the body of Orthodox doctrine. This part deals with aims and methods of biblical interpretation as
they were developed by the Greek church fathers.

The scarcity of information on this topic is even more evident at the
level of recent reference works. Less than ten pages are allocated to the
interpretation of the Scripture in Eastern Orthodoxy in post-Byzantine
times in the following three titles: David Noel Freedman, *The Anchor Bible
Dictionary* (Doubleday, 1992); Bruce M. Metzger and Michael D. Coogan,
The Oxford Companion to the Bible (Oxford University Press, 1993); and
John H. Hayes, *Dictionary of Biblical Interpretation* (Abingdon, 1999). It
is my conviction that the absence of any comparable work on this topic as
well as the ongoing interest in the history of the interpretation will make
both Orthodox and non-Orthodox readers benefit from this current book.

I dare say this project began a long time ago, in 1968, when the
Romanian Orthodox Biblical Institute in Bucharest published the *Fourth
Synodal Bible.* A mere 100,000 copies of the 1968 edition were printed
for an Orthodox population of almost 20 million. I was 13 years old at
that time. That was my first encounter with the printed Word of God, an
experience I will never forget. In communist Romania, reading and disseminating the Bible was nearly considered a crime. Except for Leviticus,
Numbers, and a few other books, I surreptitiously read the entire Bible
within one week. Visualizations from my own readings were interweav-
ing with images from frescoes and portable icons I would often see in my
local church. Words heard during Orthros and Liturgy were mingling
with printed words from the Bible. Everything became quite familiar, as
something that had always been with me, but now—for the first time—I

came to realize the majestic pervasiveness of Scripture in my tiny Eastern Orthodox universe. A desire was born to share with others the sheer joy of rediscovering the Word of God in liturgy and the biblical stories embedded in hymns and icons. The genius of Eastern Orthodox liturgy lies in its fascinating interplay of sounds, texts, and images.

Years later and worlds apart, during my doctoral studies at Harvard I was a teaching assistant to James Kugel. In his large, wonderful class of nearly 1,000 undergraduate students, questions arose regarding the Orthodox stance on various biblical issues—from canon to text witnesses and hermeneutics. Then, I felt there was a need for an introduction to the Old Testament written from an Eastern Orthodox perspective. Later, during a conversation with Michael D. Coogan, the idea of writing a survey reached maturity—a survey aiming to underscore the specificity of Eastern Orthodox Church in approaching and integrating the Old Testament into her doctrinal, liturgical, and spiritual tapestry. Historical surveys of ancient Jewish and Christian interpretations of the Bible are not new. What is new is a survey of Eastern Orthodox reception and interpretation of the Old Testament.

The term "Old Testament" in this book's title refers primarily to the Septuagint, the Greek version of the Jewish Bible, attested by fourth and fifth century Christian manuscripts. However, as will be seen throughout this work, the Eastern Orthodox Church has never closed the door to other text-witnesses, nor suppressed interpreters' efforts to dig into the unfamiliar text of the Hebrew Bible for key terms or reading variants.

While the notion of tradition is discussed amply in the first part of this book, a few remarks regarding the second part of the title, "Eastern Orthodox tradition," are warranted.

The term "orthodox" was used for the first time in the fifth century to distinguish authentic from heretical doctrine. In the sixth century, under the rule of the Emperor Justinian, Orthodox Christianity achieved its definitive character as the dominant religion of the Eastern Roman Empire. After the construction of Hagia Sophia (532–37 C.E.), Constantinople became the center of Chalcedonian Byzantine Orthodoxy. However, "Orthodox" as a term referring to the Eastern Orthodox Church was not employed until the ninth century.

Territorially, the Eastern Orthodox Church comprises the churches from the East that follow the Byzantine rite developed in Constantinople between the fourth and tenth centuries. These churches include the Greek-Byzantine Rite (Patriarchate of Constantinople, Church of Greece, Church of Cyprus), Arabic Byzantine Rite (Antioch, Jerusalem, Alexandria, Sinai), Georgian-Byzantine Rite (Churches of the Caucasus Range, subsequently absorbed by the Russian Church and forced in the nineteenth and twentieth century to employ the Slavonic Liturgy), Slavonic-Byzantine Rite (Russian, Serbian, Bulgarian Churches), and Romanian-Byzantine Rite (Romanian Church). Nevertheless, due to this geographic, linguistic and ethnic variety, oversimplifications and generalizations are unavoidable.

Chronologically, the Eastern Orthodox tradition extends from early Christian "orthodoxy" to modern Orthodoxy. Well-defined tenets of Eastern Orthodoxy can be detected already in the early phases of "orthodoxy." The uniqueness of Eastern Orthodoxy stems from its blending of ancient and modern sources into a harmonious whole. Thus, John Chrysostom's homilies can be found side-by-side with Georges Florovsky's works in any Orthodox theological discourse. Still, Eastern Orthodoxy is not a mere linearity commencing with the apostolic phase, climaxing in the patristic, and continuing with the "postpatristic" period. Rather, it is best represented by a circle, reflecting church life, with boundaries flexible enough to accommodate further soundings, reflections, and working conclusions.

Given the holistic and all embracing character of the Eastern Orthodox ethos, this book cannot be a neutral survey of how the Eastern Orthodox dealt with the Scripture in the past, much less an entirely dispassionate analysis of various ways of interpretation. As an Orthodox theologian and biblical scholar, I am part of this unfolding Eastern Orthodox tradition. Therefore, my analysis of occurrences past and present within my own faith tradition informs my own inquiry into various issues pertaining to the appropriation and interpretation of the Old Testament.

This special emphasis on Eastern Orthodox tradition distinguishes my book from a recent volume, *The Old Testament in Byzantium*, edited by Paul Magdalino and Robert Nelson (Dumbarton Oaks, 2010). The latter work seeks to examine the interrelation between the Old Testament and Byzantium at societal, cultural, and political levels. Historically and culturally Byzantium put an indelible mark on the Eastern Orthodox Church. However, the more general designation "Byzantine" cannot be identified with the much more specific reality of "Eastern Orthodox tradition," which comprises the subject of the present text.

This book addresses Orthodox seminarians and educated lay readers in an effort to articulate the characteristics of Eastern Orthodox reception and interpretation of the Old Testament, while increasing awareness of the importance of the Old Testament for their own tradition. It also fills a vacuum in scholarly literature dealing with the history of interpretation by showing to non-Orthodox readers the various ways in which Eastern Orthodoxy used the Old Testament throughout its history.

This dual audience and purpose constrains the present book to the status of a modest, initial research, while diminishing considerably its "objective" character, assuming that the notion of objectivity is applicable. For this reason, my work can merely scratch the surface of a profoundly fascinating topic. The study offers a concise yet thorough examination of the reception and interpretation of the Old Testament in Eastern Orthodox tradition. I do not offer a *vademecum* of this topic. Nor am I providing a perfect and errorless investigation. I would like my readers, however, to find in these pages a useful introduction to a topic that has never been broached as thoroughly.

The book is divided in two parts. Part I (Reception) deals with issues pertaining to the reception of the Old Testament by the early Christian and Eastern Orthodox Church. Chapter 1 (One Bible, Two Covenants) discusses the paradox that the Christian Bible hosts the "Scripture" of a different religion—that of Judaism. The unity in diversity of the Christian Bible is examined by means of the works of the church fathers. Chapter 2 (Text) emphasizes the flexible way of coping with biblical texts in Eastern Orthodoxy. While considering the Septuagint the default Bible of the Church, the Eastern Orthodox are also cognizant of the value of other text-witnesses such as the Hebrew text. Chapter 3 (Canon) underscores the peculiarity of the Eastern Orthodox Church with respect to the open-endedness of the biblical canon. Chapter 4 (Tradition) takes on a much debated topic—the relationship between Scripture and Tradition—while seeking to redeem the centrality of the former within the interpretive and operative context of the towering Tradition. Part II (Interpretation) offers the reader a rich repertoire of pertinent sources, from the literary to the visual and aural. Chapter 5 (Discursive) examines the discursive mode of interpretation—the patristic exegesis. Chapter 6 (Aural) handles the most important part of Tradition, the liturgy and the specific way to read and interpret the Old Testament—liturgical exegesis—under a wide variety of genres (e.g., scriptural lessons, psalmody, hymns, homilies, *synaxaria*). Chapter 7 (Visual) oversees the visual mode of scriptural interpretation, as reflected through church iconography (e.g., portable icons, mosaics, frescoes, manuscript illuminations).

This book has been a long time in the making.

A good portion of the writing of this book occurred during my sabbatical year 2009–2010, when I won concomitantly two fellowships: the Lilly Faculty Fellowship and the Fulbright Scholar Fellowship at the University of Athens in Greece. These fellowships provided me both with time to write and a sense of my project's importance. Special recognition is owed to the Association of Theological Schools and the Council for International Exchange of Scholars, which administer these fellowships, for their support.

I am in debt to the following colleagues who carefully read various drafts and offered substantive comments and suggestions: John Behr, Michael D. Coogan, Allan Emery, Christopher Frechette, Matthias Henze, Stefka Kancheva, Demetrios Katos, Jon D. Levenson, Maximos of Simono-petra, Carey C. Newman, Stephen Ryan, Theodore G. Stilianopoulos, and Olivier-Thomas Venard.

My heartfelt thanks are for Matthew Baker, who closely read each chapter and offered insightful comments and detailed editorial suggestions at each step of the process.

In addition, I wish to thank Theodore Niklasson, Bogue (Elias) Stevens, John Bociu, and Michael Jewler for their financial support.

Senior editor Cynthia Read, Marcela Maxfield, and Maria Pucci at Oxford University Press, Gandhimathi Ganesan at Integra, and copy-editor Marcia Youngman have my gratitude for their professionalism and unfailing patience.

To my dear wife Flora, and our beloved children, Daniel and Cristina, thank you for your love. To you I dedicate this book as a token of deep appreciation.

Glory to the long-suffering Bridegroom of the Church (*Nymphios tēs Ekklēsias*) who has always guided, strengthened, and surprised me with his unexpected and gratuitous gifts.

Eugen J. Pentiuc   Brookline, Massachusetts
April 5, 2013
The Great Lent

Abbreviations

General

b.	born
B.C.E.	Before the Common Era
C.E.	Common Era
ca.	circa
cf.	*confer*, compare
d.	died
e.g.	*exempli gratia*, for example
ed(s).	editor(s), edited by
etc.	et cetera, and the rest
f.	folio
f(f).	and the following one(s)
Gk.	Greek
Heb.	Hebrew
Ibid.	Ibidem
i.e.	*id est*, that is
inter alia	among others
l(l)	line(s)
LXX	Septuagint (the Greek Old Testament)
ms(s).	manuscript(s)
MT	Masoretic Text
NF	Neue Folge (new series)
n(n).	note(s)
no.	number

NT	New Testament
OG	Old Greek (the Greek Old Testament)
OL	Old Latin (the Latin Old Testament)
OT	Old Testament
par.	parallel
r	recto
S	Peshitta (the Syriac Old Testament)
Sam.	Samaritan Pentateuch
sic	*sicut*, thus, just as
Tg(s).	Targum(s)
UBS	United Bible Societies
v	verso
V	Vulgate
v(v).	verse(s).
vol(s).	volume(s).
vs.	versus

Primary Sources

Hebrew Bible / Old Testament

Gen	Genesis
Exod	Exodus
Lev	Leviticus
Num	Numbers
Deut	Deuteronomy
Josh	Joshua
Judg	Judges
Ruth	Ruth
1–2 Sam	1–2 Samuel
1–2 Kgdms	1–2 Kingdoms (LXX)
1–2 Kgs	1–2 Kings
3–4 Kgdms	3–4 Kingdoms (LXX)
1–2 Chr	1–2 Chronicles
Ezra	Ezra

Neh	Nehemiah
Esth	Esther
Job	Job
Ps / Pss	Psalms
Prov	Proverbs
Eccl	Ecclesiastes
Song	Song of Songs
Isa	Isaiah
Jer	Jeremiah
Lam	Lamentations
Ezek	Ezekiel
Dan	Daniel
Hos	Hosea
Joel	Joel
Amos	Amos
Obad	Obadiah
Jonah	Jonah
Mic	Micah
Nah	Nahum
Hab	Habakkuk
Zeph	Zephaniah
Hag	Haggai
Zech	Zechariah
Mal	Malachi

New Testament

Matt	Matthew
Mark	Mark
Luke	Luke
John	John
Acts	Acts
Rom	Romans
1–2 Cor	1–2 Corinthians

Gal	Galatians
Eph	Ephesians
Phil	Philippians
Col	Colossians
1–2 Thess	1–2 Thessalonians
1–2 Tim	1–2 Timothy
Titus	Titus
Phlm	Philemon
Heb	Hebrews
Jas	James
1–2 Pet	1–2 Peter
1–2–3 John	1–2–3 John
Jude	Jude
Rev	Revelation

Septuagint Additions

Bar	Baruch
Add Dan	Additions to Daniel
Pr Azar	Prayer of Azariah
Bel	Bel and the Dragon
Sg Three	Song of the Three Young Men
Sus	Susanna
1–2 Esd	1–2 Esdras
Add Esth	Additions to Esther
Ep Jer	Epistle of Jeremiah
Jdt	Judith
1–2 Macc	1–2 Maccabees
3–4 Macc	3–4 Maccabees
Pr Man	Prayer of Manasseh
Ps 151	Psalm 151
Sir	Sirach / Ecclesiasticus
Tob	Tobit
Wis	Wisdom of Solomon

Dead Sea Scrolls

CD	Damascus Document
Q	Qumran
P	Pesher (commentary)
1QpHab	Commentary on Habakkuk
4QpPsalms	Commentary on Psalms
1QIsa[b]	Isaiah[b]
4QJer[a, b, d]	Jeremiah[a, b, d]
8HevXIIgr	Naḥal Ḥever (Greek translation of the Minor Prophets)

Mishnah, Talmud, and Related Literature

b.	*Talmud Bavli* (Babylonian Talmud)
m.	*Mishnah* (Mishnah)
t.	*Tosefta*
y.	*Talmud Yerushalmi* (Jerusalem Talmud)
Meg.	*Megillah*
Nid.	*Niddah*
Pesah.	*Pesahim*
Qidd.	*Qiddushin*
Sanh.	*Sanhedrin*
Shabb.	*Shabbat*
Sof.	*Soferim*
Sot.	*Sotah*
Yad.	*Yadayim*

Secondary Sources

ABD	*Anchor Bible Dictionary.* Edited by D. N. Freedman. 6 vols. New York: Doubleday, 1992.
ACR	*Australasian Catholic Record*
ANF	*Ante-Nicene Fathers*
BA	*Biblical Archaeologist*
BASOR	*Bulletin of the American Schools of Oriental Research*
BDB	Brown, F., S. R. Driver, and C. A. Briggs. *A Hebrew and English Lexicon of the Old Testament.* Oxford, 1907

BH(K)	*Biblia Hebraica*, ed. R. Kittel
BHQ	*Biblia Hebraica Quinta*
BHS	*Biblia Hebraica Stuttgartensia*
BIOSCS	*Bulletin of the International Organization for Septuagint and Cognate Studies*
CBQ	*Catholic Biblical Quarterly*
GOTR	*Greek Orthodox Theological Review*
HALOT	Koehler, L., W. Baumgartner, and J. J. Stamm. *The Hebrew and Aramaic Lexicon of the Old Testament.* Translated and edited under the supervision of M. E. J. Richardson. 4 vols. Leiden, 1994–99
HTR	*Harvard Theological Revue*
HTS	Harvard Theological Studies
HUBP	*The Hebrew University Bible Project*
HUCA	*Hebrew Union College Annual*
IDBSup	*Interpreter's Dictionary of the Bible: Supplementary Volume.* Edited by K. Crim. Nashville, 1976
JBL	*Journal of Biblical Literature*
JETS	*Journal of the Evangelical Theological Society*
JJS	*Journal of Jewish Studies*
JPS	Jewish Publication Society
JQR	*Jewish Quarterly Review*
JSOT	Journal for the Study of the Old Testament
JSS	*Journal of Semitic Studies*
JTS	*Journal of Theological Studies*
KJV	King James Version of the English Bible
NETS	*A New English Translation of the Septuagint.* Edited by Albert Pietersma and Benjamin G. Wright. New York: Oxford University Press, 2007
NPNF[1]	*The Nicene and Post-Nicene Fathers*, Series 1
NPNF[2]	*The Nicene and Post-Nicene Fathers*, Series 2
ODB	*The Oxford Dictionary of Byzantium.* Edited by Alexander P. Kazdhan. New York: Oxford University Press, 1991

OtSt	*Oudtestamentische Studiën*
PG	Patrologia graeca [= Patrologiae cursus completus: Series graeca]. Edited by J.-P. Migne. 162 vols. Paris, 1857–86
PL	Patrologia latina [= Patrologiae cursus completus: Series latina]. Edited by J.-P. Migne. 217 vols. Paris, 1844–64
RB	*Revue biblique*
RHPhR	*Revue d'Histoire et de Philosophie Religieuses*
RQ	*Revue de Qumran*
SBL	Society of Biblical Literature
SBLEJL	Society of Biblical Literature Early Judaism and Its Literature
SC	Sources chrétiennes. Paris: Cerf, 1943–
SVTQ	*St. Vladimir's Theological Quarterly*
TEH	*Theologische Existenz Heute*
TLG	*Thesaurus linguae graecae: Canon of Greek Authors and Works.* Edited by L. Berkowitz and K. A. Squitier. Oxford, 1990
VT	*Vetus Testamentum*
VTSup	Supplements to Vetus Testamentum
ZAW	*Zeitschrift für die alttestamentliche Wissenschaft*
ZNW	*Zeitschrift für die neutestamentliche Wissenschaft und die Kunde der älteren Kirche*

The Old Testament in Eastern Orthodox Tradition

PART I

Reception

One Bible, Two Covenants

The Law and the Prophets, the Church unites in one
volume with the writings of evangelists and apostles, from
which she drinks in her faith.

TERTULLIAN, The Prescription Against Heretics 36

An Ancient Icon and Its Ageless Message
The Face with Two Looks

The pilgrim stepping into St. Catherine's Monastery on Mount Sinai has the privilege of admiring one of the oldest portable icons that outlived the fury of the iconoclasm of the eighth through ninth centuries. The icon, rendered in encaustic on panel, is known as *Christos Pantokrator*, "Christ Almighty," or simply "The Sinai Christ" (Fig. 1.1). Throughout the centuries, this icon has become the model for all the Pantocrator representations situated in the central domes or on the ceilings over the nave in Eastern Orthodox churches. Unlike the later iconic epigones executed in fresco, mosaic, or other techniques, often depicting a threatening and impassable Lord, however, the Sinai icon represents a quite peculiar Jesus, a Jesus with two different looks: a tolerant human being yet an implacable judge. The right side of his face shows a mild countenance, whereas the left displays a harsher visage, evidenced by a dilated pupil. And the effect of these two different looks is intensified by the position of the hands: while the right hand blesses the viewer, the left clasps tightly a bejeweled book, cross sealed and covered in leather.

Although the artist's original intent will probably never be recovered,[1] the basic meaning of this icon dating from the glorious reign of Justinian

FIGURE 1.1 Christ Pantokrator, portable icon, Monastery of St. Catherine, Mount Sinai.
(Photo: By permission of St. Catherine Monastery.)

(527–65 c.e.) can be decoded. Jesus is at once a compassionate friend and a stern judge, ready both to bless and to convict. The Sinai Jesus is, to quote Irenaeus (115–202 c.e.), "the Savior of those who are saved, and the Judge of those who are judged" (*Against Heresies*, 3.4.2).[2]

Apparently, the anonymous iconographer who "wrote" the Sinai portrait had grappled with the same question as the modern man, believer or nonbeliever: Who is Jesus? Was he a first-century Galilean rabbi, who met his untimely fate at the hands of cruel Roman authority in Jerusalem? An itinerant apocalyptic prophet, in perpetual conflict with Jewish authority? An enigmatic Jewish sage, given to offering contradictory wisdom sayings? A former Pharisee who taught and lived his faith in a more tolerant and inclusive way than most of his fellow party members? Or is he the incarnate Lord, the touchable "icon" of the untouchable and holy Lord (Yahweh / *Kyrios*), the Son of God made flesh and dwelling among men?

To put the matter somewhat differently: Was he the Jesus of the New Testament as recorded by the Gospels? If so, which Gospel? Was he the Jesus of the Pauline epistles? Was he the Jesus of a particular Christian tradition? Or was he the one whom biblical scholars seek to "liberate" from the Church's century-long dogmatic monopoly?

The Orthodox Church affirms that her Jesus is the same one spoken of by the Scriptures and known within the living medium of church tradition. The Sinai icon is just one small example of this living tradition. As we will see, this tradition is seasoned with liturgical flavors and choreographed by fathers, councils, and the piety of laypeople. For the Orthodox, Jesus cannot be fragmented—at the very least, a fragmented Jesus has nothing to do with the Jesus known in the church worship. *The* Jesus of Orthodox tradition is a person at once intricate and simple. A life cannot be simplified or reduced to one single facet. Yet too intricate a picture, made of too many facets, would again lead to fragmentation. The Orthodox vision embodies a balanced way between simplicity and intricacy in presenting Jesus's profile.

Just as the Sinai icon bespeaks both Jesus's compassionate humbleness and his forensic lordship, so too the most obvious element of the apostolic preaching (*kērygma*) is the fascinating mixture of weakness and strength in Jesus's persona. This alloy links all the four canonical Gospels in full circle, despite dissimilarities among them. And again, it is about the face with two looks, the hands at once blessing and wielding a cross-sealed book.

Here is Paul speaking of the *kenosis*, or "self-emptying," of the Logos become flesh, in which glory and humility are seen to coexist:

> Though he was in the form of God, did not regard equality with God as something to be exploited, but emptied himself, taking the form of a slave, being born in human likeness. And being found in human form, he humbled himself and became obedient to the point of death—even death on a cross. Therefore God also highly exalted him and gave him the name that is above every name, so

that at the name of Jesus every knee should bend, in heaven and on earth and under the earth, and every tongue should confess that Jesus Christ is Lord, to the glory of God the Father.

Phil 2:6–11

It is the same mixture of high dignity or power and weakness as in the Sinai icon. Jesus is the high priest who is capable of feeling human weaknesses:

Since, then, we have a great high priest who has passed through the heavens, Jesus, the Son of God, let us hold fast to our confession. For we do not have a high priest who is unable to sympathize with our weaknesses, but we have one who in every respect has been tested as we are, yet without sin. Let us therefore approach the throne of grace with boldness, so that we may receive mercy and find grace to help in time of need.

Heb 4:14–16

How can one depict this indescribable mix of compassion and rigor, which is glimpsed already in the first canonical Gospels? "By two different looks," replies quietly the anonymous "writer" of the Sinai icon.

Nowhere are these antinomies consisting of tensive aspects—weakness and power, humbleness and glory—better recorded than in the Fourth Gospel. Here, Jesus is able to master the natural phenomena (John 6:19) yet also sheds tears at Lazarus's tomb (John 11:35). In the words of Harold W. Attridge, "To reduce these tensive elements to indices of documentary development ignores their conceptual role. . . . The handling of the Son of Man sayings betrays a deliberate appropriation of traditions about Jesus, holding assertions about glory and suffering in an ironic tension that invites the reader or hearer of the gospel to contemplate the significance of the cross."[3]

The polarizing sayings surrounding the messianic title "Son of Man" have the same role as the face with two looks. They invite the reader to take a closer glimpse at Jesus before reducing him to either a mere human being or a strictly divine character. Like the beholder of the Sinai icon, the reader of the Gospels is invited to savor the mysterious aura of the "Son of Man" and, in doing so, to rediscover the sense of wonder a child experiences at the hearing of a fairy tale.

It is not surprising that, faced with this reality, the emerging Church was confronted from the onset with the temptation of "another Jesus"

(2 Cor 11:4) than the one preached by the apostles. The most elusive figure of human history escapes the easy and audacious construals of the human mind. Our terminology is too weak, too narrow to describe the complexity or the irreducible simplicity of Jesus of Nazareth.

In Luke's telling of the story of the Transfiguration, we learn that as Jesus was praying, "the appearance of his face became different (*heteron*)" (Luke 9:29).[4] Perhaps the "different" face is a hint at Jesus's future destiny, the one willing to identify himself with the "least" of his "brothers" (cf. Matt 25:40). Yet what is even more interesting in the Transfiguration pericope are the words conveyed by the heavenly voice: "Listen to him" (Luke 9:35). Listening takes precedence over seeing in matters of faith (Rom 10:17). The "otherness" of Jesus proposed by the Transfiguration narrative becomes a matter of faith, rather than a simple experiment mediated by seeing.

In Eastern Orthodox tradition, this perpetual, ever-puzzling "otherness" of the Lord Jesus lives on in the liturgical setting, where a wealth of media involving all the senses echo a quite intricate profile of Jesus anchored simultaneously in past, present, and future. The Orthodox see Jesus in this holistic way, with special focus on personal and communal relationship with him. Modern distinctions between a Jesus of history, a Jesus of piety, and a Jesus of this or that distinct New Testament text are foreign to Eastern Orthodox tradition and, even today, strange to Orthodox ears.

The Sinai icon is an open-ended invitation to encounter this one Jesus, whose witness is perpetuated from written to colored words. It is a tacit beckoning to plumb the mystery, the bare outlines of which the fathers gathered at Chalcedon in 451 C.E. sought to trace in their fourfold formula: "one and the same Christ, Son, Lord, only begotten, to be acknowledged in two natures, inconfusedly, unchangeably, indivisibly, inseparably (*asynchytos, atreptos, adiaretos, achoristos*)."

A Blessing Hand and a Cross-Sealed Book

But the Sinai icon is not only about Jesus's own mysterious profile, with its divine and human facets. It also shows a close relationship between Jesus and the Book.

If one takes another look, one notices that while Jesus's right hand is blessing, his left hand is holding a closed, cross-sealed book. Later Byzantine iconographers would open the book up and inscribe inside of it words uttered by Jesus as recorded in the canonical Gospels. When opened, the inscribed verses identify the tome clearly as the gospel book. But in the Sinai icon, the book is closed.

Closed also is one's access to a definitive answer to a pressing, un- avoidable question: Is it a gospel book or the entire Bible containing the two testaments? Probably the anonymous artist wanted the focus to fall on the cross marked on the cover, rather than on the book itself. Indeed, the cross functions as a central seal of the book. If one considers that the harsh look of Jesus's face is on the left side, then the cross-sealed book gripped in his left hand might connote the truth that Christ will judge according to the precepts found in the book. Or that he will judge those who resisted the book and its healing sign, the cross.

The blessing hand and the softer look of the side of Jesus's face above it tell us of his openness and willingness to be looked for, approached, and reached in a personal dialogue. The other hand, holding the closed book, speaks of the importance of Scripture in the life of those who would enter into this dialogue.

A blessing hand and a sealed book define Christianity both as religion of the book[5] and religion of a person, centered on a living ongoing dia- logue between Jesus and his followers: "And remember, I am with you always, to the end of the age" (Matt 28:20). This comes in stark contrast with the earlier cry of 2 Baruch 85:3: "We have left our land, and Zion has been taken away from us, and we have nothing now apart from the Mighty One and his Law."[6]

Christianity has always understood itself as a faith and way of life based on one person's life and sacrifice—that of Christ, and on written records containing the Word of God handed over by prophets and apostles—the books of Old and New Testaments. There is no Scripture without Christ as there is no Christ without Scripture; and this is true for all the his- torical phases of Christianity. Knowledge of Christ's person and knowl- edge of the Scriptures are interdependent elements that make up the very fabric of Christian faith.[7]

The raising of the right hand in blessing is a priestly, liturgical ges- ture, while the other hand is shown gripping tightly the cross-sealed book as if to invite and direct attention toward the precious trove. By this double gesture, the figure with the mysterious two looks suggests that one may approach him in two complementary ways. One may approach him by opening the book and reading its words—never overlooking the cross and the passion signified by it, which is the seal of the entire book, its unifying element. And one may approach him through the hand raised in priestly blessing: through personal dialogue commenced and fostered within the liturgical setting of communal worship. Two ways of discovering Christ: the written word and the liturgical worship.

The same interplay between the written word and live, personal communication is attested further by the Orthodox Divine Liturgy itself, with its two main parts: the "liturgy of the Word" and the "liturgy of the Eucharist." Like the two hands of the Sinai icon, the two parts of the Divine Liturgy are inseparable. Word and worship are two complementary, intertwining ways toward discovering and rediscovering Christ, and deciphering the enigmatic "code" of his face with its two looks. Worship without word may end up into unwanted magical practices or hollow ritualism. Yet word without worship risks becoming a bookish exercise, with no roots or fruit in reality past or present. It may even turn Christ into a lifeless object of research, disfiguring an irreducible persona into scattered little pieces of an unfinished puzzle.

The scriptural word is able to transform a redundant worship exercise into a unique dialogue, a personal relation that has its starting point in the very self-communication of God. In its turn, worship, especially Eucharistic worship, may vivify the scriptural words, creating a transparent medium between the reader and the reality that lies behind the text: the incarnate Word of God himself.

It is the strong conviction of this author, made clear throughout this work, that Eastern Orthodox tradition has always promoted and embodied, since apostolic times, the understanding that Scripture may be interpreted and transmitted not only by the written or uttered word, but also through various channels of communal worship (i.e., aural, visual, ascetic), often labeled generically as Holy Tradition. The Sinai icon directs one's attention to two channels of testimony regarding Jesus's person: the book sealed with the cross, and the liturgy in its various expressions of ritual, hymn, and icon. The latter medium of witness will be dealt with in the second part of this work. For now, we dwell on the book and its two components, the New and the Old Testaments.

The artist who painted the Sinai icon gives no clue as to the identity of the book Jesus holds in his left hand. At first sight, it is a hefty codex marked with a cross, the arms of which are flanked by four tiny tri-stellar constellations. Apparently, it represents the Christian Bible enclosing the Old and New Testaments.[8] The cross inscribed on the cover may be read as a symbol or a unifying element which keeps the two testaments together in one book. Jon D. Levenson rightly notices that "the Christian Bible includes within it a book of an alien religion."[9] In what sense, then, does the cross bring together the two books and their two covenants into one? What kind of unity is this? In what follows, we will discuss how the church authorities throughout the centuries have attempted to answer this question regarding the two parts of the Christian Bible and their interrelationship.

The Emergence of the Christian Writings
The Gospel of Salvation

The goal of this section is not to reiterate what may already be found in present scholarly works on the New Testament.[10] Thus, I will not enter here into technical discussions about the various "Christianities" (i.e., Gentilic, Jewish, Johannine) that may have informed the text of the New Testament, or the diverse literary genres that contributed to the differences so obvious between Matthew, Luke, Mark on the one hand, and John on the other, or the so-called synoptic problem and the proposed Q-source. Instead, the aim here is to take a closer look at the way in which ancient church authorities evaluated the emergence of the four canonical Gospels and their status as "Scripture." What were the central events that determined the early Christian communities to have the apostolic witness put into writing? And how did the early Church understand the differences between the resultant writings? Most importantly, how did the Church in these early centuries understand the relationship between these Gospels and the older Jewish Scriptures?

The defining aspects of Jesus's person were initially proclaimed through the apostolic kērygma: "We declare to you what was from the beginning, what we have heard, what we have seen with our eyes, what we have looked at and touched with our hands, concerning the word of life . . . we declare (*apangelomen*) to you what we have seen and heard so that you also may have fellowship with us; and truly our fellowship is with the Father and with his Son Jesus Christ" (1 John 1:1, 3). This was the eyewitness testimony of the first generation of Jesus's followers. But what triggered this oral proclamation (kērygma) to be put in writing? First, it was the fact and the testimony of Jesus's "rising up" from the dead.

For Jesus's first followers this very fact and testimony of resurrection functioned as a bridge between the "historical Jesus" and the metahistorical, ever present and eschatological Lord (*Kyrios*). Anyone who confesses him as Lord and believes that God resurrected him can enter into a living dialogue with him (Rom 10:9). The "good news" (*euangelion*) that Jesus somehow outlived, or returned to life after a violent death placed everything, his former deeds and sayings, into a new interpretive matrix. His persona was now viewed outside the small locative and temporal arena, the first century Palestine, where his short mission unfolded. Jesus was regarded as *ho Kyrios* "*the* Lord," the untouchable, as one may conclude from the postresurrectional account of his encounter with Mary Magdalene early Sunday morning in the tomb's garden (John 20:11–18).

Taking a look at Jesus's life and ministry one may notice that words and deeds denoting the two aspects of his complex personality, divine and human, are wrapped in the mystery of the central act and testimony of his coming back to life (in Greek *anastasis*, "rising up"). The uniqueness of this act and testimony, unwelcome both to Greeks who thought it useless (Acts 17:31–32) and to Jews who were awaiting an end time resurrection (Dan 12:1–4), along with chains of testimonies focusing on his divinity and humble human condition, threw every eyewitness to Jesus into one of two groups: either enthusiastic followers, or cautious Jewish believers unable to accept so many apparent doctrinal detours from their fathers' faith.

The resurrection—as published abroad through the passionate testimonials of those who claimed they encountered the risen Jesus (over five hundred individuals, according to Paul, 1 Cor 15:6, saw Jesus "at once" [*ephapax*])—became the interpretive prism through which Jesus's unique profile came to be reevaluated. Why did Jesus's passion and death have so much influence on his followers when crucifixions were done at that time almost every day? Only because this death was not the last word but was rather followed by his return to life. Neither his teachings, nor his miracles, but rather his passion, death, and resurrection left the central undeniable mark on generations of Christian confession. The Nicene-Constantinopolitan Creed, for instance, is entirely silent on Jesus's teachings and miracles. Its focus is rather on the divinity and humanity (and mortality) of Jesus, in direct connection to his glorious past, present, and future endeavors: his resurrection, ascension, sitting at the right of God the Father, coming again to judge the living and dead, and eternally reigning over his kingdom. The message of Jesus's resurrection was so unexpected, so unique, that the first generation of believers wanted it recorded. The Gospels reflect the first impact the event of Jesus's "rising up" from the dead had on the eyewitnesses. They are not sensu stricto biographies or recordings of Jesus's sayings and actions but rather briefings on the experience of the eyewitnesses to Jesus's resurrection. It is this unfathomable experience of the resurrection that is the main reason for the diversity encountered in the four gospel narratives, as well as their appearance in writings soon to be considered as having the authority of new Scriptures.

Here is Irenaeus, bishop of Lyons, pointing to the two capital events that triggered the proclamation (kērygma) of the gospel and its writing down along with its inclusion within a larger corpus of the "Scriptures":

> We have learned of the plan of our salvation from none others than those through whom the gospel has come down to us, which they did at one time proclaim in public, and, at a later period, by the will of God, handed down to us in the Scriptures, to be the ground and pillar of our faith. For it is unlawful to assert that they preached before they possessed perfect knowledge, as some do even venture to say, boasting themselves as improvers of the apostles. For, after our Lord rose from the dead, [the apostles] were invested with power from on high when the Holy Spirit came down [upon them], were filled from all [his gifts], and had perfect knowledge: they departed to the ends of the earth, preaching the glad tidings of the good things [sent] from God to us, and proclaiming the peace of heaven to men, who indeed do all equally and individually possess the gospel of God.
>
> *Against Heresies 3.3.1–2*[11]

Irenaeus speaks of two phases in the transmission of the gospel: the public proclamation and the later inscripturation. The two events that put everything in motion (the apostolic mission and the writing down of new Scriptures) were Jesus's resurrection and the descent of the Holy Spirit on the apostles at the feast of Pentecost. Those whom Irenaeus mentions as "boasting themselves as improvers of the apostles" are none other than the Gnostics, against whom the bishop of Lyons adduces the argument of the apostles' investiture with "power from on high." It is because of this gift of the Holy Spirit that the apostles, and not the Gnostics, are the carriers of the "perfect knowledge" and the heralds of the "plan of salvation."

Almost a half century earlier, Clement, the third bishop of Rome (95–97 C.E.), underscored the same basic understanding when he noted that the apostles "being fully assured by the resurrection of our Lord Jesus

Christ and full of faith in the Word of God . . . went forth with the firm assurance that the Holy Spirit gives, preaching the good news that the kingdom of God was about to come" (*1 Clement* 42.3).[12] The use of the "apostolic writings" by Clement of Rome underlines the fact that these writings were already well organized as such into a whole as early as the end of the first century c.e.

In fact, it was Paul who first linked together the faith and apostolic preaching of Christ's resurrection when he stated quite emphatically, "If Christ has not been raised, then our proclamation has been in vain and your faith has been in vain" (1 Cor 15:14). The resurrection of Jesus confers on the gospel witness its unity of essence despite all variations in its "distribution," as Tertullian (160–225 c.e.) well underlines:

> A distribution of office, not a diversity of gospel, so that they should severally preach not a different gospel, but (the same), to different persons, Peter to the circumcision, Paul to the Gentiles. Forasmuch, then, as Peter was rebuked because, after he had lived with the Gentiles, he proceeded to separate himself from their company out of respect for persons, the fault surely was one of conversation, not of preaching. For it does not appear from this, that any other God than the Creator, or any other Christ than (the son) of Mary, or any other hope than the resurrection, was (by him) announced.
>
> *The Prescription Against Heretics* 23[13]

While a single gospel (euangelion) as apostolic message (kērygma) centered on Jesus's "rising up," its fourfold variety of distribution is conditioned mainly by the diversity of authors who put that unique "gospel of salvation" in writing.[14] Irenaeus remarks:

> Matthew also issued a written gospel among the Hebrews in their own dialect, while Peter and Paul were preaching at Rome, and laying the foundations of the Church. After their departure, Mark, the disciple and interpreter of Peter, did also hand down to us in writing what had been preached by Peter. Luke also, the companion of Paul, recorded in a book the gospel preached by him. Afterwards, John, the disciple of the Lord, who also had leaned upon his breast, did himself publish a gospel during his residence at Ephesus in Asia.
>
> *Against Heresies* 3.1.1[15]

Speaking of theological differences between the four Gospels, Irenaeus suggests that the four living creatures around God's celestial throne seen by John (Rev 4:6–7) may hint at the four gospel writers and their unique testimonies:

> He who was manifested to men, has given us the gospel under four aspects, but bound together by one Spirit. . . . "The first living creature was like a lion," [Rev 4:7] symbolizing his effectual working, his leadership, and royal power; the second [living creature] was like a calf, signifying [his] sacrificial and sacerdotal order; but "the third had, as it were, the face as of a man," an evident description of his advent as a human being; "the fourth was like a flying eagle," pointing out the gift of the Spirit hovering with his wings over the Church.
>
> *Against Heresies 3.11.8*[16]

This same interpretation is found later in the third-century Latin context in the work of Victorinus, bishop of Petau,[17] and would be reflected for centuries not only in Western Christian art, but also in the Byzantine iconography, where each evangelist appears along with his zoological symbol (Matthew: man; Mark: lion; Luke: calf; John: eagle).

The four canonical Gospels have always been perceived as apostolic in origin, as intimated by the term "memorials" (Greek: *hypomnēmata*; Latin: *acta*) of the apostles found in the mid-fourth-century writing *Acta Pilati* (or, as it was called in the medieval period, *Gospel of Nicodemus*). Here is a fragment from this work, supposedly written by one of Pilate's bodyguards:

> I, Ananias, of the propraetor's bodyguard, being learned in the Law, knowing our Lord Jesus Christ from the Holy Scriptures, coming to him by faith, and counted worthy of the holy baptism, searching also the memorials written at that time of what was done in the case of our Lord Jesus Christ, which the Jews had laid up in the time of Pontius Pilate, found these memorials written in Hebrew, and by the favor of God have translated them into Greek for the information of all who call upon the name of our Master Jesus Christ, in the seventeenth year of the reign of our Lord Flavius Theodosius, and the sixth of Flavius Valentinianus, in the ninth indiction.
>
> *Gospel of Nicodemus: Part I. The Acts of Pilate. Prologue*[18]

As for the *Sitz im Leben* of these apostolic "memorials," one may adduce the testimony of Justin (100–165 C.E.) that they were read at the weekly gatherings on Sunday (*First Apology* 67). It was in all likelihood this liturgical usage that contributed to the early designation of these apostolic memorials as "Scripture," on analogy with the Torah, the Prophets, and the Writings read in the Jewish assembly of worship. Thus, Tertullian (*Against Marcion* 4.39) calls the Gospels "Scripture," underscoring that these writings are part of Holy Scripture, and Hegesippus speaks expansively of "the Scripture of the Gospels" (*Commentaries on the Acts of the Church* 1).[19]

The term "Scripture" (*graphē*) in 2 Tim 3:16 designates most likely the Jewish Bible or Old Testament alone. Obviously, "the old covenant" (*tēs palaias diathēkēs*) in 2 Cor 3:14 refers to the first covenant (i.e., the Old Testament). The expression "old covenant" is a calque after the "new covenant" mentioned already in Jer 31:31–34 (MT: *bərît ḥădāšāh*; LXX: *diathēkē kainē*). At the Last Supper, Jesus spoke of the blood of the "new covenant" (Matt 26:28: *kainēs diathēkēs*; cf. Mark 14:24; Luke 22:20; 1 Cor 11:25). In 2 Cor 3:6, Paul declares himself a minister of the new covenant. Speaking of Jesus as the "mediator" (*mesitēs*) of the same new covenant, the author of Heb 9:15 introduces the phrase "first covenant" (*prōtē diathēkē*). In the New Testament the phrase "old covenant," which appears only one time (2 Cor 3:14), refers to the reading of the Torah. In contrast, the phrase "new covenant" in the New Testament designates exclusively the religious institution of covenant, not a collection of books; for the latter, the New Testament uses the term "Scripture." The term "covenant" in Greek connotes the idea of communication and bilateralism (as suggested by the particle *dia*, "among, through," in *diathēkē*).

During the late second century, in a letter to a fellow Christian by the name of Onesimus, Melito of Sardis (second century C.E.) calls the Jewish Bible (Old Testament) "the old books" (*palaiōn bibliōn*) or "the books of the old covenant" (*ta tēs palaias diathēkēs biblia*).[20] Almost at the same time, Clement of Alexandria (d. 215 C.E.) uses the phrase *palaia diathēkē*, quoting Prov 19:17 (*Stromata* 3.6.54).[21] In some contrast, for Tertullian, the Scriptures are sources or documents of argument (i.e., evidential documents), hence his nomenclature "old and new document" (*vetus et novum instrumentum*) or "old and new testament" (*vetus et novum testamentum*).[22] Similarly, the Greek term *diathēkē*, "covenant," was rendered by Jerome (347–419 C.E.) in his Vulgate with the Latin term *testamentum*, "will, legal document," following Tertullian's alternate usage of *testamentum* and *instrumentum.* Due to the immense popularity of the Vulgate throughout the Middle Ages, this term *testamentum* influenced the translations in vernacular languages. For instance, John Wiclif (1382) renders the Greek term *diathēkē* with the English "testament." The more popular term "testament," with its legal flavoring, came to designate either of the two parts of the Christian Bible.

However, this legal flavoring fails to connote the communicative or dialogical aspect of the Greek *diathēkē*, "covenant," and instead shifts the emphasis from an initial fluid religious institution to a frozen written document. As noted, it was probably due to their liturgical usage that the apostolic writings, that later came to make up the New Testament, were first honored as "Scripture." As Frances M. Young writes, "The earthly life of Jesus was recalled in the context of cultic rites that assumed his divinity. Eventually, though probably beyond our period, the gospel books would be processed with incense in the same kind of way as a pagan idol, and with a similar cultic function, namely, to make the divine present to the worshipper."[23] Much later, the Seventh Ecumenical Council held in Constantinople in 787 C.E. would confirm this long-standing Christian reverence for the New Testament writings in its teaching that the gospel book was to be venerated equally with the icons, inasmuch as the Gospels constitute together a fourfold verbal icon of Christ. From the outset, Eastern Orthodox tradition has seen in the liturgy a powerful means to link the present, past, and future, and Jesus with his disciples together. The gospel book represents Christ's person, and is thus censed and venerated with all the pomp and reverence befitting a divine figure. The writing down of the apostles' "memorials" did not diminish the initial "astonishment" which they themselves experienced: the liturgy helped in keeping this astonishment always fresh and alive.

Christian Appropriation of the Jewish Scriptures

From the very beginning, the Jewish Bible (Old Testament) was the only Bible of the early Christians and its authority was entirely assumed, with special emphasis on prophetic dimension of the Old Testament pointing to Christ, Spirit, and community.

There have been three basic ways of looking at the Scriptures of the Jewish Bible in the history of Christianity.

First, the early Church, or what we may call the mainstream "orthodox" or "catholic" segment, viewed the Scriptures as "proof-texts" able to demonstrate the messiahship of Jesus of Nazareth. Second, some hetero-dox Christian and non-Christian groups rejected (e.g., Marcionites, Man-ichaeans) or underestimated (e.g., Gnostics) the entire Jewish Bible as having nothing to do with the gospel. Third, there were Jewish Christians known as "Judaizers" who overestimated the value of the first testament to the point of insisting on the observance of specifically Jewish rituals and practices for all Christians.

As we shall see, these differences regarding attitude to the Scriptures of Israel were from the earliest period a key criterion in distinguishing orthodoxy from heresy. In what follows, I will exemplify these three basic attitudes toward the Old Testament using the firsthand testimonies of their representative figures.

Since her very beginning, the catholic or orthodox Church appropri-ated the Jewish Scriptures, such that gradually, between 150 and 250 c.e., it became self-consciously the Church of the two testaments, old and new. This process of appropriation was a conscious[24] move of the first Chris-tians toward embracing their religious roots in Israel. At the center of this embrace was Jesus, whose Jewishness was at this point fully acknowl-edged. In addition to the continued use of the Old Testament for moral instruction, as exemplified in the *Didache,* early Christians appropriated the Jewish Scriptures in order to interpret and articulate their Christian faith on three crucial points: first, in the area of Christology, as scriptural evidence supporting Jesus's messiahship and divinity; second, as a vali-dating factor for the emerging Christian Scriptures (Gospels, apostolic epistles); and third, as evidence for the ancestry and authority of Christian doctrine.

In the third century, Origen (184–253 c.e.) mentions one of the her-meneutical maneuvers used by Christian interpreters in his time: "It is our practice, indeed, to make use of the words of the prophets, who dem-onstrate that Jesus is the Christ predicted by them, and who show from the prophetic writings the events in the Gospels regarding Jesus have been fulfilled" (*Against Celsus* 6:35).[25] The Old Testament, and especially its prophetic portions, was employed by Christians to prove that Jesus was the Christ (Messiah) prophesied in Israel. Hence, one of the main reasons why the early Church preserved the Old Testament in their Bible was that it contained "proof-texts" in support of Jesus's messiahship.

The practice Origen speaks of is as old as Jesus's ministry. One may think of that famous conversation the risen Lord had with his two dis-ciples on the road to Emmaus. Trying to downplay the puzzlement of his disciples triggered by the recent events in Jerusalem, the risen Lord brings forth the prophetic testimony of the ancient Scriptures: "Then he said to them, 'These are my words that I spoke to you while I was still with you—that everything written about me in the law of Moses, the prophets, and the psalms must be fulfilled'" (Luke 24:44). This was also the practice of the eyewitnesses who proclaimed the gospel of salvation: first, viva voce, then, in writing. Indeed, the entire New Testament is replete with Old Testament citations, having as their main purpose to "prove" Jesus's messiahship.[26]

A useful touchstone in illustrating the particular nature of this subsidiary function of the Old Testament to support or demonstrate (apodeiknymi) the veracity of the gospel is underscored by a quite interesting term found in Ignatius, bishop of Antioch (50–117 C.E.). This immediate successor of Evodius of Antioch calls the Scriptures of the Jewish Bible "the archives" (ta archaia)—a term close to Tertullian's instrumentum in its demonstrative aspect. Ignatius was asked to produce evidence from the "archives" regarding his claims; his answer was Jesus's cross, death, and resurrection are the best "archives." In other words, Jesus embodies the Scriptures of the Jewish Bible in his own life. Here is Ignatius's argument:

> I was doing my part, therefore, as a man set on unity. But God does not dwell where there is division and anger. The Lord, however, forgives all who repent, if in repenting they return to the unity of God and the council of the bishop. I believe in the grace of Jesus Christ, who will free you from every bond. Moreover, I urge you to do nothing in a spirit of contentiousness, but in accordance with the teaching of Christ. For I heard some people say, "If I do not find it in the archives (ta archaia), I do not believe it in the gospel." And when I said to them, "It is written," they answered me, "That is precisely the question." But for me, the archives are Jesus Christ, the sacrosanct archives (ta athikta archaia) are his cross and death and his resurrection and the faith which comes through him; by these things I want, through your prayers, to be justified. . . . But the gospel possesses something distinctive, namely, the coming of the Savior, our Lord Jesus Christ, his suffering, and the resurrection. For the beloved prophets preached in anticipation of him [1 Pet 1:10–12], but the gospel is the imperishable finished work. All these things together are good, if you believe with love.
>
> *Letter to Philadelphians 8.1–2, 9.2*[27]

As Frances M. Young notices, Ignatius's phrase, *ta athikta archaia*—the sacrosanct or, indeed, "untouchable" archives or records—contains "a remarkable reminiscence of the Rabbinic definition of sacred books as those which 'defile the hands'," demonstrating "that the gospel of Jesus Christ, not apparently a written gospel but what people have called the 'kerygma', has become equivalent to sacred books, within which, in any case, whatever is to be believed is found written."[28] Yet if Ignatius's main "archives" are the redemptive works of Jesus himself, nevertheless they are such on analogy with the Jewish Scriptures, and the early Church gave close attention to these Scriptures for support in interpreting and confirming those works as truly messianic.

The most important hermeneutical consequence of this missionary maneuver of utilizing the Old Testament as the source of "proof texts" for Jesus's messiahship was the predominant Christocentric typological interpretation of the Jewish Bible. It was this spiritual interpretation that enabled the ancient Scriptures of Israel to retain their status and veneration as Scripture in the Church, in spite of all the Marcionite and neo-Marcionite currents in ancient and modern times.

A second use of the ancient Scriptures of Israel by the early Church was to support the newly emerging Christian Scriptures—primarily, the Gospels and epistles. The emergence of the Gospels—the new Scriptures—determined the early Church to search for a matrix for the new offspring. The Jewish Bible was identified as the appropriate matrix of the emerging Gospels. The ethnic and religious identity between Jesus and his spiritual ancestors, prophets and sages, was the main reason for this scriptural appropriation for validation purposes.[29] By appropriating the ancient Scriptures with no interventions and modifications, the early Church meant to promote a sort of "continuum" understanding of the covenants.

Paul speaks of "covenants" (*diathēkai*) in Romans 9:4. The plural noun could refer to several covenants mentioned in the Old Testament: for instance, with Noah and his descendants (Gen 9:8–17); with Israel on Mount Sinai (Exod 19:5), at Moab (Deut 29:1), at Mount Ebal and Mount Garizim (Josh 8:30–35); with David (2 Sam 23:5), with Josiah (2 Kgs 23:3), and with Nehemiah (Neh 9–10), as well as the "new covenant" announced in Jer 31:31–34. As a distinctive feature of the Christian Church, associated especially with the new covenantal sign of the Eucharist (1 Cor 11:25), the "new covenant" stands in some contrast with the "old" (Gal 4:24–26). And yet, according to Paul, *all* these covenants, including the "new covenant," still belong to Israel, even though due to "a spirit of stupor" given by God, Israel finds itself currently in a state of being hardened (Rom 11:7–8). Note carefully that there is no obvious discontinuity between old and new covenants, and consequently between old and new Scriptures, if one takes into account Paul's remark that *all* the covenants, including the new covenant, belong to Israel.[30] In fact, there is rather a "continuum covenant," at least on the level of inscripturation.

In Origen's view, the authority of the Old Testament comes from its use by Jesus and his apostles: "The practice of the Savior or his apostles, frequently quoting illustrations from the Old Testament, shows that they attribute authority to the ancients" (*On the Principles* 2.4.1).[31] Similarly, John Chrysostom (347–407 C.E.) notices, "And mark how much honor he [Christ] showed toward Moses, again showing his agreement with the Old Testament; since indeed even by this does he make them objects of reverence. 'For they sit,' he says, 'on Moses' seat.' For because he was not able to make them out worthy of credit by their life, he does it from the grounds that were open to him, from their seat, and their succession from him" (*Homilies on Matthew* 72).[32]

All in all, from the earliest period, orthodox or catholic Christianity in its appropriation of the Jewish Scriptures followed the apostle Paul in the view that Christ himself is the unity of the two covenants, having broken down the dividing wall between Jews and Gentiles, and reconciled both in his body by means of his cross (Eph 2:14, 16).

The third purpose for the gradual and conscious appropriation by Christian Church of the Jewish Scriptures is quite different from the two preceding. This purpose is attested in the works of the early Christian apologists who sought to show the pagan philosophers of their time the superiority of Christianity over any philosophical and religious system extant in the Late Antiquity. As Jaroslav Pelikan puts it,

> This effort to demonstrate that the truth of revelation, which was also being affirmed by the pagan philosophers, had occurred first in the Old Testament was not merely a way of finding biblical support for one or another doctrine. It was also part of the campaign to prove the superiority of Christian doctrine on the grounds of its antiquity. Antiquity was widely regarded in pagan thought as lending authority to a system of thought or belief.[33]

Because their pagan critics saw the Christians as "but of yesterday,"[34] the latter had to resort to the typological explanation of the Jewish Scriptures in order to show the continuity of the "Jesus event" with the religion of ancient Israel and, thus, the old roots of the new faith. From the Christian point of view, there was a great deal of continuity indeed between Hebrew prophecy and the works and teachings of Jesus. Speaking of the Hebrew prophets, Justin Martyr notices: "In these books, then, of the prophets we found Jesus our Christ foretold as coming, born of a virgin, growing up to man's estate, and healing every disease and every sickness, and raising the dead, and being hated, and unrecognized, and crucified, and dying, and rising again, and ascending into heaven, and being, and being called, the Son of God" (*First Apology* 31).[35]

Similarly, in response to Celsus's criticism of Christianity having no ancestry and hence no authority, Origen remarks that "the writings of Moses and of the prophets, are older not only than Plato, but even than Homer and the invention of letters among the Greeks" (*Against Celsus* 6.7).[36]

Early Attitudes toward the Old Testament

Against the backdrop of the many fractions or sects that mushroomed the ecclesiastical soil, the Acts of the Apostles and *Ecclesiastical History* by Eusebius (ca. 260–341 C.E.) seem but two idealized portraits of the early Church as relatively homogenous and far from schism. The historical evidence, however, paints a somewhat different picture.

There has been always a Christianity called *catholic* (according to the whole) or, slightly later, *orthodox* (of right belief). Yet this orthodox/catholic Christianity articulated itself precisely in the struggle against heresy. The latter was understood as deviation from or denial of the unity and continuity between the incarnate Lord, as depicted in the emerging New Testament, and the Jewish Scriptures. When one thinks of those who have challenged this continuity, one recalls especially the name of Marcion and his followers. However, the Marcionites were not the only heresy to reject the first covenant and its literary records. In fact, the Marcionites are in the same league with the Manicheans, and to a certain degree, with the Gnostics.

Rejection and Underestimation

Marcionites

"I shall rend your Church, and make a permanent rent in it." With these harsh words, preserved by Epiphanius of Salamis (367–403 C.E.) (*Panarion* 42.2.8),[37] Marcion threatened the presbyters of the great Church of Rome shortly after his arrival there about 140 C.E. They were words uttered against a backdrop of debates and controversies between Marcion and Rome's clergymen on the validity of the Scriptures. According to Optatus, Marcion, "that shipmaster of Pontus, the zealous student of Stoicism" (Tertullian, *The Prescription Against Heretics* 30),[38] was apparently an ordained bishop.[39] Upon his arrival after the death of Hyginus, the eighth bishop of Rome, and prior to the enthronement of Pius I, the episcopal seat of Rome was vacant. How did it all begin?

Born about 110 C.E., the son of the bishop of Sinope in Pontus, south of the Black (Euxine) Sea, Marcion was a complex figure. From an early age, he dedicated himself to a life of chastity and asceticism. Yet Pseudo-Tertullian states that Marcion was "excommunicated because of a rape committed on a certain virgin" (*Against All Heresies* 6).[40] Some later commentators have taken this story as allegorical—the "virgin" being the Church, the rape being false teaching. Whatever the facts, this exploit led his father to expel him from the Church. After many unsuccessful attempts to regain his father's love, and under the pressure of a growing public resentment against him, Marcion set off for Rome.

One of the most famous heretics of the second century, Marcion overemphasized the discontinuities between Christianity and Judaism and between their corresponding Scriptures. For Marcion, the Father of Jesus is not the same with the God of the Jewish Scriptures. While the God of the Jewish Scriptures is a God of harsh justice and wrath, Jesus's Father is a God of love and mercy. Marcion's view can thus be considered as a form of ditheism.

In response to Marcion's dichotomy between love and justice reaching the divine being, Tertullian sought to downplay this dichotomy by introducing a quite fanciful distinction between anger and irritation: "Angry, he will possibly be, but not irritated, nor dangerously tempted; he will be moved, but not subverted" (*Against Marcion* 2.16).[41] The God of the Jewish Scriptures is not a God of anger, though he can be irritated by our sins; he remains a God of love.

However, as Pelikan notes, "Marcion's separation between the two gods was taken up into Tertullian's doctrine of the relation between the eternal, invisible Father and the Son, who had become true man in Jesus Christ."[42] Tertullian sought to explain this struggle between justice and love with regard to Marcion's teaching by transferring the whole debate to the intra-trinitarian relations between the Father and the Son. According to Tertullian:

Whatever attributes therefore you require as worthy of God, must
be found in the Father, who is invisible and unapproachable, and
placid, and (so to speak) the God of the philosophers; whereas those
qualities which you censure as unworthy must be supposed to be
in the Son, who has been seen, and heard, and encountered, the
Witness and Servant of the Father, uniting in himself man and
God, God in mighty deeds, in weak ones man, in order that he may
give to man as much as he takes from God. What in your esteem
is the entire disgrace of my God, is in fact the sacrament of man's
salvation.

Against Marcion 2.27[43]

Marcion refused such an explanation due to his docetist view of Christ
who, in his opinion, was not a true man. However, the separation between
a good God and a just yet angry God began with Marcion's exegesis of
Luke 6:43–45, where Jesus speaks of two trees, one good and the other
bad, producing corresponding fruit. According to Marcion, since the God
of the Jewish Scriptures allowed the fall of the first parents into sin, he
could not be a good or loving God. As Tertullian pointed out, Marcion
held the view that the divine statement "I create evil" (Isa 45:7) proved
beyond doubt that the God of the Jewish Scriptures was the source of evil,
and since Christ showed a "pure benevolence," the God revealed by him
had to be a "new and strange divinity" (Tertullian, *Against Marcion* 1.2).

Both Irenaeus (*Against Heresies* 1.27) and Tertullian (*Against Marcion*
1.2) describe Cerdo as the spiritual predecessor of Marcion, anticipating
what the master would teach. In Pelikan's view,[44] this description was
meant to disparage Marcion's originality. Nevertheless, even those writers most hostile to Marcion agree that his aversion to the Jewish Scriptures began with his own exegesis of the New Testament passage where
Jesus speaks of the new wine poured into old wineskins (Luke 5:37 and
par.). This exegesis was done prior to Marcion's Roman excommunication
and his association with Cerdo. Thus, Tertullian is right when he writes,
"Marcion's special and principal work is the separation of the Law and the
gospel" (*Against Marcion* 1.19).[45]

This separation or dichotomy between the gospel and the Law is reflected also in Marcion's doctrine of creation and salvation. For Marcion's,
God's salvation is limited to humankind and even here to the soul alone,
sex and childbirth being altogether unclean. This is why Marcion despised the rest of creation. Tertullian asks the Marcionites rhetorically

on what authority they dare to vilify those "poverty stricken elements" (*paupertina*) of the creation from which the very Lord chose "beggarly elements" (*mendicitatibus*), namely, the bread and the wine, for the sacrament of Eucharist. As Tertullian exclaimed, "How hard is this obstinacy of yours! You vilify the things in which you both live and die" (*Against Marcion* 1.14).[46]

Marcion's rejection of the Old Testament as Christian Scripture also entailed an exclusively literal or historical interpretation of the Jewish Scriptures. Rejecting any allegorical or typological interpretation, Marcion came to conclusion that the Old Testament did not prophesy at all Christ's coming and suffering on the cross. For instance, all the texts regarding the offspring of David were to be referred not to Christ, but to Solomon. In response to this rejection of allegory, Tertullian shows that not all passages in the Scriptures can be explained literally:

> Another characteristic will be, that very many events are figuratively predicted by means of enigmas and allegories and parables, and that they must be understood in a sense different from the literal description. For we both read of "the mountains dropping down new wine," [Joel 3:18] but not as if one might expect "must" from the stones, or its decoction from the rocks.
>
> *Against Marcion* 3.5[47]

In fact, it may have been its strict aversion to the Jewish Scriptures that contributed in part to the popularity of the Marcionite movement, a popularity testified in the substantial number of treatises *Adversus Marcionem*.[48] As Pelikan states, "Marcion did not found a school but a church."[49] Marcion's sect, founded circa 144 C.E. when Marcion was 34 years old, after he had already been excommunicated by the Church of Rome, was characterized by strong ecclesiastic and ascetic overtones, making it a serious competitor to the orthodox Church at a time when the doctrinal terms of ecclesiastical communion were still not very clearly defined. Well organized with bishops and presbyters, it is possible that the Marcionite Church may have been viewed by many as the true *ecclesia ex gentibus*, with no ties at all with Jews and their Scriptures.[50]

Prior to his excommunication in Rome, Marcion was active in Asia Minor, where he encountered for the first time the Pauline corpus. It was at that point that he began to teach about the irreconcilability between the teaching of Paul and the mainstream Christianity of his time, so connected to the Old Testament. The Epistle to Galatians was especially revelatory for Marcion, with its opposition between faith and the works of the Law, between Paul's teaching and that of the Judaizers (Jewish Christians). In Marcion's view, the only true apostle of Christ was Paul; all others had mutilated the gospel.

In contrast, according to Irenaeus, it was Marcion who "dared openly to mutilate the Scriptures" (*Against Heresies* 1.27).[51] Ironically, however, though there is no consensus regarding Marcion's influence in the making of the biblical canon, it is generally agreed that Marcion represents the first Christian—albeit heretical—attempt to create a canon. Marcion's Bible was the product of two actions: rejection of the entire Old Testament, and mutilation of the New Testament. His Bible consists of the following Scriptures: *Gospel* (a mutilated and reworded Luke with the omission of the first chapters), the *Apostolikon* (ten Pauline letters) and Marcion's own work *Antitheses* (a list of "contradictions" between the Old and the New Testaments). The Pauline epistles received by him were as follows: Galatians (the charter of Marcionism), 1–2 Corinthians, Romans, 1–2 Thessalonians, Ephesians (known by Marcion under the name of Laodicians), Colossians, Philippians, and Philemon. He excluded from the New Testament the pastoral epistles, the catholic epistles, Hebrews, Acts, and the Apocalypse.[52]

Marcion was not a deep theologian. His doctrine might be summed up in one word, *discontinuity*—a separation or dichotomy on multiple planes: gospel and Law, Old and New Testament, creation and salvation, God the Father and Christ.[53]

Apelles, a Gnostic, is considered the most famous and creative disciple of Marcion (Tertullian, *The Prescription Against Heretics* 6.30). After some years spent in Alexandria, Apelles returned to Rome. Tertullian in his heightened taste for scandal in cases of heretics states that Apelles had been attached to a virgin Philumene, who eventually became a prostitute. Apelles believed that Philumene was inspired; as Hyppolitus records, "he deems her a prophetess" (*Against Heresies* 10.20). According to Pseudo-Tertullian, Apelles authored a book entitled *Reasonings* (*Sillogismoi*) "in which he seeks to prove that whatever Moses has written about God is not true, but is false" (*Against All Heresies* 6).[54] Thus, Apelles deviated from his master, Marcion: it is not that the God of the Old Testament was a god of justice and wrath but rather that the portrait of him penned by Moses did not reflect the reality of this God.

By the fifth century c.e., the Marcionites would begin to be absorbed by the Manicheans. Although Marcionism was condemned by a council held at Rome in 260 C.E., the heresy continued to exist for several centuries in the East and had sympathizers in the West as late as the Middle Ages. Noteworthy at the end of these reflections on Marcion are the words of John Clabeaux: "The vociferous insistence of anti-Marcionite Christianity on the validity of the Old Testament within the canon is a point which should not be missed in our time. Since rejection of the Old Testament was an essential feature of Marcionism, it is straining the point only a little to say that among Christians today there are many virtual Marcionites."[55] Adolf von Harnack (1851–1930) may be considered a modern Marcionite by his radical statements against the Old Testament, which, in his view, cannot be equated with the New Testament in terms of canonicity. Hence, underscores Harnack, the Old Testament should not have any authority in Christianity.[56]

Gnostics

Gnosticism was probably one of the most important heresies confronted by early Christianity. The evidence from both Christian heresiologies and Gnostic documents themselves point toward Gnosticism as a conglomerate of syncretistic religious-mythical and philosophical ideas conjugated in a bizarre way with magical practices. Due to its syncretistic propensities, Gnosticism succeeded in molding itself to various religious matrices: the austere Judaism, the fancy and intricate Greco-Roman religious mosaic, and the rising Christianity.[57]

Greek language and philosophy constituted an important vehicle in the spread of Gnostic ideas. Middle Platonism had a great impact on Gnosticism, especially in the area of mediation between the singular being of God (*theos*) and the diversity of the created world (*kosmos*), which was seen as a degradation from spirit (*pneuma*) to matter (*hylē*) accompanied by an alienation of the spirit. In the Gnostic milieu, the Platonic duality between spirit and matter, soul and body, God and world was only intensified.

The nomenclature "Gnostic" or "Gnosticism" is relatively new, being the creation of modern historical scholars, but the name "Gnosis" (knowledge) was used by those belonging to various Gnostic groups to emphasize the fact that they followed in their daily lives the guidelines of the esoteric knowledge, the only thing able to save the soul from material corruption. Early Christian writers tended to enumerate the Gnostics according to their founders or masters (e.g., Valentinians). As can be observed especially in the work of Clement of Alexandria, *gnōstikos* (good at knowing) is a term that some Christians claimed for themselves to indicate an ease with the redemptive knowledge found through faith in Christ. In a similar sense, "The Gnostic" (*ho gnōstikos*) is also the title of a treatise written by Evagrius Ponticus (b. 345 C.E.) on the qualities of an ideal monk. In relationship to catholic Christianity, Gnosticism may be regarded as a chapter in the former's convoluted history.

According to the Gnostics, the physical creation of the world occurred by mistake and was accomplished by a lesser god, a demiurge, without the approval of the highest God. In order to correct this mistake, the perfect God inserted in humanity a "spark" (called sometimes "soul" or "spirit"). Through this divine spark, human beings are enabled to draw into contact with the perfect God. The redeeming "knowledge" (*gnōsis*) is granted to practitioners either through heavenly messengers or myths. After criticizing the Gnostics for having replaced Christian baptism as the initiating sacrament with their own understanding of *gnōsis* as a cosmic redemptive *instrumentum*, Irenaeus speaks in detail about the Gnostic view on redemption:

> These hold that the knowledge of the unspeakable Greatness is itself perfect redemption. For since both defect and passion flowed from ignorance, the whole substance of what was thus formed is destroyed by knowledge; and therefore knowledge is the redemption of the inner man. This, however, is not of a corporeal nature, for the body is corruptible; nor is it animal, since the animal soul is the fruit of a defect, and is, as it were, the abode of the spirit. The redemption must therefore be of a spiritual nature; for they affirm that the inner and spiritual man is redeemed by means of knowledge, and that they, having acquired the knowledge of all things, stand thenceforth in need of nothing else. This, then, is the true redemption.
>
> *Against Heresies* 1.21[58]

Generally speaking, the Gnostics' contribution is more at the theological than biblical level. As Marcion was the catalyst for the shaping of the orthodox biblical canon by his harsh criticism and rejection of the Old Testament along with the mutilation of the New Testament, so the Gnostics determined the orthodox thinkers, such as Irenaeus, Clement of Alexandria, and Origen, to articulate their theological agendas.

Unlike Marcion, the Gnostics did not exactly promote their own biblical "canon," nor did they reject the Old Testament as a whole.[59] They did indulge, however, in their own open canon with a definite tendency for the esoteric and eclectic, especially in their choice of the Gospels of Didymus, Judas, and Thomas as carriers of Jesus's genuine sayings over the Gospels of the mainstream Church (Matthew, Mark, Luke, and John). The Gnostics showed a milder attitude toward the Jewish Scriptures by insisting on the diverse origin of the laws contained in these Scriptures. Yet very similar to Marcion, the Gnostics demonstrated a hostile attitude toward the God of creation, who they also styled as the "God of the Jews."

Their almost exclusive preference for highly oblique allegorical interpretations was probably the main reason why the Gnostics did not reject the Jewish Scripture outright and, as a matter of fact, the New Testament also. In contrast to Marcion, whose literal interpretation of Jewish Scriptures brought him to the radical conclusions exposed in the previous section, the Gnostics perceived an allegorical potential. Unlike the typological readings of Clement and Origen, however, the Gnostics in allegorizing the Jewish Scriptures tended to show a denial or else indifference to the historicity of the events recorded by them.

In the Gnostics' view, some parts of the Old Testament were inspired by a seed of *plērōma* planted in the world, whereas others (especially the laws and the prophecies) were inspired by a lesser god, a demiurge. If the Simonian Gnosticism assigned some of the prophecies to the angels responsible for the creation of the world, Saturninus attributed some of these prophecies to Satan himself. Their infatuation with Hebrew names of God (primarily *'ĕlōhîm*) brought the Gnostics to the conclusion that the Supreme God cannot be equated with the God of creation or the God of the Jews.

With regard to the Gnosticism professed by Simon Magus, Cerinthus and Saturninus, the only evidence comes from the church fathers— most especially, Irenaeus. A more advanced type of Gnosticism is that of Valentinus. The main source of evidence for Valentinus' views is the *Gospel of Truth*[60] attributed to him. Another Gnostic ostracized by the church fathers is Basilides, roughly contemporary with Valentinus and Marcion.

One of the most famous Christian Gnostics of the second century was Ptolemy, a disciple of Valentinus. He lived and taught in Rome. His works are extant only in fragmentary form: one portion of an exegetical work, preserved by Irenaeus (*Against Heresies* 1.8.5), and a letter to Flora, a non-Gnostic Christian woman, preserved by Epiphanius (*Panarion*

33.3.1–7, 10).[61] The letter is one of the clearest expositions of Gnostic doctrine on the Law of the Old Testament.

The *Letter to Flora* is only the beginning of Ptolemy's teaching to Flora. It was written as an introduction to Valentinian Christianity for the uninitiated.[62] According to this letter, the correct interpretation of the Bible depends on one's view on divine inspiration. The orthodox err because they state that the Law was given by the perfect God, while the Law is imperfect.

To Flora's inquiry concerning the origin of the Old Testament Law, Ptolemy states that the Law cannot be attributed to the perfect God the Father nor to the devil. Rather, it may be divided into three groups of precepts corresponding to three different authors: an inferior god (the demiurge occupying a middle position between the perfect God and the devil), Moses, and elders. Further, the laws attributed to the inferior god are to be divided into three sections: the pure legislation of the Decalogue, which was not to be destroyed but fulfilled by the Savior; the laws mixed with evil (e.g., the vengeance law), which were abolished by the Savior; and finally, the laws symbolizing a higher reality (i.e., the regulations concerning the circumcision, Sabbath, Passover). On the last group of laws, Ptolemy comments in his *Letter to Flora*:

> Since all these were images and allegories, they were transformed when the truth appeared. Outwardly and in bodily observance they were abrogated; spiritually they were adopted, with the names remaining the same but the actions altered. The Savior did command us to offer sacrifices, not of dumb animals or their odors but of spiritual hymns, praises, and thanksgiving, and charity and beneficence to our neighbors. He wants us also to have a circumcision, not of the bodily foreskin but of spiritual heart—and to keep Sabbath, for it is his will that we desist from evil works. And to fast—but it is his will that we keep not the bodily fast but the spiritual, which includes abstinence from all evil.
>
> Epiphanius, *Panarion 33.5.8*[63]

However, remarks Ptolemy, some of these typical laws, such as fasting, are still observed by Christians in their original material garb.

As already noted, the Gnostics did not reject the Old Testament outright. They did, however, prepare the path for the Manichaeans, who would go to extremes in their treatment of the Jewish Scriptures.

Manichaeans

Manichaeism was the major world religion to be born out of the dying Near Eastern Gnosticism in Late Antiquity soon after the third century c.e. The birthplace of this religion was Mesopotamia. So powerful was the influence of Manichaeism in the Christian world that even throughout the Middle Ages all other dualistic heresies, such as those of the Bogomils and Albegensians, were labeled by Christian heresiologists as "Manichaeism." However, Manichaeism was not a mere Christian heresy, but a distinct religion of its own.

The founder of this oriental religion, the Iranian prophet Mani (216–77 c.e.), sought to found a universal and missionary religion by combining elements taken from Christianity, Zoroastrianism, and Buddhism. His religion spread quickly. Already in his lifetime, the prophecy of Mani reached India in the east, and the Roman Empire in the west.

Mani was born on April 14, 216 c.e. in Ctesiphon, southeast of Mesopotamia. At first he belonged, like his father, to a Judeo-Christian baptismal sect characterized by Gnostic and ascetic tendencies. After receiving two angelic visions that revealed a new teaching to him at age twelve and nineteen, Mani severed his ties with his baptismal sect. Not coincidentally, the central idea of Mani's teaching was that redemption comes not through baptism but through a sharp separation, both physical and moral, between light and darkness, spirit and matter, good and evil. As with all the Gnostics, the key question that propelled the extreme dualism of the Manicheans was that of the origin of evil. More precisely, the question is thus: Is evil a substance or, as Augustine was later to assert, the mere absence of good?

Mani's Church was divided into two groups: the elect and the auditors. The elect were vegetarian, abstinent, poor, and involved daily in a moral combat with evil. With the help of the *Nous* (Mind), which is to be found in the Manichaean teachings,[64] the elect could reach redemption. The role of the *Nous* was to assist the elect in discerning the sharp dichotomy between light and darkness and to sustain them in moral combat. The Manicheans believed that those not awakened by the *Nous* would be punished with reincarnation into animal bodies, to be relegated finally to the Kingdom of Darkness. Mani's Church was hierarchical, led by a pope (Mani's successor), twelve apostles, seventy-two bishops, and three hundred sixty elders.

Regarding the Christian Scriptures, Mani rejected the whole of the Old Testament, but preserved most of the New. He rejected the Acts of the

Apostles, however: in his opinion, the mention of the descent of the Holy Spirit at Pentecost in Acts did not fit his own claim to be the Paraclete promised by Jesus at the Last Supper (John 14:16, 26).

An informative view into the extreme ingenuity with which the Manicheans collected and interpreted scriptural texts can be found in the anti-Manichean writings of Augustine. Of these, *Reply to Faustus the Manichaean* especially stands out. Written about 400 C.E., this work is Augustine's response to his former Roman master Faustus,[65] who dared to express harsh criticisms of Old Testament and even the New whenever the latter contradicted his own ideas. Besides rejecting the Old Testament in its entirety, Faustus's teaching was also replete with anti-Judaic overtones. Faustus despised the patriarchs, Moses and the prophets of the Old Testament, on moral grounds; he also held that the Gospels in their current form were not the work of the apostles but rather of some later Judaizing forgers.

Although in his own time his critique was seen as quite strong and well founded, Augustine's answers to Faustus are somewhat evasive, and only partially satisfactory, often betraying a poor understanding of the relation between the two testaments. To Faustus's difficult and pertinent questions, Augustine replies by resorting to an allegorical and symbolical interpretation of the sayings and actions recorded by the Old Testament. The work is important mainly from the point of view of biblical criticism.

Faustus rejects the Old Testament because it leaves no room for Christ. "When a vessel is full, what is poured on it is not received, but allowed to run over." The New Testament represents the full vessel. If one adds the Old Testament to the New Testament then its content will run over. Faustus continues: "For to pour gall on honey, or water on wine, or alkaline on vinegar, is not addition, but adulteration. This is why we do not receive the Old Testament." He states ironically, "We leave the Old Testament to your Church [i.e., that of Augustine], that, like a bride faithless to her spouse, delights in the letters and gifts of another" (*Reply to Faustus the Manichaean* 15.1).[66]

On Manichean views of the Old Testament, book twenty-two of *Reply to Faustus the Manichean* is the most important of the entire treatise.[67] Faustus brings forward two key points of criticism. First, the Old Testament statements about God are lies if the god of the Jews is to be viewed as good. Second, the crimes and sins committed by the patriarchs and prophets do not reflect well on their moral character.

In response to these accusations, Augustine interprets the Old Testament statements about God in a symbolical, allegorical way. Likewise, he argues, the "crimes" or sins of the patriarchs could be interpreted by appealing to the customs of those days (e.g., Jacob having four wives was permissible in his time), or as deeds reported with no approbation from either God or the writers of the Old Testament (e.g., the incest of Lot), or finally, as symbolic acts prefiguring future events regarding Christ and his Church (e.g., Hosea marrying a prostitute). In the case of Moses killing the Egyptian who was beating a Hebrew, Augustine again interprets it allegorically, as hinting at Christ killing the devil to defend his brother, namely, humanity. In addition, Augustine notes, the Scriptures often condemn the sins of its main cast of characters while praising their good deeds (e.g., the case of David). Faustus is therefore wrong to conclude that if the mainstream Church accepts the Old Testament Scriptures, then this means that it must praise all the deeds recorded by them.

Throughout his reply, Augustine uses a hermeneutical principle one may call "difference in times" in order to link the two testaments together. This principle allows Augustine to explain the differences between the Old and New Testaments while also discerning a progressive revelation of God in his dealings with humanity. Thus, God allows certain human customs (e.g., sexual behavior) in the past (Old Testament times) while forbidding the same after the incarnation of the Logos (New Testament times). So no Christian is allowed to cite Abraham's behavior vis-à-vis his maidservant Hagar to excuse his own sexual relation with his female servant.

The Manicheans also suggested that the Old and New Testaments were at odds with one another on various topics. For instance, the Old Testament preaches violence, while the New Testament teaching translates into love and peace. Augustine's reply to this was that even in the New Testament we find differences between various statements of Jesus. On the one hand, Jesus orders his disciples not to carry any purse with them, while on the other hand, the same Jesus tells them to acquire a purse.

As a general conclusion, we may note that the Manicheans followed the literal interpretation of Scripture, while the mainstream Christian writers used the allegorical. Moreover, it may be argued that Augustine, in his very attempt to defend the Old Testament, despoils it of any inherent historical value. He comes close to reducing the Old Testament to a mere compendium of messianic prophecies that were fulfilled in Christ and historical statements whose complete meaning was revealed post factum through Christ's coming. In Augustine's own words, "We have repeatedly shown at great length, that the precepts and symbols of the Old Testament contained both what was to be fulfilled in obedience through the grace bestowed in the New Testament, and what was to be set aside as a proof of its having been fulfilled in the truth now made manifest" (*Reply to Faustus the Manichaean* 22.6).[68]

Overestimation

Jewish Christians

In Gal 2:14, Paul accuses Peter of hypocrisy. Peter, who upon his arrival at Antioch was eating with Gentile Christians, separated himself from them when some Jewish Christians sent by James made their appearance. In Paul's view, Peter's attitude conveyed a wrong message: Gentile Christians should be compelled to "live like Jews" (*ioudaïzein*).[69]

In our discussion of early Christian sects that overestimated the importance of the Old Testament to Christian faith, we prefer over the more restrictive term "Judaizer" a designation used by Jerome: "Jewish Christians" (*Commentary on Zechariah* 3.14.91).[70] This designation as adopted here should be understood along the lines of the definition offered by Joel Marcus: "Torah- and praxis-centered" Christianity (ethnically Jewish or non-Jewish). Marcus rightly remarks that this emphasis on Torah led to a variety of Christologies among Jewish Christians, sometimes reaching even a certain "de-emphasis on the importance of Christology."[71] According to this definition, the Jewish or non-Jewish ethnic origin of these Christian groups ranks second after their primary focus on the observance of Torah and its ritual precepts. Jewish Christian groups such as Ebionites, Nazarenes, and Elchasaites shared Jewish practices but not necessarily theology in common. Jewishness, in the ancient world, was conveyed above all through orthopraxy: circumcision, Sabbath, kosher food, and so on. Moreover, the criterion demarcating between a Christian Jew and a non-Christian Jew was the acceptance or refutation of Jesus's messianic claim (Epiphanius, *Panarion* 29.7.2).

The core of the Jewish Christians' preaching is represented in Acts 15:1: "Then certain individuals came down from Judea and were teaching the brothers, 'Unless you are circumcised according to the custom of Moses, you cannot be saved.'" According to a hint given in Col 2:14, the observance of the Sabbath day and kosher food prescriptions along with the already mentioned circumcision represented the three cardinal points of the Jewish Christians' message to Gentiles who embraced the gospel of salvation. The Jewish Christians overemphasized the Mosaic Law and the Old Testament, its revelatory matrix. They were not asking for a refutation of the New Covenant in Christ, in the way the Marcionites demanded the Old Testament's rejection. Nevertheless, their overemphasizing the Law sometimes led to a de-emphasis on Christology and a tilting of the balance between Old and New Testaments toward the former. This was a sort of reverse Christian supersessionism, this time with the Old Testament superseding the New. Here, the Old Testament becomes the criterion of truth for all the New Testament assertions. We may contrast this view with the teaching of Ignatius of Antioch discussed earlier in this chapter. Ignatius speaks of Jesus's death and resurrection as his own "archives" and as such the true criterion over the Old Testament "archives" employed by the Jewish Christians as the main criterion of veracity for Jesus's messiahship.

Despite the Apostolic Council in Jerusalem (ca. 48 c.e.) and its guidelines (Acts 15), the Jewish Christians in Galatia continued to preach the need for the Gentiles to observe the entire Mosaic Law. These "all zealous for the Law" folks (Acts 21:20) became a great obstacle and danger for Paul's mission to the Gentiles in Asia Minor and Greece. Paul's message to the Gentile Christians in Galatia (Gal 5:1–6) emphasizes the freedom resulting from Christ's salvific work. Circumcision cannot save. Only faith in Christ working through love can do this. Paul also attacks these same Torah-observant missionaries to the Gentiles in his letter to the Philippians (see 3:2–3, where the Jewish Christians are called "dogs"). The Jewish Christians are also targeted in 2 Corinthians (11:5, 22–23).

The mere fact that many writings of the New Testament deal with the issue of Torah observance demonstrates the significant influence of Jewish Christianity in the apostolic period. The death of the most influential apostles Paul, Peter, and James by the early 60s and the first Jewish revolt against the Romans (66–70 c.e.) created a gulf between the first and second generation of Christians. The Jewish Christians sought to fill this gap by insisting on the Law as guarantor of theological continuity. To this end, the Epistle of James, written toward the end of the first century, emphasizes the Law while downplaying Christology.[72] As Marcus rightly notes,[73] however, not all Jewish Christians came to choose between a high view of Torah and a high view of Jesus. For instance, Matthew, who was probably a Jew by birth, succeeds in wedding quite well faith in Jesus's divinity (Matt 1:23; 28:16–20) with a high view of the Law (5:17–20).

The destruction of Jerusalem Temple (70 C.E.), where Jewish Christians gathered for worship, was an important factor contributing to the eventual marginalization of this group that represented the mass of Christians at least in the area surrounding Jerusalem. Yet the influence of this group continued for the first quarter or so of the second century. In the East, the *Didache*, a late first or early second century document apparently originating in Syria, Palestine, or Egypt, could have been written by a Jewish Christian writer. In Syria, the influence of Jewish Christianity was very strong. It is reflected in the translation of the Peshitta.[74]

Jewish Christianity's sway was not limited to the East. Writings such as *1 Clement* and the *Shepherd of Hermas*, both written in Rome at the end of the first century, beginning of the second century, show clear Jewish traces. The *Dialogue with Trypho*, composed by Justin Martyr in Rome about mid-second century, also testifies to Jewish Christianity's continued importance. Justin was born in Samaria and traveled to Asia Minor and Rome. His work mirrors the concerns of local churches in Palestine, Asia Minor, and Rome regarding Jewish Christianity.

The main respondents to the Jewish Christian claims—Justin, Barnabas, Melito, and Origen—had to answer a difficult question: Why did the mainstream Christians employ the Jewish Bible as Christian Scripture while also neglecting most prescriptions of the Law? The answer of these representatives of early orthodox Christianity was consistently the same: The Torah in its cultic aspects had a temporary validity, being restricted to the period prior to the coming of Messiah.

Speaking of Jewish Christians, Justin Martyr distinguishes between those who observe the Law while not imposing its observance on the Gentiles and those who seek to require the Gentile Christians to follow the Mosaic prescriptions. Here is a fragment from *Dialogue with Trypho* (47):

And Trypho again inquired, "But if someone, knowing that this is so, after he recognizes that this man is Christ, and has believed in and obeys him, wishes, however, to observe these [institutions], will he be saved?" I said, "In my opinion, Trypho, such one will be saved, if he does not strive in every way to persuade other men, I mean those Gentiles who have been circumcised from error by Christ, to observe the same things as himself, telling them that they will not be saved unless they do so. This you did yourself at the commencement of the discourse, when you declared that I would not be saved unless I observe these institutions."[75]

Ebionites

By the end of the second century, the impetus of the Jewish Christians began to decrease and they were known only as a sect, the Ebionites. Epiphanius (*Panarion* 30.2) suggests that the Ebionites fled Jerusalem for Pella before 70 C.E. The earliest literary evidence of this sect is found in Irenaeus, who labeled this group "heretical" because they lived according to the "Judaic way of life," including circumcision, and also doubted the virgin birth (*Against Heresies* 1.26.2; 5.1.3).[76] Apparently, while teaching a human parentage of Jesus, the Ebionites sacrificed Christ's divinity to the monotheistic faith they saw proclaimed by the Jewish Scriptures. According to Irenaeus, the Ebionites rejected Paul's view on the Law:

> Those who are called Ebionites agree that the world was made by God; but their opinions with respect to the Lord are similar to those of Cerinthus and Carpocrates. They use the Gospel according to Matthew only, and repudiate Apostle Paul, maintaining that he was an apostate from the Law. As to the prophetical writings, they endeavor to expound them in a somewhat singular manner: they practice circumcision, persevere in the observance of those customs which are enjoined by the Law, and are so Judaic in their style of life, that they even adore Jerusalem as if it were the house of God.
>
> *Against Heresies* 1.26.2[77]

Some time after Irenaeus, Hippolytus of Rome (170–235 C.E.) also tells us that the Ebionites believed that Jesus was named *Christ* "because he obeyed the Law; the Ebionites were therefore also to obey the Law so that they could become Christs" (*Refutation of All Heresies* 7.22).

Regarding the etymology of the name, the Ebionites, there are several opinions among early church writers. Tertullian suggests that this name should be related to the founder of the sect, Ebion (Hebion). For Origen, the name of the sect says something about its members who are "poor in understanding,"[78] since they were emphasizing that Jesus was sent only to the Jews (*On the Principles* 4.38; *Against Celsus* 2.1). One may mention here that since the discovery of the Dead Sea Scrolls, the term Ebionites has been compared with the "poor ones" (*'ebyōnîm*) referring to the members of the Qumran community (1QpHab 12, 3, 6, 10). In 4QpPsalms

(4Q171), the Qumran community is termed "the congregation of the poor ones ('*dt h'bynym*)."

Origen was the first (*Against Celsus* 5.61; cf. Eusebius, *Ecclesiastical History* 3.27) to distinguish between two groups of Ebionites: those who accepted and those who rejected the virginal birth of Christ. In the fourth century, Epiphanius calls the former Nazarenes and the latter Ebionites.[79] While the Nazarenes shared a high Christology, with Jesus as Son of God born of a virgin, the Ebionites had a low Christology, seeing Jesus as a mere man born of Mary and Joseph. It has been suggested that while the Ebionites may have looked to the Epistle of James (limited, low Christology and anti-Paulinism), the Nazarenes could be traced back to the Gospel of Matthew.[80]

Epiphanius (*Panarion* 30) also attributes some of the Pseudo-Clementine literature to the Ebionites. The most representative parts of this literature, using the literary genre of ancient secular romance, are the *Homilies* and *Recognitions*.[81] The core teaching of the *Homilies* (twenty in number) may be summed up as follows: Christian revelation is merely a restoration of Mosaic revelation. However, the sacrifices of the old covenant are a Mosaic concession to Israel that Jesus came to abolish (*Recognitions* 1.36–39).[82] For Pseudo-Clement, the Christian faith was intended by Moses. The coming of the Gentiles was in order because this way the number revealed to Abraham (Gen 15) was fulfilled by Gentiles, replacing those among the Jews who did not receive Christ.

As for the scriptural canon, the Ebionites accepted the Gospel of Matthew (which they termed the *Gospel According to the Hebrews*)[83] while rejecting the Pauline letters. The Gospel of the Ebionites, as mentioned by Epiphanius (*Panarion* 30.13), began with the baptism of Jesus by John. Epiphanius also suggests that the Ebionites rejected parts of the Pentateuch (*Panarion* 30.18.7), as well as the Prophets and Psalms (30.25.2), though this is uncertain.

Pelagians

I list the Pelagians under "Overestimation" for the mere fact that they placed the Old Testament on parity with the New Testament, which was equated with overvaluing the first covenant.

Under the threat of the Goths, culminating with the sack of Rome on August 24, 410 c.e., Pelagius and his disciple Celestius left Rome in 409 c.e. for Hippo and then Carthage. Here Augustine met Pelagius at the council of 411 c.e. convoked by Count Marcellinus to put an end to the controversy with the Donatists. However, Augustine did not have the chance to speak with Pelagius on those occasions (*On the Proceedings of Pelagius* 22.46). Shortly after, Pelagius went to Palestine, where he found favor with bishop John of Jerusalem, but his disciple remained in Carthage. In Carthage, under the influence of Rufinus the Syrian, Celestius drew attention for himself in Christian circles for his views regarding the topic of original sin. At a synod in late fall 411 c.e. at Carthage, Celestius was accused of disseminating these six theses:

1. Adam was created mortal and sinning or unsinning could not change his destiny.
2. Adam's sin had an impact on him alone and not on the whole human race.
3. Infants at the time of baptism are in the same condition as Adam prior to his transgression.
4. Humans do not die due to Adam's transgression, and they will not rise again due to Christ's resurrection.
5. The Law leads people to the kingdom of heaven in the same way as does the gospel.
6. Even prior to Christ's birth there were men without sin.

The synod finally excommunicated Celestius since he would not abjure these theses. These six charges are listed in two sources: Marius Mercator, *Commonitory against Celestius* and Augustine, *On the Proceedings of Pelagius* 11.23 (in a different order).[84] Augustine mentions in his *Retractions* (2.45) how a synod was held in Palestine in 417 c.e., where Pelagius was called to expose his teachings but his accusers were absent on the day of Pelagius's appearance; the synod thus issued no official condemnation against him. Augustine's reason for writing his treatise *On the Proceedings of Pelagius* (ca. 417 c.e.) was to discard the presumption that since Pelagius was acquitted his opinions were automatically approved by the bishops present at that synod.

In chapters 14 and 15 of the *Proceedings*, Augustine seeks to refute Pelagius's thesis on the parity between the Law and the gospel. For Augustine, the distinction between the two testaments lies with the nature of their promises. If the Old Testament's promises are centered on earthly realities, the New Testament's promises concern the heavenly realities such as the kingdom of heaven.

The Juxtaposition of Old and New Testaments

Scriptural Supersessionism

The ubiquitous and long-lasting Christian supersessionism[85] and its theological implications for the ongoing Jewish-Christian dialogue will be touched on sporadically throughout this work. Here, I would like to deal only with those aspects of supersessionism pertaining to the relationship between the Old and New Testaments: namely, the continuities and discontinuities between these two canonical corpora from a Christian hermeneutical standpoint.[86]

From the onset, one may notice an interesting paradox. On the one hand, the Christian Bible, as it stands, consists of Old and New Testaments as two juxtaposed yet quite distinct corpora. As tense as it might seem, there is a unity of two collections of books within one Bible, the Christian Bible, that is. For the common Christian reader of Holy Writ, the linking element between the two testaments lies with the very Christ event at the center of a succession of historical events commonly labeled the "history of salvation."[87] The terms "old" and "new" attached to the term "testament" (*diathēkē*, which in Greek means primarily "covenant") should be understood as chronological qualifiers defining a mild and time-related supersessionism. On the other hand, the Christian apologists and theologians, beginning with the second century and long after, have repeatedly employed rhetoric that emphasizes a sort of structural supersessionism in which the New Testament superseded and, to a certain degree, if not entirely, replaced the Old Testament (i.e., the Jewish Scriptures).[88] Thus, for Tertullian, "continuance of the Old Testament has been buried in Christ" (*On Fasting: In Opposition to Psychics* 14).[89] This supersessionist viewpoint consigned Jews to a dead-end situation that could be terminated only by conversion to Christian faith. This viewpoint is still upheld in some Eastern Orthodox Christian circles. According to this view, if Israel has a contribution to the Christian faith, that contribution is exclusively related to the Old Testament times and almost restricted to the righteous figures of the Old Testament having an interpretive impact on the New Testament messianic fulfillment. The living Israel has been totally ignored if not rhetorically demonized.[90] For many of Eastern Orthodox Christian faithful, Paul's kind references to Israel in Rom 9–11, are to be relegated to the overidealized Israel of the Old Testament period. In this context, a pertinent question arises: How, then, could the current "dead" Israel—with its deep roots in the patriarchs, the prophets and the covenants—be a source of life and nourishment for those branches that have been grafted on—namely, the followers of Jesus?

I personally think that Eastern Orthodox hierarchs should take a clear, courageous, and well-articulated stand to amend such erroneous yet popular and resilient views among the faithful of their Churches. The work of teachers in Eastern Orthodox seminaries is not enough to discard these perilous teachings spread through various channels if the bishops are not vocal enough in condemning anti-Judaic feelings while promoting a healthy environment for genuine Jewish-Christian relations.

A concrete step in this direction can be taken in the area of liturgical life. The Orthodox Church, as a whole, and especially and more effectively the hierarchs, should revise and discard anti-Judaic statements and allusions from hymnography and from liturgy itself, as a matter of fact. The poetry of Eastern Orthodox hymns is too sublime to be marred by such low sentiments echoing from a past dominated by religious quarrels and controversies. Just a frugal look at the Orthros service on Good Friday will make any honest believer wonder if some of the hymns are appropriate for such a holy day, or indeed for any day of the liturgical year.

For instance, on Holy Friday, when we commemorate Christ's prayer of forgiveness for those who crucified him, "Father, forgive them; for they do not know what they are doing" (Luke 23:34), the Church is still praying for "the murderers of God, the lawless nation of the Jews" (Beatitudes, *sticheron*), in a way that has little if nothing to do with forgiveness: "But give them, O Lord, their reward, for they devised vain things against you [cf. Ps 2:1]" (*antiphon*).

A similar problem has been faced by the Roman Catholic Church in her liturgical tradition. Shortly after his election, Pope John XXIII interrupted the Good Friday liturgy of 1959 at the moment of the "prayer for the Jews," *Oremus et pro perfidis Judaeis* ("Let us pray for the perfidious Jews") and asked the celebrant to repeat the prayer without the word "perfidious." The result of such a dramatic act was the removal of the adjective *perfidis*, "faithless, perfidious" from the Roman Missal.[91]

Having said this, I am not calling here on a quick and in toto revision of the Eastern Orthodox liturgy, but rather for an ongoing serious reflection and congenial discussion on those anti-Judaic statements in hymnography, which are not and should not be part of such a sophisticated and Christ-centered tradition as is the Orthodox. I am deeply cognizant of the fact that there are strong and passionate voices on each end of the spectrum. On the one hand, there are folks urging for immediate individual or group-based actions. Unfortunately, such a drastic and brusque move will lead to an unnecessary division within the Church with regrettable consequences hard even to imagine. On the other hand, there are stark defenders of the status quo: Liturgy is the *lex orandi*, higher even than the *lex credendi* (theology), so there must be no liturgical revision at all. Painfully enough, such a position continues to convey a wrong message to the non-Orthodox. Both extremes, as life may prove it, are perilous and should be avoided. However, the significant number of believers, even among theologically educated folks, who support the "conservative" view, worries me because it shows an increased level of insensitivity toward Jews who suffered also due to this kind of "soft" and "inoffensive" anti-Judaic rhetoric encountered in hymns or homilies (see Chrysostom's *Eight Homilies Against the Jews*). It is my strong conviction that theologians and clergy have a duty to cultivate the basic human values among believers. Doing so, we can hope that one day, the Church as a whole, starting with the grass-roots level, will reach that stage of maturity and sensitivity so needed for a serious, well balanced, peace building, and sustainable revision.

As one can easily observe, the "fulfillment theology," or more pejoratively, "replacement theology," with its supersessionist overtones, withstands the symbiotic yet tense unity between the two testaments, turning the Old Testament into a lifeless, dusty, and mostly useless archive. Here, I may add, as with other aspects of church life, there is an obvious dichotomy between popular and theological levels of Eastern Orthodox tradition. In many cases, theological reflection does not harmonize with the sentiments that should be evoked by the reality of actual church practice. For instance, in the case discussed here, the very juxtaposition of the two testaments within the Christian Bible stands in opposition to the supersessionist intimations that permeate theological treatises and biblical interpretations throughout the church history.

Speaking of the two planes of Christian tradition, Jaroslav Pelikan argued that the litanies of the Church preserve the initial articulation of faith more faithfully than its formal dogmatic statements.[92] While appropriating the Jewish Scriptures as proof-texts or pointers toward the Christ event, the first apologists and theologians had the unmediated opportunity to compare closely the Jewish Scriptures with their own emergent writings centered on the "gospel of salvation" and were thus able to notice various continuities and discontinuities between the two surging canonical corpora. While celebrating the flurry of continuities under the triumphant banner of "messianic fulfillment," the Christian writers tried hard to downplay the discontinuities by resorting to various hermeneutical procedures, such as allegorical interpretation.

Continuity with the Scripture of ancient Israel is claimed by both Christianity and Judaism. This continuity is a matter of interpretation and not of readily apparent objective textuality. However, there is a difference between these communities of faith as regards the nature of the scriptural continuity. The pertinent remark of Jon D. Levenson that "there is more continuity between the [Hebrew] Bible and its rabbinic interpretation than between the Bible and its early Christian interpretation" must be seriously weighed. By claiming for itself the status of "New Israel" along with a new corpus of sacred books, the New Testament, Christianity underwent a "quantum leap" which is absent in rabbinic Judaism. The latter has no particular theological motivation to "deny the pluriform character of the Hebrew Bible,"[93] the result being Judaism's more obvious continuity with the Jewish Scriptures.

In his seminal study, "Qumran and Supersessionism—and the Road Not Taken," Krister Stendahl takes on the much-debated topic of Christian supersessionism, showing that the very claim to be the only legitimate scriptural continuity is the driving force behind supersessionism. For a better illustration of this thesis, Stendahl compares the early Church with the Qumran community and its claim for scriptural continuity with the Jewish Scriptures:

> The Qumran texts and that whereof they speak can sharpen the analysis needed in a search for better ways. For in those texts one can see with great clarity that the driving force behind supersessionism is the claim to the true, authentic, and only legitimate continuity to the inherited history. At Qumran we see this claim intensified by high voltage eschatology with all the habits of demonizing the Other that comes with the territory; and the heightened standards of purity add weight to the claim as it is buttressed by divinely authorized (re)interpretation, (re)assessment and (re) adjustment of that tradition to which one claims to be the legitimate heir. The claim to exclusive continuity is the very spine of supersessionism.[94]

I concur, to a certain degree, with Stendahl in his assertion regarding the close relationship between supersessionism and the Christian claim for the legitimate continuity. But one must ask: What about Marcionism, an extreme form of Christian supersessionism that began with an anti-Law attitude—that is, a rigorous claim for rather scriptural discontinuity between the "gospel of salvation" and the Jewish Scriptures? To reconcile Stendahl's observation with this question, one should distinguish between various sorts of supersessionism: mainly, between a harsh supersessionism induced by a Christian (but most often, heretical) emphasis on scriptural discontinuity (as in Marcion's rejection of Old Testament) versus much softer forms of supersessionism caused primarily by an exclusive Christian claim to scriptural continuity with the first testament.

In the following passage, Tertullian speaks of the abrogation of the Law and the establishment of the gospel as marking the "period of separation" or supersession, namely, the old Law being superseded by the new Law. The Christian apologist argues against the Marcionites who, ironically, could not accept that the old Law had been annulled by its very author:

> The epistle which we also allow to be the most decisive against Judaism, is that wherein the apostle instructs the Galatians. For the abolition of the ancient Law we fully admit, and hold that it actually proceeds from the dispensation of the Creator, a point that we have already often treated in the course of our discussion, when we showed that the innovation was foretold by the prophets of our God. Now, if the Creator indeed promised that "the ancient things should pass away," [compare Isa 43:18, 19 and 45:17 with 2 Cor 5:17] to be superseded by a new course of things which should arise, while Christ marks the period of the separation when he says, "The Law and the prophets were until John" [Luke 16:16]—thus making the Baptist the limit between the two dispensations of the old things then terminating—and the new things then beginning, the apostle cannot of course do otherwise, (coming as he does) in Christ, who was revealed after John, than invalidate "the old things" and confirm "the new," and yet promote thereby the faith of no other god than the Creator, at whose instance it was foretold that the ancient things should pass away.
>
> *Against Marcion* 5.2[95]

The extreme form of this harsh suppersessionism is the rejection of the entire Old Testament which we discussed above with reference to the anti-Law attitudes of Marcionites and Manichaeans.

In the following section, I will succinctly review the main types of scriptural continuities and discontinuities along with New Testament and early Christian evidence.

Continuities and Discontinuities

Fulfilling the Law and the Prophets

"Do not think that I have come to abolish (*katalysai*) the law or the prophets; I have come not to abolish but to fulfill" (Matt 5:17).

Given the repetition of the verb *katalyō*, "to put down, loosen; to destroy, annul, abolish," in negative form, one should agree that the accent in this text falls not on the abolishment of the Law but rather on its fulfillment. Jesus seeks to dismiss all the accusations that he would neglect or abolish the Torah. To this goal, he asserts emphatically that he never intended to annul the Torah's observance. As a proof, he declares that whatever he is doing is toward the fulfillment of the Torah. A difficult question remains though: What did Jesus understand by fulfilling the Law? The meaning cannot be gleaned solely from the semantic analysis of the Greek verb *plēroō*, "to fulfill, accomplish, finish." One might take a closer look at the context, primarily to the following v. 18. The mere juxtaposition "Law or Prophets" would make one think of a fulfillment of the old prophecies and a messianic orientation attached to the observance of the Law. According to some ancient and modern commentators, the saying should be understood "in the sense of bringing it [the Law] to its intended meaning in connection with the messianic fulfillment"[96] accomplished by Jesus.

> The Son of God, who is the author of the Law and the Prophets, did not come to abolish the Law or the Prophets. He gave the people the Law that was to be handed down through Moses, and he imbued the prophets with the Holy Spirit for the preaching of the things to come. Therefore he said, "I have come not to abolish the Law and the Prophets but to fulfill them." He fulfilled the Law and the Prophets in this way: He brought to pass those things that had been written about him in the Law and the Prophets. Hence, when he drank the vinegar offered him on the cross, he said, "It is finished" [John 19:30], evidently to show that everything written about him in the Law and the Prophets had been completed, even including the drinking of vinegar. He fulfilled the Law at any rate when he completed by the sacrament of his passion the once prefigured

mystery of the paschal meal. Consequently the apostle says, "For Christ our paschal lamb has been sacrificed" [1 Cor 5:7].

Chromatius, *Tractate on Matthew* 20.1.1–2[97]

However, such an interpretation is not supported by this logion's immediate context. Jesus's words recorded by Matt 5:17–18 reflect rather a un- or anti-Pauline position, emphasizing the *halakhic* rigorism among his followers.[98]

The Antiquated Covenant

"In speaking of 'a new covenant', he has made the first one obsolete. And what is obsolete and growing old will soon disappear" (Heb 8:13).

The author of Heb 8:8–12 cites Jer 31:31–34 in conformity with the Septuagint text (Jer 38:31–34) in Codex Alexandrinus with some variations. The cited passage, embedded in Jer 30–33, a long section of oracles referring to the future fate of the exiled Israelites, speaks of the new covenant and its main characteristics. First, the new covenant will be inscribed not on stone but on heart (vv. 10–11). Second, this new covenant will entail effective forgiveness of sins (v. 12). In v. 13, the author of Hebrews concludes from the mention of a "new" (*kainē*) covenant in Jer 31:31–34 that the "first" (*prōtē*) covenant became "antiquated" (*pepalaiōken*) and "aged" (*gēraskon*), thus "close to vanishing" (*engys aphanismou*). However, this is a mere exegetical conclusion and no inference about the old covenant or Law being abrogated or abolished is warranted by this text, the focus of which is on the shining promises of the new covenant.

Note, however, Justin Martyr's interpretation of "old" and "new" laws, where the old Law has been annulled by the new Law:

> For the Law promulgated on Horeb is now old, and belongs to yourselves alone; but *this* is for all universally. Now, Law placed against Law has annulled (*epause*)[99] that which is before it, and a covenant which comes after in like manner has put an end to the previous one; and an eternal and final Law—namely, Christ—has been given to us, and the covenant is trustworthy, after which there shall be no Law, no commandment, no ordinance.
>
> *Dialogue with Trypho* 11[100]

Even though not cited elsewhere in the New Testament, Jer 31:31–34 had a significant impact on the Christology of the Hebrews while also exercising a great influence on both Qumran (cf. CD 6:19; 8:21; 20:12) and early Christian communities (cf. Matt 26:28; Mark 14:24; Luke 22:20; 1 Cor 11:25; 2 Cor 3:6) in shaping their own claims for being the eschatological covenant community heralded in the Old Testament oracle.[101]

A Pedagogue toward Christ

"Therefore the Law was our pedagogue toward Christ, so that we may be justified by faith. But after the faith has come, we are no longer under a pedagogue" (Gal 3:24–25, author's translation).

Even though Paul never speaks of an ultimate abolition of Torah (Law), this verse depicts the Law as a pedagogue whose task in antiquity was to guard the pupil on its way to school. The ancient "pedagogue" (*paidagōgos*), usually a slave, has nothing to do with our modern understanding of the pedagogue as directly involved in the process of education. In antiquity the term pedagogue was not identifiable with "teacher" (*didaskalos*). Paul's usage was strongly influenced by the Hellenistic Judaism, where the ancient pedagogue was there to warn and chastise the pupil, to correct him by using a rod. The duty of the pedagogue ceased when the pupil reached the age of puberty.[102] Thus, likewise here, the Law has to cease with the coming of Christ. The Law represents the necessary backdrop of the gospel, meant to bring freedom instead of slavery of the Law: "But after the faith has come, we are no longer under a pedagogue" (Gal 3:25).

How did Paul come to this association between pedagogue and Law? From the time of Plato, the concept of "education" (*paideia*) had been combined with that of "law" (*nomos*). This was a common feature during the Hellenistic Judaism (4 Macc 1:17). Nevertheless, though associated with pedagogue, the Law is devaluated in Paul's passage. This semantic transformation appeared first in the Cynic-Stoic diatribe literature, which made its way into the Hellenistic Judaism from which Paul likely borrowed the main features of his description of Law as a pedagogue.[103]

A question arises at this juncture. Did the Law have a preparatory value? Did the Law prepare the way "toward" Christ? Or was it a mere guardian "until" the coming of Christ? The answer to this question depends on the meaning of Gk. *eis* ("toward" or "until") and Paul's view on Law as a pedagogue. If the latter is quite easy to grasp from the historic-cultural context, the meaning of the preposition *eis* is still debated; hence, the difficulty of reaching a general consensus on the connotation of these two verses. Yet, because Paul never pleads for a complete abrogation of the

Law, one may keep both aspects of the Law (custodian and preparator) in consideration.

The preparatory, instructional function of the Law is underscored among ancient commentators by Theodoret of Cyrus (ca. 393–457 C.E.): "Now it was necessary that the Law be given, as it fulfilled our need of a custodian. And it freed us from our previous impiety, taught us knowledge of God and then brought us to Christ the Lord as though to some wise teacher, so that we might be instructed by him in perfect learning and acquire the righteousness that is through faith" (*Epistle to the Galatians* 3.24).[104]

While noticing no opposition between Law and grace, Chrysostom shows that abiding by the Law after the coming of Christ is to ignore the temporary character of the Law as custodian: "Now if the Law was a custodian and we were confined under its direction, it was not opposed to grace but cooperated with it. But if it continues to bind us after grace has come, then it is opposed to grace. . . . Those who maintain their custody at this point are the ones who bring the child into the greatest disrepute. The custodian makes the child ridiculous when he keeps him close at hand even after the time has come for his departure" (*Homily on Galatians* 3.25–28).[105]

In some contrast, an anti-Judaic overtone may be detected in Marius Victorinus's interpretation of Paul's words, "That faith has come" to mean that Christ himself has come—the implication being that only then did faith arise. Christ's coming signals the "time for us to believe in him in whom is all salvation, in contrast to the Jews, who did not believe" (*Epistle to the Galatians* 2.3.25–26).[106]

The next voice is quite singular within the ancient supersessionist choir. Responding to those who rejected the Old Testament (e.g., Marcion, Celsus), Archelaus, a bishop in fourth century Roman Mesopotamia, states that the Jewish Scriptures stand in "perfect harmony" with the New Testament. However, he then raises a rhetorical question: Should "the boy who is brought by his pedagogue to the teachers of learning when he is yet a very little fellow ought to hold that pedagogue in no honor after he has grown up to manhood?" One may note that Archelaus's view on the honor the Christians should give to the Old Testament differs from Chrysostom's point of view that still being subject to the Law after Christ's coming is "ridiculous." For Archelaus, Moses was the guardian father, the pedagogue who cared for and instructed Israel during its slavery in Egypt and afterward during its pilgrimage in the wilderness. However, even after the very revelation of God himself, Israel still has to honor Moses, its old pedagogue. Paraphrasing Jesus's remarks at the end of the parable of Lazarus and the rich man (Luke 16:29–31), Archelaus makes his point quite clear: "'They have Moses and the prophets.' For if they received not these, so as to have their course directed by him, i.e., Moses, as by a pedagogue, they would not be capable of accepting the doctrine of the superior master" (*The Acts of the Disputation with the Hesiarch Manes* 41).[107]

Irrevocability of the Old Covenants

"They are Israelites, and to them belong the adoption, the glory, the covenants, the giving of the law, the worship, and the promises; to them belong the patriarchs, and from them, according to the flesh, comes the Messiah, who is over all, God blessed forever. Amen" (Rom 9:4–5).

The plural "the covenants" (*hai diathēkai*) hints at Paul's earlier phrase, "covenants of the fathers in Judaism" (Rom 4:18). Paul asserts that the covenants, including the "new covenant," belong to the "Israelites." They are open to the Gentiles but they do belong to the Israelites. The possessive *ōn*, "theirs, belonging to them," accents this idea.[108] However, in Rom 9:6–8, Paul speaks of an "Israel within Israel"—the distinction here is "between believing and physical Israel" or between "children of the flesh" and "children of the promise."[109] Closely connected to the covenants is "the giving of the Law" (*hē nomothesia*—the term occurs only in Rom 9:4 in the entire New Testament). This Law should be upheld (Rom 3:31) since it belongs to Israel's history and supports the concept of righteousness by faith (Rom 3:21). Therefore, those who embrace the gospel should not despise the Law, for through this Law they can enjoy the gospel's better promises.[110]

Interpreting Rom 9:4, Origen notices that the covenants were given frequently; thus, the status of Israel as receptacle and inheritor of these covenants was never lost but rather renewed:

> "The covenants" and "the giving of the Law" seem to be much the same thing. But I think there is this difference between them, that the Law was given once, by Moses, but covenants were given frequently. For every time the people sinned and were cast down, they were disinherited. And every time God was propitiated and he called them back to the inheritance of their possession, he renewed the covenants and declared them to be heirs once more.
>
> *Commentary on the Epistle to the Romans* 9.4[111]

"As regards the gospel they are enemies of God for your sake; but as regards election they are beloved, for the sake of their ancestors; for the gifts and the calling of God are irrevocable" (Rom 11:28–29).

If "the gifts" (*ta charismata*) in Rom 11:29 refer to the ten attributes of Israel in Rom 9:4–5, then the gifts including the covenants and the giving of the Law are in fact irrevocable. This teaching has not always been soundly maintained, however, by Christian exegetes. Note, for instance, Theodoret of Cyrus's anti-Judaic interpretation on the revocability of Israel's gifts. Theodoret uses kings Saul and Solomon as illustrations for his thesis:

> Paul says this in order to encourage the Jews. In fact, of course, God did revoke the good gifts which he gave. . . . King Saul, for example, who received spiritual grace which later deserted him [see 1 Sam 15:26; 28:6]. Likewise Solomon, who received peace through the kindness of God, but after his transgression was deprived of grace [see 1 Kgs 11:6–13]. And then, there are the Jews themselves, who always had their prophets to take care of them but who at the preswent time have been deprived of them.
>
> *Interpretation of the Letter to the Romans*[112]

In some contrast with what is found here in Theodoret, we listed above several New Testament texts along with early interpretations regarding the Christian claims for continuity between the two testaments, claims that generated a sort of soft, mild supersessionism centered on the antithesis "Old-New Israel." Here, the "old" refers to the Old Testament Israel while the "new" alludes to the Church.

There is also a peculiar variant of supersessionism, commonly coined "dispensationalism." This scriptural reductionism is aimed to sift the Jewish Scripture in quest for a curriculum of texts considered seminal for Christian readership. During the fifth century c.e. especially, this quest was an important preoccupation among the Christian interpreters and theologians. Thus the *Apostolic Constitutions* (probably late fourth century c.e.) made a distinction between the laws promulgated after the Golden Calf event (Exod 32) and the laws given before (e.g., the Decalogue [Exod 20] and the Covenant laws [21:1–23:19]), requiring the Christian believers to abide by those laws given prior to Exod 32 unless they were ceremonial. Thus, Cyril of Alexandria (376–444 c.e.) divides the Christian Bible in five periods. The first three periods (Moses, Joshua, Judges) are "impure" for Christians. During the fourth period (prophets) the Law was "purified." The fifth period, represented by Christ, brings the purification and spiritualization of the Law to a climax.[113]

Questioning the Supersessionist Views of the Past

On the sensitive topic of continuities and discontinuities within the Christian Bible, Jon D. Levenson notices the Christian community's "eagerness to discover a deep continuity between the two testaments of the Christian Bible," and goes on to say,

> I am not, please note, arguing that the Church should adopt the classical Jewish understanding of Israel, only that it should acknowledge the sources of that understanding in the Old Testament and not subordinate the Old Testament to the New quite so hastily and quite so thoroughly. That a Christian document would try to find things in the Old Testament that point to the New is readily understandable. But what about the things in the Old Testament that do *not* point to the New?[114]

Downplaying the scriptural discontinuities by an exaggerated quest for typologies and a consistent disinterest in the plain, historical meaning of the Jewish Scriptures has often led ancient Christian interpreters to harsh supersessionism. This type of supersessionism translates into a tensed relationship between the two testaments, going from the moderate (the New Testament structurally superseding the Old) to the extreme (rejection of the intrinsic value of the Old Testament), as well as a daring interference into the inner religious life of Judaism. The latter aspect of this supersessionism is prescriptive, implying Christian dictation directed to Jewish believers as to how they should conduct their worship, what sacred text to use, and what biblical interpretation to follow.[115] As Matthew Levering well notes, "Debating the claim that the Messiah has definitively fulfilled and reconfigured Torah is one thing; denying that Rabbinic Judaism can define what counts as the practice of Rabbinic Judaism is another."[116] And the latter attitude is a crude, harsh type of Christian supersessionism, which should be entirely decried.

In Krister Stendahl's view, a way out of the continuity-based supersessionism is to acknowledge that the "new things emerge" and discontinuity might coexist with continuity. Stendahl mentions a "benevolent typology" as an alternative to the supersessionist way followed by the Christian Church in the past:

> The logic of this thinking could actually have opened up a future in which Christianity could have both seen itself and been seen by Israel and the Nations as a "Judaism for Gentiles." But this was one road not taken. In such a model the supersessionism would have been overcome by a benevolent typology: There is a familiar shape to God's ways with the world, God's ever repeated attempts at the mending of what was broken, even restoring the imago dei in which humanity had been created. Such a benevolent typology would rejoice and marvel in the analogous shape of Passover and Easter, of Aqedah and Golgotha, of Sinai and the Sermon on the Mount. But the supersessionist drive forced typological interpretation into adversary patterns where the younger had to trump and trounce the older.[117]

In contrast, in his fine work, *The Death and Resurrection of the Beloved Son: The Transformation of Child Sacrifice in Judaism and Christianity,* Jon D. Levenson considers Judaism and Christianity as "two rival midrashic systems, competing for their common biblical legacy."[118] For this reason, Christian scriptural supersessionism cannot and *should not* be entirely discarded: it is part of the church history and her centuries-long hermeneutical legacy, argues Levenson. What the Christian *can* do is to renounce triumphalism, adopting a refreshing modesty while reading the Old Testament. Ephrem the Syrian's daring remark should be a continuous reminder for all Christians who embrace quite passionately the *theologia gloriae* while consciously neglecting its quintessential complement, the *theologia crucis*: "Humility is so powerful that even the all-conquering God did not conquer without it" (*Homily on Our Lord* 41).[119]

Although Levenson's cautiously balanced and insightful remarks are offered in response[120] to the 2002 document of the Pontifical Biblical Commission, *The Jewish People and Their Sacred Scriptures in the Christian Bible*, they may be directed also both to the supersessionism of Eastern Orthodox as well as the modern inclination toward relativism and "inclusiveness" at the expense of enduring age-old traditions. I would say that between a mild supersessionism that cannot be entirely avoided and Christian triumphalism, the latter should be easily discarded. This would help Christian and Jews to foster a genuine dialogue with a reciprocal understanding and respect for each other's tradition. In Levenson's view, losing one's identity in order to embrace a politically correct relativism is to depart from the truth, while the rejection of the claim that there is absolute truth means taking away the basis of any religious system.[121] It is thus as eschewing such political correctness that Levenson urges the following:

> If the Catholic Church is to combat that widespread and cultur-
> ally prestigious reduction and the concomitant loss of identity, it
> needs to approach the understanding of Israel in both testaments
> of its Bible with more openness and more humility than *The Jewish
> People and Their Sacred Scriptures in the Christian Bible* displays. For
> the difference between Judaism and Christianity is not the differ-
> ence between particularism and universalism. It is the difference
> between two particularisms, each of which makes, in its own way,
> universal claims.[122]

A lasting manifesto against scriptural supersessionism is inscribed in the very bipartite structure of the Christian Bible that reflects, as mentioned previously, the popular reflection of tradition. The only qualifier attached to the scriptural structure is the chronological criterion. The Old Testament comes first, prior to Christ event, being followed by the New Testament. There is no further qualification, no theological evaluation of either corpus inherent in the structure of the canon. Only a solemn, silent unity in diversity: one Bible, two covenants. As Theodore G. Stylianopoulos notices, "If they [Christians] call the Hebrew Scriptures 'Old Testament, it is not to devalue its revelatory significance. Rather, it is to affirm their own understanding of the gracious acts of the living God, the Father of Jesus Christ, and to bear witness to their own experience of the new covenant in Christ which fulfills the first covenant."[123]

The Christian Bible: Unity in Diversity

Georges Florovsky insists on the unity of the Bible with reference to the difference between the Greek and English names of the scriptural corpus: "It was no accident that a diverse anthology of writings, composed at various dates and by various writers, came to be regarded as a single book. *Ta biblia* is of course plural but *the Bible* is emphatically singular. The scriptures are indeed one Holy Scripture, one Holy Writ. . . . There is one composite and yet single story—from Genesis to Revelation."[124]

In concluding this chapter, we offer some general remarks on this unity in diversity that defines the Christian Bible. Below are the main reasons why ancient Christian interpreters perceived their Bible in terms of both unity and diversity.

How did this "arranged marriage" between Old and New Testaments begin? According to Tertullian, the union between Law, Prophets, Gospels, and epistles was possible due to the Church's work of uniting all these various writings in "one volume." The term "Church" used here designates the whole body of believers as well as the two levels, theological and popular, of the living Christian tradition.

The Christian Bible is a sort of tensile unity, if one takes into account the time frameworks, addressees, literary genres, and theologies of either collection of writings. Tertullian himself hints at this tensile "marriage" when he writes about the dialectical unity between Law and gospel, "So likewise the gospel is separated from the Law, whilst it advances (*provehitur*) from the Law—a different thing (*aliud*) from it, but not an alien one; diverse, but not contrary. Nor in Christ do we even find any novel form of discourse" (*Against Marcion* 11).[125] The mere fact that the Old Testament is more or less the Jewish Scripture and the New Testament is the Christian Scripture should make one think of two religions, Judaism and Christianity, being brought together into one book sealed by a cross, the emblematic sign of the latter, as seen in the Sinai Christ icon with which we began.

Things are different in the world of modern biblical scholarship. As Krister Stendahl well notices, the dominant contemporary interpretation of the fact that the Christian Bible is a two-testament work is entirely alien to the thought world of ancient Christianity. Today, however, this division has "academic-sociological dimensions. Old and New Testament scholars keep different company. Even in the Society of Biblical Literature they seldom take part in one another's sessions. For scholarly purposes the Bible of the Christian Church is not any longer a unified whole."[126]

Auctor Primus

Perhaps the most common and resilient assumption held by ancient Christian interpreters is that the two testaments, even though written in different periods of time and configuring scripturally two distinct communities of faith, proclaim one and the same God, the creator of heavens and earth, the Father of Jesus Christ. This God is not only proclaimed but he is also the *auctor primus*, the main author of the entire Christian Bible.

For Cyril of Jerusalem (315–86 C.E.), the unity of the two testaments is conferred by the fact that the Creator is the same God as the Father of Jesus Christ, and the same God is witnessed by both testaments:

> We worship, therefore, as the Father of Christ, the Maker of heaven and earth, "the God of Abraham, Isaac, and Jacob" [Exod 3:6]; to whose honor the former temple also, over against us here, was built. For we shall not tolerate the heretics who sever the Old Testament from the New, but shall believe Christ, who says concerning the temple, "Did you not know that I must be in my Father's house?" [Luke 2:49] and again, "Take these things hence, and make not my Father's house a house of merchandise" [John 2:16], whereby he most clearly confessed that the former temple in Jerusalem was his own Father's house.
>
> *Lecture 7. The Father 6*[127]

According to Ambrose of Milan (ca. 340–97 C.E.), Scripture's unity is assured ultimately by the same Spirit at work in both Old and New Testaments. As one may notice, Ambrose extrapolates the assumption mentioned above to the Spirit:

> But no one will doubt that the Spirit is one, although very many have doubted whether God be one. For many heretics have said that the God of the Old Testament is one, and the God of the New Testament is another. But as the Father is one who both spoke of old, as we read, to the fathers by the prophets, and to us in the last days by his Son [Heb 1:1]; and as the Son is one, who according to the tenor of the Old Testament was offended by Adam [Gen 3:17], seen by Abraham [Gen 18:22–23], worshipped by Jacob [Gen 28:17]; so, too, the Holy Spirit is one, who energized in the prophets [2 Pet 1:21], was breathed upon the apostles [John 20:22], and was joined to the Father and the Son in the sacrament of baptism [Matt 28:19].
>
> *Three Books on the Holy Spirit 1.4.55*[128]

Cyril of Jerusalem gives the assumption of God's singularity in both testaments a Trinitarian garb:

There is One God, the Father, Lord of the Old and of the New Testament: and One Lord, Jesus Christ, who was prophesied of in the Old Testament, and came in the New; and One Holy Spirit, who through the prophets preached of Christ, and when Christ came, descended, and manifested him. Let no one therefore separate the Old from the New Testament; let no one say that the Spirit in the former is one, and in the latter another; since thus he offends against the Holy Spirit himself, who with the Father and the Son together is honored, and at the time of Holy Baptism is included with them in the Holy Trinity.

Lecture 16 3–4[129]

John of Damascus (b. ca. 676; died between 754 and 787 C.E.) states similarly, "It is one and the same God Whom both the Old and the New Testament proclaim, who is praised and glorified in the Trinity: 'I came, says the Lord, not to destroy the Law but to fulfill it'" [Matt 5:17] (*An Exact Exposition of the Orthodox Faith* 4.17).[130]

The Crux of God's Revelation

John Chrysostom sees in the two covenants "two sisters and two maidens" serving the same Lord: "The Old anticipated the New and the New interpreted the Old. Often I said that two Covenants, two sisters and maidens, serve (wait upon) one Master. The Lord is announced by the prophets; Christ is proclaimed in the New; the new things are not new; for the old things anticipated [them]; the old things are not put out; for they are interpreted in the New" (*In illud: Exiit edictum*).[131]

This patristic assumption that Christ is the linking point of the two covenants may be further debated as part of the ongoing dialogue between Christians and Jews. For Orthodox Christianity, however, the centrality of Christ within the Bible is realized, supported, and propped up by such construals as prophecy-fulfillment, anticipation-reality, and complementarity. Below one may find some textual evidence supporting these hermeneutical presuppositions followed by ancient Christian interpreters.

The eighteenth letter sent in 381 C.E. from Constantinople to Pope Damasus is Jerome's earliest expository letter. In it, Jerome interprets Isaiah's vision (Isa 6) in an original way that is not the traditionally Trinitarian explication of the passage. The cantankerous writer uses the imagery of the two seraphim representing the two testaments with Christ in center sitting on a throne. "Some of my predecessors," Jerome writes, "make 'the Lord sitting upon a throne' God the Father, and suppose the seraphim to represent the Son and the Holy Spirit. I do not agree with them, for John expressly tells us [John 12:41] that it was Christ and not the Father whom the prophet saw." And again, "The word seraphim means either 'glow' or 'beginning of speech,' and the two seraphim thus stand for the Old and New Testaments. 'Did not our heart burn within us,' said the disciples, 'while he opened to us the Scriptures?' [Luke 24:32]." Jerome then speaks of the unity of the sacred books. "Whatever," he asserts, "we read in the Old Testament we find also in the gospel; and what we read in the gospel is deduced from the Old Testament. There is no discord between them, no disagreement. In both Testaments the Trinity is preached."[132]

Prophecy and Fulfillment

Polycarp of Smyrna (69–155 C.E.) underlines the prophetic value of the Old Testament—prophecy being here understood as predication, foretelling: "So, then, let us serve him with fear and all reverence, just as he himself has commanded, as did the apostles, who preached the gospel to us, and the prophets, who announced in advance the coming of our Lord [Acts 7:52]" (*Letter to Philippians* 6.3).[133]

The same idea that the Old Testament prophets announced in advance the passion of Christ is found in the following ancient Christian writing composed about 130 C.E.:

> What, then, does the prophet again say? "A band of evil men have surrounded me, they have swarmed around me like bees around a honeycomb [Ps 21(22):16(17)]; 117(118):12]," and "for my garments they cast lots [Ps 21(22):18(19)]." Therefore, inasmuch as he was about to be manifested and to suffer in the flesh, his suffering was revealed in advance. . . . Understand, therefore, children of joy, that the good Lord revealed everything to us beforehand, in order that we might know to whom we ought to give thanks and praise for all things.
>
> *Epistle of Barnabas* 6.6–7, 7.1[134]

In Augustine's view, "We receive the Old Testament, therefore, not in order to obtain the fulfillment of these promises, but to see in them predictions of the New Testament; for the Old bears witness to the New" (*Reply to Faustus the Manichean* 4.1–2).[135] Nevertheless, concludes the bishop of

Hippo, the entire Old Testament should be "regarded with admiration and reverence and followed with implicit reliance" (*Reply to Faustus the Manichean* 16.20)[136] due to its prophetic sayings and figures.

Although prophecy-fulfillment is quite popular among the church fathers,[137] there are some weaknesses with this construal. First, it rests on a quite subjective and limited selection of Old Testament Scriptures. Books like Job, Ecclesiastes, Song of Songs, Proverbs, and Nahum seemingly do not fit this hermeneutical framework.

Second, as much as the early fathers struggled to find one-to-one matches between Old and New Testaments, there are still a considerable number of prophecies in the Jewish Scriptures that remain resistant to this construal. Not all the Old Testament prophecies were fulfilled through Christ's coming. Many of so-called royal prophecies would remain to be fulfilled at the end of time. Levenson is correct in noting this:

> The failure of Jesus to return and fulfill the old messianic expectations (despite reports of his resurrection) only heightened the eschatological understanding of the royal theology, already attested in Judaism. The extravagant promises would become reality at the end of time, but not before. On this reading, Judaism and Christianity, despite their irreconcilable difference on the identity of the messianic king, agree on a point that the Commission[138] seems to have missed: the hyperbole of the royal psalms and the messianic prophecies will remain just that until kingdom come.[139]

In the same vein, one may mention as an illustration that the Old Testament vision of world peace remained unfulfilled.

Third, as Brevard S. Childs remarks, the construal of prophecy-fulfillment has been repeatedly and almost exclusively rehearsed on the Greek text as opposed to the Hebrew text of the Jewish Scriptures, which was mostly ignored.[140]

Foreshadowing and Realization

Pondering the epistles to the Corinthians (especially 1 Cor 10) and Hebrews (mainly chapter 13), Theodoret of Cyrus declares rather emphatically, "All the Old Testament, so to say, is a type of the New" (*Dialogues: The Impassable* 3).[141] The authors of the New Testament, primarily Paul and those responsible for the final form of the four canonical Gospels, saw in the Jewish Scriptures both a prelude and anticipation (prefiguration) of the gospel narrated events, persons, institutions, objects—all were seen as types of corresponding elements in the New Testament. As already noted, the possible danger here in this model of anticipation-reality is that of emptying the Old Testament of its own historical reality and intrinsic significance or value.

For Ignatius, the Old Testament figures, events, and prophetic sayings all have an anticipatory function, pointing to Christ, the center of scriptural unity:

> I have taken refuge in the gospel as the flesh of Jesus and in the apostles as the presbytery of the church. And we also love the prophets, because they anticipated the gospel in their preaching and set their hope on him and waited for him; because they also believed in him, they were saved, since they belong to the unity centered in Jesus Christ, saints worthy of love and admiration, approved by Jesus Christ and included in the gospel of our common hope [1 Tim 1:1].
>
> *Letter to Philadelphians* 5.1–2[142]

According to Origen, the Old Testament refers figuratively to Christ:

> But with respect to the Son of God, although no one knows the Son save the Father, yet it is from sacred Scripture also that the human mind is taught how to think of the Son; and that not only from the New, but also from the Old Testament, by means of those things which, although done by the saints, are figuratively referred to Christ, and from which both his divine nature, and that human nature which was assumed by him, may be discovered.
>
> *On the Principles* 1.3.1[143]

Methodius of Olympus (d. ca. 311 C.E.) maintains that the New Testament is superior to the Old Testament because "the Law is a kind of figure and shadow of things to come, but the gospel is truth and the grace of life. Pleasant was the fruit of the prophets, but not so pleasant as the fruit of immortality which is plucked from the gospel" (*Discourse* 9: *Tusiane* 3).[144]

For Chrysostom, the episode of Moses who prayed on mountain being sustained by his two disciples (Exod 17) is an "anticipation of the cross": "Thus Moses also prevailed over Amalek when he displayed the figure of the cross: and one may observe countless things happening in the Old

Testament descriptive by anticipation of the cross" (*Against the Marcionists and Manichaeans* 3).[145] Similarly, "It was necessary too that many things should prepare the way for Baptism; yes, thousands of things; those, for instance, in the Old Testament, those in the Pool, the cleansing of him that was not sound in health, the deluge itself, and all the things that have been done in water, the baptism of John" (Chrysostom, *Homilies on the Epistle of St. Paul to the Colossians: Homily 5*).[146]

In Augustine's view, "Those also who have before us expounded the divine oracles, have spoken largely of the symbols of the sacrifices of the Old Testament as shadows and figures of things, then future" (*Letter* 102.17).[147] But not only Old Testament figures and events have an anticipatory function. According to Augustine, even the precepts can have such a function. The bishop of Hippo makes the distinction between "moral" and "symbolical" precepts of the Old Testament. While the former precepts have always had a religious value, the latter were given to Israel as "a shadow of future things." Even though Christians are not required to follow the "symbolical precepts," they should be aware of them as a type of future realities.

Scriptural Complementarity

The claim for scriptural complementarity is perhaps the strongest blow stricken against supersessionism. Unfortunately, this construal is but sporadically attested in ancient Christian interpretations.

Origen is one of the few interpreters who articulated the complementarity between Old and New Testaments with profundity. Perhaps the Church's greatest anti-Marcionite theologian, Origen insists on the fact that there is only one God in the entire Scripture whose main attributes are love and justice. These divine attributes, he argues, are complementary to one another; hence, the complementarity between the two covenants (testaments), if one thinks in terms of the harsh dichotomy between "Law" and "grace" as mediated by Moses and Jesus respectively (John 1:17): "By all which it is established, that the God of the Law and the Gospels is one and the same, a just and good God, and that he confers benefits justly, and punishes with kindness; since neither goodness without justice, nor justice without goodness, can display the (real) dignity of the divine nature" (*On the Principles* 2.5.3).[148]

That the division into two testaments based on the above dichotomy is an oversimplification may be proven with textual evidence from the Old Testament itself. For instance, Exod 34:6–7 speaks of God's enduring mercy, love, and compassion while accenting the divine commitment for justice. Paradoxically, despite God's gracious and forgiving move toward man's frailty, sin will not go away unpunished, or closer to the Hebrew wording, "Surely, he will not acquit [*the guilty*]" (v. 7). In addition to this early Israelite credo, one may adduce Hosea, an eighth-century B.C.E. prophet. In Hos 11:8–9, God's inner struggle between love and justice is solved rather dramatically. Surely, at the end of God's deliberation over a punishable Israel's fate, his love triumphs, but with what great price—his heart being torn apart![149] In a nutshell, love and justice as well as the Old and New Testaments in the Christian Bible cannot and should not be disunited for they complement each other in a tensed yet benign way, the only way which allows us a glimpse into God's own mysterious existence.

For Augustine, complementarity is detectable in the very scriptural fabric of both testaments: "In the Old Testament there is a veiling of the New, and in the New Testament there is a revealing of the Old" (*On the Cathechizing of the Uninstructed* 4.4.8).[150] In consequence, explains Augustine, heavenly promises were veiled in earthly promises. "And it is for this reason that God made the Old Testament, because it pleased God to veil the heavenly promises in earthly promises, as if established in reward, until the fullness of time; and to give to a people which longed for earthly blessings, and therefore had a hard heart, a law, which, although spiritual, was yet written on tables of stone" (*A Treatise against Two Letters of the Pelagians* 3.10).[151]

A caveat is well warranted here. Properly understood, the real complementarity between Old and New Testaments should in no way be considered a linear and merely reciprocal equation between two canonical corpora. One may have Jewish Scriptures without New Testament. The enduring presence of Judaism as a vibrant community of faith proves this fact. However, as the ancient Church made dogmatically clear in her ancient struggles with Marcionism, if one is to follow the orthodox faith, one may not have a New Testament alone without Jewish Scriptures. Rejecting or undervaluing the Jewish Scriptures is to neglect the fountainhead whence the New Testament originates, "For whence do Marcion and Manichaeus receive the gospel while they reject the Law? For the New Testament arose out of the Old, and bears witness to the Old; if then they reject this, how can they receive what proceeds from it?" (Athanasius, *To the Egyptian Bishops* 1.4).[152]

To summarize, since the early times of apostolic kērygma, Jewish Scriptures have been appropriated and employed by Christian writers as proof-texts or pointers toward Christ event. This missionary usage went hand in hand with a persistent claim for legitimate continuity between the two covenants (testaments).

Concomitantly with the quest for continuities, Christians came unavoidably upon discontinuities. This complex process entailed a spectrum of scriptural supersessionism, ranging from soft to harsh, along with a creeping triumphalism in theological-social arena. However, at the level of the popular self-reflection of Christian tradition, a tensed scriptural unity was promoted by the very juxtaposition of the two testaments within the surging Christian Bible. This unity was perceived as rotating around two basic assumptions: (1) one and the same God as the author and ubiquitous figure of both testaments, and (2) Christ as the hermeneutical key to the unity of Scripture, shown in the relation of prophecy and fulfillment, anticipation and reality, and the complementarity between the two testaments.

While learning from the lessons of the past and considering current critiques and comments, Eastern Orthodox may indeed find good theological reasons to preserve the "soft" supersessionism of their tradition while at the same time renouncing the more noxious triumphalism. This new and refreshing attitude must be conjoined with a much deeper consideration of Jewish Scriptures, as both an independent canonical corpus for Judaism and as a body of writings that has been appropriated by Christianity as Holy Scripture along with the New Testament.[153]

2

Text

So earnest and assiduous was Origen's research into the divine words that he learned the Hebrew language, and procured as his own the original Hebrew Scriptures which were in the hands of the Jews. He investigated also the works of other translators of the Sacred Scriptures besides the Seventy.

EUSEBIUS, Ecclesiastical History 6.16.1

SINCE HER INCEPTION, the Church appropriated and employed the Greek translation of the Jewish Scriptures known under the name of Septuagint. The uninterrupted use of the Septuagint in the eastern side of Christianity during its long history may lead one to the erroneous conclusion that the Septuagint represents the only official and authoritative Old Testament text of the Eastern Orthodox Church. Turgid phrases like "the Old Testament text of the Orthodox Church has been and remains the Septuagint" are to be found in various printed and digital pamphlets aimed at introducing general readership to the tenets of Orthodoxy. Yet this expedient sketch is far away from truth.

The historical reality is more complex and thus resistant to such an oversimplification. From the onset, it must be emphasized that the Septuagint was originally a Jewish undertaking. This caveat is quite necessary. As the centuries have elapsed, the Septuagint has become part of Christian literature and ethos. Nonetheless, ordinary churchgoers today are inclined to see this translation as "*the* Bible of the Church" from the very beginning, as a Christian translation, due to the New Testament quotations and theological concepts deriving from it.

Indeed, the Septuagint played and continues to play an important role in the life of the Eastern Orthodox Church. It is truly "*the* Bible of the Church." Despite its high popularity, however, the Septuagint has never reached the level of canonical authority in Eastern Orthodoxy enjoyed by the Vulgate in the Roman Catholic Church prior to the Second Vatican Council. Unlike the Latin Bible, the Septuagint has never become the "official" or "authoritative" text. No council in the East has ever sanctioned the text as such. Early translations in vernacular languages done in various Orthodox lands also witness to this fact. Up to nineteenth century, the basis for most of these translations was commonly the Greek Septuagint, though there are examples of early use of the Latin or Hebrew text as a basis for translation,[1] not because the Septuagint was an "official" text, but rather for the mere reason that the early Church and the Church of ecumenical councils made extensive use of it. Also, beginning with Justin's time there has been a continuous suspicion on the part of the Christians that the Jews corrupted the Hebrew Scriptures in order to blur the messianic prophecies referring to Christ, hence the increasing Christian attachment to the Old Greek Bible.

The flurry of early translations (Syriac, Coptic, then Gothic and Armenian in the fourth century, Ethiopic and Georgian in the fifth century) following the appropriation of the Old Greek Bible by the early Church shows that the association of Christianity with Greek as its sacred or original language occurred later, during the fourth century, when the Church came to be associated with the empire and its capital Constantinople, the New Rome. This linguistic contiguity was further enforced later by post-Renaissance Western scholars interested in the original Greek text of the New Testament and then again by modern historians of religions quick to relate every religious system to a particular linguistic group.

The Orthodox Church as a whole has never authorized a certain text or translation of the Scriptures. This fact conveys the enduring Orthodox tradition's modus operandi regarding the Bible and related questions such as inspiration and canon.[2] On the whole, Eastern Orthodoxy has historically showed a tendency to be flexible as regards the biblical text and its inherent potential to be disseminated in various languages and dialects.

Hebrew Text

Although during the early patristic period the exposure of the Christians to the Bible was done almost solely via translation (Greek, Latin, Syriac, Coptic, etc.), the first section of this chapter will be allocated to the Hebrew text as the first and foremost carrier of the Jewish Scripture.

The textual evidence for the Hebrew Bible (the biblical texts written in Hebrew and Aramaic) may be divided into two scribal traditions: proto- or pre-Masoretic (exclusively consonantal text) and Masoretic (consonantal text accompanied by vowel-signs and other reading helpers).

Proto-Masoretic

Initially, Hebrew biblical writings were copied and transmitted exclusively as consonantal texts. For centuries, the biblical texts have been written only with consonants and no vowels at all. Pronunciation was a matter of oral tradition carried on from teachers to pupils via memorization. The vowels were inserted mentally into the consonantal text each time a reader was musing over the sacred text.

Emanuel Tov[3] divides the transmission of the Hebrew text (proto- and Masoretic) into three phases. The borders of Tov's periodization are dictated merely by the availability of textual evidence.

The first period of text transmission extends from the (unclear) beginnings of the proto-MT until the destruction of the Second Temple (70 C.E.). During this long period, proto-MT is marked by internal differences in the textual transmission. The evidence comes from Qumran (texts written between 250 B.C.E. and 68 C.E.), Masada (before 73 C.E.), and Wadi Murabba'at (around the time of second Jewish revolt, 132–35 C.E.), among others.

Despite many differences that exist between the members of the proto-MT group, this group is nevertheless characterized by an internal unity more obvious than for any other group of extant textual witnesses, including the LXX and its recensions. This internal unity of the proto-MT, evidenced from the onset of the transmission process, reflects the punctilious care of the scribes for the sacred text. It is likely that these scribes had close ties with Temple circles, leading them to favor the standardization of the text. The Temple had professional "correctors" or "revisers" (*maggihim*). The Talmud makes reference to the work of those correctors when it urges, "When you teach your son, teach him from a corrected scroll (*sepher muggah*)" (*b. Pesah.* 112a); or "My son, be careful, because your work is the work of heaven; should you omit (even) one letter or add (even) one letter, the whole world would be destroyed" (*b. Sot.* 20a).[4]

The textual standardization of the proto-MT should be understood as a process during which erroneous readings were gradually removed and other manuscripts not agreeing with the standardized text were discarded.

But this textual process is not to be imagined as a mere transition from pluriformity to uniformity. In Adam S. van der Woude's words, "the text of the Old Testament passed down to us is not the product of a drastic recension or of a historical accident. It is a basically faithful representation of the tradition by the spiritual leaders of early Judaism which is grounded on theological considerations and possibly also stimulated by the influence of the Alexandrian grammarians."[5]

The second period of text transmission, from the destruction of the Second Temple until the eighth century c.e., is characterized by a higher degree of textual consistency due primarily to the end of the Second Temple and major socio-religious changes succeeding this event. The significant improvement in textual consistency is evidenced by the similarities between the MT (e.g., *Codex Leningradiensis* of 1009 c.e.) and proto-MT (e.g., Naḥal Ḥever and Wadi Murabba'at texts), ancient translations (e.g., Targumim, Peshitta, LXX's recensions such as Aquila, Symmachus, the fifth column of Origen's Hexapla, Vulgate), and biblical quotations in the rabbinic literature (e.g., *piyyutim*, "liturgical hymns").

Masoretic

The third period of text transmission, marked by complete textual unity, spans between eighth century and the end of the Middle Ages. The textual evidence for this period is offered by the Masoretic manuscripts and biblical citations in the medieval commentators. At this point, the MT became a completely standardized text.

Since its beginnings, mainstream Judaism has considered MT *the* original, unaltered, text of the Bible. Yet such a belief is challenged by the historical fact that vowels were added later during the rabbinic period. As a response to this criticism, the defenders of MT's internal unity argue that the late addition of the vowels by the Masoretes relied on an accurate oral transmission.

The phrase "Masoretic Text"[6] designates a group of manuscripts deriving its name from the Masoretic apparatus added to the consonantal text beginning with the seventh through the eleventh century. The tenth century represents the peak of the Masoretic activity with the input of the Ben Asher family of Tiberias. But given the fact that almost all the printed editions of the Masoretic Text depend on copies produced by members of the Ben Asher family, the term MT is imprecise. A term like Masoretic "Texts" or "group" would better reflect the complex reality. In addition, the MT is catchall term, similar to LXX, referring to a multitude of textual traditions. It is impossible to postulate with certainty that there would have ever been a single prototype for this group designated *"the* MT."

The texts grouped under the generic phrase Masoretic Text (MT) at a certain moment in time were preferred by the orthodox, mainstream Jewish group, over other textual traditions. Nevertheless, as Emanuel Tov cautions, "When evaluating the different texts one should disregard this situation, for the preference of MT by a central stream in Judaism does not necessarily imply that it contains the best text of the Bible. Both the Hebrew parent text of LXX and certain of the Qumran texts reflect excellent texts, often better than that of MT."[7] The large number of textual witnesses testifying for a single proto-MT as early as the second century C.E. should not be considered a criterion of evaluating a text. The wide representation of the proto-MT was determined by socio-political-religious factors rather than a vote on the textual value of this particular text. The same remark is true with any textual witness to the Old Testament, including LXX, or other literary documents in public circulation as a matter of fact.

In any event, the Qumran texts should not be automatically considered a reflection of the MT's *Vorlage.* They could very well have been pristine texts parallel to the one(s) that would be eventually standardized and considered today as the *Vorlage* of the MT. For instance, 1QIsa[b] discovered in 1947 and dated to 50–25 B.C.E. is textually almost identical with *Codex Leningradiensis*, one thousand years younger than the former, but this resemblance does not make this Qumran scroll sine qua non the MT's direct parent.

Between the second and third periods of the Hebrew text transmission one may place the prodigious activity of the Masoretes. The Masoretic activity (i.e., vocalization, cantillation marks, accents, and self-checking apparatuses) played a major role in the textual standardization of the MT.

With respect to their work on the text of the Jewish Bible, the Masoretes may be divided into several groups. *Soferim*, the scribes, are the ones who copied the consonantal text; the *naqdanim*, "pointers," were responsible for vocalization, namely, by creating and inserting the vowel-signs within the consonantal writing; and *bale ha-massorah*, "masters of the Masorah" (the Masoretes), the ones who gathered all necessary information in the Masoretic apparatus.[8]

The rabbinic interpretation of the term *soferim*, literally, "counters," as deriving from the Hebrew root *s-p-r*, "to count," speaks volumes of the strong desire and diligent work of these Masoretes to design and observe various mnemonic techniques for self-checking in order to avoid or correct inherent mistakes. "The ancients were called *soferim* because they counted every letter in the Torah. They said that the *waw* in *ghwn* (Lev 11:42) is the middle consonant in the Torah, *drš drš* (Lev 10:16) the middle word and *whtglḥ* (Lev 13:33) the middle verse" (*b. Qidd.* 30a).[9] One can imagine the sedulous scribe checking all the quantifiable details to see if they were reflected properly in his copy. If not, he would return and count again all the consonants, words, and lines to locate his mistakes (commonly due to haplography or dittography).

The entirely vocalized and accented text along with a very detailed apparatus found in *Masorah parva* ("Small Masorah"—lateral marginal notes) and *Masorah magna* ("Great Masorah"—upper or lower marginal notes) was the new interface offered by the Masoretes to both readers and scribes of the sacred text.[10] In particular, the vocalization not only contributed to a more precise and standardized pronunciation of the Hebrew words, but it also prevented the consonants from being lost or altered during the process of textual transmission.

Later, continuously accruing annotations were gathered in separate volumes. The main focus of these collections was the Hebrew orthography. By resorting to such noninvasive procedure, while following reverently the oral tradition, the Masoretes proved once again, as their precursors who transmitted heedfully the proto-MT, that they were exceedingly wary not to alter the consonantal framework of their Scriptures.

By inserting vowel- and accent-signs into the consonantal framework, the Masoretes offered indirectly their own interpretation of the text. The accent-signs (or cantillation markers) were meant to lead the flow of ideas within a literary unit. Thus, the Masoretic activity had a willy-nilly exegetical import.

The liturgical division of the Hebrew text may be adduced as another, indirect way of stabilizing the text during its age-honored transmission.

The Torah was divided (ca. eighth century C.E.)[11] into fifty-three or fifty-four *parashot*, "sections," to be read in the synagogue throughout the entire liturgical cycle, according to the Babylonian one-year liturgical cycle, and 154 or 167 *sedarim*, "sequences, portions," based on the Palestinian triennial cycle.[12] The division in *sedarim* was already reflected in the LXX.

The current division into chapters was introduced in 1214 by Stephen Langton, Archbishop of Canterbury. The oldest preserved copy that contains this division is the Paris manuscript of the Vulgate (*Biblia* or *Exemplar Parisiense*, thirteenth century). Afterward, the division was exported into the manuscripts and printed editions of the Hebrew Bible.[13] It is said that Robert Stephens introduced the division into verses, first for the Greek and Latin texts of the New Testament in 1551, and then for the printed edition of the whole Bible, the Vulgate, published in 1555. As a caveat, this division of the Bible in chapters and verses is late and quite artificial from an exegetical point of view. Thus in order to grasp the intended (historical or plain) meaning of a text one should leave aside this modern division and try to discern rather the literary boundaries of the unit under examination.

Manuscripts

The oldest preserved MT manuscript is the *Codex Cairensis* (895 C.E.) that comprises only the Prophets. The *Aleppo Codex* (three-fourths of this manuscript have been kept), dated to ca. 925 C.E., was published in a facsimile edition by Moshe H. Goshen-Gottstein (Jerusalem, 1976).

One may also mention here a tenth-century codex from the Karaite synagogue in Cairo containing the Pentateuch alone, and *Codex Leningradiensis*, dated to 1009 C.E., which covers the Old Testament in its entirety. According to the colophon of *Leningradiensis*, a single person, Samuel ben Jacob, was responsible for copying the consonantal text of the entire Jewish Bible and adding the vowels along with the Masorah.

Printed Editions

The first printed complete text of the Jewish Bible appeared in 1488 in Soncino (close to Milan). This edition was followed by the multilingual or polyglot Bibles, the first of which was the *Complutensum* published by Francisco Ximénes de Cisneros in Alcalá (Spain) in 1514–17.

The Rabbinic Bibles are those that combine the MT with rabbinic commentaries (e.g., Rashi, Ibn Ezra, Kimchi) and Targums. The first two Rabbinic Bibles were published by the press of Daniel Bomberg in Venice (1516–17 and 1524–25). Characteristic of the *Second Rabbinic Bible*, known also as the *Bible of Jacob ben Chayyim*, was that it added for the first time the Masorah to the Hebrew text. The *Second Rabbinic Bible*, following the Ben Asher system, became the most influential standard printed Bible, by preserving the *textus receptus* (received text) of the MT.

The most complete critical edition of the MT thus far is *BH* edited by Rudolph Kittel (all the editions up to 1951 are termed *BHK* after their editor; in the 1951 edition Qumran data were added) or the fourth edition *Biblia Hebraica Stuttgartensia* (*BHS*) edited by Wilhelm Rudolph and Karl Elliger (Stuttgart, 1967–77). The *BHS* represents the classroom Bible. It enjoys great popularity among biblical scholars. The base text for *BHS* is the *Codex Leningradiensis* and the apparatus contains readings from other Hebrew manuscripts as well as various textual witnesses (e.g., OG, S, V).

The *Biblia Hebraica Quinta* (*BHQ*), the fifth edition of the *BH*, was designed to replace the *BHS*. The *BHQ* is a diplomatic edition based on *Codex Leningradiensis*, which contains the *Masorah magna* and *parva* while textual variants are discussed in the footnotes. The following fascicles have been published thus far: *Five Megilloth* (2004); *Ezra and Nehemiah* (2006); *Deuteronomy* (2007); *Proverbs* (2009); *The Twelve Minor Prophets* (2010).

The *Hebrew University Bible Project* (*HUBP*) is another diplomatic edition, based on *Codex Aleppo*. Three full volumes have been published: Moshe H. Goshen-Gottstein, ed., *The Hebrew University Bible: The Book of Isaiah* (Jerusalem, 1995); Chaim Rabin, Shemaryahu Talmon, and Emanuel Tov, eds., *The Book of Jeremiah* (Jerusalem, 1997); and Moshe H. Goshen-Gottstein, Shemaryahu Talmon, and Galen Marquis, eds., *The Book of Ezekiel* (Jerusalem, 2006).

Among the differences between *BH/BHS* and *HUBP* one may list the following: (a) *BH* and *BHS* rely on the complete, yet not the most representative, Ben Asher system of vocalization (i.e., *Codex Leningradiensis*), while *HUBP* is based on Aleppo, the best, yet incomplete representative of this system of vocalization; (b) *BH* and *BHS* contain conjectural emendations, while *HUBP* is free of them; (c) *HUBP* does not evaluate the textual data as does the *BH* and *BHS* through various notations with abbreviated Latin forms: for example, *l(ege)*, "read," *dl = delendum*, "omit," *ins(ere)*, "insert," *pr(aemitte)*, "place before"; (d) in contrast with *BH* and *BHS*, *HUBP* contains data from rabbinic sources and medieval codices, indicating differences in consonants, vocalization, and accents.

Greek Text

The Septuagint is one of the greatest achievements both linguistically and culturally. It is the oldest large-scale translation of a Semitic corpus of sacred texts into an Indo-European language. It is also the first written translation of the Jewish Bible.

From the onset one should underscore that the Septuagint was not the Scripture that Jesus and his immediate disciples knew. The appropriation of the Septuagint was done gradually along with the proclamation of the gospel outside Palestine and the Gentile element outnumbering the Jewish component in the apostolic Church.

In the area of modern biblical studies, the Septuagint has always been used in those instances where the Hebrew text would offer but difficult and obscure readings. Nevertheless, as Marguerite Harl[14] well emphasized, the Septuagint should be considered as a work of its own right. During the reception process by the early Church, Septuagint became "un oeuvre autonom, détachée de son modèle." In other words, the Septuagint may be employed with no relation whatsoever to MT. As a matter of fact, the Septuagint was intended for Greek-speaking readers with no knowledge of Hebrew at all.

The name Septuagint comes from Latin *septuaginta*, "seventy," as an abbreviation of *interpretatio septuaginta virorum*, "the translation by the seventy men." The Latin term was influenced by the Greek *hoi hebdomēkonta*, "the seventy," used by second-century Christian writers to designate the Greek translation of the Old Testament. The Greek name found in Christian manuscripts from the fourth century on is *kata tous hebdomēkonta*, "according to the seventy." The common siglum for this Greek translation is the Roman numeral for seventy, LXX.

The connotation of the term "Septuagint" differs from manuscript to manuscript, from community to community. Thus, when it appears in Jewish sources, "Septuagint" refers to the Torah (Pentateuch) alone. Beginning with Justin Martyr, Christian sources suggest that "the Seventy" translated into Greek all the books of the Bible accepted by Christians. Yet even among Christian communities there are differences of opinion regarding the scope of the term Septuagint. This situation is reflected in the fourth–fifth century C.E. LXX manuscripts (codices) that contain beside the books of the Hebrew Bible various writings labeled differently in the three main branches of Christianity today.[15]

Scholars employ the term "Old Greek" (OG) for the original translation and "Septuagint" (LXX) as an all-embracing term for the original Greek translation of the Jewish Scripture used in Palestine as well for the whole collection of sacred Greek writings in the current form.[16] The term Septuagint is also employed to designate the critical editions of the Greek translation listed below.

Letter of Aristeas

The nomenclature (Septuagint) itself is an echo of old legends about seventy (or seventy-two) translators who rendered the Hebrew Law (Pentateuch) into Greek. These legends are found primarily in the pseude-pigraphical *Letter of Aristeas to Philocrates* (*Pseudo Aristeas*), a Hellenistic Jewish work.[17]

According to the *Letter of Aristeas*, Demetrius Phalereus, king Ptolemy II's librarian in Alexandria, requested Eleazer, the high priest of the Temple in Jerusalem, to provide skilled translators along with the Torah scrolls to be dispatched to Alexandria. Aristeas, the purported author of the letter, was one of the king's emissaries sent to Jerusalem. High priest Eleazer selected six men from each of the twelve tribes, and sent all seventy-two translators along with a large escort and various gifts to Alexandria. Having arrived in Alexandria, the translators were welcomed with a banquet for a number of days during which the king entertained and discussed with the Jewish sages theological and ethical matters. Afterward, the translators were moved to the island of Pharos connected by a causeway to Alexandria. There, the Jewish sages worked seventy-two days on the first Greek translation of the Law. The completed translation, read aloud in front of a great assembly of Jews in Alexandria, was well received by the attendees as a beautiful and devout rendition. A copy was prepared to be read by the Jews in their communities. In the end, a curse was uttered by priests and elders against any who would dare to alter the text of the translation.

Scholars agree that the *Letter of Aristeas* was not written in the third century B.C.E., as it purports, but rather toward the end of the second century B.C.E. as a manifesto defending both Judaism and the Greek translation of the Law. At that time, Jews were confronted with massive Hellenization, dividing them into groups for or against the Greek language, and eventually for or against the Greek translation of their own Scriptures. The *Letter of Aristeas* served as a reminder regarding the concrete circumstances generative of the Septuagint. In defending the translation, the *Letter of Aristeas* underscores its authority by telling the readers that the Hebrew scrolls were brought from the Temple of Jerusalem, the high priest himself was involved in the process, and sages representing the whole confederation of the Israelite tribes living in the homeland were used as translators. Remarkably, the whole episode of making of this translation is compared with the giving of the Law on Mount Sinai.

Despite its legendary garb and lack of authenticity, the *Letter of Aristeas* contains some reliable information. The letter states that the Jewish Law (Torah) was translated into Greek in Alexandria during the reign of king Ptolemy II Philadelphus (285–47 B.C.E.). Such a detail about the need for a Greek translation of the Jewish Law in the Diaspora during the Hellenistic period is quite convincing. The letter also states that the translation was done by Jewish sages that came from Jerusalem to Egypt. Nevertheless, the language of the translation betrays traces of the kind of Greek spoken in Egypt, not Palestine.

According to the letter, the translation was produced at the request of the king's librarian who wanted to enrich the Alexandrian library with a Greek translation of the Jewish Law. Most scholars reject this explanation as a legendary feature. The true reason for such a high scale translation is still debatable. The common assumption is that it was done for practical reasons. Most Jews in Alexandria had ceased to speak the language of their ancestors; hence, the need for a translation of their Scriptures in the most spoken language of the time, Hellenistic Greek. The same reason obtains for the Aramaic translations (targumim) done in Palestine. It is possible that both types of translations, Greek and Aramaic, first circulated orally, being occasioned by liturgical gatherings.[18]

Nevertheless, there may also have been academic purposes for the translation, for the use of Jewish students and scholars. Supporting proof for such a supposition is found in the translators' choice for literal renditions of difficult passages in the Hebrew Scriptures.[19] The letter's detail concerning the king's care and support for such a cultural-religious enterprise seems reliable. In any event, the Septuagint served both the Jews in the Diaspora for their liturgical and spiritual life, and the pagan culture at large, in enabling it a glimpse into Jewish religion via the Scriptures rendered in Greek (cf. Acts 8:26–40). Both operative directions, toward Jews and Gentiles, assisted the Christian Church in rapidly appropriating and further spreading the Jewish Scriptures outside Palestine.

In any event, *the* Septuagint (with the definite article) is a misnomer,[20] suggesting a literary homogeneity that is not the case with this translation. Rather than being the work of one single author, done in a limited period of time, and in one location, the LXX spanned over more than two centuries, involved many translators working independently, and was not accomplished entirely in Alexandria. As a historical fact, the Law (Pentateuch) was translated in Alexandria around mid-third century B.C.E. and the rest of the Jewish Scriptures were rendered during the following two hundred years.[21] Regarding the Law (Pentateuch), one may say that each of its books was done by a single translator or a single team of translators. Other books, especially the Minor Prophets, Isaiah, and Jeremiah, were translated by several individuals or teams of translators. As for the translation itself, this was in some cases literal (e.g., the Pentateuch) and in others quite free (e.g., Daniel, Job).[22]

Jewish and Christian Reception of the *Letter of Aristeas*

The Jewish historian Josephus is one of the fewest ancient authors who reproduced the *Letter of Aristeas* literally with no alteration (*Antiquities* 12:1–118).[23] Josephus's purpose was to justify Judaism for a Hellenistic Roman audience. Thus, he was not so much interested in the translation itself, but rather in the harmonious relationship that existed between a Jewish high priest (Eleazer) and a Hellenistic Egyptian king (Ptolemy II).

Earlier, Philo introduced for the first time some embellishments to the core of the *Letter* (*Life of Moses* 2.25–44). Philo added the legendary detail of how the Jewish translators, though working separately, managed to come up with exactly the same literal rendition due to divine dictation. He also asserted that the Greek translation, as its Hebrew original, was inspired by God: "They, as inspired men (*enthousiēntes*), prophesied, not one saying one thing and another, but every one of them employed the same nouns and verbs, as if some unseen prompter had suggested all their language to them" (*Life of Moses* 2.37).[24]

The same idea of divine inspiration[25] with regard to Septuagint may be deduced from a second-century C.E. interpretive tradition included in *b. Sefer Torah* 1.8, which mentions seventy Jewish translators rather than the seventy-two as attested in the *Letter of Aristeas*. This rabbinic gloss contains references to the seventy elders who accompanied Moses to the Mt. Sinai prior to the promulgation of the Torah (Exod 24:1–2, 9–11), and to those seventy elders who shared with Moses the same spirit of prophecy (Num 11:10–25). By this comparison, the seventy translators were to be regarded as prophets inspired by God while working on the translation. The Greek name *hoi hebdomēkonta*, "the seventy," for the LXX was probably crafted on this early Jewish interpretation.

According to Emanuel Tov,[26] the idea that the Septuagint itself—not only the translators, as mentioned in Philo—was inspired, has its origins in Christian sources. Unlike the Jews who could choose between Hebrew and Greek versions, Gentile Christians had to rely on the Greek version alone, the Greek language being the lingua franca of the day; hence, the emphasis on the inspired character of the Septuagint and indirectly on its soteriological authority. As the inspired and only widely utilized text in the early Christian Church, the Septuagint became for many church fathers and teachers more reliable than the Hebrew text. In their view, the Septuagint enjoyed such a high position because it was a *praeparatio evangelica*, a providential act hereby God prepared the Gentiles to receive Jesus of Nazareth as their Lord and Savior.[27] In addition, there was also the claim that the Septuagint matches quite well the New Testament, culturally, linguistically, and religiously.[28] Yet, as Emanuel Tov rightly notices,[29] this claim does not square with the fact that the New Testament used both the LXX and Jewish recensions (Aquila, Symmachus, Theodotion) in quoting the Jewish Bible.

Regarding the use of LXX by the New Testament writings, the closest quotations appear in the Gospel of John, Luke-Acts, and the catholic epistles. Many of the non-LXX quotations are closer to MT and this situation obtains especially with those texts where LXX and MT presuppose two different *Vorlage*'s. In these cases, the likelihood is that the New Testament author quoted from proto-Theodotion a revision of the LXX (first century B.C.E.) to bring the latter into literal closeness to the Hebrew text (proto-MT) extant in Palestine at that time. It is commonly accepted that Matthew and Paul quoted extensively from proto-Theodotion and other revisions of the LXX. The similarities between Matthew and Paul and the proto-Theodotion are so visible that the assumption that the two New Testament authors borrowed the Old Testament quotations directly from the Hebrew text[30] or from their own renditions of the Hebrew text into Greek seems quite unlikely.[31]

Among ancient Christian writers, Justin Martyr is one of the first to mention the Greek translation in a larger narrative context dealing with Hebrew prophets (*First Apology* 31). According to Justin's account, king Ptolemy sent to king Herod (sic!) for a copy of the Hebrew prophecies. Being unable to read Hebrew, Ptolemy sent again for translators and the books were translated in Greek. Justin is the first author who claims that the Septuagint was the Greek translation of the entire Jewish Bible—not only of the Law (Pentateuch), as suggested by the *Letter of Aristeas*. Unlike Philo, Justin is completely silent on the fact that the translators worked separately. Apparently, Justin's purpose was to defend the veracity of the Septuagint before the Jews who rejected Christian claims regarding the messianic prophecies of the Old Testament, which were not restricted only to the Torah (cf. Isa 7:14); this would seem to explain Justin's reference to the Septuagint as including the entire Jewish Bible and not only the Pentateuch.

Similarly to Justin, Irenaeus (*Against Heresies* 3.21.2; see Eusebius, *Ecclesiastical History* 5.8.11–15) defends the inerrancy of the Septuagint text when compared with other Jewish versions. According to Irenaeus, the Septuagint preserved the messianic prophecies much better than the other versions. Irenaeus follows Philo's claim that the Septuagint is inspired because the translators worked separately and yet produced exactly the same translation. The same Spirit who inspired the prophets and the apostles inspired the translators; thus, the inspired Septuagint connects the prophets with the apostles within the Christian Bible. Moreover, what better proof for the Septuagint's superiority than the Gentiles' approval of its inspired character? The inferiority of the other Greek translations lay with their novelty. According to Irenaeus, "The apostles, who are older than the new translators Theodotion and Aquila, and also their followers, preached the words of the prophets just as they are contained in the translation of the elders. Thus is the same Spirit of God who spoke through the prophets of the coming of the Lord, who properly translated through the elders what was really prophesied, and who preached the fulfillment of the promise through the apostles" (*Against Heresies* 3.21.3; Eusebius, *Ecclesiastical History* 5.8.15).[32]

Not long after Irenaeus, Clement of Alexandria accents the inspired character of the Septuagint that turned this translation into a "prophecy in Greek" (*Stromata* 1.149.3).

Eusebius of Caesarea is known for his concern for accuracy in listing the names of the bishops of the ancient apostolic Churches. With regard to the *Letter of Aristeas*, he shows the same punctiliousness by reproducing the document with no additional material.

The longest account of the story among the ancient Christian writers is preserved in Epiphanius of Salamis (*On Measures and Weights* 3–11). According to Epiphanius, Ptolemy kept the seventy-two translators (divided in pairs) in a state of quasi-confinement, providing for them separate cooks. Their cells were equipped with small holes in the roof, rather than regular windows, through which food was delivered. Each pair of translators received a book. Having finished it, each pair received another book. At the end of their work, the translators presented thirty-six copies perfectly identical to one another.

John Chrysostom insists on the usefulness and necessity of the Septuagint for both Jews in Alexandria who did not speak Hebrew, and Gentiles who would receive Christ and the Old Testament messianic prophecies via this translation.[33]

According to Cyril of Jerusalem, the way chosen by king Ptolemy II Philadelphus to bring the Jewish written lore unaltered to Alexandria was the best. Cyril notices that Ptolemy "judged it much nobler, not to get the books from the possessors by force against their will, but rather to propitiate them by gifts and friendship; and knowing that what is extorted is often adulterated, being given unwillingly, while that which is willingly supplied is freely given with all sincerity, he sent to Eleazar, who was then high priest, a great many gifts for the temple here at Jerusalem, and caused him to send him six interpreters from each of the twelve tribes of Israel for the translation" (*Lecture 4. Of the Divine Scriptures* 34).[34]

Jerome provides in his *Prologus in Pentateucho* an altogether different account of the Septuagint. For Jerome, the Septuagint designates the translation into Greek of the entire Bible. In order to heighten the veracity of his own translation, Jerome suggests that the commissioner king Ptolemy Lagus, Ptolemy II Philadelphus's father, was a Platonist and the translators in their desire to please him distorted the sacred text by producing a faulty translation. Jerome argues that the story about the cells of the translators is a legendary element, since it does not appear in ancient Jewish sources (i.e., Philo, Josephus). He also casts doubts on the detail about the separation of the translators and their possession of the prophetic spirit: neither Aristeas nor Josephus, notices Jerome, had anything to say about this.[35]

In contrast to Jerome, Augustine's excessive reverence for the Septuagint made the latter embrace even the errors of this translation. Ps 87(88) is the case on point. Even though in v. 11(10) the Hebrew text ("shadows") is more intelligible in the context, Augustine advances a sui generis interpretation based on the Greek wording ("physicians"):[36]

The following verse, "Shall physicians revive them, and shall they praise you?" [Ps 87/88:11/10] means, that the dead shall not be revived by such means, that they may praise you. In the Hebrew there is said to be a different expression: giants [Heb *rephayim* "shadows, dead spirits"] being used where physicians [Gk *iatroi*] are here: but the Septuagint translators, whose authority is such that they may deservedly be said to have interpreted by the inspiration of the

Spirit of God owing to their wonderful agreement, conclude, not by mistake, but taking occasion from the resemblance in sound between the Hebrew words expressing these two senses, that the use of the word is an indication of the sense in which the word giants is meant to be taken.

Ennarationes in Psalmos[37]

Septuagint Manuscripts and Printed Editions

The earliest evidence for the Septuagint comes from the Judean Desert and dates back to the second century B.C.E. It consists of fragments of Exodus (7Q1 = Exod 28:4–7), Leviticus (4Q1 19 = Lev 26:2–16), Deuteronomy (4Q1 22 = Deut 11:4), the Letter of Jeremiah (7Q2). One of the most important textual evidences from this region is the late first century B.C.E. Naḥal Ḥever scroll of the Minor Prophets (8ḤevXIIgr),[38] which was revised against the Hebrew text. As a passing remark, the presence of LXX fragments among the Dead Sea Scrolls testifies to the early spread and use of the Greek translation by Greek-speaking Palestinian Jews prior to the rise of Christianity.

The earliest Christian manuscripts date to the late first century–second century C.E. Distinguishing Christian from Jewish manuscripts for this period is problematic. However, almost all manuscripts from the third century C.E. onward are Christian. One of the most important (prior to Origen's Hexapla, at least) is Papyrus 967 of the *Chester Beatty Papyri*,[39] dated to the late second–early third century C.E. It is a codex containing fragments from Ezekiel, Esther, and Daniel (in the LXX not Theodotion form). These fragments on papyri or parchment scrolls or codices are the forerunners of the complete LXX Bibles.

A distinguishing mark for any Christian LXX manuscript is the ubiquitous use of *Kyrios* (Lord) for the Hebrew *tetragrammaton* (in consonantal transliteration YHWH), while Jewish scrolls continued to exhibit the divine name either in Hebrew characters (paleo or square script)[40] or in Greek transliteration.[41] Origen (*Commentary on Psalms* 2.2) and Jerome (*Prologus Galeatus*) mention this practice in their days. The discovery of two small fragments (1 Kgs 20:9–17 and 2 Kgs 23:12–27) from the Greek translation of Aquila on a sixth century palimpsest found in 1897 in the Cairo *genizah*[42] proves the reliability of the two writers' testimony.[43] This distinction goes back to the first century C.E., helping one to differentiate between a Jewish and Christian manuscript fragment, and between its use in Church or synagogue.[44] However, Robert Hanhart[45] argues that the easiness with which Old Testament sayings about *Kyrios* (YHWH) were applied to Jesus proves that the Septuagint had originally rendered the *tetragrammaton* with *Kyrios*. Yet his argument is not quite solid, as one can well reply that those Septuagint copies the New Testament writers used were already partially "Christianized" and the switch from the use of the *tetragrammaton* in one form or another to its rendition as *Kyrios* had by that time already occurred. In Albert Pietersma's view, the presence of some form of *tetragrammaton* in Jewish Septuagint manuscripts was not original, but rather the result of the revisionist recensions.[46] In any event, the debate is still open and no definitive conclusion has been reached thus far.

The first Bibles containing both testaments are uncials on codices dating back to fourth–fifth centuries c.e. There are three such preserved codices: (1) Vaticanus, fourth century; lost most of Genesis; no marks of heavy revisions; usually taken as a base text for diplomatic critical editions; (2) Sinaiticus, fourth century; incomplete Pentateuch and historical books mostly lost; a reliable unrevised LXX text; (3) Alexandrinus, fifth century; almost complete; marked by revisions; Isaiah is probably the most reliable text compared with other LXX manuscripts.

Besides the uncials, there are also a great number of minuscule manuscripts (most numerous) dating from ninth to fifteenth century.

The Reformation brought with it a renewed interest in the *Hebraica veritas* ("Hebrew truth") and a heightened care for the text due to the stress on scriptural inerrancy. At the same time, the Septuagint was used to correct doubtful readings of the Hebrew text. It was an opposite process compared with Origen's attempt to correct the Septuagint via the Hebrew text. The Renaissance with its return to classical antiquity brought also an increased interest in the Septuagint.

The first printed editions of the Septuagint were actually the Polyglot Bibles (the *Complutensian* [Alcalá, Spain, 1514–17], the *Sixtine* [Rome, 1587]).

A critical edition of the Septuagint used by students and ministers is the one produced by Alfred Rahlfs (Stuttgart, 1935). It is based on the three major codices (Sinaiticus, Alexandrinus, Vaticanus). This edition became the basis for all subsequent editions of LXX.

The critical edition par excellence is the *Göttingen Septuagint* (1931–). This edition does not follow a particular textual tradition. Rather, the editors picked the best readings in the manuscript tradition based on the Hebrew text. The goal of the editors was to offer the best text while recognizing that they were not able to recover the original form in every particular point. Publication of this edition is still under way.

Later Greek Translations

From her inception, the Church opted for the Septuagint, with the result that soon this translation of the Jewish Scriptures became the standard text. The common view is that the extensive use of the Septuagint by Christians to support their messianic claims about Jesus determined the Jews to discard the old version while producing new translations for their own use in the synagogue. One may notice that the Septuagint has never been the version for both Jews and Christians simultaneously.

Besides the Christian appropriation of the Septuagint, there would have been another factor for the emergence of later Greek translations.[47] At the beginning of Christian era, the Dead Sea Scrolls show a certain textual fluidity concerning the Hebrew text, hence the need for new translations in Greek to keep up with this pluriformity as well as with the gradual standardization of the Hebrew text.[48]

The fact that as early as first century B.C.E. there was more than one Greek translation (e.g., proto-Theodotion) shows that attempts were made within Judaism itself to accommodate the LXX to the ongoing changes undergone by the Hebrew text. If this holds true, then the necessity for new translations arose primarily within Judaism.[49] Thus, the second-century C.E. Greek translations might be regarded more or less as revisions of the LXX. Sometimes, as in the case of Aquila and Symmachus, they are new recensions of an older revision (e.g., proto-Theodotion).[50]

The LXX ceased to exercise its influence on Judaism from the end of the first century C.E. onward, after the differences between the LXX and the Hebrew text in Palestine were noticed, and following the New Testament's use of the LXX. The last sign of the LXX's influence in the Jewish sphere may be detected in its central position in Josephus's work toward the end of the first century C.E.

Interestingly enough, the sole reference to LXX in the Talmud, *b. Meg.* 9a, contains two juxtaposed and contradictory evaluations. On the one hand, the positive evaluation depicts the LXX as an inspired translation. This is probably the older interpretive layer of the *baraita* (rabbinic gloss). One the other hand, the negative evaluation is hinted at in those fifteen places where the *baraita* notes a discrepancy between the Greek translation and the Hebrew text.

The rabbis even established a day (the eighth of Tevet) for fasting and mourning, warning pious Jews of the desecration of the Scriptures by LXX translators. This injunction, which was canceled in the Middle Ages, is however not found in the main sources of *Megillat Ta'anit Batra*, but in a late addition to the scroll.[51] Moreover, the post-Talmudic text from the tractate *Soferim* speaks of the LXX making in terms of the building of the golden calf (Exod 32): "It happened once that five elders wrote the Torah for king Ptolemy in Greek, and that day was ominous for Israel as the day when which the golden calf was made, since the Torah could not be accurately translated" (*Sof.* 1.7).

Theodotion

The older terms, proto-Theodotion,[52] indicating an early revision of the LXX, and Theodotion of Hexapla, were recently replaced by a newer term, *kaige*-Theodotion, coined by Dominique Barthélemy according to one of this recension's feature, the rendition of Hebrew *gam*, "also," with Greek *kaige*, "at least." The *kaige*-Theodotion recension is a revision of the LXX preserved in the scroll of the Minor Prophets. The scroll, dated to the first century B.C.E., was discovered in the Judaean desert at Naḥal Ḥever in 1952, and published by Barthélemy in *DJD* VIII (plate 21).[53]

Among this recension's distinguishing features one may mention its inclination for literality (to a certain degree, similar to Aquila), even to the extent of transliterating Hebrew words (especially terms for animals, vegetation, etc.) rather than translating them into Greek.

Characteristic of Christian Septuagint, in the case of the Book of Daniel, is the replacement of the LXX with the (proto-) Theodotion text (about second century C.E.). In the second half of the second century C.E., Justin's Daniel is quite similar to the recension of (proto-) Theodotion.[54] Nevertheless, this replacement was not implemented at once and overall.[55] The LXX of this book is still represented in the Syro-Hexapla.

Nowadays, it is commonly thought that the pre-Christian *kaige*-Theodotion recension formed a base for the second-century C.E. recensions of both Aquila and Symmachus.

Aquila

According to the Palestinian Talmud (*y. Meg.* 1:11 [71c]), Aquila (Hebrew *'qyls hgr*, "Aquila, the foreigner") was a pupil of R. Eliezer and R. Joshua.

However, *b. Meg.* 3a states: "The Targum of the Pentateuch was composed by Onqelos the proselyte under the guidance of R. Eleazar and R. Joshua." Thus, since the end of nineteenth century, "Aquila the proselyte" has been identified with "Onqelos the proselyte," the author of the homonymous targum.[56] However, the mere similarity in names and translation approaches is not a convincing argument to accept such identification.

Around 125 c.e., Aquila produced a literal translation, very close to the Hebrew text.[57] Aquila's translation approach was based on Rabbi Aqiba's principle that every word and even letter-sign of the Hebrew Scripture carries some important meaning. Due to its literalness and careful sense of precision, Aquila's recension was well received among the rabbis. Aquila is the only Greek translation that generated ten quotations in the Palestinian Talmud and Midrashim; it finds no such mention, however, in the Babylonian Talmud.[58] Earlier, Origen noted that Akylas (i.e., Aquila) "is preferred by those Jews who know Hebrew, as being the most successful translator of all" (*Letter to Julius Africanus* 4).[59]

Justinian's novella 146 (titled *Peri Hebraiōn*, "On Jews"), issued on February 13, in the year 553 c.e., allows the Jews within the confines of the Byzantine empire to use in their synagogues only two Greek versions of the Scripture: the Septuagint (presumably, the Christianized copies) and the translation of Aquila.[60]

The Aquila recension may be found in Hexapla fragments and in some sixth-century palimpsests from Cairo *geniza*.

Symmachus

At the end of the second century or beginning of the third century c.e., Symmachus brought out a new recension of the Greek text.[61] According to Eusebius and Jerome, Symmachus was an Ebionite. His work is a moderately literal translation (close to *kaige*-Theodotion) that seeks to find matching Greek idioms for Hebrew phrases. This recension is attested only in a few Hexapla fragments.

Septuagint Recensions

As a matter of fact, the church fathers and other early Christian writers used predominantly the Septuagint while mentioning the other Greek translations which were designated as "Later Versions," "Hexaplaric Versions," "the Three (translators)," or simply, "Aquila," "Symmachus," and "Theodotion," sometimes labeled with the initials of their names,

$α'$, $σ'$, $θ'$. Only small fragments of these translations have been preserved,[62] though some textual evidence may be gleaned from patristic
quotations and marginal notes in various manuscripts.

Some church fathers and writers refer to *ho hebraios*, "the Hebrew
(translator?)" or *to hebraikon* "the Hebrew (translation?)," *ho Syros*, "the
Syrian (translator?)," and *to samar[e]itikon*, "the Samaritan (translation?)."
To this list of mere names, too scant to conclude much regarding these
recensions, one may add the three textual witnesses to the Septuagint
used by Origen in his Hexapla: namely, the *Quinta* ("the Fifth"), *Sexta*
("the Sixth"), and *Septima* ("the Seventh").[63]

Origen's Hexapla

Unlike other ancient Christian apologists resorting to the *Letter of Aristeas*
and overloading it with more legendary features in an assiduous effort to
defend the Septuagint's veracity and superiority over other versions,
Origen was among the few to recognize the textual and literary difficulties
surrounding the Greek translation of "the Seventy." Among these difficulties was the fact that the Greek translation contained more books than the
Jewish canon. Also problematic was the fact that some Greek renditions
seemed to be shorter than their corresponding text in the Hebrew Bible.
Other later Greek translations were also very different from the LXX.

About 240 C.E., Origen, the dauntless teacher of the famous school of
Alexandria, surnamed *Adamantios* (Greek, "invincible, adamant, steel")
for his untiring energy, produced a magnum opus on six columns, titled
Hexapla. It took him twenty-eight years to accomplish such a Herculian
task (about six thousand leaves or twelve thousand pages). During this
time, he was financially supported and encouraged by a patron named
Ambrosius. Here is Jerome's account on the making of Origen's Hexapla:

> He [i.e., Origen] was so assiduous in the study of Holy Scriptures,
> that contrary to the spirit of his time, and of his people, he learned
> the Hebrew language, and taking the Septuagint translation, he
> gathered the other translations also in a single work, namely, that of
> Aquila of Ponticus the Proselyte, and Theodotian the Ebonite, and
> Symmachus an adherent of the same sect who wrote commentaries
> also on the Gospel according to Matthew, from which he tried to
> establish his doctrine. And besides these, a fifth, sixth, and seventh
> translation, which we also have from his library, he sought out with
> great diligence, and compared with other editions.
>
> *The Lives of Illustrious Men* 54[64]

Out of the Hexapla's six columns, the first two were allocated to the Jewish Scriptures, with Hebrew characters (consonantal text only) and Greek transliteration. The other four columns contained, in this order, Aquila, Symmachus, Septuagint (OG), and Theodotion (i.e., *kaige*-Theodotion). The fifth column included Origen's "annotated" version of the OG, in which Origen made notations regarding the pluses (indicated with an *obelos*, "obelisk") and minuses (marked with an *asteriskos*, "asterisk") of the Septuagint compared to the Hebrew text. The minuses in the Septuagint were filled in with material from the other columns, especially from the sixth (*kaige*-Theodotion).[65]

Origen mentions neither the translation story of the Septuagint nor the legendary detail regarding its inspiration. Nonetheless, he seemingly recognizes the unique value of the Septuagint as a translation made under God's providence and used as an authoritative text in the Church.[66] On the other hand, Origen is one of the few ancient Christian writers who rightly estimated the Hebrew text. As Martin Hengel notes, by the preeminent position of the Hebrew text in Origen's Hexapla, "the church was continually reminded that the LXX is only a translation that can never exceed the Hebrew original in dignity, but must, rather, always succeed it."[67]

The objective of Origen's huge enterprise was to survey the differences between the Hebrew text and the Greek Bible (OG) of the Church, and to revise the OG by comparing it with the extant Hebrew text and with the help of the other Greek translations, primarily the *kaige*-Theodotion (one of the earliest revisions of the OG). The Septuagint thus edited in the fifth column was labeled the "Hexaplaric recension" of the Greek text.

According to Origen's own testimony, special attention was granted to the Septuagint and its revision to serve better the needs of the Church:

> This, if it be not arrogant to say it, I have already to a great extent done to the best of my ability, laboring hard to get at the meaning in all the editions and various readings; while I paid particular attention to the interpretation of the Seventy, lest I might to be found to accredit any forgery to the churches which are under heaven, and give an occasion to those who seek such a starting-point for gratifying their desire to slander the common brethren, and to bring some accusation against those who shine forth in our community.
>
> *Letter to Julius Africanus* 5[68]

In fact, Origen wanted to correct the LXX lest the Church be accused of using an erroneous version of the Scripture. Obviously, Origen's work meant to be apologetic in its nature, resetting the LXX as the Church's Bible while recognizing the textual preeminence of the Hebrew Scripture. Writes Origen:

> But why should I enumerate all the instances I collected with so much labor, to prove that the difference between our copies and those of the Jews did not escape me? In Jeremiah I noticed many instances, and indeed in that book I found much transposition and variation in the readings of the prophecies. Again, in Genesis, the words, "God saw that it was good," when the firmament was made, are not found in the Hebrew [Gen 1:8], and there is no small dispute among them about this.
>
> *Letter to Julius Africanus 4*[69]

Origen's Hexapla was preserved in the library of Caesarea of Palestine. Never copied in its entirety, it was lost during the seventh-century Islamic invasion. Only the Hexaplaric recension (i.e., the fifth column) was frequently reproduced. Pamphilius (d. 409 c.e.), the director of Caesarea's library, as well as the church historian Eusebius of Caesarea contributed to the wide distribution of the Hexaplaric recension. No complete text of this recension was, however, preserved. Nevertheless, there are some witnesses to it, among which, *Codex Colberto-Sarravianus* (fourth–fifth century c.e.) and Syro-Hexapla (worked by bishop Paul of Tella in 616–17 c.e.).[70]

Post-Hexaplaric Revisions

The most important post-Hexaplaric[71] recension is that of Lucian of Antioch, dating from about 300 c.e.[72] The Lucianic recension done on an existing Greek text of the Old and New Testaments was rediscovered in the nineteenth century in some minuscule manuscripts coined b,o,c$_2$,e$_2$ in the *Cambridge Septuagint.*

Lucian's recension, probably based on the fifth column of Origen's Hexapla, is stylistic in nature. It was used by Antiochene writers such as Chrysostom and Theodoret of Cyrus.

The Lucianic revision is detectable in the Book of Psalms and New Testament. Both these literary corpora present signs of stylistic revisions and a great deal of literary homogeneity. Other traces of Lucianic revision may be found in the Prophets and historical books of the Old Testament.[73]

The Hexaplaric and post-Hexaplaric recensions of the LXX indicate a certain standardization of the text. They represent a shift of the LXX from a Jewish to a Christian medium of transmission.

Other Textual Witnesses
Samaritan Pentateuch

Contrary to popular belief, the Samaritans did not separate from the Jews until the Hasmonean times (second century B.C.E.) when the sanctuary on Mt. Gerizim was plundered by the Jerusalem high priest John Hyrcanus. At the time of separation, the Samaritans took with them the Pentateuch, preserved in the form of a second Hebrew recension, the Samaritan Pentateuch.[74]

The oldest fragment manuscript in codex format of the Samaritan Pentateuch is dated to the beginning of the twelfth century. Discovered in 1846 and preserved in the Cambridge University Library, the Nablus (Shechem) Scroll, also known as the Abisha Scroll, is a compilation of fragment manuscripts. The oldest fragment, covering Num 35–Deut 34, dates back to the eleventh century.

The fact that the Samaritan manuscripts were written in paleo-Hebrew script, which predates the Assyrian (or "square") script in which the MT manuscripts were transmitted, conferred on the former an antique aura of originality.[75] Nevertheless, as it has meanwhile been proven, an old script is not sine qua non a token of originality when dealing with textual transmission.

Brought from Damascus to Europe by Pietro della Valle in 1616, the Sam. was published for the first time in the Paris Polyglot Bible (1629–45).

Among modern printed editions, one may mention Avraham Sadaqa and Ratson Sadaqa, eds., *Jewish and Samaritan Version of the Pentateuch*.

One may detect two overlapping layers in the Samaritan Pentateuch: the Samaritan layer, reflecting distinct characteristics of Samaritan religion and ideology; and the pre-Samaritan layer, betraying textual similarities with the manuscripts found in the Judean desert, especially the Qumran Scrolls. Due to this twofold interface, scholars prefer to call this textual witness the pre-Sam. rather than more traditional term, the Sam.

After the discovery of the Qumran Scrolls, the term pre-Sam. came to designate non-Samaritan texts such as the Qumran texts, with which the former show a high degree of similarity. It is quite likely that one of the Qumran texts reflected the textual base for the true pre-Sam. textual tradition leading to the two-layer Samaritan manuscripts dated to the beginning of the twelfth century.[76]

Two points make the Sam.—more specifically, its pre-Sam. layer—especially valuable. First, it witnesses, along with some Qumran Hebrew manuscripts, to the New Testament quotations of the Septuagint. Second, along with a number of unrevised Jewish medieval manuscripts, the Sam. reflects a form of Hebrew text very popular and well spread during the second century B.C.E. and first century C.E.

There are some six thousand places where the Sam. differs from the MT. Many of these differences are simply orthographical in nature or with no impact on meaning. Significantly, the Sam. concords with the LXX against the MT in some one thousand nine hundred instances.[77]

Unlike other textual witnesses, primarily the proto- and the MT, where one can notice the scribes' great care in copying, the pre- and the Sam. show a great deal of liberty in dealing with the biblical text. Some of the changes found in the Samaritan texts are due to the scribes' tendency toward harmonization, as well noted by Emanuel Tov.[78]

Early Christian interpreters show very little awareness of the Sam. However, it is worth noting that Origen often cited a Greek translation of the Sam. known as the *Samaritikon*.[79]

Peshitta

The name Peshitta (Syriac, "simple, plain [translation]")[80] distinguishes this translation from the Syro-Hexapla, a rendition of the Greek Hexapla into Syriac done by Paul of Tella early in the seventh century C.E. The Jewish and Christian elements at the interpretive level of the S cast indecisiveness over the origin of this textual witness. The common view is that the S was produced during the mid first–second century C.E. from a Hebrew text. The Hebrew source of the S is much closer to the MT's *Vorlage* than to the Hebrew source of the LXX.

The oldest manuscript of S preserved in London British Library dates to 459–60 C.E. In the fifth century C.E., the Syrian Church divided into two branches, the East Syriac and the West Syriac. Among the West Syriac mss. of S, the most important is Codex Ambrosianus, a sixth–seventh century manuscript kept at the Ambrosianus Library in Milan.[81] Given the late date of these manuscripts, the biblical quotations in Syriac church fathers such as Ephraem the Syrian (d. 373 C.E.) and Aphraates (fourth century C.E.) are of great value in assisting the text critic to reconstruct earlier phases in Syriac textual tradition.

No trails of revision or standardization have been detected in the early S transmission. If until the ninth–tenth century the S manuscripts exhibited a great deal of variance, after that date, the high degree of similarity among them implies a single exemplar, an archetype, from which these later manuscripts derived.

A critical edition, based on Codex Ambrosianus, is now being published by the Peshitta Institute of the University of Leiden.[82] The modern English translation of the Peshitta by George M. Lamsa, *The Holy Bible from Ancient Eastern Manuscripts,* based on an unreliable text of the Peshitta, will be replaced in the near future by the *New English Annotated Translation of the Syriac Bible* (NEATSB), sponsored by the Peshitta Institute and published by Brill. In addition, the Gorgias Press is launching a new English translation accompanied by the Syriac text of the Peshitta and titled *The Antioch Bible.*

The Peshitta has a well-positioned place among the other textual witnesses and its importance for the textual critic is given by the mere fact that the language of this translation, Syriac, is closely related to Hebrew, both belonging to the Semitic linguistic family.

Vetus Latina

While Greek enjoyed the lingua franca status in the Mediterranean region, Latin was used uninterruptedly in some parts of the Roman Empire such as Italy, Gaul, and North of Africa (especially Carthage). The African Pope Victor (189–98 C.E.) masterminded the linguistic shift from Greek to Latin in Rome itself. Already in the second century C.E., when the LXX became the Christian Bible par excellence, a need for a Latin translation was felt.

The OL gained a great importance for the Septuagint studies precisely as it reflects a phase earlier than that of the major manuscripts of the Greek text. Thus, the OL may assist the scholars to reconstruct the OG prior to its major revisions. Christian authors such as Tertullian and Cyprian of Carthage (third century C.E.) made use of Latin translations of the LXX.

When detected in Jerome's Vulgate, the OL readings differ from both textual witnesses, the LXX and MT. Pierre-M. Bogaert[83] suggests that the

OL of Jeremiah, where it is well preserved (e.g., Jer 39 and 52), attests the oldest form of LXX, which in its turn reflects one of the earliest forms of Hebrew text, much older than the MT's *Vorlage*. The Jeremiah texts studied by Bogaert are shorter than those found in the Septuagint. (In these particular cases, Vaticanus and Sinaiticus show traces of revision based on the Hebrew text.)

Vulgate

The Vulgate began as a revision by Jerome of the Psalms in the OL, known as *Psalterium Romanum*, and of the Psalms in the Hexapla, known as *Psalterium Gallicanum*. Jerome's own translation of the Hebrew Old Testament was accomplished between 390 and 405 c.e. The name of his translation, Vulgate (Vulgata), comes from Latin adjective *vulgatus*, "commonly known, in general circulation," hence a "popular" rendition of the Bible. Jerome's Hebrew source is generally close to the MT's *Vorlage*.

Augustine's mistrust in Jerome's use of proto-MT as a basis for translation determined the latter to be cautious in his daring endeavor. The fear of the bishop of Hippo that this translation could bring a new schism between Greek and Latin Churches made things even harder for Jerome. One may notice that between Augustine and Jerome there was a great difference of attitudes with respect to the Septuagint. In Augustine's view, the Septuagint was inspired, the Church's authoritative version. In contrast, Jerome was more reserved as regards the matter of inspiration. Since Jerome did not have the luxury of dictionaries or grammars of Hebrew, he had to rely on the Septuagint, Aquila, Symmachus, and Theodotion, as well as on some information from Jewish sources. These were his lexica and grammar books. Consequently, the Vulgate is not from beginning to end a Latin translation of the Hebrew text; often, it is simply another recension of the OG, but in Latin. Jerome himself admits this alternation between translation and revision during his work as a translator:

> The canon of the Hebrew Truth [*Hebraica veritas*—The Old Testament as translated directly from the Hebrew]—except the Octoteuch [the first eight books of the Old Testament] which I have at present in hand—I have placed at the disposal of your slaves and copyists. Doubtless you already possess the version from the Septuagint which many years ago I diligently revised for the use of students.[84] The New Testament I have restored to the authoritative

form of the Greek original. For as the true text of the Old Testament can only be tested by a reference to the Hebrew, so the true text of the New requires for its decision an appeal to the Greek.

Letter 71: To Lucinius 5[85]

The Vulgate was established over against the OL as the standard Latin Bible by the eighth or ninth century. However, it was not until the Council of Trent—on April 8, 1546, to be exact—that Jerome's work was officially recognized as the authoritative version of the Roman Catholic Church "in matters of faith and morals."[86] Yet even this conciliar statement did not refute the importance of other versions (i.e., the Hebrew text and the Septuagint). Moreover, the OL Psalter remained in liturgical use within the Roman Catholic Church.

The Tridentine decree regarding the doctrinal and moral authority of the Vulgate entailed the recognition of an official edition of the Latin text. This edition remained for almost a half-century. In 1592, Clement VIII published a new edition of Jerome's Vulgate, known as the *Clementine* edition. This edition would stood firm as the official Latin text of the Roman Catholic Church until 1979, when it was replaced by the *Nova Vulgata*, a revision of Jerome's Vulgate based on Hebrew, Aramaic, and Greek. The new revision reflected the enormous growth in Roman Catholic biblical studies in the decades following the 1943 encyclical of Pope Pius XII, *Divino Afflante Spiritu,* which had flung open the doors for the use of textual criticism and translations from the original biblical languages among Roman Catholic scholars. A critical edition of the Vulgate was also published by the Benedictine Order between 1926 and 1986.

Targums

The Aramaic word *targum,* "translation, interpretation," came to designate the Aramaic translations (targumim or targums) of the Hebrew text. The Tgs. were highly appreciated by Jewish Medieval biblical commentators. Moreover, the Rabbinic Bibles incorporate the text of the Tgs. in parallel with the MT. There is no way of knowing precisely when the Tgs. appeared for the first time, although fragments of Tgs. were found at Qumran. The Hebrew source of the Tgs. is very close to the MT's *Vorlage.* The Tgs. were published in critical editions such as Alexander Sperber, *The Bible in Aramaic.*

The Tgs. are divided into three groups according to the three divisions of the Hebrew Bible. Among the Tgs. on Torah, Targum of Onqelos is perhaps the best known. With regard to the date of its composition, the scholars are divided among three possibilities: first, third, or the fifth century c.e. The text of the Onqelos reflects the Hebrew of the MT. In terms of interpretation—since all the Tgs. are interpretations rather than simply translated texts—Tg. Onqelos offers a plain interpretation. Among the Palestinian Tgs., one may list the Jerusalem Tg. 1 (or Tg. Pseudo-Jonathan). The Tg. Jonathan to the Prophets is ascribed by tradition to Jonathan ben 'Uzziel, a disciple of Hillel the Elder.

A very old targum is the Job Tg. already in use at the time of Gamaliel the Elder (first half of the first century c.e.).

The Authority of the Septuagint
The Bible of the Church

The relationship between identity and textuality is an already established axiom. Communities are shaped by texts. Moreover, texts are reshaped by communities. This holds true especially for Judaism and Christianity, which are "textual communities," that is, groups formed around a text and its interpreters.[87] The Scriptures have for both communities generative and legitimizing functions.

The adoption and appropriation of the Septuagint as primary Bible of the Eastern Orthodox Church proves the relationship between identity and textuality. A good example here is the impact of Septuagint (conceptually and lexically) on the liturgical life of the Church. For instance, the whole Eastern Orthodox hymnography is infused with concepts and terms derived from the Greek translation. This relation between identity and textuality is echoed and underscored in the outright question posed by Brevard S. Childs: "Why should the Christian church be committed in any way to the authority of the Masoretic text when its development extended long after the inception of the church and was carried on within a rabbinic tradition?"[88]

For Eastern Orthodox Church, the Septuagint has first of all a religious value. It is *the* Bible witnessing to all phases of the church history, beginning with the New Testament and apostolic times through to church fathers, ecumenical councils and beyond. The Septuagint is doubtlessly the Bible of the undivided Church. All the dogmatic statements of the ecumenical councils were crafted with a theological lexicon whose biblical correlate and source was the Septuagint.

The early Church inherited from early Judaism the view on the parity between Hebrew and Greek texts while considering any correction of the LXX as unnecessary.[89] For Augustine both textual witnesses (Hebrew and Greek) have the same authority, offering complementary views on various facets of God's fathomless revelation.[90] Commenting on Jonah's prophecy on Nineveh's imminent ruin (Jonah 3:4), Augustine sees no contradiction between the two versions, but rather a complementary relationship validated by the allegorical interpretation of the passage. With Nineveh representing the Church of Gentiles, the "forty days" (Hebrew text) refer to the risen Lord's fortieth day ascension and "three days" (Greek text) hint at Christ's third day resurrection (*City of God* 18.42–44).[91]

To take a step further, Epiphanius of Salamis argues that the Septuagint is more accurate than the Hebrew text. In Epiphanius's view, the seventy-two translators reached this high degree of textual accuracy by omissions and additions. The repetitions in Hebrew were eliminated, while the additions in the Greek text were considered needful to explicate the difficult Hebrew wording. The Septuagint, through clarity and conciseness, is superior to Aquila and other late Greek translations (*On Weights and Measures* 22–38).

One may adduce here Jerome's pertinent remark suggesting two possible reasons for the popularity of the Septuagint: "The Septuagint has rightly kept its place in the churches, either because it is the first of all the versions in time, made before the coming of Christ, or else because it has been used by the apostles (only however in places where it does not disagree with the Hebrews)" (*Letter 57: To Pammachius on the Best Method of Translating*).[92]

The debate surrounding the authority of the biblical text surfaced in the East after the seventeenth century, simultaneously with the debate on the extension of the biblical canon, both debates occurring against the backdrop of theological disputes between Roman Catholics and Protestants with regard to the Vulgate in relation to the Hebrew text. These disputes had a direct impact on Orthodox, who separated into two groups: the supporters of the Septuagint and those of the Hebrew text.

Within this context of polemics about canon and texts, the *Rudder* (Greek, *Pedalion*), codified canon law by Nicodemus the Agiorite (1749–1809),[93] mentions the Septuagint (in general terms, not referring to a specific manuscript) as *the* Old Testament of the Eastern Orthodox Church.

All the legendary embellishments found in church fathers and writers are rehearsed in the *Rudder* arguing for the inspired character of the LXX, and hence the abiding authority of this translation. Oddly enough, the Rudder grants more credence to a "paraphrase" (i.e., the Tgs.) than to the textual base—the Hebrew text! The document responds to the critique that the Septuagint does not follow the Hebrew text by emphasizing that the latter was corrupted and the former was based on a Hebrew text different than the one in circulation at that time. In addition, the compilers of the *Rudder* are silent on Origen's Hexapla and his honest intention to survey the differences between LXX and the Hebrew text of his time. The three late Greek translations (Aquila, Symmachus, Theodotion) are discarded altogether due to the fact that they were done by Jewish proselytes who in their work intentionally obfuscated the Old Testament prophecies referring to Christ. Yet the *Rudder* ignores the fact that the Book of Daniel has been preserved and transmitted in Theodotion version. Moreover, the Vulgate cannot be trusted because of its many errors. Thus, concludes the *Rudder*, the Septuagint and the Peshitta are to be considered the most authoritative texts in the Eastern Orthodox Church.

In sharp contrast to the *Rudder*'s view on LXX's singularity, the Greek Enlightenment humanist scholar Adamandinos Korais proposed in 1808 to the British and Foreign Bible Society a translation from Hebrew into Modern Greek. Korais was also pleading for the introduction of Hebrew in the curriculum of Greek schools. Nevertheless, this favorable current for Hebrew text and language ended shortly upon the foundation of the Greek state (1828–30), when the Church separated from the direct jurisdiction of the Ecumenical Patriarchate and became the "Church of Greece," and upon the arrival in Greece of the first Protestant missionaries in 1810.

As for the "inspiration of the Septuagint," it has been always tacitly recognized in the East. This recognition was even further underscored after the Protestant publication of a translation of the Old Testament from Hebrew into Greek in 1834. The fact that the evangelical missionaries helped with the distribution of this translation put the Orthodox Church in Greece in the defensive mood. The Greek theologian Constantine Oikonomos, who was initially on the side of Korais, became a fervent opponent of the translation. Oikonomos thus wrote a treatise defending the inspiration of the Septuagint.[94] This was the time when the Orthodox Church in Greece became the protector of the Greek national traditions. Any attack against the Church's "traditional" views was considered an attack against the national security. In 1911, the Greek constitution forbade the translation of the Bible into Modern Greek as well as any form of proselytism.[95]

Were the Orthodox to introduce on the agenda of the long projected Pan-Orthodox Council[96] a serious discussion about the Septuagint and its inspired status and take decision on whether this textual witness could become the official version for the Eastern Orthodox Church, two important questions would have to be answered: (1) How much credit should one accord to those legendary embellishments added by Christian writers to a pseudepigraphon such as the *Letter of Aristeas*? (2) Which one of the manuscripts or recensions of the Septuagint (or a mix of them) should be selected so that the Orthodox might be able to say with clean conscience that the chosen manuscript or recension is the only text that has been used throughout history by church fathers and writers? Meanwhile, the presence of the Theodotion (*kaige*-Theodotion) for the Book of Daniel in almost all the LXX manuscripts remains a serious problem for the proponents of the LXX as *the* official version of the Church.[97]

Besides being the Bible of the Church, so dearly embraced by the Eastern Orthodoxy, the Septuagint has at least three major intrinsic merits we try to summarize in the following paragraphs.

A Different *Vorlage*

The discovery of the Dead Sea Scrolls[98] reopened the discussions on the relationship between the two most important textual witnesses, the Masoretic Text and the Septuagint.

Based on the ongoing analysis of Qumran texts (Hebrew and Greek) dating to the third century B.C.E.–first century C.E., the current consensus is that the text of the Septuagint either reflects a Hebrew/Aramaic *Vorlage* different from the one mirrored by the MT, or is the product of various editorial interventions introduced by the Greek translators, or that it was simply corrupted by scribal mistakes piled up during the transmission. Or the Septuagint could be the product of all three of these factors combined.[99] This last explanation represents a major shift from a not so remote past when students of the Hebrew Bible considered the Septuagint a free translation-interpretation, a type of midrash, done on a Hebrew text quite similar if not identical with the MT's *Vorlage*.

Emanuel Tov argues that the MT's *Vorlage* was fostered within the Temple circles. One would expect that the Hebrew scrolls used for the LXX originated in the same circles. A close comparison of the LXX with

the MT suggests large-scale differences between these two main textual
witnesses. Why texts of the MT family were not used for the Greek translation is a conundrum. One thing seems clear, however. The Hebrew manuscripts used for the Septuagint could have not been sent to Alexandria by
a high priest (Eleazer) along with other sages as mentioned in the *Letter of
Aristeas* (paragraph 176) for the mere reason that a high priest would have
promoted a text of the MT family connected to the Temple circles. For
instance, it is well known that the LXX of Jeremiah is shorter with some
two thousand seven hundred words than the MT of the same book.
Interestingly enough, in the Qumran library there were found both, a
longer (4QJer[a]) and a shorter (4QJer[b,d]) version of the Hebrew text of this
book.[100] With regard to Jeremiah, Tov raises the question: Why did the
LXX translators resort to a text of the tradition of 4QJer[b,d] instead of 4QJer[a]
(dated about 200 B.C.E.—almost the same time as the LXX's beginnings)
of the MT family? There are a few possible answers. It could be that the
LXX translators opted for an older text or that the pre-MT edition did not
exist at the time of the translation. According to Tov, during the third and
second centuries B.C.E., pre-MT manuscripts were embraced by some circles, while other circles used different, older manuscripts. However, this is
just the beginning of unraveling the mystery of Hebrew manuscripts used
by the LXX translators.[101]

Older Layers of Redactionality

There is another intriguing factor that makes the Septuagint a significant
object of research especially in the area of literary (redaction) criticism. As
Emanuel Tov notices, "When comparing the LXX evidence with that of
the other sources, we found that beyond MT, the LXX is the single most
important source preserving redactionally different material relevant to
the literary analysis of the Bible, often earlier than MT." A similar yet limited redactionality obtains with some early Hebrew biblical texts found at
Qumran. In Tov's view,

> The preservation of redactionally different material in the LXX was
> ascribed to two factors or a combination of them: (1) the idiosyn-
> cratic nature of the Hebrew manuscripts used for the translation
> not shared by the circles which embraced MT; and (2) the relatively
> early date of the translation enterprise (275–150 B.C.E.) involving
> still earlier manuscripts which could reflect vestiges of earlier

editorial stages of the biblical books. These factors may explain the special nature of the LXX in different ways, but sometimes they need to be combined.[102]

That the Septuagint could contain elements dating back to early periods in the literary history of the biblical books, elements that are absent in the MT, has since the nineteenth century always been a point of attraction for scholars working in the area of literary criticism.

According to Mogens Müller, the Septuagint is not merely a translation reflecting a Hebrew *Urtext*, but it is also a "witness to the process of transmitting tradition."[103] In Müller's view, the text of Old Testament was generally fixed by the third century B.C.E. with the exception of some books or fragments where the text shows fluidity. The best example is the Book of Daniel whose process of enrichment by way of new traditions came to a transient halt by the middle of second century B.C.E. However, this process continued long after this date; hence the major textual differences between Septuagint and Theodotion. Eventually, for no particular textually evaluative reason, the Theodotion will supplant the Septuagint text of Daniel in all the Septuagint manuscripts. This phenomenon of textual fluidity, together with the shift that occurred with the rise of Jewish sectarianism during third and second century B.C.E.[104] should be seriously considered when discussing the relationship between Hebrew and Greek textual witnesses, especially for the books of Jeremiah, Job, and Proverbs. One may want to discard the common misconception that translation is a method and a reflection of preserving texts in the form the translator had at his disposal. As a matter of fact, the process of shifting traditions continued even after the first Septuagint copies were put in circulation. The emergence of Qumran commentaries (second–first century B.C.E.) is a sign that the text has already received a final form and by consequence become authoritative.

Early Biblical Interpretation

It goes without saying that between the LXX translator (*interpres*) for whom the interpretational element is due to the ambiguity of the Hebrew text, and the Tg. translator (*expositor*) where the explanatory gloss is deliberately inserted, there are as many interpretive registers as there are translations (e.g., from Greek into Latin, Syriac, Armenian, Coptic, etc.). In a nutshell, the LXX presents both literal (verbatim) and paraphrastic renderings.

Every translation is more or less an interpretation of the primary text. Thus LXX value is twofold, as a translation and interpretation. This is true with any translation modern or ancient. Much more does this obtain with ancient translations as attested by Greek, Latin, Hebrew, and Aramaic lexicographic evidence. Notably, in all these languages the verb "to translate" has also the meaning "to interpret": *hermēneuō* (Greek), *interpretari* (Latin), *targēm* (Aramaic), *paššēq* (Hebrew).[105]

Eastern Orthodox Views on Hebrew Text

In general lines, the Eastern Orthodox Church is not against the use of Hebrew text. Nonetheless, with few exceptions, Eastern Christian writers, ancient and modern, have accorded minimal attention to the Hebrew textual witness.[106]

Early church writers were fully aware that in working on Septuagint texts they were availing themselves of a translation with its inherent deficiencies. As an illustration of the patristic awareness on difficulties related to the Septuagint as a translation of a Hebrew original are the following authorities.[107]

Among the church writers and fathers who had some exposure to Hebrew one may mention Julius Africanus (160–240 C.E.). In his only preserved complete letter to Origen, Africanus speaks of the fact that the Greek translation carries on the pun that has no relevance in the Hebrew original wording:

> And when the one said, "Under a holm-tree" (*prinos*), he answered that the angel would saw him asunder (*prisein*); and in a similar fashion menaced the other who said, "Under a mastich-tree" (*schēinos*), with being rent asunder (*schēistēnai*). Now, in Greek, it happens that "holm-tree" and "saw asunder," and "rend" and "mastich-tree" sound alike; but in Hebrew they are quite distinct. But all the books of the Old Testament have been translated from Hebrew into Greek.
>
> *Letter to Origen*[108]

For Jerome (*Letter 18: To Pope Damasus*), Hebrew represents "man's original language";[109] hence, the exceeding value of the Old Testament written originally in Hebrew. Speaking about the Hebrew text, Jerome states:

The Hebrew Scriptures are used by apostolic men. . . . Our Lord and Savior himself whenever he refers to the Scriptures, takes his quotations from the Hebrew; as in the instance of the words, "He that believes on me, as the Scripture said, out of his belly shall flow rivers of living water" [John 7:38; a quote from Prov 18:4 or Isa 58:11] and in the words used on the cross itself, "Eli, Eli, lama sabachthani," which is by interpretation "My God, my God, why have you forsaken me?" not, as it is given by the Septuagint, "My God, my God, look upon me, why have you forsaken me?" and many similar cases. I do not say this in order to aim a blow at the seventy translators; but I assert that the apostles of Christ bare [Sic] an authority superior to theirs. Wherever the Seventy agree with the Hebrew, the apostles took their quotations from that translation; but, where they disagree, they set down in Greek what they had found in the Hebrew.

Apology against Rufinus 2.34[110]

In his commentary on Isaiah, Theodoret of Cyrus uses the Hebrew text in addition to the Septuagint and the late translations of Aquila, Symmachus, and Theodotion. He terms the former as "the Hebrew" (*ho Hebraios*) or "the Hebrew Scripture" (*hē Hebraikē graphē*). According to Demetrios Trakatellis, Theodoret's "objective in such quotations is to discuss words or phrases that appear in the Hebrew but not in the Septuagint text or to explain the precise meanings of difficult terms."[111] Charles Kannengiesser points out that Theodoret of Cyrus admits to having used a lexicon of Hebrew names for identifying the correct meaning of certain Hebrew proper names such as Neasar (*synechomenos*, "held together"). Theodoret calls this glossary *tēs tōn hebraikōn onomatōn hermēneias ho biblos*, "the book of the interpretation of Hebrew names."[112]

Procopius of Gaza (465–527 c.e.) interpreting Isaiah[113] brings into discussion several Greek and Hebrew variants of the biblical text. With respect to Isa 9:6(5),[114] he notices the difference between Septuagint and the other three Greek versions:

Symmachus reads: "And his name will be called glorious (*paradoxasmos*), purposive (*bouleutikos*), mighty (*ischyros*)"; Aquila: "wonderful (*thaumastos*), counseling (*sumbouleōn*), mighty (*ischyros*)"; Theodotion: "wonderful (*thaumastos*), counseling (*sumbouleōn*), mighty (*ischyros*)." All [the versions] are in agreement when they render the word "God" (*theos*) present in the Septuagint with the word "mighty" (*ischyros*), in this manner showing reverence and not assign the name "God" (*theos*) to a born child (*paidiou*). Nevertheless, the Seventy, considering the sayings about him as befitting God, naturally rendered the term *Ēl*[115] found in Hebrew with "God" (*theon*).[116]

A little below in his commentary, Procopius underscores the agreement between Septuagint and the Hebrew text: "For 'God Almighty' (*theon ischyonta*), the Hebrew version has *'ēl gibbōr*."[117]

In his *Second Homily on the Obscurity of the Old Testament*, John Chrysostom notices the insurmountable difficulties each translation carries with it:

> What, then, is the second reason why the Old Testament is more difficult than the New? We do not have the Old Testament written for us in our native tongue: while it was composed in one language, we have it read in another language. That it is to say, it was written originally in the Hebrew tongue, whereas we received it in the language of the Greeks, and whenever a language is rendered into another language, it involves great difficulty. All who are versed in many languages are aware of this, how it is not possible to transfer the clarity naturally contained in the words when moving to another language.[118]

The Greek translation, concludes Chrysostom, as imperfect as any translation may seem, has been the main means through which those from nations came to adore Christ.

On the same line of thought with Chrysostom, Photius (810–93 C.E.), the learned Patriarch of Constantinople, in his *Amphilochia. Question 152: What is the Obscurity of the Scripture?*, lists ten deficiencies related to the translation of the Old Testament from Hebrew into Greek giving rise to what he calls the "obscurities" of the Holy Writ:

> The obscurities of the Divine Scriptures may have various causes. First, because each language converted in another language loses its own sequence (*heirmos*). Second, because the translators were ignorant of synonyms of the Hebrew language: as in the case of the *kalos* that means different things according to the place of the

accent. . . . For *kalos* accentuated on final syllable means "nice" or "attractive"; in case of virtues, "fitting." Yet, *kalos* accentuated on first syllable means the "roar of a ship." . . . Third, there are the Hebrew words that cannot be rendered with Greek words, but they were left in place, as in Jeremiah [MT Jer 29:26; LXX Jer 36:26] prison (*apokleisma*) [Hebrew] *sinōch*. Fourth, often a mere jot can produce obscurity, "as for the good ones, they will be the inhabitants of the earth," if one would not put a comma after "good" [Prov 2:21]. Fifth, even the difference in accent, as "the beginning of wisdom, seek the wisdom" [MT Prov 4:7] would not be understood if one would not change the accent from *archē*, "beginning" to *archē*, "it [the wisdom] had ruled." Sixth, many times the Hebrews indicate with a single ending both numbers, singular and plural, as with "God" and "gods." Seventh, often there are differences in person, as, addressing Abraham, should be read, "I know (*egnōn*) that you fear God," instead of "you know" (*egnōs*). Eighth, by using opposite genders, i.e., "moon" (*selēnē*) and "sea" (*thalassa*), both feminine in Greek, are masculine nouns in Hebrew. Ninth, often they leave some words out, as in "mountains go up, valleys go down," where the word "like" (*hōs*) is missing. The whole phrase (referring to the waves) would read, "they [the waves] are going up like mountains and go down like the valleys." Tenth, the books having been burnt during the exile, they [the Jews] sent reciprocally from Jerusalem to Babylon the sayings of God, while [the Babylonians?] lying in ambush they removed the books, but they [the Jews] wrote them again with a script unintelligible to the foreigners; hence, the obscurity. Until later the inspired Esdras remembered all and put [them] in writing.[119]

And a little bit further same Photius notices:

In addition, the cause of the obscurity is that the Old Testament was not conceived in Greek language, but underwent changes from Hebrew into that [language]. It is natural with any language that is translated into a foreign language to bring with it obscurity and ambiguity. Besides, the Mosaic laws were initially uttered in Hebrew, hence only the Jewish nation at that time could draw near to the knowledge of God; the other nations were thrown away into idolatrous folly. Since Christ was almost to appear and call to himself the inhabited world (*oikoumenēn*), and since at that time the Greek language was in use by the Gentiles, the language of the Hebrews was exchanged with that of the Greeks, within a period of time not more than one hundred years before the coming of the Savior, when Ptolemy was king in Egypt.[120]

In this passage, Photius concords with Chrysostom in the pertinent observation that a translation, no matter how good might be, remains a translation, with the major handicap of being unable to mediate the full meaning of the original wording.

In conclusion, in the case of text, as in that of canon, Eastern Orthodox tradition shows a high degree of flexibility. On the one hand, there is a sort of continuity in the usage of the same textual witness, the LXX, that has become the most emblematic biblical text for ancient and modern Eastern Orthodox interpreters and theologians. On the other hand, there is no hindrance at all from church authority over the use of Hebrew or other textual witnesses. Nevertheless, I would like to see within the Eastern Orthodox tradition more concrete steps in raising the awareness of the exegetical and theological value of the MT in conjunction with Q, Sam., S, just to mention a few of the precious textual witnesses. I am dreaming of a day, and hope that this will happen sooner than later, when Philo's appeal to his readers will become a reality and those seeking God's word in Scripture will hold both versions, Hebrew and Greek, in "reverence as sisters" (*Life of Moses* 2.40).

3

Canon

*Learn diligently, and from the Church, what are the books
of the Old Testament, and what those of the New. And,
please, read none of the apocryphal writings. For why you,
who do not know those which are acknowledged among
all, trouble yourself in vain about those which are disputed? Read the divine Scriptures, the twenty-two books
of the Old Testament, these that have been translated by
the Seventy-two Interpreters.*

CYRIL OF JERUSALEM, Lecture 4: Of the Divine Scriptures 33

IT IS NOT the purpose of this chapter to offer an exhaustive treatment
of the problem of biblical canon.[1] Rather, I want merely to situate this
topic within the Eastern Orthodox tradition while reflecting on some of
its similarities and differences with Jewish views and Western Christian
stances.

Toward Scriptural Canonization
Canon and Its Meanings

The English word "canon" derives from the Greek term *kanōn*. Most interestingly, *kanōn* is a word which the Greek took from Hebrew *qāneh*, "cane
stick" (having behind it the Akkadian *qanūm*, with the same basic meaning). The ancient Greek polis used the word *kanōn* to designate the ideas
of "accuracy" (*akribeia*) and "truth" (*alētheia*) in politics and arts (sculp-
ture, music). In the New Testament, the word "canon" has a general connotation of "spiritual norm or standard" (Gal 6:16). This general meaning

of "norm" or "rule" can be also found in a mid-first century C.E. Jewish work written by a Pharisee, 4 Macc 7:21 (author's translation): "Philosophizing on the whole rule (*kanona*) of philosophy."

Following the New Testament usage, early Christian writers employ the term *kanōn* to designate the "rule" or "guideline" of right Christian faith. Thus, Irenaeus accuses the Valentinians of distancing themselves from the "rule of faith" (*kanōn tēs pisteōs*) (*Against Heresies* 1.22.1), with special reference to the baptismal creed, known also as the *kanōn alētheias*, "rule of truth." Similarly, in the Latin sphere, Tertullian relates this "rule" to the baptismal creed: "With regard to this rule of faith (*regula fidei*), it is that which prescribes belief that there is one God, and that he is none other than the Creator of the world, who produced all things out of nothing through his own word" (*The Prescription Against Heretics* 13).[2] No second or third century author, however, employed the word "canon" to designate a scriptural corpus as sanctioned by the Church.

For Clement of Alexandria, the *kanōn ekklesiastikos*, "ecclesiastical rule," is the exposition of the Scriptures as interpreted by Christ. Further, it is "the unity and harmony of the Law and the Prophets with the covenant delivered at the coming of the Lord" (*Stromata* 6.15).[3]

Origen is the first among early Christian authors for whom "canon" is not as definite as the baptismal creed but rather a metaphor for the general faith held by orthodox Christians. The ideal reader of Scripture is the one who always holds fast to the "rule of the heavenly church" (*kanonos tēs ouranious ekklēsias*) (*On the Principles* 4.2.2).[4]

The Alexandrian grammarians were the first to use "canon" for a "list." In fact, they put together all sorts of "canons" such as lists of spellings, proper names, kings, countries, etc. In his *Chronological Canons* (*chronika kanones*), Eusebius offers a comparative chronology comprising six different nations, following the Alexandrian model.[5] Yet no one until late fourth century thought to use "canon" for a list of sacred Scriptures.

The Making of the Jewish Scripture

The making of the Jewish Scripture occurred in three consecutive steps.[6]

Scrolls of individual writings or collections were put together into bigger collections. First came the Law (Torah),[7] whose final redaction and collection was concluded around 400 B.C.E. After this were the Prophets (Nebiim) collected about 200 B.C.E.[8] Finally, the Writings (Kethubim) were completed as collection by 100 C.E.[9] The prologue of

Sirach (Ecclesiasticus), composed sometime between 132 and 116 B.C.E., mentions a tripartite division of the Hebrew Bible: Law, Prophets, and "others like them" (vv. 1–2); "the reading of the Law, the Prophets and the other writings of our fathers" (vv. 24–25).

Philo (20 B.C.E.–50 C.E.) mentions that the sect of the *Therapeutes*, when they gathered together, brought with them the scriptural corpus. This corpus, says Philo, consisted of "laws and the sacred oracles of God enunciated by the holy prophets, and hymns, and psalms, and all kinds of other things by reason of which knowledge and piety are increased and brought to perfection" (*On the Contemplative Life* 3.25).[10]

Josephus (37–101 C.E.), in *Against Apion* (1.38–42), written about 90 C.E., goes beyond the vague tripartite division of the Hebrew Bible in noting that the Jews have twenty-two sacred books (i.e., five books of the Law, thirteen books of the Prophets, and the other four books), similar to the twenty-two consonants of the Hebrew alphabet. The presence of numbering in connection with the books of the Hebrew Bible is a proof of scriptural canonization by the time of Josephus, prior to the end of the first century C.E. The thirteen books of the Prophets include the following: Joshua, Judges and Ruth, Samuel, Kings, Chronicles, Ezra and Nehemiah, Esther, Job, Isaiah, Jeremiah and Lamentations, Ezekiel, Minor Prophets, and the Book of Daniel. The last section of the Hebrew Bible (Psalms, Song, Proverbs, and Ecclesiastes) supports the assumption that Josephus follows the order of the books attested by the Septuagint.

The Jewish apocalyptic 4 Ezra (end of the first century C.E.) mentions twenty-four sacred books. This number corresponds to Josephus's "twenty-two," but with Ruth and Lamentations dissociated from Judges and Jeremiah, respectively. These twenty-four books are to be distinguished from the other seventy books that should be kept "secret" because they are to be read only by "wise" people.[11] "During the forty days, ninety-four books were written. And when the forty days were ended, the Most High spoke to me, saying: Make public the twenty-four books that you wrote first and let the worthy and the unworthy read them; but keep the seventy that were written last, in order to give them to the wise among your people" (4 Ezra 14.44–46).[12]

The Council of Jamnia (or Jabneh), supposedly around 90 C.E., is often mentioned as a key moment in the canonization of the Jewish Scriptures.[13] From the onset, one may notice that unlike Christianity, Judaism has no councils or canons.[14] The "decisions" of the Jamnia "Council"[15] (or, more accurately, "meeting-place") are recorded in *m. Yad.* 3.5, where one reads that the Song of Songs and Ecclesiastes "defile the hands,"[16] that is, these books are sacred and inspired. But this discussion does not necessarily imply the occurrence of a council, nor did it put an end to the canon debate that was unfolding within Judaism. Later, canonical questions rise around Ruth and Esther (*b. Meg.* 7a).

According to Mogens Müller,[17] the formation of the Old Testament canon was fixed at the time of the New Testament. The proof for such a suggestion is found in the New Testament itself. Note the text of Matt 23:35 mentioning the blood of Abel up to the blood of Zacharias, the son of Berachias. These names and examples are taken from the first and last books of the Jewish Bible, Genesis (4) and 2 Chronicles (24:20–22), assuming that Zacharias is the son of Jehoiadah. Thus, the New Testament text witnesses to a canonical sequence that appears only later on in the Jewish Bible: beginning with Genesis and ending with 2 Chronicles. It is important to note here too that the New Testament distinguishes quite regularly between canonical and noncanonical by introducing the canonical books with the qualifier "Scripture" or the technical formula "It is written."[18]

Prerequisites and Criteria of Scriptural Canonization

Some concerns of the ancient Greek polis[19] culture and philosophy are considered today prerequisites of Christian scriptural canonizing process. Among the most important prerequisites, one may mention the following.

Authorship. The anonymity of ancient world and the "corporate mentality"[20] of Semitic culture were challenged with the birth of Christian Gentile Church in the desire to name the author of a given writing. This drive toward authorial attribution was characteristic of the culture and philosophy of the ancient Greek polis, and thus part of the enculturation of Christian Church in the thought patterns of the Greek polis. An early example of such enculturation[21] coming from Judaism is Josephus, who was the first ancient Jewish writer to ascribe the first five books of the Hebrew Bible "to Moses" (*Against Apion* 1.39). In contrast, in the Hebrew Bible itself, only two books (Deuteronomy and Job) out of the thirty-nine mention their authors. Yet another such example of transition from the ancient Semitic anonymity to the Greek quest for authorship is found in Ecclesiasticus (Sirach), a book not contained in the Jewish Bible of today. In Sir 50:27 "Jesus son of Sira Eleazer of Jerusalem" is named as author of this book.[22]

Cataloging. The need to catalog all the scrolls in the *Mouseion* ("Shrine of the Muses"), the famous library of Alexandria founded by Ptolemy II Soter in 283 B.C.E., is directly related to the notion of authorship. During Alexandria's golden days (280–40 B.C.E.), the library contained several hundred thousand volumes. Callimachus of Cyrene (305–240 B.C.E.), the director of the *Mouseion*, created a catalogue or index (Greek: *pinax*; Latin: *tabula*) of thousands of scrolls in the library indicating their titles and authors. Callimachus and his co-workers went even further in creating biographical sketches of each author appended with a list of his "genuine" (*gnēsioi*) and "spurious" (*nothoi*) writings. It is perhaps notable that Callimachus's cataloging activity took place more or less contemporaneously with the making of the first rendition of the Hebrew Law into a foreign language—Greek, that is.[23]

Codex versus scroll. The transition from scroll to codex format around the beginning of the second century C.E.[24] was a necessary step toward scriptural canonization. Since with the codex all the Scriptures were located in one single "volume" (*teuchos*) or codex-book, it was much easier to craft and compare "canons" (i.e., canonical lists) than it had been previously, when Scriptures were written on scrolls and preserved often in jars in various locations, but never in one single place, between two covers, as a single collection. The introduction of the codex format, in which the text runs on both sides, also contributed to the speeding up of the canonization process: scribes were obliged to decide which books should go inside the binding as well as what sequence should be followed.

Significantly, Christianity adopted the codex very early while the Judaism preserved the scrolls. Even in synagogues today, the Torah is read from a scroll rather than a codex (book) format. No wonder, then, that the first canonical lists are to be found in Christian authors such as Melito of Sardes (second century C.E.) and Origen (third century C.E.), while in Judaism such lists appear no earlier than the third century C.E.[25]

Early Christian authors speak of "canonical" or "canonized" books, rather than a scriptural "canon"—a single, closed collection. Numbering, where it appears, is not so important, and always is borrowed from Jewish sources (e.g., Josephus).[26]

According to Eusebius (*Ecclesiastical History* 3.25.6),[27] canonical books—here he refers primarily to the New Testament—should be "true, genuine, and well authenticated." "True" means that the writing teaches the gospel of Jesus Christ. "Genuine" points to one of the Twelve Apostles or the apostle Paul as author, in contrast with the "spurious" books whose apostolic authorship could not be proven. "Well authenticated" means acknowledged by consistent use in orthodox Churches. Eusebius's criterion of authenticity is uninterrupted "complete succession," which he reconstructs and demonstrates for four touchstone episcopal sees: Rome, Alexandria, Antioch, and Jerusalem. Similar to Josephus's "prophetic succession," Eusebius speaks of "apostolic succession." For those "novel" writings whose apostolic succession could not be demonstrated, Eusebius added two additional criteria: style and theological content. If the style and theological content of a "novel" writing is close to the style and theological content of a "genuine" writing, then the "novel" writing should be treated as genuine. For instance, the Coptic Gospel of Thomas proposes a much different theology than the one offered by the four Gospels universally acknowledged as genuine at least since the time of Irenaeus.

Regarding the criterion of style, a good example may be gleaned from Origen's *Homily on the Epistle to the Hebrews*. In this homily, Origen observes that while Hebrews is Pauline in thought or ideas, the epistle's educated style of Greek, so different from the blunt style of Paul, makes one think of a second author (editor). For this token, Origen ascribes Hebrews to Clement of Rome or Luke. Later on, Eusebius follows in the footsteps of his master Origen, using style as a criterion for authorship.

Early Views on Canon

From the onset, it must be underscored that the notion of canon is often used with no rigor at all, and merely out of sheer convenience. Much ink has been spilled on this controversial topic of biblical canon.[28] Usually, the canon is treated as the result of a historical process, as a matter of history, which needs a historical analysis.

It might be interesting and refreshing to use a different methodology: a synchronic analysis of terms and divisions of the Jewish Bible, as evidenced by Jewish and Eastern Christian authors in the first millennium. It is arguable that the way in which the Jewish Bible was seen as a collection of books divided into various parts influenced greatly the acceptance or refusal of "other" or "outside" books—namely, the additions to the Septuagint—from the much desired "canonical" status. The methodology followed here goes beyond mere historical-comparative presentation, reaching the level of semantic analysis of, and theological inquiry into, the book names and divisions crafted to describe the rich and irreducible content of the Jewish Bible.

Thus far, most canon research has sought to understand the quasi-canonical status of additions to the Septuagint as due to various presupposed historical factors. This approach is reflected for instance in the "double canon" hypothesis, postulating a narrow Palestinian canon versus a wider Alexandrian canon identical with the Septuagint corpus as attested by fourth–fifth century c.e. codices.[29] According to the proponents of this hypothesis, the early Church opted for the Alexandrian canon on account of linguistic reasons alone—hence, such proponents would say, the almost exclusive use of the Septuagint (including the so-called LXX additions) by the New Testament writers, church fathers, and the Church at large in her liturgical services. The "double canon" or "Alexandrian canon" hypothesis aimed to explain the sources of the current divergence between Judaism and Protestantism (with their shorter, Palestinian type canon) on the one hand and Roman Catholicism (with its larger, Alexandrian type canon) on the other. However, the "double canon" hypothesis received a lethal injection due to its inability to prove the assumption that the geographical separation between Palestinian and Alexandrian Judaism was paralleled by a linguistic and theological division. Moreover, the proponents of this hypothesis have completely overlooked the Eastern Orthodox position, which does not fit neatly into either canon type. In fact, this sophisticated and to a certain degree ambiguous position still present in Eastern Orthodoxy represents a solid argument against the late "double-canon" hypothesis.

Eastern Orthodoxy has much to offer to the intricate and much debated issue of Old Testament canon. This chapter seeks to show how the Eastern Orthodox tradition succeeded in preserving the early position on canon as evidenced in ancient sources beginning with the late second century b.c.e. prologue to Sirach, through the early Christian writers, and ending in the eighth century c.e. with the synthesis of John of Damascus. As will be seen, the current Orthodox position on canon still looks very similar to the Damascene's concluding remarks. Nevertheless, the main goal of this chapter is to detect the time-honored mechanisms behind this peculiar way of looking at the Scriptures.

Why the current situation with narrow, larger, and in-between canons? It is the argument of this chapter that the answer is to be found in the additions to the Septuagint and within the Jewish Bible itself—more precisely, in the early, second century b.c.e. tripartite division of the Jewish Bible. This argument is based on the assumption that there has always been a tension between two important and early well-defined divisions (sections): the Torah (Law) and the Prophets. In addition, one may detect a certain delay in defining or labeling the third division (attested with a technical term, Kethubim ["Writings"], as early as the third century C.E.). This delay left the third group of books, termed variously, "the other," "the remaining books," as the "open" end of the Scriptures, offering an indirect invitation to other "outside" books to join on various degrees the "canonical" (normative) chorus of Scripture.

In this long period of delay (second century B.C.E. to third century C.E.), each of the two well-defined divisions, Torah and Prophets, determined the terminology, position, and subdivisions of the third division of the Jewish Bible. When Torah (Law) was seen as the towering element within the Jewish Bible, then everything was "subordinated" to its irresistible influence, and the entire corpus was viewed as a "formative" entity, whose first goal was to shape out, form, and instruct its readers, hearers or (in the case of Scripture-based iconography) beholders. In contrast, when the Prophets were seen as the focal point of the Jewish Bible then the remaining material was regarded as "historic," and the function of the entire corpus was rather considered "informative," revealing God's will and design for human history.

What do these functions of the Jewish Bible have to do with the additions to the Septuagint? Apparently, the third group, still seeking its self-identity, has been already around at the end of the second century B.C.E. Thus, the Jewish Bible was already concluded as a normative corpus at that time, and discussions around the additions were concerned with their status as "Scriptures"—not their inclusion as part of a closed collection. Were these additions "Scriptures" or not? If the Scripture's function was "formative," then any addition to the Septuagint with a certain "formative" outlook (e.g., Sirach) would have been considered a candidate to the "scriptural" status. But if, on the contrary, Scripture's primary role was seen as "informative" and Israel's prophets were regarded as channels of God's revelation inside history, then "Scripture" was already closed with the activity of last prophet, Malachi (mid-fifth century B.C.E.), according to Josephus. Thus, no addition to the Septuagint had any chance to be admitted into the category of "Scripture."

In a nutshell, the tendencies toward a shorter or wider scriptural corpus have stood always in dialectical tension. This tension, well attested in the ancient writers examined below, is still present in modern Eastern Orthodox theologians, who may argue for either of the two tendencies without any interference from church authority, which has never defined its official position on the scriptural canon in any ecumenical or Pan-Orthodox council. The present work identifies what may be called the "official" Eastern Orthodox position as located precisely at this point of tension, thus maintaining the balance between "formative" and "informative" tendencies in approaching the Scripture.

This following discussion will show how these tendencies crafted the two main views on canon encountered in Eastern Christian writers, but with a marked longstanding preference toward the formative function of Scripture. Our focus is on Eastern Christianity during the first millennium and its struggles to preserve the inherited Jewish (Pharisaic) Bible, while having to deal with the Septuagint as part of its own growing tradition. In the absence of a clear definition produced by ecumenical councils, the lists and statements offered by ancient authorities provided below give us the best and most authoritative picture of the Eastern Orthodox understanding of scriptural canon. The formation of a list implies acceptance of a book as a particular type of book. However, the lists do not absolutely agree across all geographic areas, and so cannot make any universal claim on behalf of the whole Church. On the other hand, unlike the lists, the patristic statements tell us nothing about canonicity in stricto sensu or a "canon" as a closed collection of Scriptures. They only signal whether a book was considered worthy of "reading" at certain point in time—that is, whether that book was considered "normative" or "formative" (i.e., canonical in a broader sense).

Ecclesiasticus (Sirach)

The prologue to Ecclesiasticus, written ca. between 132 and 116 B.C.E., divides the Jewish collection into three distinct sections: "Law" (*nomou*), "Prophets" (*prophētōn*), and "the other succeeding them" (*tōn allōn tōn kat'autous ēkolouthēkotōn*), "other books of the fathers" (*tōn allōn patriōn bibliōn*), or "the rest of the books" (*ta loipa tōn bibliōn*). The purpose of this collection is to mediate Israel's tripartite "instruction and wisdom" (*paideias kai sophias*).

The prologue avers that after having studied the Law, the Prophets, and the other books of the fathers, Jesus ben Sirach (around 180 B.C.E.) decided to write "something pertaining to instruction and wisdom" (*ti tōn eis paideian kai sophian anēkontōn*). He consciously modeled his writing on the Book of Proverbs.

The bridge between the almost-concluded tripartite Jewish collection and the "outside" books conventionally termed "additions to the Septuagint"—some composed in Hebrew, others in Greek, but all eventually rendered into Greek—consists of two key-terms "instruction and wisdom." The grandson of Sirach makes his case clearly enough. If Israel's tripartite collection—still open at that time, with the third group vaguely termed "other books of the fathers"—is about "instruction and wisdom," then any book "outside" this collection, if it meets the requirement of mediating "instruction and wisdom," could be "accepted" within the aforementioned collection. Even though not clearly stated, the "language" criterion is implied by the prologue's reference to Sirach's work being initially composed in Hebrew.

The sentence, "Not only this book [Sirach in Greek], but even the Law itself, the Prophets, and the rest of the books," may imply that the prologue's author placed the book of his grandfather, Jesus ben Sirach, on the same level with the three divisions of the Scripture. The rationale of such elevation is summarized in the following points.

1. Israel's tripartite collection mediates "instruction and wisdom" primarily for Jewish people, while works such as Sirach's writing aim at the same goal, "instruction and wisdom," but primarily "for those outside" (*tois ektos*)[30] the circle of experts or learned men. Indirectly, the prologue commends Jesus ben Sirach for writing his book: it is a "duty" (*deon*) for those who have reached instruction and wisdom to share these qualities with those "outside" Israel by writing similar works especially for them. Jesus ben Sirach was a professional scribe (Sir 38:24: Heb. *sōphēr*, Gk. *grammateus*), which at that time meant wise man or sage (Heb. *ḥākām*). So "outside" refers to those outside the guild of "scribes" and "sages"—common folks.

2. The prologue implies that the Book of Sirach was initially written in Hebrew, as those books contained by the tripartite collection.

3. There is a certain "subordination" of all other writings (inside or outside the collection) to the Law. The final goal, reached by instruction and wisdom, is a "living within the Law" (*ennomou biōseōs*).

4. If a book mediates instruction and wisdom and moves the reader to the observance of the Law, and a life based on the Law, then that book should be approached with "good attitude and attention" (*eunoias kai prosochēs*).

5. The fact that the last group of writings was not still defined by a special term, but rather switching back and forth between some vague terms ("other books" or "the rest of the books"), was probably regarded by this translator as an invitation to add extra writings to a corpus not yet defined.

6. The prologue refers also to the difficulties in translating a work from Hebrew into Greek. This quite long explanation within the prologue may be read as a preemptive attack against potential detractors of Greek Sirach as close neighbor to the tripartite collection. Instead, the author of the prologue begs "indulgence" (*syngnōmēn*) from Sirach's readers.

7. The author of Sirach is the only writer of the Old Testament who signed his work with his full name, "Simon ben Jesus ben Eleazar ben Sirach" (Sir 50:27). This could have been considered a strong point toward the special place of this book.

Sirach, one of the earliest and longest additions to the Septuagint, enjoyed a "quasi-scriptural" status. Near the end of the first century c.e., the Pharisaic rabbis excluded the Book of Sirach from the Jewish Scriptures, perhaps on theological grounds (for example, the denial of retribution in the life to come, which was considered quite similar to the Sadducees' views; also, the hint of epicurean tendencies found in the book). About 250 c.e., the Tosephta (*Yad.* 2:13) considers Sirach a noncanonical writing. In spite of this more or less formal rejection, the book is quoted eighty-two times in the Talmud in favorable terms, sometimes with the technical formula "it is written" (e.g., *Nid.* 16b) reserved only for quotations from canonical texts. In Christian lists, Sirach is listed besides Wisdom of Solomon as a special book.

Philo of Alexandria

Philo lists three groups of books under the rubric of "Sacred Scriptures" (*hierois grammasi*): (1) "laws" (*nomous*); (2) "divine sayings declared through prophets" (*logia thespisthenta dia prophētōn*); and (3) "hymns" (*hymnous*) and "the other (writings)" (*ta alla*) (*On the Contemplative Life* 3.25, 28–29).[31] Philo's division ("laws, prophets, hymns and others") is a rough equivalent of Josephus's tripartite division. As in case of Josephus, whom we will consider next, one may notice here a certain subordination of scriptural material to the "laws" (plural!), with a special emphasis on the educational or instructional purpose (function) of the Scriptures. Their reading, underscores Philo, leads to an increase in "understanding and piety" (*epistēmē kai eusebeia*), similar to Jesus ben Sirach's wording, "instruction and wisdom."

As for the third group, "hymns and the other [writings]," one can detect two simultaneous tendencies. On the one hand, there is a tendency toward finding a specific term to designate the entire group, "hymns" or "psalms" (cf. Luke 24:44). On the other hand, by choosing the vague term "the other," there is a tendency to keep this section as flexible and inclusive as possible.

Interestingly, even though Philo was familiar with the Septuagint, and that the third group of his division looks pretty flexible and inviting, he never quotes from or hints at the additions to the Septuagint. Philo represents an interesting case, between "narrow" and "wider" canons, with the "formative" function of the Scripture clearly underlined.

Flavius Josephus

Josephus's tripartite division of Scriptures is well defined, much better than the one in Sirach's prologue: "Five (books) of Moses" (*pente Mōyseōs*), "the prophets (*prophētai*), who were after Moses, wrote down what was done (*prachthenta*) in their times," and "hymns to God and precepts for the conduct of human life" (*hymnous eis ton theon kai tois anthrōpois hypothēkas tou biou*).[32]

The emphasis on "history" and "prophecy," Israel's long-time office, reflected in the expanded title of the second section and in the name of "Moses" as substitute for the more traditional term "Law," is counterbalanced by the "subordination" of the third section, consisting of "hymns" and "precepts of life" to Moses' Law. According to Josephus, the twenty-two books constitute the "record of the entire history" (*tou pantos chronou tēn anagraphēn*).

The tension between "formative" and "informative," or more precisely, between the "framed" or closed and loosely "open-ended" understandings of Scripture, evidenced by Eastern Christian authors, finds the first and best illustration in Josephus's description of the tripartite collection of the twenty-two "trustworthy" (*pepisteumena*) books. Paradoxically, Josephus's intent was to set a *terminus ad quem* for the Jewish collection of God's inspired writings: the time of Persian king Artaxerses (mid-fifth century B.C.E.).[33]

Nevertheless, by defining the third part as containing "precepts of life for human beings," Josephus prepared the way for later Christian views regarding the normativeness or quasi-canonicity of the additions to the Septuagint. Thus, later Christian writers, as for instance Athanasius, called these additions *anaginōskomena*, "readable," for the "religious edification" of the newcomers to Christian faith.

In Josephus's criterion, the "outside" books—those writings that are not numbered among the twenty-two "trustworthy"—can be distinguished as follows: (1) they were written "from the time of Artarxerxes until our time" (i.e., Josephus's time, first century c.e.); (2) they "were not considered worthy of the same trust" (*pisteōs d'ouch homoias ēxiōeai*) as the twenty-two books; (3) the lesser degree of "trustworthiness" is due to the fact that these writings cannot prove "the exact succession of the prophets" (*tēn tōn prophētōn akribē diadochēn*) as the "twenty-two."

Justin Martyr

Having noticed the difference in Scriptures between Judaism and Christian Church, Justin Martyr is the first author to suggest the principle of Church's "self-sufficiency" in determining her Scripture (or canon in a broader sense).

Justin's evidence (*Exhortation to the Greeks* 13)[34] hints at certain "rules written by holy men for instruction" (*ta pros didaskalian hypo tōn hagiōn andrōn graphenta dikaia*). The "books" (*bibliōn*) containing these rules were "produced" (*prokomizesthai*) by and "preserved" (*sōzomenōn*) in the "synagogue of the Jews" (*tōn Ioudaiōn synagōgēs*). These books, says Justin, "pertain" (*prosēkei*) to Christians. And all this process of producing and preserving the sacred writings is considered the "work of divine providence" (*theias pronoias ergon*).

This is the first clear evidence of the "subordination" of the entire scriptural material extant in the Jewish Bible to the New Law, the gospel, that is. Thus, in Justin's wording, the biblical books contain "rules" (*dikaia*). The use of the term "rules," instead of the technical word "Law" (*nomos*) with regard to the Jewish Law is likely intentional. These "rules" were written by "holy men" (*hagiōn andrōn*), not by "prophets," and their main purpose is "instruction" (*didaskalian*). By "subordinating" the Jewish Scriptures to the New Law, and defining their main function as "instruction," Justin is indirectly inviting other revered books, containing rules (such as the Septuagint additions), to return from exile and join the educational chorus of Jewish Scriptures, now under Church's roof.

Melito of Sardis

The first Christian list of Jewish Scriptures was compiled by Melito, Bishop of Sardis (capital of Lydia) in about 160 c.e., who traveled to the East (i.e., Palestine) to produce an "accurate account" (*akribeian*) of the biblical collection (Eusebius, *Ecclesiastical History* 4.26.13–14).[35] As a true researcher, Melito compares Christian with Jewish views on canon. His list has an interesting makeup. As for the terminology ("Law and Prophets" [*tou nomou kai tōn prophētōn*]) and number, Melito's list is, with the Book of Esther being left out, almost identical with a Pharisaic Jewish Bible. As for the sequence of books, more precisely, the intercalation of Wisdom (of Solomon), an addition to the Septuagint, with the Jewish Scriptures, the list is quite similar to the Septuagint's fourth–fifth century codices.

Melito is the first Christian author to use the term "Old Testament" for the entire collection of books. Moreover, the expressions "the old books" (*tōn palaiōn bibliōn*), "the books of the Old Testament" (*ta tēs palaias diathēkēs biblia*), imply that the Church at that time had a canon of the New Testament at least in its incipient phase. Slightly later, around 200 c.e., Tertullian is the first one to use the actual phrase "New Testament" for the collection of books (the phrase *diathēkēn kainēn* designating a "new covenant" is used in Jer 31:31 [LXX]).[36]

Melito's gloss "and the Wisdom [of Solomon]" (*hē kai Sophia*) within a collection otherwise quite "Jewish" in its exclusiveness is noteworthy. If the list was discussed by Melito with Christian and Jewish authorities, then the situation in the late second century Palestine becomes quite interesting. This piece of information—an addition to the Septuagint among the "twenty-two" Jewish Scriptures—weakens considerably the so-called double-canon hypothesis relying on the assumption that there was a demarcating line between the Palestinian and Alexandrian collections (canons). What Melito's list shows, in fact, is that such a demarcation perhaps never existed, at least in the late second century c.e. Palestine, and that the early Jewish views on canon were more flexible than had been previously thought. Moreover, one can discern a certain formative orientation of the entire scriptural corpus.

Origen

Origen states that the Jews have twenty-two canonical books, yet his list, preserved by Eusebius (*Ecclesiastical History* 4.35),[37] contains in fact only twenty-one. It is also the first time, in a Christian work, when the Hebrew names of biblical books are mentioned. The order of books is closer to the Septuagint than to the Jewish Bible; for instance, Daniel is placed among Prophets, after Jeremiah.

As in Melito's case, Origen's list makes use both of the Septuagint and the Jewish Bible. From the Septuagint, Origen takes the sequence of books, offering both their Hebrew and Greek names (e.g., Genesis— *Beresith*, Exodus—*Welesmoth*, etc.). A special case obtains with the books of "Kings." The books are called by the Septuagint's term "Kingdoms" (*Basileiōn*) and by the Hebrew names: "Samuel, 'the one chosen by God'" (*Samouēl 'ho theoklētos'*) and "the king of David, which means 'kingdom of David'" (*Ouammelch dauid hoper estin 'basileia Dauid'*).

As an illustration of the "outside" books, Origen lists the Maccabees, mentioned by their Hebrew name, *Sarbeth Sabanaiel*. This is the first mention of the term "outside" (*exō*) with explicit reference to the additions to the Septuagint, which were not part of the twenty-two canonical books handed down by the Jews.

Athanasius of Alexandria

In the *Festal Epistle* 39 written in 367 C.E., Athanasius distinguishes between three groups of books: (1) "canonized" (*kanonizomena*); (2) "non-canonized" (*ou kanonizomena*) or "readable" (*anaginōskomena*); and (3) "apocrypha" (*apokrypha*). Nevertheless, the "apocrypha" of Athanasius are different from Origen's "apocrypha" (i.e., difficult canonical books which are to be kept away from unprepared readers). Athanasius's "apocrypha" are books not even worthy to be mentioned and which belong to the "heretics" (*hairetikōn*).

Athanasius has skillfully kept the two functions (informative and formative) of the Scriptures together. Moreover, he speaks of the twenty-two "books of the Old Testament" (*palaias diathēkēs biblia*) as the "fountains of salvation" (*pēgai tou sōtēriou*), because "only in these the doctrine of godliness (*eusebeias didaskaleion*) is proclaimed." In other words, the "canonized" (kanonizomena) books are the ones that assure the "informative" function of Scriptures. In addition, Athanasius notices, "there are other books outside of these (*hetera biblia toutōn exōthen*) indeed noncanonized (ou kanonizomena), but prescribed by the fathers to be read (*tetypōmena de para tōn paterōn anaginōskesthai*) by those who newly join us, and who wish to be instructed in the word of godliness (*katēcheisthai ton tēs eusebeias logon*): the Wisdom of Solomon, and the Wisdom of Sirach, and Esther, and Judith, and Tobit, and that which is called the Teaching of the Apostles, and the Shepherd." These "readable" (anaginōskomena) books that bespeak the "formative" function of Scriptures, though not included in the canon (understood in a narrow sense), must be distinguished from the third category of books, namely, the "apocrypha" (apokrypha) that are "an invention of heretics," who "assigned them a date, that so, using them as ancient writings, they may find occasion to lead astray the simple" (*Festal Letter 39*).[38]

Athanasius differentiates between the "canonical" leading to "the doctrine of godliness" and the "noncanonical" facilitating "the instruction of godliness." Both groups of books aim to bring their readers to "godliness" (*eusebeias*), but their means are different. In case of the "canonicals," the means is "doctrine" (*didaskaleion*), namely, in an "informative" way. In case of the "noncanonicals," the means is "instruction" (*katēcheisthai*); thus, a "formative" way.

Pertaining to the anaginōskomena, Athanasius does not follow the Septuagint's way of "intercalating" the "canonical" with "noncanonical" as found in the fourth–fifth century Septuagint manuscripts.

Interestingly, in the *Festal Letter 39*, the Book of Esther is placed among the "noncanonicals," between Wisdom of Sirach and Judith. This shows how flexible was at that time the boundary between "canonical" and "noncanonical" (or anaginōskomena). Nevertheless, "none should add to these [canonical books], or take out from them." With this last warning, Athanasius inclines toward a "closed" list (canon) regarding the Jewish Scripture. His position is quite articulate within an Eastern Christian context marked by discrepancy between practice (most Eastern fathers quote extensively from the noncanonicals)[39] and theory (none of these fathers dared declare the noncanonicals on par with the canonical books appropriated from the Jewish Scripture).[40]

Cyril of Jerusalem

Cyril of Jerusalem (*Lecture 4* 33–36)[41] is the first Christian author to divide the Old Testament into four groups of books: Law, historical books, prophetic books, and books written in verse. With slight modification, this will later become the classical Christian division (Pentateuch, Prophets, Histories, Wisdom literature) in contrast with the Jewish well-settled tripartite division (Torah, Prophets, Writings). With the exception of the historical books (seven in number), all the other groups number five books each, perhaps a hint at the "subordination" of the Prophets and the poetical books to the Law.

According to Cyril, only twenty-two books are "acknowledged" (*homologoumena*) and "read in church with boldness" (*en Ekklēsia meta parrēsias anaginōskomena*). These books have the authority of "pious" (*eulabesteroi*) and "wise" (*phronimōteroi*) people ("apostles, bishops of old time, and presidents of the Church"—*apostoloi kai hoi archaioi episkopoi hoi tēs Ekklēsias prostatai*) who "handed down" (*paradontes*) these books for the use of the Church.

Cyril uses the term "apocrypha" for both Athanasius's "noncanonicals" or anaginōskomena and proper "apocrypha." In spite of the austere structure, Cyril's list is not entirely identical with the Rabbinic Bible, because it contains the two noncanonical additions to Jeremiah, namely, the Epistle of Jeremiah and Baruch. According to Cyril, Christians must not read the apocryphal books. One may add that Cyril shows a great esteem toward the Septuagint, the work of the same Holy Spirit who produced the Scriptures in the first place. Nevertheless, the additions to the Septuagint written in Greek or translated from Hebrew into Greek are indirectly considered "apocrypha."

Epiphanius of Salamis

Epiphanius provides three lists pertaining to Scripture and canon.

1. List 1 (*Panarion* 8.6)[42]

   The "canonical books" number twenty-seven, representing twenty-two consonants of the Hebrew alphabet plus five consonants that have special forms at the end of a word. Epiphanius recognizes the Jews as the first recipients of these twenty-seven canonical books, "These were given to Jews (*dotheisai tois Ioudaiois*) by God."

   Outside these twenty-seven canonical books, Wisdom of Solomon and Wisdom of Sirach are listed among the "disputed" (*amphilektōn*). These books should be distinguished from "apocrypha" (*enapokryphōn*). Two other "noncanonical" books, the Epistle of Jeremiah and Baruch, are listed together with the Book of Jeremiah and Lamentations.

2. List 2 (*Panarion* 76.5)[43]

By placing the two wisdom books (Solomon and Sirach) at the end of
the New Testament list of twenty-seven canonical books, Epiphanius
considers them not a part of the New Testament corpus, but rather
outside the canonical books of both testaments. However, the phrase
"in short, all divine writings" (*pasais haplōs graphais theias*) at the end
of the second list may designate all previously mentioned books, including the two wisdom books. If it holds true, this "inclusive" twist
would sharply contrast with Epiphanius's "Jewish-like" view found in
the other two lists where the two wisdoms are placed among the "disputed" or simply called "useful" and "helpful" books.

3. List 3 (*On Measures and Weights* 3–4)[44]

In the third list, Epiphanius returns to the more common number
twenty-two, while dividing the entire Old Testament into "Four Pentateuchs" with two books remaining "behind" (Ezra-Nehemiah and
Esther). This restructuring of the twenty-two Scriptures into four
groups of five (*pentateuchs*) reflects on the "subordination" of the rest of
the Old Testament books to the Law. Moreover, notices Epiphanius, the
Psalter has also a "pentateuchal" structure: "The Hebrews also divided
the Psalter into five books, as if it was another Pentateuch." This "pentateuchal" rethinking and restructuring of the entire Old Testament
helped the "outside" books (i.e., anaginōskomena), considered "good"
for "instruction," to be eventually assimilated with the canonical books,
at least at the collection level, as part of the Scripture. Early Septuagint
codices testify to this reevaluation of the "outside" books. However,
as in the case of Athanasius's list, the "formative" function of the Old
Testament is counterbalanced here by the sequence of the four pentateuchs, namely, Law, poetical, historical, and Prophets, with the last
Pentateuch, that of the "Prophets," precluding any intrusion of "formative" Scriptures from "outside" into the rigorous "twenty-two" corpus.

Regarding the "noncanonical" books, Epiphanius lists two books initially written in Hebrew and then translated into Greek (i.e., Wisdom of
Solomon, and Wisdom of Sirach). These books are called "useful and helpful" (*chrēsimoi kai ōphelimoi*), a phrase which corresponds to Athanasius's
"noncanonical" or "readable." Nevertheless, they are not part of the twenty-
two canonical books, which is "why they [the Israelites] did not place them
into the AARON,[45] that is, in the ark of the covenant." This is an interesting
argument, which hints at the Diaspora as the provenance of these books.

Council of Laodicea (ca. 363 C.E.)

Canon 59 of the Council of Laodicea reads: "No private psalms nor any noncanonical books may be read in Church, but only the canonical ones of the New and Old Testament."

Canon 60, whose genuineness is highly questioned, lists twenty-two books of the Old Testament following the inherited sequence: Law, historical, poetical, prophetical books. Regarding the Psalms, the canon expands: "the book of one hundred and fifty Psalms," thus leaving Ps 151 of the Septuagint out of the biblical canon. Baruch and the Epistle of Jeremiah, even though not found in the Jewish Bible, are intercalated among the canonical, as actually additions to the Book of Jeremiah. Some of the controversial books such as the books of Maccabees, Wisdom of Solomon, and Revelation are altogether omitted.[46]

The two conciliar canons make a sharp distinction between the "canonical" books, which are set "to be read" (*anaginōskesthai*) in the Church, and the "outside" books, namely, "noncanonical" (*akanonista*) and "individual psalms" (*idiōtikous psalmous*), "which must not be read in the Church" (*ou dei legesthai en tē Ekklēsia*).

The Council of Laodicea precedes the *Festal Letter 39* by Athanasius (367 C.E.) that distinguishes between the "noncanonical" also called anaginōskomena ("readable") and "apocrypha" which must not be read by Christians. Athanasius's clear-cut distinction was needed since according to Laodicea's canon 59, both "noncanonical" and "private (individual) psalms" must not be read in the Church.[47]

Note that the Council of Laodicea is a local council with no ecumenical (universal) authority for the Eastern Orthodox Church. At the same time, however, the canons of this council were approved by the Council in Trullo, 692 C.E., a council given quasi-ecumenical status through the inclusion of its canons together with the Acts of the Fifth and Sixth Ecumenical Councils, thus, the name Quinisext ("Fifth-Sixth") Council.

As a note of contrast with the Council of Laodicea, the Synod of Rome in 382 C.E., convened during the reign of Pope Damasus I (366–84 C.E.), moved in a completely different direction and issued the *Decretum de libris recipientis et non recipientis*. The extant text, however, known as the *Decretum Gelasianum* (due to its erroneous attribution to Pope Gelasius [ca. 492–96 C.E.]), was probably composed or revised by an Italian church man in the sixth century C.E. In any case, the article on the approved books is introduced by the sentence, *Nunc vero de scripturis divinis agendum est, quid universalis catholica ecclesia recipiat et quid vitare debeat* ("Now truly the divine Scriptures must be discussed, which the universal catholic church receives, and which writings must be avoided").[48] The additions to the Septuagint (i.e., Tobit, Judith, Sirach, Wisdom of Solomon, and 1 and 2 Maccabees) are listed among the approved books.

In addition, the local synods of Hippo (393 C.E.) and Carthage (397 C.E.) accepted a definite number of Old Testament books including some of the additions to the Septuagint. The list promoted by the synod of Carthage opens with this line: *Ut praeter scripturas canonicas nihil in ecclesia sub nominee divinarum scripturarum* ("Outside of canonical writings nothing should be read in Church under the title of divine Scriptures"). The list contains Tobit, Judith, 1 and 2 Maccabees, and "five books of Solomon" (i.e., the canonical Proverbs, Song of Songs, and Ecclesiastes, plus two additions to the Septuagint: Wisdom of Solomon and Sirach). At the end of this list there is a pertinent remark: "Let this also be made known to our brother and fellow bishop, Boniface of Rome, or to other bishops of those parts, for the confirmation of this canon; for we have learned from the Fathers that we should read these in church."[49]

These extended lists including additions to the Septuagint reflect the great influence of Augustine in the West. In the *On Christian Doctrine* (2.8.12), the bishop of Hippo defends the Septuagint additions by proposing the use of a book by a significant number of Churches as a criterion of canonicity: "Now, in regard to the canonical Scriptures, he must follow the judgment of the greater number of catholic churches."[50]

On the contrary, in the *Prologue to the Kings*, Jerome calls the additions to the Septuagint (i.e., Wisdom, Sirach, Judith, Tobit, and Maccabees) "apocryphal," while including them in his Vulgate.[51] These books—and Jerome names Wisdom of Solomon and Sirach as an illustration—are to be read "for the edification of the people, [but] not to give authority to doctrines of the Church" (*Preface to Proverbs, Ecclesiastes, and Song of Songs*).[52] As one may notice, the same discrepancy between theory and practice encountered in most of church fathers and teachers is found here also in Jerome.

Beyond the first section of the Bible, the Law (Torah), Jerome and Augustine differ substantially both as regards division and content. Augustine's list closely follows the Septuagint tradition with the Law (Torah) followed by "histories," "poetry" (Psalms and wisdom literature) and "oracles" of the prophets. As for content, Augustine is the first Christian writer who lists all the books (disputed and undisputed) without making any distinction between them. Note that in both, Jerome's Vulgate and Augustine's list, the additions to the Septuagint are interspersed or intermingled with the "undisputed books."

Amphilochius of Iconium

Born of a Cappadocian family, Amphilochius is perhaps the first author who distinguishes between "Scripture" and "canon." "Not every book that acquired the status of a revered 'Scripture' is 'infallible'" (*ouh hapasa biblos asphalēs hē semnon onoma tēs graphēs kektēmenē*). Thus, Scriptures like the Epistle of Jeremiah, Baruch, or the two wisdoms, found in several lists (but not in Amphilochius's), should not be automatically considered "infallible" (*asphalēs*) or "canonical." Amphilochius's "canonical" list (*Iambics to Seleucus*)[53] is identical with the Rabbinic Bible, containing no noncanonical books at all. The criterion of canonicity according to Amphilochius is authenticity: spurious writings, even those that might come close to the words of truth found in canonical Scriptures, are not to be considered canonical.

Amphilochius's list is the closest of any early Christian author to the Jewish scriptural corpus. While naming and grouping the Old Testament books according to the Septuagint usage (e.g., "and of Kingdoms four books" [*basileiōn te tessaras biblous*]), Amphilochius follows to a certain degree the Jewish tradition, considering, for instance, Hosea as the "first" (*prōton*) prophet (so in the Jewish Bible's arrangement of the twelve Minor Prophets), and Leviticus "the middle book" (*tēn mesēn biblon*) or the center of the Pentateuch.[54]

Interestingly, Amphilochius also employs poetical names describing the content of some books, such as Job, "crowned in the contests of many sufferings" (*stephthentos athlois poikilōn pathōn*) or Psalms, "soothing remedy for the souls" (*emmeles psychōn akos*).

Amphilochius's division of the Old Testament books, namely, Pentateuch, Writings (poetical books), Prophets, precludes any intrusion of outside "noncanonical" Scriptures into "canonical" space of the Old Testament. The last group, the Prophets, functions as a buffer against any attempt of noncanonicals that fail to prove their authenticity or "prophetic" authorship to get closer to the canonical Scriptures.

Gregory Nazianzus

Following on the footsteps of his cousin Amphilochius of Iconium, Gregory Nazianzus represents perhaps one of the most extreme views pertaining to the Old Testament canon. While still embracing the Jewish practice by dividing the "ancient books" (*archaias biblous*) of the Old Testament into three groups ("historical," "poetic," and "of prophetic Spirit"), he dares to replace the customary term "Law" for the five books of Moses (Pentateuch) with a new title: "historical" books, gathering together in one category the Pentateuch, the Major Prophets, and Ruth. The new sequence, with the "prophetic" group displaced from the second to the third position, echoes a tendency to solve the tension between "Law" and "Prophets" by conferring preeminence to "historical" (*historikai*) and "of prophetic Spirit" (*pneumatos prophētikou*) as two ends of the Old Testament. This maneuver creates a quite interesting situation. On the one hand, the "informative" function supersedes the "formative" role of the Old Testament. On the other hand, with the "poetic" Scriptures not anymore on third position, as in the Jewish Bible, the tripartite corpus looks well framed and closed to any intrusion of "outside" noncanonical material. Hence Gregory's list as Amphilochius's in fact, makes no mention of the Epistle of Jeremiah, Baruch, or the two Wisdoms, the noncanonical books most often found in the early lists. As in Amphilochius's case, any book "outside" (*ektos*) the twenty-two canonical books should be considered noncanonical, or as Gregory labels it "not among the genuine ones" (*ouk en gnēsiais*) (*Carmina Dogmatica* 1.1.12).[55]

Gregory's emphasis on history goes as far as mentioning the biblical books not according to the traditional terminology but rather after the author's name. For instance, he cites the poetic books in this way, "There are five poetic books: first Job, next David . . . ," instead of "Book of Job, Book of Psalms. . . ." Jewish influence is also seen further in the name "Kings" (*basileōn*) instead of the Septuagint's promoted heading "Kingdoms" (*basileiōn*).

John of Damascus

The description provided by John of Damascus is almost identical to the three lists prepared by Epiphanius of Salamis. The two writers form an arch over centuries, witnessing to Eastern Christianity's struggle to maintain and transmit the tension extant within the very Jewish

Bible itself, between the two foci, "Law" and "Prophets," which had already been spoken of as two well-defined groups of divinely inspired Scriptures in Jewish sources as early as the second half of the second century B.C.E.

John (*An Exact Exposition of Faith* 4.17)[56] follows the Jewish practice by dividing the whole scriptural corpus into twenty-two or twenty-seven books (if one takes into account the consonants with special graphemes at the end of a word). Like Epiphanius, he places a special emphasis on the "Law" since the twenty-two books are grouped into "Four Pentateuchs" and two remaining books. Thus, at the end of the period of the Seven Ecumenical Councils, one may detect a slight preference for the "formative" function of the Scriptures, with an indirect invitation to those formative noncanonical books to join the canonical chorus, especially in the areas of catechesis and liturgy.

Neither Epiphanius nor John of Damascus mention anything about Lamentations, Epistle of Jeremiah, or Baruch. Perhaps Lamentations was automatically counted with Jeremiah. But then what about the Epistle of Jeremiah and Baruch? Were they treated similar to Lamentations, or were they simply discarded as noncanonical?

John lists the two Wisdoms (Solomon and Sirach) as "virtuous and noble" (*enaretoi men kai kalai*), similar to "useful and helpful" (*chrēsimoi kai ōphelimoi*) in Epiphanius's terminology. However, adds John, these books are not among the twenty-two "encovenanted books" (*tas endiathetous biblous*) because the Hebrews "did not place them in the ark" (*oude ekeinto en tē kibōtō*).

After the First Millennium

All the canons and lists of the Old Testament found in Christian sources of the first millennium and discussed above have the approval of the Council in Trullo (692 C.E.) and of the Seventh Ecumenical Council (787 C.E.). One may add though that the approval given was not specific but general because there were various opinions in those canons and lists of Old Testament books ratified by the above-mentioned councils. In fact, it was the very tension between two tendencies intrinsic to the Jewish Bible (i.e., narrow and wide scriptural corpora, "formative" and "informative" functions of the Scripture) that received the conciliar approval first in 692 C.E.

The Reformers

Following their main desideratum to retrieve the spirit of the apostolic Church, the Reformers made a methodological error by confounding the early (Pharisaic) Judaism of the time of Jesus with the rabbinic Judaism of the fourth century C.E. onward. Thus, they opted for a narrow scriptural corpus made of thirty-nine books (identical with the extension of the *Biblia Hebraica*). The "outside" books (i.e., the Septuagint additions) were labeled "apocrypha." Nevertheless, the Reformers did not go so far as to reject the "apocrypha" from their Bibles, but rather preserved them at the end of the Old Testament. Thus, they were not intermingled with the thirty-nine books of the Jewish Bible as in the case of the fourth–fifth century Septuagint codices, Vulgate, and those Christian canonical lists coming from either East or West. The final position of the Septuagint additions in the Reformers' Bibles bespeaks the diminishing value of these books, now treated only as an "appendix."

In Luther's translation of the Bible of 1534, the Septuagint additions are found at the end being introduced by a qualifying statement, "Apocrypha: these are books which are not held equal to the Sacred Scriptures and yet are useful and good for reading."

The Reformed Church by her *Confessio Gallicana* (1559) and *Confessio Belgica* (1561) rejected altogether the Septuagint additions from the Scripture. The Lutheran Church did not issue any official canonical list. The sixth article among the *Thirty-Nine Articles* (1571) of the Church of England states that the Septuagint additions may be read "for example of life and instruction of manners," but should not be utilized for "establishing doctrine." Later, in order to appease any conflict between various fractions, the British Bible Society decided in 1827 not to include the disputed books in future publications of the Bible.[57]

Today, one may detect a slow but sure return of Protestantism to a more accepting attitude toward the Septuagint additions. These books should be considered for their intrinsic value as a bridge between the two Testaments. Many of the teachings (e.g., resurrection of the dead, angelology, etc.) encountered in the New Testament find their incipient expression in the Septuagint additions. A number of Protestant theologians have recently requested that the Apocrypha be placed again at the end of canonical books, as was the practice with the Reformers' Bibles.[58]

Tridentine Roman Catholic Views

The trenchant attitude of the Reformers determined the Roman Catholic Church to take a clear-cut decision with regard to the biblical canon, especially to the place of the Septuagint additions. In opposition to the Protestant views, the Roman Catholic Church accepted definitively the Septuagint additions at the Council of Trent (1545–63).[59] The council adopted the wider canon, following on the footsteps of Augustine. The official list accepted at Trent numbers forty-six Old Testament canonical books, that is, thirty-nine called "protocanonical" of the Hebrew Bible, and a number of seven additions to the Septuagint (i.e., Tobit, Judith, Wisdom of Solomon, Sirach, Baruch, and 1 and 2 Maccabees) and three additions to the "protocanonical" (Letter of Jeremiah, Additions to Daniel, and Additions to Esther), all called "deuterocanonical" (the term was coined by Sixtus of Sienna in 1566).[60] The council in its fourth session (1546) decrees: "Henceforth the books of the Old Testament and the New Testament, protocanonical and deuterocanonical alike, in their entirety and with all their parts, comprise the canon and are held to be of equal authority."[61]

Augustine's criterion of canonicity (the use of a book by many significant Churches) was the moving force that led to the official decision at Trent. The participants also took Jerome's Vulgate as the absolute norm for church usage. The council condemns everyone who does not read these books according to the Vulgate, thereby linking canonicity to a specific text witness.[62] This was the first time an official and so widely abiding church authority had ever required readers to employ a certain textual version of the Bible. For the Roman Catholic Church, the Council of Trent is considered an ecumenical council, universally binding; thus, the First Vatican Council (1869–70), also regarded as ecumenical by Rome, reaffirmed the decree of Trent. In contrast, the Eastern Orthodox Church has never "canonized" a particular text, even though preferences for various translations (primarily the Septuagint) have been in evidence within the mosaic of Eastern Orthodoxy throughout its long history.

Eastern Orthodox Approaches

The polemics of the sixteenth and seventeenth centuries between Protestants and Roman Catholics were centered on Protestant presupposition that accepting the Septuagint additions would be interpreted as supporting Roman Catholic doctrines, such as purgatory (2 Macc 12:44–45).

The Eastern Orthodox Church found herself in the middle of these polemics. Given the ambiguity in terminology used in the past (e.g., Athanasius's threefold division of writings) the Orthodox continued to oscillate between Protestant and Roman Catholic views, pleading for a narrow or a wider scriptural corpus.

It is important to note that there is no evidence of any earlier controversy between the Latins and the Greeks regarding the extension of the canon. The Council of Florence (1438–41), in addressing "the Greeks," places the Septuagint additions on par with the thirty-nine books of the Jewish Bible. This list of canonical books approved at Florence was adopted by the participants at the Council of Trent in the sixteenth century.

The sixteenth century local councils and confessions (*homologiai*, "confessions" crafted on Protestant model) listed below sought to bring some precision to the discussion, while at the same time unfortunately distancing themselves from the ambiguous yet quite rich and profound expressions of Eastern Orthodox tradition.

The Confession of Cyril Loukaris (1629)

Cyril Loukaris was born in 1572 in Crete. While studying and traveling in Europe, he arrived in Switzerland where he came in contact with the Reformed Church and liked her teachings. In 1602, Cyril was elected Patriarch of Alexandria, and in 1621 Patriarch of Constantinople. As patriarch in both these two sees, he maintained a dialogue with Protestant theologians and sent students to Protestant universities in Europe. Cyril died in 1638, strangled at the behest of the Sultan for high treason; his lifeless body was thrown into the Bosphorus.

The Confession of Cyril was written in Latin in 1629, and then, in 1631, in Greek with additions; it was published in both languages in 1633 in Geneva. Heavily Protestant in content, Cyril's Confession is a plain exposition of basic Calvinist teaching: justification by faith alone, predestination, reduction of seven sacraments to two, rejection of icons, rejection of church infallibility. Unsurprisingly, this confession ushered in a long series of controversies. In keeping with its general Protestant character, in the appendix to the second (Greek) edition, Cyril excluded the additions to the Septuagint (called by him "apocrypha") from the list of canonical books.

Synod of Jerusalem (1672)

The Synod of Jerusalem was convened by the Greek Orthodox Patriarch Dositheos Notaras in March 1672 on the occasion of consecration of the Church of Nativity in Bethlehem (hence its alternative name, the "Synod of Bethlehem").[63] This was one of the most important Orthodox councils in modern times, and to a certain degree comparable to the Council of Trent for the Roman Catholic Church. Sixty-eight bishops and ecclesiastics, including some from the Church of Russia, attended the synod.

The Acts of the Synod of Jerusalem consist of six chapters and the Confession of Dositheos. The Confession of Dositheos (i.e., *Chapter VI of Acts and Decrees of the Synod of Jerusalem*), signed by the Jerusalem patriarch along with other council participants on March 16, 1672, was intended to be a response to Loukaris. The Acts of this council were later signed by the other five patriarchates of Constantinople, Alexandria, Antioch, Jerusalem, and Moscow.

The Orthodox participants at the Synod of Jerusalem argued that Cyril's Confession was a forgery by Calvinists and quoted large sections from Cyril's homilies in order to prove their point. The Confession of Dositheos proclaims the Orthodox faith in eighteen decrees and four questions. This confession aims to respond to the chapters and questions of the 1629 Confession of Cyril Loukaris. Question III of the Dositheos's Confession (*What Books do you call Sacred Scripture?*) thus states:

Following the rule of the Catholic Church, we call Sacred Scripture all those which Cyril [Loukaris] collected from the Synod of Laodicea, and enumerated, adding thereto those which he foolishly, and ignorantly, or rather maliciously called Apocrypha; to wit, "The Wisdom of Solomon," "Judith," "Tobit," "The History of the Dragon," "The History of Susanna," "The Maccabees," and "The Wisdom of Sirach." For we judge these also to be with the other genuine Books of Divine Scripture genuine parts of Scripture. For ancient custom, or rather the Catholic Church, which has delivered to us as genuine the Sacred Gospels and the other Books of Scripture, has undoubtedly delivered these also as parts of Scripture, and the denial of these is the rejection of those. And if, perhaps, it seems that not always have all been by all reckoned with the others, yet nevertheless these also have been counted and reckoned with the rest of Scripture, as well by Synods, as by how many of the most ancient and eminent theologians of the Catholic Church; all of which we also judge to be Canonical Books, and confess them to be Sacred Scripture.[64]

As one may see here, the Confession of Dositheos moves toward the modern Roman Catholic view regarding the Septuagint additions. Where Cyril Loukaris followed the Protestant Reformers in considering these books "apocrypha," Dositheos appears to imitate Trent and calls them "canonical." Both patriarchs move away from the nuanced terminology of Athanasius, for whom the Septuagint additions were at once "noncanonized" (ou kanonizomena) and "readable" (anaginōskomena), thus useful for instruction.

Later Orthodox Confessions

This oscillation between Roman Catholicism and Protestantism with regard to the extension of the biblical canon can be detected in two other confessions. On the one hand, the Confession of Peter Mogila (1643), Metropolitan of Kiev, though not sanctioning the apocrypha, quotes often from the Septuagint additions (e.g., Tobit 12:9 on alms).[65] The Confession of Mogila attacked both the Jesuits and the Calvinists. On the other hand, the Confession of Metrophanes Kritopoulos (1625)[66] numbers only twenty-two canonical books (similar to Josephus's numbering) of the Old Testament, and (similar to the Protestant view) clearly excludes the Septuagint additions from the canon, which it mentions by name: Tobit, Judith, Wisdom of Solomon, Sirach, Baruch, and the Maccabees. The confession of Kritopoulos has never received ecclesiastical approval, however, and was ignored by the Synod of Jerusalem. It should be added here too that the important Russian Catechism of Philaret, Metropolitan of Moscow (1823), rejects the Septuagint additions from the list of canonical books for the reason that these books "do not exist in Hebrew," but "they have been appointed by the fathers to be read by proselytes who are preparing for admission into the Church" (Athanasius). More recently, however, the anaginōskomena have been returned to the Russian Bible published in Moscow in 1956.

None of the confessions and statements discussed above should be considered as representing the Eastern Orthodox tradition as a whole. They were crafted under the pressure of several controversies between Roman Catholicism and Protestantism at a time when, due to political and cultural factors, Orthodox theological education was at an all-time low. Thus, they often simply repeat the Roman Catholic responses to Protestants, or vice versa. According to Miltiadis Konstantinou, these views having been articulated by external theological confrontations cannot claim to be binding resolutions on biblical canon for the entire Eastern Orthodoxy.[67]

Remarks

Given the past hesitations of the Christian East with respect to the biblical canon, the issue of canon has remained unsettled. The popularity of Septuagint in the East and the liturgical use of the anaginōskomena did not change this situation. John Meyendorff notices:

> In spite of the fact that Byzantine patristic and ecclesiastical tradition almost exclusively uses the Septuagint as the standard Biblical text and that parts of the "longer" canon especially Wisdom are of frequent liturgical use Byzantine theologians remain faithful to a "Hebrew" criterion for Old Testament literature, which excludes texts originally composed in Greek. Modern Orthodox theology is consistent with this unresolved polarity when it distinguishes between "canonical" and "deuterocanonical" literature of the Old Testament, applying the first term only to the books of the "shorter" canon.[68]

Similarly, Petros Vassiliadis suggests that the canons of Council of Trullo (692 C.E.), which confer to the former patristic and conciliar statements on biblical canon the universal status, "leave the issue of the number of the canonical books of the OT (and to an extent some of the NT too [e.g. Apocalypse]) unsettled. It may not be an exaggeration to state that the undivided Church has not solved the issue of, and therefore not imposed upon her members, a canon of the Bible."[69] In light of Eugene Ulrich's definition of canon, the last part of Vassiliadis' quote makes perfect sense. Ulrich distinguishes three elements in the definition of canon: (a) books, i.e., the material reality of the scrolls (not the textual form of the books); (b) reflective judgment of a community of faith that examines and ratifies its authoritative books; and (c) a closed list (a definite number of books entering that collection). Ulrich concludes, "If the canon is by definition a closed list of books that have been considered, debated, sifted, and accepted, then talk of an open canon is confusing and counterproductive; it seems more appropriate to speak of a growing collection of books considered as sacred scripture."[70]

If one takes into account the clear-cut definition of biblical canon proposed by Ulrich, that the biblical canon is a "closed list" of books tied to the notion of institutional "authority," then strictly speaking only the Roman Catholic Church can claim for herself a biblical canon: a closed list of forty-six books of the Old Testament, officially endorsed by the Council

of Trent. Ulrich's definition does not apply to the views held by Eastern
Orthodox Churches, as there has been no Ecumenical or Pan-Orthodox
council (Laodicea in 363 C.E. and Jerusalem in 1672 were but local councils) to decree on a definite number of books considered canonical (i.e., a
closed list). Rather, the Eastern Orthodox Churches have an "open canon"
or, more precisely, to use Ulrich's technical term, a growing "sacred
Scripture" that consists of thirty-nine books of the Jewish Bible and a
number of ten (or so) additions to the Septuagint called anaginōskomena,
"readable."[71]

Theodore G. Stylianopoulos uses the phrase "closing of the canon"
while adding that this is "not a rigid principle in the Orthodox Church because the classic Christian tradition never dogmatized the exact number
of scriptural books and always valued many other writings and liturgical
texts in addition to the canonical collection of Scriptures."[72] Stylianopoulos includes the anaginōskomena in the canon by noting that "the Orthodox Old Testament maintains the most inclusive canon of the ancient
Church which embraces, together with the ten Readable Books, forty-nine
books. In addition, a few other writings mentioned above, such as the
Prayer of Manasses and Psalm 151, are accorded some value within the
Orthodox tradition."[73]

Speaking of the "openness" of the canon in the Orthodox Church,
Savvas Agouridis remarks that

> Holy Scripture is not law but "witness," and its writers are not leg-
> islators but "witnesses." If for instance an archaeological pickaxe
> were to uncover an authentic epistle of Paul the Apostle, no one
> would imagine excluding it from the canon. Neither is there the
> least doubt that the discovery of new texts from early Christianity
> would pose any problem whatsoever regarding the essence of faith.
> Through such a new possession our knowledge and spiritual expe-
> rience would simply be enriched in a truly authentic and genuine
> way.[74]

One may add here Harold P. Scanlin's pertinent observation, clearly supported by the evidence in the sources discussed above:

> It is important to recognize that the Eastern Churches approach the
> issue of biblical canon from their own perspective. First, Eastern
> Churches are autocephalous, that is, each national church tradition

can make autonomous decisions, including decisions regarding the biblical canon. . . . Further, the relationship between Scripture and Tradition is considered differently than Scripture-Tradition discussions in the West. A related issue is the Eastern hermeneutic, characterized in the term theoria. . . . Finally, it is important to recognize the crucial role of liturgical use of Scripture.[75]

The Notion of Authority

The requirement of an official and universal authority in Eastern Orthodoxy to define the biblical canon is still debatable. There are voices that would say that the liturgical use is sufficient to turn a "Scripture" into a "canonical" item. Others will remain adamant on the position that without an ecumenical or pan-Orthodox council there is no biblical canon (i.e., closed list authorized by the entire ecclesiastical body).

Liturgical Use

It is a truism that liturgical life lies at the core of what we call the Eastern Orthodox *phronēma* (ethos). No doubt, liturgy is the life of the Church, the pulsating energy that sets the entire body of the Church in motion. *Lex credendi* (theology) is naturally interrelated with *lex orandi* (liturgy). Theology and worship are twin sisters in a reciprocal and perennial engagement. Any doctrinal statement, any view of the biblical canon should stem naturally from the liturgical and Eucharistic experience of the Church.[76] As Petros Vasiliadis reminds us, early Christians received the Scripture in the Church, in relation to Eucharist:

> The Church told them what Scripture was. In the first three centuries of Christian history a lengthy process of testing was needed in order to distinguish between those books which were authentically "canonical" Scripture, bearing authoritative witness to the Church's self-understanding, and above all to Christ's person and message; and those which were "apocryphal," useful perhaps for teaching, but not a normative source of doctrine. Thus, it was the Church (in her ecclesial rather than institutional form) that had decided which books would form the Canon of the New Testament. A book is part of Holy Scripture not because of any particular theory about its date and authorship, but because the Church had treated it as canonical;

it is debatable whether that treatment was juridical, i.e. through a proper conciliar process, or experiential, i.e. "Eucharistic" in the above mentioned sense.[77]

Speaking of anaginōskomena, Vassiliadis adds that the liturgical use of these books in Eastern Orthodox tradition endowed them with a special aura of authority: "In view, however, of their wide use in the liturgy their authority can hardly be differentiated from the so-called canonical books of the Bible. It is also to be noted in addition that the Orthodox *Anagignoskomena* do not exactly coincide with the *Deuterocanonical* books (only seven) of the Catholic Bible."[78] I might add here that the anaginōskomena are to be distinguished from the "canonical books of the Bible"—hence, the openness of the Eastern Orthodox "canon" (or more precisely "sacred Scripture").

In a similar vein of thought, Scanlin uses the word "function" to define the canon in Eastern Orthodox tradition:

> Orthodox *theoria* [an inspired vision of the presence and purpose of God within history and within the church] recognizes Scripture as canonical, that is, as normative for the faith and life of the church, but it also stresses the role of the revelation of the living Word of God in a synergistic, dynamic revelation. Accordingly, canon is defined in terms of function; all Scripture that functions in the dynamic relationship of God's revelation may be said to possess canonical authority. The use of Scripture in the liturgy and worship of the church is, accordingly, that which defines the extent of the canon. . . . Canon is functional rather than descriptive; it is the church's recognition that the sacred texts accepted as canonical function as the means of divine revelation, both as a historical event as well as spiritual bridge linking past and present.[79]

According to Demetrios J. Constantelos,[80] these are the anaginōskomena used in Greek Orthodox worship, in order of their frequency: Wisdom, Judith, Sirach,[81] Song of the Three Children, Tobit, Baruch, Susanna, 4 Maccabees, 1 Esdras, and 1 and 2 Maccabees.

In his well-balanced study on anaginōskomena books, Elias Oikonomos touches one of the most puzzling situations: the obvious discrepancy between theory and practice within the Eastern Orthodox tradition: "On the basis of Athanasius's arguments, the Orthodox Churches have retained the deuterocanonical writings, and have reaffirmed this position in the seventeenth century. These writings can accordingly be freely used in church practice, but may not be made the basis of dogmatic decisions. Such a position remains true both to the ancient decisions, and also to traditional freedom in this respect."[82]

Conciliar Statements

We may briefly note that a pan-Orthodox Council was projected in the eve of the Second Vatican Council (in 1959). Consequently, several conferences were held to prepare the agenda of the synod.

The First pan-Orthodox Conference of Rhodes in 1961 announced the goal of the "Great and Holy Council." The Second Conference of Rhodes, in 1963, debated the question of whether to send Orthodox observers to the Second Vatican Council.

The Fourth Pan-Orthodox Conference at Chambesy in 1968 selected six themes from the Rhodes list as a working agenda for the "Great and Holy Council." These were: (1) modes of divine revelation: Scripture and Tradition; (2) participation of laity in worship and church life; (3) accommodation of fasting to modern life; (4) marriage impediments and uniformity in practice; (5) date of Pascha; and (6) *akribeia* and *oikonomia*. The first theme, on Scripture and Tradition, was discarded with no further explanation from the agenda at the First Pan-Orthodox Preconciliar Conference at Chambesy in 1976. A new list of ten topics for the future Great and Holy Council was devised, with no reference to the theme of Scripture and Tradition.

Text and Canon

We must mention here also the confusion that exists between text and canon. That the Eastern Orthodox Church has always used the Greek text of the Septuagint[83] does not mean necessarily that she adopted the whole list of books (forty-nine or so) contained in the Septuagint as her official canon. Here one must question the oversimplification of Constantelos's suggestion that the use of the Septuagint and the citations of canonical and noncanonical books by Christian authors of the first four centuries would plead for the existence of a wider canon in early Church. Constantelos concludes rather hastily, "Today the Greek speaking church subscribes to the longer canon, making no distinction between protocanonical and deuterocanonical."[84] For Constantelos, the contemporary Orthodox Church continues to use these books "because this collection of Old Testament books was the official Scripture used by the Apostolic Church. The early Church as a Greek speaking church, both in the eastern and the western parts of the Roman Empire, used the Greek translation of the Alexandrian Jewish canon, the Septuagint."[85]

Unlike the Roman Catholic Church, where the extent of the canon was contoured by medieval manuscripts of the Vulgate, the Eastern Orthodox Church, in spite of all her exuberant dedication to the Old Greek version, has never confounded the text with the canon, by canonizing the particular make-up of her favorite version.

Formative or Informative?

From an Eastern Orthodox perspective, so anchored into the liturgical life of the Church, there is no stringent need for a Pan-Orthodox council to decide in favor of the one or the other of the two tendencies discussed here, "formative" and "informative" or "wide" and "narrow" scriptural corpora. Both polarities remain strongly rooted in Orthodox faith and practice, where they are held in dialectical tension. Orthodox theology and practice find good reasons to continue in maintaining this tension inherited from prerabbinic Judaism and the early Church, instead of attempting to solve it in a reductionist way, thus repeating those attempts in the seventeenth century by allying Orthodoxy either to the Roman Catholic extended canon or Protestant narrow corpus. A discussion of the Eastern Orthodox position regarding the additions to the Septuagint based on thorough analysis of historical and theological data is entirely warranted; but a rushed move toward a formal canonization of the Septuagint additions will translate into something different than the older praxis of the Eastern Orthodox Church. This would be a continuation of the phenomenon Georges Florovsky diagnosed and decried as the Latinizing "pseudomorphosis" of post-Byzantine Orthodox theology.[86]

The "openness" of the biblical canon inherent in Eastern Orthodoxy makes of this tradition an interesting locus, a median place between the Protestant narrow canon (similar to rabbinic Judaism) and the Roman Catholic wide canon. Eastern Orthodox "sacred Scripture" is not primarily a "source" of divine revelation—a static reality, a closed list from A to Z—but rather a "means" or "channel" by which God's uncontrollable, eternal Word is "breathing"[87] through, so that human lives may be shaped and reshaped as part of that "instruction in righteousness" mentioned in 2 Tim 3:16–17.

The difference of emphasis on informative or formative uses of Scripture that delineates Eastern Orthodoxy and the Western variants of Christianity can be encountered at the level of biblical canon. If one accents the number of books making up the Scriptures, then emphasis is set on information: a definite collection of books "recording" God's entire revelation. In contrast, if the external boundaries of the Septuagint additions to an inherited fixed canon (Jewish Bible) are flexible the accent falls on formative function of the Scripture viewed as a means of building and fostering man's relationship with God.

Due to this wide understanding of Scripture, a treasure trove of instructions, the Eastern Orthodox definition of canon or rather of canonical books does not necessarily need a conciliar authority as warrantor of canonicity. The liturgical use of a biblical book can turn this book into a normative yet not a "canonical" (in narrow sense) Scripture. That is why at the grass roots level of Orthodox theology, even those books "outside" the Hebrew Scriptures and found only in the Septuagint are rightly called anaginōskomena ("readable") due to their use in liturgy. Liturgy has always been for Eastern Orthodox a laboratory where characters are shaped out and strengthened based on events, figures, and sayings contained in the Scriptures—where genuine relationship on both horizontal and vertical levels is built and continuously nurtured.

4

Tradition

Let the inspired Scripture be our arbiter (diaitēsatō), *and the sentence* (psēphos) *of truth will be given to those whose dogmas are found to agree with the divine words.*

GREGORY OF NYSSA, On the Holy Trinity, and of the Godhead
of the Holy Spirit: To Eustathius

OSCAR CULLMAN WAS right: "On the old problem of 'scripture and tradition' everything possible would seem to have been said."[1] Nevertheless, from an Eastern Orthodox point of view, there are a few brushstrokes that should be added to the generally accepted picture.

From the onset, one might suggest, with the risk of overgeneralizing, that there are three distinct ways of looking at Tradition. First, there is "Scripture and Tradition"—two sources or means of God's revelation, as espoused in older Roman Catholic sources. Second, there is "Scripture alone" (*sola scriptura*), defining Protestantism since the time of Luther—although older and newer discontenting voices here do claim the need for a tradition of sorts. And third, there is the old patristic view, well anchored in the apostolic tradition and shooting its twigs vigorously again today, which might be encapsulated in the phrase, "Scripture *(with)in* Tradition." If Tradition is conceived as the life of the Holy Spirit in the Church, Scripture might be imagined as the Church's pulsating heart, always radiating life and sustenance to the members of the body, always challenging it to dialogue with the living Word of God. Aural, visual, and discursive interpretations elaborated throughout the time are the fruit of this dynamic dialogue between the Word and its followers *within* the wide and multifaceted context of Church's life.

Ecclesial Framework
The Church as *Locus Scripturae*

Due to its canonical configuration and interpretation, one may say that "The Bible is foremost the book of the church and the church's history."[2] The nascent Christian community appropriated the Jewish Scriptures while weaving interpretive rules out of a certain ethos, tradition or way of life and thinking whose perpetuation has been dear to its heart from the beginning.

Scripture did not arise in a vacuum. Nor did the Scripture come without hermeneutical assumptions which are inherently part of the "appropriation" process. As Theodore G. Stylianopoulos remarks: "Just as theology cannot be separated from history, so also Scripture as a holy book cannot be disjoined from the communal context in which it originated, took shape, and was variously used. These contexts are namely, Israel and Church."[3] Thus also, Paul D. Hanson observes, "The most appropriate context for the theological interpretation of the Bible is the living community of faith, which for Christians is of course the church."[4]

To insist on the Church as the proper field of interpretation of the Christian Scripture is not to say that everything is fixed, or that the Church has some kind of interpretive monopoly over the living Word of the Bible. On the contrary, as R. W. L. Moberly observes, "Whenever there are structures, communities, and patterns of life whose identity is in some fundamental way defined by a particular textual corpus, there should always be a healthy two-way interaction between text and community. . . . If the interaction cannot be revived, the tradition is moribund and its end is at hand, and differently structured patterns of thought and life will be adopted (for better or worse)."[5]

In fact, the Church has been formed and informed by the Scripture since her inception. It is the Church's continuous responsibility to interact with the sacred text in order to keep the Tradition alive. Where there is Scripture, there must also be a community abiding to a set of rules regarding interpretation, if that Scripture is to be rightly understood and lived. This was the case both in the early Church and rabbinic Judaism. As Georges Florovsky writes:

> Scripture belonged to the Church, and it was only in the Church, within the community of right faith, that Scripture could be adequately understood and correctly interpreted. Heretics, that is—those outside of

the Church, had no key to the mind of the Scripture. It was not enough just to read and to quote Scriptural words—the true meaning, or intent, of Scripture, taken as an integrated whole, had to be elicited. One had to grasp, as it were—in advance, the true pattern of Biblical revelation, the great design of God's redemptive providence, and this could be done only by an insight of faith.[6]

In the Church, the Scripture was acknowledged as "sacred" text. The sacred text was read and interpreted as "canonical," normative for Church as regards belief and living. Moreover, the Scripture belongs to the Church as witnessing to God's revelation that is still unfolding in the Church, the body of Christ:

> Only within the experience of the Church is the New Testament truly and fully alive. Church history is itself a story of redemption. The truth of the book is revealed and vindicated by the growth of the Body. . . . The sacred history of redemption is still going on. It is now the history of the Church that is the Body of Christ. The Spirit-Comforter is already abiding in the Church. No complete system of Christian faith is yet possible, for the Church is still on her pilgrimage. And the Bible is kept by the Church as a book of history to remind believers of the dynamic nature of the divine revelation, "at sundry times and in divers manners."[7]

Florovsky is saying in the passage just quoted that the Church preserved the Bible to teach her members about the dynamic, living character of God's revelation still at work in the Church. Inasmuch as God's revelation is unfolding or recapitulated within the Church, the Church herself is part of God's revelation too.

This ecclesial character of Scripture is underlined by many ancient writers, as early as Irenaeus onward, with the emphasis that heretics, outsiders to the Church (*ekklēsia*), have no right to use the Scripture. The switch from orality to textuality in the formation of Scriptures, both Jewish and Christian, occurred within specific communities of faith that preserved their foundational memories and gradually turned them into liturgical acts. As Theodore G. Stylianopoulos remarks,

> In the Orthodox perspective, what established the Church was not the gospel as such, but the original acts of revelation experienced

by specific men and women drawn together by the Spirit to form the early Church. The gospel as a saving message has intrinsic power but no voice of its own. There could be no gospel apart from Mary Magdalene, Peter, James, Paul, Barnabas and the others who proclaimed the good news. . . . The gospel was never a disembodied, floating message that could exist or act apart from the Church in which it is lived and to which it leads. Moreover, empowering and increasing the Church, the gospel from earliest times was seen as tradition, indeed the heart of the apostolic tradition as St Paul declares, using the explicit language of *paradosis* or tradition 1 Cor 15:1–11.[8]

Neither traditionalist readers nor modern historical scholars can avoid context when dealing with a text. While traditionalist readers place the text within the traditional context of their community of faith and study this text based on a set of hermeneutic assumptions inherent in that tradition, historical critics attempt to analyze the text within the original historical, cultural, and religious context in which it was generated. John A. McGuckin's criticism of the claims of modern historical biblical research to "objectivity" is well taken: even the historical critics employ a toolkit of presuppositions characteristic of historical critical methods and literary theory.[9] Again, both camps of readers deal with the text within a context and bring in their peculiar assumptions. In other words, no reader can eschew entirely *eisegesis*, inference of the reader's meaning into the text. Everything depends on the reader's initial intent in approaching the text: either to discover how the text came about in its original context, or to discern the perennial meaning of the text—the latter being an inquiry based on community's belief that the text represents the eternal Word of God.

Apostolicity, *Episcopē* and *Laos*

Two important events in the life of the early Church triggered a rather quick transition from oral proclamation (kērygma)[10] to the first written documents (Gospels, Acts, Epistles). These were the death of the first apostles (James, Peter, and Paul) in the sixties and the destruction of Jerusalem and its Temple in 70 C.E.

Along with the writing down of the Gospels, one may notice a tendency in the early Church toward centralization and standardization of her structures. Already by the early second century C.E., the bipartite structure evidenced in the pastoral epistles (*episcopos*, "overseer" [1 Tim 3:1–13] or *presbyteros*, "elder" [1 Tim 5:17–20]/*presbyteroi*, "elders" [Tit 1:5–7], and *diakonos*, "deacon" [1 Tim 3:1–13])[11] is quickly replaced by a tripartite configuration ("elders" and "deacons," both subordinated to one "overseer" [bishop]). This new threefold structure is attested in the epistles of Ignatius of Antioch.[12] From a primarily economic-administrative function,[13] the episcopal office moves now to a more liturgical and authoritative status. According to Ignatius, the validity of Baptism and Eucharist was assured by the presence of the episcopos (bishop), who to some extent fills the empty seat left by the apostles.

In Ignatius's exhortation to the community in Magnesia, the bishop was "presiding in place of God." The threefold structure (bishop, presbyters, and deacons) is paralleled by God, the Council of the Apostles, and Jesus Christ:

> Be zealous to do all things in harmony with God, with the bishop presiding in the place of God and the presbyters in the place of the Council of the Apostles, and the deacons, who are most dear to me, entrusted with the service of Jesus Christ, who was from eternity with the Father and was made manifest at the end of time. . . . Let there be nothing in you which can divide you, but be united with the bishop and with those who preside over you as an example and lesson of immortality.
>
> *Epistle to the Magnesians 6.1–2*[14]

Interestingly, Ignatius is quite adamant regarding the duty of believers to stay united with the bishop and to give respect to him as the sign of unity. Yet he is completely silent regarding the bishop's actual function, apart from representing God or Jesus Christ as the concrete token of unity.[15]

According to the fourth century document *Constitutions of the Holy Apostles*, the primary function of the bishop was to interpret the Scriptures, underscoring the harmony between the Gospel, the Prophets, and the Law. But in order to interpret the Scriptures, he had first to study them. Hence, the exhortation: "Be careful, therefore, O bishop, to study the word, that you may be able to explain everything exactly, and that you may copiously nourish your people with much doctrine, and enlighten them with the light of the Law; for God says: 'Enlighten yourselves with the light of knowledge, while we have yet opportunity [Hos 10:12]'" (*Constitutions 2.2.5*)[16]

In order to defend the authenticity of her faith against various forms of Gnosticism, the orthodox mainstream Church had to appeal to "verifiable episcopal succession and continuous tradition."[17] This episcopal succession has remained a touchstone of Orthodoxy ever since. Yet if it is the bishops' unique role to teach definitively on behalf of the whole Church, it must also be stressed that in Orthodox teaching the entire Church (ekklēsia)—"people of God" (*laos tou Theou*), both hierarchy and laity—is in fact the "tradents"[18] of authentic apostolic tradition. The emphasis on the entire body including the laity makes the Eastern Orthodox point of view somewhat unique within the denominational concert. Nevertheless, since the Second Vatican Council, however, the Roman Catholic Church has also moved closer to Eastern Orthodoxy on this issue, with a new vision of the Church as *communio* and an affirmation that the "Christian people as a whole are the tradents of tradition."[19]

John A. McGuckin explains the role of the bishop within this symphony of the whole people of God:

> The "maintenance" of the sacred tradition is the responsibility of the whole church. Its holistic conscience of the faith (sometimes referred to in Latin as *sensus fidelium*) makes it alert to the preservation of apostolic order from heterodox dissidence of all types. Within that charism of the *sensus fidelium*, however, the office of bishop as teacher and defender of the true faith is particularly elevated within Orthodoxy. This, and the eucharistic presidency of the churches, are the primary offices of the episcopate, wherein the bishops serve as stewards and ministers of church unity and fidelity.[20]

The "people" (*laos*) itself is the "guardian of piety" (*hyperaspistēs tēs thrēskeias*), as mentioned in the Encyclical Letter of the Eastern Patriarchs from 1848. This function of the people does not downplay the role of the bishop as a teacher. It means only that the power of teaching granted to the bishop by the one high priest Jesus Christ in the sacrament of orders is one of the functions of the Church as a whole. When a bishop teaches, he represents the whole Church. When he speaks, he does not speak from himself but on behalf of the Church (*ex consensu ecclesiae*). If the bishop in his teaching deviates from the Church's tradition the people have the authority to accuse and depose him.[21]

The Roman Catholic Church supplemented this consensus ecclesiae criterion with the teaching office of the bishops and pope (*magisterium*). However, in earlier centuries, as today in Eastern Orthodoxy, "The true and authentic *consensus* was that which reflected the mind of the Catholic and Universal Church—*to ekklēsiastikon phronēma.*"[22]

For Eastern Orthodox, Roman Catholic, and Anglican denominations, the apostolic succession or the uninterrupted line of duly ordained bishops together with the identity of teaching from the time of the apostles to the present is what confers on Church's ministry authority in matters of faith, morals, and administration of sacraments. In a nutshell, apostolic succession is what makes Church's communities—clergy and laity together—tradents of apostolic tradition.

The model of ecclesial authority based on a merely linear historical "apostolic succession" has also been questioned by some recent Orthodox theologians, however. These theologians include Nicolai Afanasiev, who puts the Eucharist at the center of ecclesiology, and John D. Zizioulas, who in building critically on Afanasiev roots the foundation of Eucharistic ecclesiology in the intra-Trinitarian relationship between the Father, the Son, and the Spirit. In Zizioulas's understanding, the apostolicity of the Church is no merely historical institution but is a work of the Spirit and an image of the last things, constantly renewed by the Eucharistic *epiclesis.*[23]

In any case, whether one refers to a focalized and linear-historical understanding of apostolic succession as guarantor, or to a stereoscopic vision in which the episcopate is seen as instantiated within the broader network of ecclesial communion, one should look at Scripture, Church, and episcopate as inextricably linked and having a common foundation in the original apostolic "deposit." As Georges Florovsky writes:

> Indeed, Scripture itself was the major part of this Apostolic "deposit." So was also the Church. Scripture and Church could not be separated, or opposed to each other. Scripture, that is—its true understanding, was only in the Church, as she was guided by the Spirit. . . . The task of the interpreter was to disclose the word of the Spirit: *hoc observare debemus ut non nostras, cum docemus, sed Sancti Spiritus sententias proferamus* [we must be careful when we teach to present not our own interpretation but that of the Holy Spirit ([Origen] *In Rom.,* 1.3.1)]. And this is simply impossible apart from the Apostolic Tradition, kept in the Church.[24]

Since the Church is the only authentic depositary of the apostolic proclamation (kērygma), it is the Church that has both the mandate and the authority to interpret the Scripture. And the reading of the gospel in church is not simply liturgical recitation. It is a living proclamation of the Logos, made flesh and exalted at the right side of the Father, through the continuous abiding of the Spirit in the Church. The proclamation of the Word of God in Church through the life-giving mediation of the Spirit generates the Tradition that is the life of the Church in the Spirit.

In what follows below, we consider the nature of this Tradition as the interpretive medium of the Eastern Orthodox reading of Scripture.

Tradition as Life and Journey of the Church

The Russian Orthodox theologian Vladimir Lossky wrote: "Tradition (*paradosis, traditio*) is one of those terms which, through being too rich in meanings, runs the risk of finally having none. . . . As soon as precision is desired, the overabundant content has to be broken up and a group of narrow concepts created, the sum of which is far from expressing that living reality called the Tradition of the Church."[25] The terms paradosis (from Gk. verb *paradidōmi,* "to hand over") and traditio (from Latin *tradere,* "to deliver") designate primarily an action—the handing over or transmitting of Tradition. One may infer that Tradition is a somewhat fluid reality, easier to describe than to define—not a static thing, but a dynamic process still unfolding.

Tradition is not something lost in the past and then retrieved by the Church; it is not "archaeology." Tradition is the "living connection" of believers with the historical and eschatological "fullness of experience," uniting them both with God and with fellow believers across time within a single communion. There is a reciprocity between Church and Tradition. The Church is the locus and living witness of this living experience of the Spirit among believers. Thus, the Church is not only an archive of words, symbols, and events of the past constituting the so-called history of salvation, but also, by the presence of the Spirit, the locus where the eternal Word of God is heard and "touched," and God's creative and redemptive power re-experienced and proclaimed.[26]

The Tradition is this rich, never exhausted life of the triune God experienced by believers within the Church through various elected media of sacraments, hymns, readings, interpretations, icons, asceticism, and social involvement. Abraham Heschel's insightful definition of time may

apply quite well to Church and Tradition in their essential function of
media by which one may glimpse God's eternal life: "To men alone time
is elusive; to men with God time is eternity in disguise."[27] One may dare
to relate Heschel's statement to the Church and say that for believers the
Church is God's kingdom in disguise, and church tradition, the living experience of this yet to be unveiled kingdom.

As a preview of what follows, one may notice a certain pattern in the
historical expression of church tradition. First, there is the oral "proclamation" (kērygma) of the Word of God made flesh. Then, there is the
"rule of faith" (*kanōn pisteōs*), more normative and better contoured in
its content. Finally, there is a move slowly toward "codification" of Tradition, beginning with the conciliar statements codified by Justinian in
the mid-sixth century C.E. and culminating with a process of "screening,"
"filtering," and compartmentalization of the entire Tradition (understood
more or less as a deposit rather than a process open to accretion) done
at various times and culminating with the seventeenth century. We will
conclude this section by considering recent attempts by Orthodox theologians to restate anew for our time the dynamic character of Tradition as
the life of the Church.

Kērygma

The earliest form of Christian tradition was the "proclamation" (kērygma)
or the "tradition" (paradosis) of the apostles. Even though Scripture in
its written form became the *norma normans,* apostolic tradition is even
earlier than the New Testament itself. As James I. H. McDonald notes,
the term kērygma "may refer to preaching as an activity or as the content
of proclamation, and sometimes it is not easy to decide which meaning
predominates."[28]

The apostolic kērygma, expressing the unity of early Christian proclamation, is the interpretation of the Christ-event through the lens of the
first eyewitnesses, the apostles; it is the first, fresh impression handed
over both orally and in written form.

In the following fragment, Papias (b. second half of first century C.E.),
bishop of Hierapolis, a witness from the age of the apostles, states that
being forced to choose between various "evidences," he will opt always
for "the word of a living and abiding voice"—the apostolic tradition—as
the only medium able to convey the unique and living voice of the ever-
present Lord:

If, then, any one came, who had been a follower of the elders, I questioned him in regard to the words of the elders,—what Andrew or what Peter said, or what was said by Philip, or by Thomas, or by James, or by John, or by Matthew, or by any other of the disciples of the Lord, and what things Aristion and the presbyter John, the disciples of the Lord, say. For I did not think that what was to be gotten from the books would profit me as much as what came from the living and abiding voice.

Eusebius, Ecclesiastical History 3.39.4[29]

Sometime earlier, Paul urged the Thessalonians to "stand firm and hold fast to the traditions (*paradoseis*) that you were taught (*edidachthēte*) by us, either by word of mouth or by our letter" (2 Thess 2:15). These traditions (paradoseis) were the firsthand apostolic interpretations of the Lord's proclamation. Thus, in the New Testament context, tradition in its positive sense means transmission and reception of the living preaching of the apostles. Paul asks the believers in Thessalonia to stay away from anyone who does not live "according to the tradition (paradosin) you received from us" (2 Thess 3:6): the tradition transmitted by Paul and other apostles is the only one genuine going back to the Lord; everything else is wrong. Hence, Paul's exhortation: "Hold to the standard of sound teaching (*logōn*) that you have heard from me, in the faith and love that are in Christ Jesus. Guard the good treasure (*parathēkēn*) entrusted to you, with the help of the Holy Spirit living in us" (2 Tim 1:13–14). 1 Cor 15 further specifies the Christological interpretation of the Old Testament as a crucial mark of this apostolic tradition to which Paul refers.[30]

Rule of Faith

The notion of "rule of faith" (Gk. *kanōn*[31] *pisteōs* or Latin *regula fidei*) as the norm of right interpretation of Scripture was born during the second-century disputes between mainstream Christians and Gnostics or other heretics.[32] The rule served as an expression and test of orthodoxy. The idea of orthodoxy arose through the efforts of heresiologists who set the boundaries between the early Christian Church and Judaism. They named each other "Judaizers" and *minim* (i.e., gentiles or Christians). In effect, their work was to eliminate the ambiguity of boundaries and to demarcate two distinct religions: Christianity and Judaism.[33] In the Christian camp, the heresiologists targeted nonmainstream Christians as well as pagans.

Following Alain Le Boulluec's perspective on orthodoxy and heresy as notions and not things, Daniel Boyarin considers orthodoxy and heresy as coeval. Boyarin's interpretation is different from the traditional account of Christian orthodoxy as a descending line originating in the teaching of Jesus and transmitted via the apostles to the bishops, with heresy viewed as a later encroachment upon the mainstream catholic tradition. On the other hand, the interpretation Boyarin draws from Le Boulluec also diverges from the well-known and controversial argument of Walter Bauer that heresy antedated orthodoxy.

Through the work of Justin Martyr, the word *hairesis*, "heresy," came to designate a group of people whose ideas and beliefs were considered "outside established or recognized tradition." The proximate goal of heresiology was to contour the "whatness" or identity of Christian faith. It is possible that Justin was not prompted by Jews or Gnostics to define certain teachings as heretical, but rather by a natural impulse to define the identity of the Christian teaching that he himself espoused. "It is no accident," remarks Boyarin, "that the alleged 'inventor of heresy' is also the author of 'one of the earliest texts [*Dialogue with Trypho*] which reflects a self-consciously independent Christianity,' or, as I would prefer to put the same point, one of the earliest texts that is self-consciously engaged in the production of an independent Christianity."[34]

Christianity introduced the notion of religion as is defined today, referring to a group of people related, not by geography or ethnicity, but rather by a set of *beliefs*. What is *Christianismos,* or "Christian"? Boyarin relates: "The vehicle to answer that question was, again for these Christians, orthodoxy and heresy. 'In' was to be defined by correct belief; 'out' by adherence via an alleged choice to false belief. This notion that identity is achieved and not given by birth, history, language, and geographical location was the novum that produced religion, having an impact, I suggest, on the whole semantic system of identities within the Mediterranean world."[35]

Quite similarly, Georges Florovsky asserts: "Tradition was in the Early Church, first of all, an hermeneutical principle and method. Scripture could be rightly and fully assessed and understood only in the light and in the context of the living Apostolic Tradition, which was an integral factor of Christian existence. . . . It was not a fixed core or complex of binding propositions, but rather an insight into the meaning and impact of the revelatory events, of the revelation of the 'God who acts.'"[36]

If, however, Tradition was not a "complex of binding propositions," but rather "insight" into the acts of God as witnessed by the Scriptures, nevertheless, as Frances M. Young notes, from the time of Irenaeus or even earlier the Church used "creed-like statements and confessions" as the "hermeneutical key to public reading of Scripture." The shift from scrolls to "notebooks" (codices) adopted by Christians during the second century c.e. exposed the Scripture to the "private piracy" or "private eso-teric interpretations of the heretics."[37] In response, the early Church ap-pealed to Tradition in order to uncover the "perspective" (*hypothesis*) and the "unifying purpose" (*skopos*) of the Scripture as a whole. As Irenaeus (*Against Heresies* 2.28.3)[38] put it, the goal of Tradition was to "perceive" (*aisthanomai*) "one harmonious melody" (*hen symphōnon melos*) (i.e., the inner harmony), "throughout the polyphony of [Scripture's] utterances" (*dia tēs tōn lexeōn polyphōnias*). The difference between mainstream or-thodox Christians and heretics was that the former, through this living Tradition, were able to look at the Scripture as a symphonic whole, while the latter employed isolated texts to support their teachings.[39]

For Irenaeus, the Christian Bible has its own hypothesis ("pers-pective"), identifiable with the "rule of faith" or the "rule of truth," which provides the proper Christological interpretation of the Scripture—rendering, in Irenaeus's below cited analogy, "the likeness of the king." In contrast, Irenaeus compares the heretics with cultured individuals who extracted verses from Homer out of context and try to put them together in a new narrative, the final product being a patchwork with an entirely new meaning, at odds with the original text:

> What simple-minded man, I ask, would not be led away by such verses as these to think that Homer actually framed them so with reference to the subject indicated? But he who is acquainted with the Homeric writings will recognize the verses indeed, but not the subject to which they are applied, as knowing that some of them were spoken of Ulysses, others of Hercules himself, others still of Priam, and others again of Menelaus and Agamemnon. But if he takes them and restores each of them to its proper position, he at once destroys the narrative in question. In like manner he also who retains unchangeable in his heart the rule of the truth which he received by means of baptism, will doubtless recognize the names, the expressions, and the parables taken from the Scriptures, but will by no means acknowledge the blasphemous use which these

men make of them. For, though he will acknowledge the gems, he
will certainly not receive the fox instead of the likeness of the king.
But when he has restored every one of the expressions quoted to its
proper position, and has fitted it to the body of the truth, he will lay
bare, and prove to be without any foundation, the figment of these
heretics.

Irenaeus, *Against Heresies* 1.9.4[40]

Commenting on the same passage, John Behr rightly notices, "According
to Irenaeus, his opponents have based their exegesis upon their own
'hypothesis', rather than that foretold by the prophets, taught by Christ
and delivered ('traditioned') by the apostles."[41]

In Frances M. Young's view, the "rule of faith" and the creed were
not mere summaries of the biblical narrative: "They provided, rather, the
proper reading of the beginning and the ending, the focus of the plot and
the relations of the principal characters, so enabling the 'middle' to be
heard in bits as meaningful. They provided the 'closure' which contemporary theory prefers to leave open. They articulated the essential hermeneutical key without which texts and community would disintegrate in
incoherence."[42] The "rule of faith" can be compared to a frame for a canvas
made of various scriptural texts. Interpreters can enjoy a great deal of liberty provided they pay attention to the framework.

Apostolic and Ecclesiastical Tradition

Thus far, we have mentioned only "apostolic tradition" and its immediate
sibling, the "rule of faith." Now a question is warranted: is apostolic tradition coterminous with what is labeled "ecclesiastical tradition"?

In the view of Oscar Cullmann,[43] there is a great gulf between these
two concepts. While Roman Catholics distinguish between "tradition"
(*traditio activa*), which is a function of the Church, and "traditions" (*tradi-
tiones passivae*)—namely, the formulae themselves—the Reformers speak
only of the former: "tradition" as a function of the Church. It must be
noted here, however, that no such neat scholastic distinction between
"tradition" and "traditions" obtains within Orthodoxy. As the life of the
Church herself, Tradition cannot be reduced to one aspect (i.e., ecclesiastical formulae), but rather encompasses various facets of this rich life:
doctrinal definitions, canons, liturgy, iconography, hymnology, ascetical
practices, and so on.

Oscar Cullmann argues against the Roman Catholic identification of the apostolic tradition with the ecclesiastical tradition by underscoring the uniqueness of the apostolic office. The apostles belong exclusively to the period of incarnation: they did not appoint other apostles, but bishops; the apostles bear a direct witness to Christ, the Church indirect; the postapostolic Church is led by bishops, not apostles. As a critique of Cullmann's insistence on the discontinuity between apostolic and ecclesiastical traditions one may adduce Clement of Alexandria. In his *Stromata*, Clement emphasizes the unity between "apostolic" and "ecclesiastic" with reference to "orthodoxy in doctrines." As Clement writes, "Our Gnostic[44] then alone, having grown old in the Scriptures, and maintaining apostolic and ecclesiastic orthodoxy in doctrines, lives most correctly in accordance with the gospel, and discovers the proofs, for which he may have made search (sent forth as he is by the Lord), from the Law and the Prophets. For the life of the Gnostic, in my view, is nothing but deeds and words corresponding to the tradition of the Lord" (*Stromata* 7.16).[45]

Similarly, in Florovsky's view, the two qualifications of church tradition, "apostolic" and "patristic" (or "ecclesiastical"), cannot be separated. The transition from "apostolic" to "patristic," from kērygma to *dogma*, was done by "an inner urge, an inner logic, an internal necessity" on the part of the Church for the purpose of a better articulation of the initial simple faith of the apostles. Florovsky concludes: "Indeed, the teaching of the fathers, and the dogma of the Church, are still the same 'simple message' which has been once delivered and deposited, once for ever, by the apostles. But now it is, as it were, properly and fully articulated. . . . Fathers are not only witnesses of the old faith, *testes antiquitatis*. They are rather witnesses of the true faith, *testes veritatis*."[46] In order to be kept alive in the Church, the apostolic tradition needs the patristic supplement. And, if I may add, the apostolic-patristic needs the creative neopatristic synthesis so dearly advocated by Florovsky. The unifying principle for all these phases (or better, *modi operandi*) is the Spirit alive and active in the Church during her journey (cf. John 14:26; 16:13).

One may still hear, however, Cullmann's persistent voice: "The written witness of the apostles is for us the living element which continually brings us anew face to face with Christ."[47] Yet as much as Cullmann insists on the direct eyewitness of the apostles—hence the unique value of the "apostolic" tradition—one should not forget that even this direct witness is not, as Cullmann intimates, a calque of Jesus's words and deeds. As any other human endeavor this eyewitness is an interpretation. And this eyewitness-interpretation as it comes to us has itself been "traditioned": a closer look to the Gospel of Matthew, for instance, will allow one to discern various layers of tradition. Thus, both apostolic and ecclesiastical traditions are interpretations of the same unique Christ-event.

For Cullmann, the mid-second century c.e. represents the boundary between the apostolic and postapostolic tradition. This coincides with the emergence of the "rule of faith" as a summary of the apostolic faith and the formulation of the apostolic canon. Nevertheless, as Florovsky reminds us, the Tradition remains always the same, mirroring in its definitions the apostolic witness:

> Not everything within the Church dates from apostolic times. This does not mean that something has been revealed which was "unknown" to the apostles; nor does it mean that what is of later date is less important and convincing. Everything was given and revealed fully from the beginning. On the day of Pentecost Revelation was completed, and will admit of no further completion till the Day of Judgment and its last fulfillment. Revelation has not been widened, and even knowledge has not increased. The Church knows Christ now no more than it knew him at the time of the apostles. But *it testifies of greater things*. In its definitions it always unchangeably describes the same thing, but in the unchanged image ever new features become visible. But it knows the truth not less and not otherwise than it knew it in time of old. The identity of experience is loyalty to tradition. Loyalty to tradition did not prevent the Fathers of the Church from "creating new names" (as St. Gregory Nazianzen says) when it was necessary for the protection of the unchangeable faith. All that was said later on, was said from catholic completeness and is of equal value and force with that which was pronounced in the beginning. And even now the experience of the Church has not been exhausted, but protected and fixed in dogma. But there is much of which the Church testifies not in a dogmatic, but in a liturgical, manner, in the symbolism of the sacramental ritual, in the imagery of prayers, and in the established yearly round of commemorations and festivals. Liturgical testimony is as valid as dogmatic testimony. The concreteness of symbols is sometimes even more vivid, clear, and expressive than any logical conceptions can be, as witness the image of the Lamb taking upon Himself the sins of the world.[48]

As one can see from the quoted passage, the apostolic tradition has found expression not only in the apostles' witness to the Christ-event, but also in the ecclesiastical tradition of the dogmas; and not only in these discursive modes of expression, but also in the polyphonic testimony of the liturgy. Later in this book, we shall consider some of the rich symbolic articulations of the liturgy, both aural (hymnographic) and visual (iconographic). These rather intuitive or poetical modes of interpretation remind us, as Florovsky notes, that not everything in the Tradition understood as Church's life and journey can be codified or dogmatically fixed. Yet for now, we must consider first the move toward codification of the Tradition.

Toward Codification of the Tradition

A first step toward a codification of Tradition was taken around mid-second century C.E. with the appearance of the "rule of faith," already covered in the previous section. This was the time when the idea of a norm was attached to Tradition.

The second really important movement toward codification of Tradition, but of a rather different kind, was Justinian's *Novella 131*. As Wolfhart Pannenberg observes:

The church and empire took a momentous step beyond this stage when they made a codification of dogmas legally binding, thus not merely presupposing their truth but establishing it. This kind of codification terminated and silenced the process of reception relative to official doctrinal promulgation. A move in this direction might be seen already in the 4th century. A climax came in 545 during the prolonged conflict over the validity of the Council of Chalcedon (451). In that year Justinian declared that the *dogmata* of the first four councils carried an authority equal to that of the holy Scriptures.[49]

Novella 131 issued by emperor Justinian in the year 545 C.E. reads:

Therefore We order that the sacred, ecclesiastical rules which were adopted and confirmed by the four Holy Councils, that is to say, that of the three hundred and eighteen bishops held at Nicea, that of the one hundred and fifty bishops held at Constantinople, the first one of Ephesus, where Nestorius was condemned, and the one assembled at Chalcedon, where Eutyches and Nestorius were anathematized, shall be considered as laws. We accept the dogmas of these four Councils as sacred writings, and observe their rules as legally effective.

Novella 131. Chapter I: Concerning Four Holy Councils[50]

Taking a closer look at this imperial document, one may accept up to a point the leveling of the *dogmata* with the sacred Scriptures.[51] One may also agree with emperor's theological decision on the orthodoxy of the first four ecumenical councils. However, one has to consider Justinian's attempt to legally codify religious statements (dogmata) as a fault. Behind the legal codification, there was a growing assumption that God's revelation in Jesus Christ could be fully encapsulated in formulae.

Along with this assumption the need for religious coercion was born. Aimed at harmony regarding the dogmata, religious coercion had fatal consequences, especially in the Western Church. As Pannenberg elaborates: "Religious coercion is an attempt to force consensus about the truth of dogma and in this way to establish the truth itself. Consensus, it is thought, can serve as a mark of truth because the universality of truth expresses itself in agreement of judgment. That agreement is then to be forcibly achieved by religious coercion. Yet only a consensus that arises free from any coercion can be advanced as a criterion of truth."[52] This kind of consensus "free from any coercion" may be detected in the formula of Vincent of Lerins (fifth century C.E.), *curandum est, ut id teneamus quod ubique, quod semper, quod ab omnibus creditus est,* "What is believed everywhere, at all times, by everyone is what it should be believed." Thus, a dogma or doctrine belongs to the Church only when it is embraced everywhere, at all times, and by all believers.[53] Vincent distinguishes between content and formulation. If the latter may change, the former must remain unchanged. However, as Pannenberg also points out, "Holding to the faith content in spite of variations in its formulation seems to demand an additional authority by which to test and decide the issue."[54]

Especially in the East, this "additional authority" has always been the "people of God" (laos tou Theou), which in harmony with their bishops assembled in synod discern the dogmata of the Church. A *theologoumenon* (respected theological opinion) that emerged *within the Church* is discussed by bishops gathered in a synod. If approved by the synod as dogma it goes back to the Church. If the people of God embrace that dogma, it is accepted as an authentic expression of church tradition, or the *ekklēsiastikon phronēma* ("ecclesiastical mindset"). The truth does not become a dogma, unless it has been experienced and certified from within the Church. For a truth to become a dogma of the Church, it must necessarily go through the communion of the Church in her totality, and not only through a few people—be they theologians in the current (academic) sense, bishops, or charismatic ascetics. The principle of *koinonia* ("communion") is observed when the people of God receive and accept whatever was decided in council. Thus, the Church as a whole is involved in formulating and accepting her dogmata.

Theodore G. Stylianopoulos notices that in the East, the "traditionalist" period (sixth through eighteenth centuries) is characterized by "an archaizing loyalty to the church fathers and a maximalist devotion to tradition."[55] Even a great mind like Maximus the Confessor (ca. 580–662 C.E.) suggested the true exegetes should rely on the God-inspired fathers more than on their acumen. So high was the interpretive authority of the "fathers" that canon 19 of the Council of Trullo (692 C.E.) prohibited new interpretations of Scripture besides the patristic ones, in preaching. Nevertheless, this period did not lack entirely in great and creative writers. One may mention here two: Symeon the New Theologian (tenth century) and Kosmas Aitolos (eighteenth century), both of whom made fresh and direct use of the Scripture without being carried away by the strong torrent of a more codified and standardized tradition.

The seventeenth century[56] represents a key moment in the codification of Tradition. Through the doctrinal confessions of Dositheos of Jerusalem and Peter Mogila, and the conciliar decisions of local councils of Constantinople (1638) and Jerusalem (1672), Scripture was almost completely subordinated to ecclesiastical authority. In the same direction, the wider canon (including the anaginōskomena books)[57] was embraced while the private reading of Scripture by faithful was forbidden.[58] This new development was based on notions such as Church's "infallibility" and the theory of "two sources" of revelation, "Scripture and Tradition." These notions are not traditionally Eastern Orthodox but rather Roman Catholic in their origin.[59] As John A. McGuckin notes, "tradition, as it came to be understood in the later West, was reduced to being a matter of the 'sources of authority' for Christian faith. . . . This was a doctrine that even affected some Orthodox theologians in the eighteenth to nineteenth centuries, though in reality it is not so much true to Orthodoxy as redolent of Latin scholasticism."[60]

Quite apart from later Western influence, however, some tendency toward uniformity and codification can be detected early on, particularly when contrasted with the fluidity of religious opinions emblematic of Judaism. According to Daniel Boyarin, "'Judaism(s)' and 'Christianit(ies)' remained intertwined well past the first half of the second century until Rabbinic Judaism."[61] Both religions, orthodox Christianity and rabbinic Judaism, at the end of Late Antiquity produced their defining books or collections (i.e., a collection of church fathers and the Babylonian Talmud). Boyarin distinguishes between these two textual collections along the following lines: Patristic literature is a collection of tracts by named authors, while the Talmud is anonymous; it is a sacrilege for the Talmud to assign authors to its constitutive parts. "Talmud is a single text with many authors (or, rather, no author). The very idea of an author seems anathema to the Babylonian Talmud."[62] Further, while the church fathers seek *homonoia* (same mindset—harmony—thus tending toward reductionism in their dealings with Scripture, which in its deep textuality is stubbornly polyvalent),[63] the Talmud "seems to revel in the irresolution of disagreements among its contending speakers without an authorial voice even to tell us who is right and who is wrong."[64] Thus *polynoia* (manifold mindset) is the main characteristic of the Talmudic literature. Where the ideal of the Christian interpreters was a kind of monody, its many authored texts speaking with one voice, the ideal of the Babylonian Talmud was of one many-voiced text with no author. At a time when dialectic was being increasingly demonized by Christian orthodox writers, Talmudic narrators, using the same tropes and topoi—for instance, of dialecticians as "shield-bearers"—were raising forever unresolved dialectics to the highest level of religious discourse.[65]

Christian tradition was moving slowly but steadily from the "life of the Church" to "textuality," or to the ideal of a single "book," as in Augustine's dream (*Against Julian* 2.10.37) imagining all the bishops from the East and West gathered, not in one place, which would require traveling, but rather in a book that could itself travel to everyone. Boyarin comments on Augustine's musing:

This citation [Augustine's dream], I think, is sufficient to evoke the fascinating similarity of the cultural world that produced the Babylonian Talmud, also a collection of the sayings of many "excellent" rabbis over centuries and in different places made into a book that travels in space and time to the faithful. And this powerful similarity also points up the enormous difference in the mode of discourse of the two new books: one voice versus many voices, but both, I warrant, in support of the "same" kind of project, the production of a bounded, concerted orthodox "religion."[66]

The same tendency toward the textualization of Tradition is seen in the Christian East. As Virginia Burrus observes, "In Athanasius's texts—in his sensitivity to 'textuality' itself—we sense something of what Richard Lim describes as a late-antique trend toward a 'growing reliance on textual authority.'"[67] The tendency toward textualization was occasioned by the First Ecumenical Council held at Nicaea in 325 C.E. Unlike other councils, Nicaea left no *acta*. Burrus suggests that Athanasius, based on extant materials, put in writing ex post facto the acta of the Council of Nicaea. In doing so, Athanasius created a model for the other councils to produce their own acta. Moreover, Athanasius contributed to future Christian textual practices including the collection of the "church fathers," considered as the book of the books.[68]

Recent Western scholarship commonly sets the beginning of the codification of "church fathers" in the fifth–sixth century when Christians were looking backward to the thoughts of earlier "fathers" as genuine witnesses to Christian truth.[69] The concept of "select fathers" was then born.[70] Much later, the eighteenth century—the age of the encyclopedists—brought to fruition the *Philokalia* of Nicodemus, a collection of select treatises from a millennium of church fathers pertaining to prayer and the ascetic life, with deep implications for Eastern Orthodox hermeneutics.[71]

Components of the Tradition

Due to the process of codification one may speak today of certain definite "components" of the Tradition. Unlike Western Christianity replete with creedal statements, encyclicals and other official documents carrying the authority of various commissions of experts and final hierarchical approval, Eastern Orthodox Christianity still exhibits a certain freedom, flexibility, and open-endedness in theological expression. This situation is due partly to the character of Tradition understood as an unfolding journey or life of the Church, in spite of all the Western influences beginning with the Counter-Reformation period. The emphasis of Eastern Orthodoxy has tended to be more on worship and praxis than elaborate scholastic articulations of its faith. This distinct point must not be too exaggerated, however. Orthodox theology is at once *apophatic*, resistant to formulations while centered in worship, and *kataphatic*, proclamatory—concerned for accurate expression of the essential points of doctrine. In other words, Orthodox theology is "simultaneously formal and charismatic,"[72] reflecting a sense of Tradition that is both the life of the Church and the deposit of faith "once given to the saints."

If an Orthodox has to answer a catechism-like question such as, "What are the components of Tradition that should be understood as constituting the deposit of faith?" the response would be something like this. Holy Tradition consists of (but is never limited or reducible to) the following:

1. Scripture (Old and New Testaments)
2. Liturgy and ritual practices (symbols, hymns, homilies)
3. Creeds and professions (*ektheseis*) of the ecumenical councils
4. Lives of the saints
5. Patristic writings including biblical commentaries
6. Lives, sayings, and teachings of desert fathers, ascetics, and saints
7. Iconography
8. Symbolic books[73]

These items listed above are not only components of Tradition but also sources of authority, the bulwarks in Eastern Orthodoxy.

If Tradition is the life of the Church and the work of the Church is ordered toward communion, Tradition is unavoidably liturgical. "'Liturgy,' in the wide and comprehensive sense of the word," remarks Georges Florovsky,

> was the first and initial layer in the Tradition of the Church, and the argument from the *lex orandi* [Rule of worship] was persistently used in discussion already by the end of the Second century. The Worship of the Church was a solemn proclamation of her Faith. The baptismal invocation of the Name was probably the earliest Trinitarian formula, as the Eucharist was the primary witness to the mystery of Redemption, in all its fullness. The New Testament itself came to existence, as a "Scripture," in the Worshipping Church. And Scripture was read first in the context of worship and meditation.[74]

At the very heart and center of the Tradition is to be found the Scripture; yet the first context of Scripture is the liturgy.

The life of the Church, however, cannot be reduced to Scripture and liturgy. Throughout her history, needs and crises arise for the Church, which require consultation. The purpose of the first, pre-Nicene councils, was to preserve the unity of the Church. The authority of these councils was granted by their conformity with the apostolic tradition. In fact, everything in the Church—tradition, bishops, councils, interpretation of Scripture—should be traced back to the apostolic tradition in the quest for authenticity and authority.

The Second Ecumenical Council in Constantinople (381 C.E.) accentuated the hermeneutical role of the conciliar authority of the Church. Conciliar authority could go beyond exegetical work and rely heavily on living Tradition. The adoption of the nonbiblical Athanasian term *homoousios*, "of the same essence," at the First Ecumenical Council in Nicaea (325 C.E.)[75] and its insertion in the Nicene-Constantinopolitan creed conveyed the Church's message that Tradition seeking the skopos (unifying purpose) of Scripture, rather than a literalist and detailed interpretation of the text, should have the last word, as the highest authority when judging between correct and erroneous interpretation, between orthodoxy and heresy.[76]

There has been no clear and consistent theory of conciliar authority throughout the centuries of tradition, especially in the era of the imperial ecumenical councils of the first millennium. As Georges Florovsky pointed out,

> Councils were never regarded as a canonical institution, but rather as occasional *charismatic events*. . . . And no council was accepted as valid in advance . . . those councils which were actually recognized as "Ecumenical," in the sense of their binding and infallible authority, were recognized, immediately or after a delay, not because of their formal *canonical* competence, but because of their *charismatic* character: under the guidance of the Holy Spirit they have witnessed to the Truth, in conformity with the Scripture as handed down in Apostolic Tradition. . . . there was *no theory*. There was simply an *insight* into the matters of faith.[77]

Nevertheless, in spite of this lack of any clearly biding theory of councils themselves, these insights articulated by the councils universally accepted by the Eastern Orthodox Church are regarded as binding and adequate expressions of Orthodox tradition. Here Michael Prokurat spells out an important truth: "All ('Chalcedonian') Orthodox Churches look to the Seven Ecumenical Councils, and related local councils, as definitive of Holy Tradition, as a statement of faith over time, as a norm of 'orthopraxy,' etc.; and the decisions of these Councils are very much alive today, from the Nicene-Constantinopolitan Creed to iconography."[78]

Centrality of Scripture within Tradition
Biblical Authority

As John Breck notices, "The Bible is a living book as well as a book about life. If it is read appropriately, it can become in Christian experience a vehicle for conveying life-giving knowledge of God. Yet through the working of the Holy Spirit in the interplay between text and reader, it can become as well a medium for communion with the God who reveals himself in and through it."[79] Reading the Scripture is not a simple reading; it is in fact a dialogue initiated by Christ with us through this medium of "God's breathing" (1 Tim 3:16).[80] The fathers of the Church were quite clear about this. In the words of Jerome, "Do you pray? You speak to the Bridegroom. Do you read? He speaks to you" (*Letters* 22.25).[81]

Although the concept of "biblical authority"[82] is a modern construal, the "centrality of Scripture" has always been a tenet of Christian theology, with ramifications in other areas of theological discourse such as inspiration, revelation, canonization, interpretation, and the unfolding work of the Spirit. "Even if a dead person rises," wrote John Chrysostom, "even if an angel descends from heaven, the Scriptures are more worthy of belief than any of them. For the Master of the angels, the Lord of the dead and the living, himself has given the Scriptures their authority" (*Fourth Sermon on Lazarus and the Rich Man*).[83] From an Eastern Orthodox perspective, the authority of the Bible is not reduced to a mere proclamation, but involves a great variety of uses of Scripture: liturgical, homiletical, catechetical, doctrinal, spiritual, and academic.

In his concise and fine contribution "Biblical Authority in Eastern Orthodoxy,"[84] Theodore G. Stylianopoulos reviews the theme of biblical authority in Eastern Orthodoxy under three periods: (1) classical period (first–fifth centuries); (2) traditionalist period (sixth–eighteenth centuries); and (3) modern period (nineteenth–twentieth centuries).

During the classical period, the first challenge was the "Christological appropriation" of the Hebrew Scriptures by the early Church. The Law lost its centrality for the Christ-event that became, in its place, the hermeneutical key to scriptural interpretation. Paul (Gal 3:19–26), Matthew (Matt 5:17–18), the author of Hebrews (Heb 7:18–19), and the author of the *Epistle of Barnabas* (*Barnabas* 9.4) tried to respond to the question: How is the new revelation related to the Jewish Scripture? In the Christological hermeneutical response given by second-century mainstream Christianity to Gnostic groups, Jewish Scripture preserved its authoritative status as the arbiter of truth. Justin Martyr is perhaps the most illustrative case of second-century Christological interpretation of Old Testament prophecies.

Probably the most logical explanation why Scripture and not theological formulae should be placed at the center of Church's life is stated by Georges Florovsky. As he writes: "Theology witnesses back to the revelation. It witnesses in diverse manners: in creeds, in dogmas, in sacred rites and symbols. But in a sense Scripture itself is the primary response, or rather Scripture itself is at once both the Word of God and the human response—the Word of God mediated through the faithful response of man."[85] Scripture takes precedence over theology because while the former contains both revelation and interpretation, the latter is narrower, being only interpretation. Florovsky's remark fits quite well with Gregory of Nyssa's description of Scripture as being the "arbiter" of doctrinal debates, as quoted in the epigraph of this chapter.

From an Eastern Orthodox perspective, Scripture, as God's word dressed in human words, should always be the arbiter of truth in the Church's formulation and acceptance of dogmatic definitions. Jaroslav Pelikan underscores well Florovsky's statement cited above that the Word of God found in the Scripture makes this collection of sacred texts unique in its centrality among other components of the Holy Tradition: "Christian doctrine also proved again and again that it could not live by philosophy alone, but had to turn to the word of God in the Old and New Testament."[86] Such primacy of the Scripture means also that, as Theodore G. Stylianopoulos has well stated,

> the Church does not possess the Bible in such a way that it can do whatever it pleases with it, for example through virtual neglect or excessive allegorisation. . . . In its canonical status, scripture occupies the primacy among the Church's traditions. . . . The Bible as the supreme record of revelation is the indisputable norm of the Church's faith and practice. . . . The neglect of the Bible and the

silencing of its prophetic witness are inimical to the Church's evangelical vibrancy and sense of mission in the world. . . . The Church
in every generation is called to maintain the primacy and centrality
of the Bible in its life, always attentive, repentant and obedient to
God's word.[87]

Despite a growing importance accorded to a Tradition more and more
codified and turned into a "deposit of faith," Scripture has always maintained its centrality in the deep fabric of Eastern Orthodoxy, even though
most of the time camouflaged in various components of Tradition.[88] Here
is John of Damascus's description of Scripture as a "very fair garden" dis-
playing "varied sounds":

> All Scripture, then, is *given by inspiration of God is also assuredly*
> *profitable* [1 Tim 3:16]. Wherefore to search the Scriptures is a work
> most fair and most profitable for souls. For just as the tree planted
> by the channels of waters, so also the soul watered by the divine
> Scripture is enriched and gives fruit in its season [Ps 1:3], I mean,
> orthodox belief, and is adorned with evergreen leafage, I mean,
> actions pleasing to God. . . . Wherefore let us knock at the very fair
> garden of the Scriptures, so fragrant and sweet and blooming, with
> its varied sounds of spiritual and divinely-inspired birds ringing all
> round our ears, laying hold of our hearts, comforting the mourner,
> pacifying the angry and filling him with joy everlasting. . . . But
> let us not knock carelessly but rather zealously and constantly: lest
> knocking we grow weary. For thus it will be opened to us. If we
> read once or twice and do not understand what we read, let us not
> grow weary, but let us persist, let us talk much, let us enquire. . . .
> Let us draw of the fountain of the garden perennial and purest
> waters springing into life eternal [John 4:14]. Here let us luxuri-
> ate, let us revel insatiate: for the Scriptures possess inexhaustible
> grace.
>   John of Damascus, *An Exact Exposition of the Orthodox Faith* 4.17[89]

Interplay of Scripture and Tradition

In matters of faith, Scripture has been considered always the "arbiter" and
the "sentence of truth" (Gregory of Nyssa). Its preeminence has never been

a matter of debate in Eastern Orthodoxy. The biblical authority, to invoke this modern concept, has always been accepted. Nevertheless, given the early confrontations of mainstream orthodoxy with heresies and Judaism (more precisely, the Judaizers) on hermeneutical grounds, the primary concern of the Church was to safeguard its unity in the proclamation of the gospel. To this end, the interpretation of Scripture was placed under the guidance of the Church. Thus, orthodox interpreters, like good actors, have to follow their director's guidelines.

One can hardly imagine a believer in the fourth or fifth century, at the climax of the so-called golden age of the church fathers, reading the Scripture at home from Genesis to Revelation. Information on the copying process in the time of Constantine is, however, scant. Obviously the fifty copies of the Bible commissioned by the emperor were destined for church (not individual) use. For believers, the main access to the Bible was through Tradition—the multifaceted manifestation of church life through the aural, visual, and textual media of liturgy, iconography, preaching, commentaries, and ascetic writings.[90] "To treat the Bible in isolation from the tradition of the church, as it was located in the ancient rule of faith, baptismal confessions, and conciliar creeds, would have been incomprehensible to the Christian pastors and thinkers of the patristic age."[91]

For instance, the creeds were vehicles that preserved the scriptural lore at the aural level. Cyril of Jerusalem reports that in his time not many had the leisure and learning to read and understand the Christian Scripture; the creeds were summaries of faith based on Scripture that could be memorized and recited.[92] Each article of the Jerusalem Creed, as Cyril expounds them, is so thoroughly grounded in biblical authority that, as the bishop insists, his hearers must not accept anything without reference to the Sacred Scriptures: "Even to me, who tell you these things, give not absolute credence, unless you receive the proof of the things which I announce from the Divine Scriptures. For this salvation which we believe depends not on ingenious reasoning, but on demonstration of the Holy Scriptures" (*Lecture 4* 17).[93] Cyril's intention was to assure the catechumens that nothing in the Jerusalem Creed was contrary to the biblical message.[94] Being schooled in the creed was the first step not only in learning what the Bible meant but also in preparing these candidates to read the Bible with insight.[95]

The church fathers understood Scripture and Tradition in reciprocal, complementary terms. Nonetheless, Scripture had a preeminence of place. Its central position in the Church's life and Tradition has never been contested. Yet, out of pastoral concern, the church fathers always insisted that Scripture should not be taken out of Church's traditional proclamation and worship. At the same time, the Tradition was not thought as an addition to the Scripture or a secondary revelatory source.[96] As Georges Florovsky soberly underlines: "We cannot assert that Scripture is self-sufficient; and this not because it is incomplete, or inexact, or has any defects, but because Scripture in its very essence does not lay claim to self-sufficiency. We can say that Scripture is a God-inspired scheme or image (*eikon*) of truth, but not truth itself. . . . If we declare Scripture to be self-sufficient, we only expose it to subjective, arbitrary interpretation, thus cutting it away from its sacred source."[97]

The centrality of Scripture within the church tradition so characteristic of Eastern Orthodoxy has nothing in common with the Protestant dictum of sola scriptura. As Pannenberg shows, sola scriptura was directed against the Roman Catholic teaching that the *salutaris veritas* (truth of salvation) lies in both "written books" (Scripture) and "nonwritten traditions" (Tradition). According to the Roman Catholic teaching, biblical statements are supplemented by later tradition that validates the Church's dogmas, going beyond the testimony of Scripture. However, the Second Vatican Council revised this teaching by underscoring the unity between Scripture and Tradition and defining the Scripture as the source and norm of the Church's doctrine and piety.[98]

Tradition cannot add anything essential to Scripture. What the Tradition can do is to provide the lens for reading Scripture in its canonical intentionality. Tradition represents the Church's unfolding life under the guidance of the Spirit. And the Church is the first stage of God's ongoing self-disclosure to humanity. There is a natural interrelation between Scripture, Church, and Tradition. That is why, as Florovsky rightly states, "Real interpretation of Scripture is Church preaching, is tradition."[99]

One may mention also that it was in response to the Protestant sola scriptura teaching that the Council of Trent in 1545 formulated the doctrine of "two sources," Scripture and Tradition, in juxtaposition and contrast. This doctrine exercised a great influence on Orthodox theology and hermeneutics. During the seventeenth century, Protestant theology absolutized the Scripture as the unique and supreme arbiter of truth. In response, the Roman Catholic and to a certain degree also Eastern Orthodox theologians reacted by overemphasizing church tradition as the preeminent criterion of truth.

One of the most insightful definitions of Tradition from a recent Eastern Orthodox authority is found in the 1976 *Moscow Agreed Statement*.[100] As the statement clarifies, Tradition is the "entire life of the Church in the Holy Spirit," expressed in doctrine, worship, canonical discipline, and spiritual life. With its various expressions, Tradition remains always the "single and indivisible life of the Church." And the statement goes on underlying the "supreme importance" of the "dogmatic" expression of Tradition that remains essentially unchangeable, even though its formulations are adjustable. New terminological usages should be tested by Scripture and the dogmatic definitions of the ecumenical councils. The *Moscow Agreed Statement* also speaks of certain "liturgical and canonical expressions of tradition" which remain unchangeable due to the fact that they "embody the unchangeable truth of divine revelation and respond to the unchanging needs of mankind." The centrality of both Scripture and Holy Tradition is affirmed: "The Church cannot define dogmas which are not grounded both in Holy Scripture and in Holy Tradition, but has the power, particularly in Ecumenical Councils, to formulate the truths of the faith more exactly and precisely when the needs of the Church require it." As Kallistos Ware well notices, Tradition according to *Moscow Agreed Statement* is changeless in its "inner essence" but changing in its "outward formulations." Tradition is "dynamic and creative, not static and inert." "Tradition is a principle of continuity, and yet equally is a principle of growth and regeneration."[101]

Notably, the *Moscow Agreed Statement* defines Tradition as "life of the church in the Holy Spirit," thus differing from Vladimir Lossky's definition, "the life of the Holy Spirit in the church." While the latter definition restrains the life-giving work of the Holy Spirit to church's confines, the former views the Church as moving under or in the Holy Spirit whose activity cannot be limited by time or space. "We confess that the tradition of the Church is a living one in which the Spirit continues his work of maintaining the true witness to the Revelation of God, the faith once delivered to the saints" (*Moscow Agreed Statement*, Part Three, paragraph 13).[102]

Tradition as the life of the Church in history is also a journey. It is a journey of the entire Church, hierarchy and people, as the extended body of the exalted Lord, where the Holy Spirit is the protector, the guide, and the mediator of God's unfolding revelation through "words, acts, and symbols."[103] Scripture is the heart of this moving organism or living body that sets and keeps everything in motion, the heart pumping blood with nutrients to all the members of the body. The Spirit impregnates the body with life. Tradition is the journey of the enlivened body of the church toward the *eschaton* (end of time). It is a journey in which the whole Trinity is involved: the Father in his unfolding revelation, Christ the Good Samaritan journeying with and saving his people, the Spirit vivifying the body and leading it according to God's will through Church's sacraments. Tradition is the journey of the exalted Lord Jesus with his disciples (as promised in Matt 28:20), protected and led by the Holy Spirit (John 14:26; 16:13). With this understanding, Eastern Orthodoxy does not absolutize the Church, nor does it dare it to circumscribe the inscrutable Spirit of God to a preconceived framework, whether of Tradition or Scripture.

Regarding the relation between Scripture and Tradition in Eastern Orthodoxy, the *Moscow Agreed Statement* (3.9) states, "Any disjunction between Scripture and Tradition such as would treat them as two separate 'sources of revelation' must be rejected. The two are correlative. We affirm (1) that Scripture is the main criterion whereby the Church tests traditions whether they are truly part of the Holy Tradition or not; (2) that Holy Tradition completes Holy Scripture in the sense that it safeguards the integrity of the biblical message."[104] As Kallistos Ware points out, the wording of the *Statement* represents a shift from the terminology of Metropolitan Philaret (Drozdov) of Moscow (1782–1867) that Scripture "*is* the Word of God." Rather, the *Statement* prefers to say that Scripture "*expresses* the Word of God." Ware concludes: "The Scriptures cannot be identified unconditionally with the uncreated Word of God."[105]

A few observations here are warranted. The binomial "Scripture and Tradition" used by the *Statement* is more Roman Catholic than Eastern Orthodox in tenor. To quote John Breck: "Orthodoxy sees the relationship between the two in a way that can be described not as Scripture *or* Tradition, or Scripture *and* Tradition, but Scripture *in* Tradition. This is because Scripture is Tradition, in the sense that the New Testament writings are a part of Tradition and constitute its normative element. Those writings came forth from the Church's life and proclamation and they have continued through the ages to be measure, rule or 'canon' of Christian faith."[106] I might slightly alter Breck's phrase by saying that Scripture *within* the Holy Tradition fits quite well the Eastern Orthodox view on Tradition understood primarily as the very life of the Church in the Spirit. *Within* more accurately than *in* intimates that the Holy Tradition or the unfolding life of the Church led by the Holy Spirit is thoroughly imbued with Scripture. In other words, Scripture is to be found not only *in* one place, but everywhere *within* Tradition. As Kallistos Ware remarks, "Tradition is not something 'added' to the Scripture. Tradition includes Scripture, and Scripture exists within Tradition."[107]

Scriptural authority is interrelated with Tradition and the life of the community. The sacred text creates and nurtures community while the latter interprets the former as part of its unfolding life. In the words of Frances M. Young,

> for those who accept scriptural authority, the world of the text gives meaning to the world outside the text. Conversely, the world out-side the text enables the meaning inside the text to be discerned. We are not talking about "eisegesis" so much as the inevitable pro-cess of hermeneutics. An authoritative text is understood to refer to the world in which people live, and so its meaning is bound to be received or contested in the light of the plausibility structures of the culture which receives the text.[108]

For a better understanding of the Orthodox view on the relationship be-tween Scripture and Tradition, I propose the following analogy: Scripture as a textbook and Tradition as a set of explanatory handouts.

Scripture, most especially the Old Testament, may be compared to a daring and untamable textbook. Holy Tradition in all its avatars—conciliar statements, writings of church fathers, liturgy, iconography, ascetic teaching—functions as guiding handouts of the textbook. Following this analogy, one may note a certain complementarity or reciprocity. Handouts aim to summarize and explain the salient points of a textbook. Similarly, Tradition, based on Scripture, complements the latter by condensing and illuminating its content. Nevertheless, the handouts, however complete and clear they may appear, will never be able to exhaustively elucidate all the angles of scriptural trove or provide an all-encompassing and self-sufficient summary of Holy Writ. The handouts do necessarily depend on a textbook and they are always in state of revision and improvement. If the latter to a certain degree can stand by itself, the handouts always need the textbook as their irreducible point of departure and reference.

Thus, one may speak of the centrality of Scripture. Scripture is central not only because it is the basis for all the further handouts, namely, the manifestations or compartments of Tradition. The centrality of Scripture consists in its very nature, its "untamable" character. The "handouts" of Tradition are counterparts to an unbridled textbook. Of course, there are "sections" of the Tradition that come closer to Scripture in their untamable depths. For instance, in some contrast with the discursive vein of conciliar statements and most patristic commentaries, iconography and hymnography may be regarded as the most flexible, creative, and poetical expression of church tradition. Yet the truth remains that there are two rhetorical tendencies, one of Scripture and one of Tradition. The rhetorical mode of Scripture is based on ambiguities, apparently contrasting statements, and anecdotic language, whereas the rhetoric of Tradition has often tended toward reductive organizational schemes and precise definitions.

In contrast with Tradition's greater tendency to define, Scripture has invariably remained the same untamed, and untamable, source of wonder. It does not explain so much as offer a lavish array of ways of thinking and doing. Scripture is an open textbook, an endless reservoir of wisdom in the making, at times posing more questions than answers. Along with R. W. L. Moberly, we may characterize the relationship between Scripture and Tradition observed here in these ruminations in terms of a "hermeneutical dialectic of biblical text and post-biblical faith."[109] The Church has been formed and informed by the Scripture since her inception. It is the continuous responsibility of the Church to interact with the sacred text in order to keep the Tradition always alive.

PART II

Interpretation

5

Discursive

The whole divinely inspired Scripture may be likened, because of its obscurity, to many locked rooms in one house. By each room is placed a key, but not the one that corresponds to it, so that the keys are scattered about besides the rooms, none of them matching the room by which it is placed. It is a difficult task to find the keys and match them to the rooms that they can open.

ORIGEN, Philocalia 2.3: On Psalm I

GIVEN THE OUTSTANDING number of fine monographs and studies on patristic exegesis of the Bible,[1] the scope of this chapter is restrained to only a few sketchy remarks on this vast topic that have significant import throughout my work.[2]

At the present time, there is still a seemingly impassable gulf between patristic hermeneutics and historical-critical methods. In a "neopatristic" approach (Florovsky), some kind of synthesis between ancient and modern modes of biblical interpretation is a must for any Orthodox biblical scholar who takes seriously the incarnational model for a sound exegesis aimed at encountering the Word of God dressed in human garments. Hence, the great challenge for any Orthodox student of the Bible is to strike a balance between the contributions of modern historical criticism seeking to describe accurately the various human garments, and the path of insight found in patristic soundings of the Word of God "who conceals himself" (Isa 45:15).

Not a few issues pertaining to patristic exegesis may be treated under the rubric of Tradition. For instance, the centrality of Scripture within the Tradition and the patristic evidence shedding light on the intricate relation between Scripture and the components of a Tradition ever moving toward codification were discussed in detail.[3] There is no need here to reiterate what was already said.

The contribution of the church fathers with regard to the Scripture was basically threefold. First, they "defined" the canon. In the East, the patristic handling of the biblical canon was quite flexible and diverse, hence its ongoing open-endedness in the Eastern Orthodoxy.[4] Second, the fathers drew the doctrinal teachings of the Church—Christology, trinitarian theology, and so on—from the Scripture and corroborated them in their own theological works or conciliar statements. Third, as biblical interpreters, they produced substantial theological and spiritual works with a tremendous pastoral applicability. This ubiquitous emphasis on pastoral application makes patristic exegesis to a certain degree unique within the concert of other ancient and modern methods of interpretation. Nowhere else have the ancient or modern interpreters proven to be as eager as these church fathers to explicate the text for the theological, spiritual, and moral nourishment of their communities.

The last of these three contributions constitutes the topic of the present chapter. One may signal out already that the excess of a high allegorization of biblical texts, while underestimating or even eschewing historical and literary contexts, represents probably one of the obvious downsides of patristic interpretation as a whole. Having said this, it would be an irremediable mistake to discard the entire interpretive contribution of the church fathers based on this shortcoming while overlooking the profound theological and spiritual-pastoral import of their interpretive labor.

Assumptions of Patristic Exegesis

According to Anthony Thiselton, theoretical hermeneutics "entails critical reflection on the basis, nature and goals of reading, interpreting and understanding communicative acts and processes."[5] One should distinguish between the modern theoretical discipline of hermeneutics founded by Friedrich Schleiermacher in the nineteenth century and hermeneutics as the very act of interpretation.[6] Along the lines of the latter, Garret Green has remarked, "theological hermeneutics began in the Garden of Eden, as any careful observer of the serpent, that subtle hermeneut of suspicion, will at once recognize."[7]

Hermeneutical preoccupations at the level of theoretical reflection can be, however, also detected in the Christian Bible. For instance, there is the two-way principle found in Luke 24:27, 32—that texts can explain present events and the latter can illuminate old texts. Similarly, there is Paul's insistence on Christ as the hermeneutical key to read the Jewish Scriptures (2 Cor 3:15–16). Sophisticated hermeneutical reflections are found already in two of the Church's earliest great theologians, Origen (*De principiis* 4.1) and Irenaeus (*Against Heresies* 1.8.1).[8]

Concerted hermeneutical reflection as a quasi-philosophical or theological discipline is, however, a modern development triggered especially by questions associated with the historical self-consciousness of the Enlightenment and nineteenth-century historicism. Given the relative paucity of explicit textual evidence on how the church fathers reflected on their own ways of interpreting Scripture, one may want to reconstruct a tentative list of hermeneutical assumptions or principles that guided their exegesis of the sacred text.

In his collection of ancient interpretations on Torah, James L. Kugel delineates four assumptions that both ancient Jewish and Christian commentators observed in their interpretive activity.[9] What follows is a brief summary of Kugel's remarks on the four assumptions of the ancient interpreters, along with my own comments.[10]

The Bible Is Cryptic

One of the commonalities between ancient Jewish and Christian interpreters was that they both looked at the Scripture as to a cryptic, codified document. In other words, the true meaning is hidden beyond what is said on the surface of the text. The main role of the interpreter is to decipher that hidden meaning. Thus, for the ancient Christian interpreters, Abel murdered by his brother is not simply the first human victim, but rather a foreshadowing of Christ, innocence being the hermeneutical bridge between the two figures separated by time. Gradually, the need for specially trained interpreters developed. Thus, trained interpreters, able to "lead"[11] their audience (hearers or readers) to the deep meaning of the sacred text, came to be held in high esteem. Hence, the authority given to these interpreters placed them sometimes in juxtaposition to the very text itself.

The Bible Is Relevant

The Bible was always regarded as a book of instruction (1 Cor 10:11). This didactic character makes the Bible a work of outstanding relevance for its readers. Unlike other samples of ancient literature (e.g., the Babylonian epic of creation *Enuma elish*), the Bible more or less clearly invites its readers to take an attitude, to follow its precepts, to model their lives according to the good examples put forward. Those beautiful hymns dedicated to Ishtar had no afterlife, while David's Psalms have been continuously recited in synagogue and church liturgy. Certainly, through the work of ancient interpreters the relevance of Scripture was significantly promoted. Thus, figures belonging initially to Israel's history (e.g., Abraham, Jacob, Moses, David) became, through the pen of ancient Jewish and Christian interpreters, universal models to be followed, or else foreshadowings of persons and realities that have already come into being or yet to come.

A similar situation obtained with the old prophecies. Interpreters read these prophecies as addressing their own time. For instance, Qumran yielded a number of *pesharim* (inter alia, the *pesher*-fragments on Hosea and Habakkuk), "actualized interpretations," that show the Essenes' preoccupation with keeping the old Hebrew prophecies relevant for their time. In these pesharim, Hosea, Habakkuk, and others were depicted as referring to a Palestine occupied by Roman troops, a situation never foreseen by those prophets in their days. Similarly, the New Testament authors (most especially in Matthew and Hebrews) made many prophetic texts actual and relevant by using them in relation with Jesus's life and work. This Christological relevance of the old prophecies was consistently maintained and further developed by the work of the patristic interpreters who were assiduously searching the Old Testament for typologies.

The Bible Is Perfectly Harmonious

The belief in the perfectly harmonious fabric of Scripture means that there is no mistake in the Bible (i.e., biblical inerrancy).[12] Ancient interpreters are always prompt to solve any problem of apparent historical inaccuracy or textual contradiction by resorting to various hermeneutical maneuvers. For ancient interpreters, each text can elucidate any other text no matter if these texts come from different authors, different parts of the Bible, or different times. According to ancient interpreters, there is a basic harmony underlying the whole Scripture and transcending all apparent contradictions between individual texts. Thus, the primary role of an interpreter is to search and find this basic harmony. Nevertheless, such a search has led to excessive harmonizing maneuvers meant to downplay the inherent polyphony of the Jewish Scriptures. Due to this insatiable hermeneutics of harmonization, the rich chromatic diversity of the scriptural tableau has often been reduced to one dominant color.

The patristic interpreters, especially the Antiochenes, were interested to find the hypothesis (perspective) of a book or the skopos (unifying purpose) of a particular text (e.g., a psalm). Athanasius accused the Arians of reading the Scriptures as individual texts while missing the skopos or *dianoia* (mind, inner meaning) of Scripture as a whole. The greatest mistake of the Arians was that they missed the "intent of the divine Scriptures" while concentrating exclusively on the grammatical meaning of individual texts. This "intent of Scripture" was to be found in a condensed way in the "rule of faith"[13] that was "transmitted from fathers to fathers." Discerning the unitive "mind" (dianoia) of Scripture was considered prerequisite for a proper interpretation of individual passages or books.[14]

Zealous accent on the perfect harmony of Scripture led both Jewish rabbis and Christian ancient fathers also to the conclusion that the Scripture is "omnimeaningful." Differently put it, each text, sentence or word of Scripture would have a significance that is to be identified by the diligent interpreter. The doctrine of the "omni-significance" of the Bible took deep roots particularly on the Jewish side of ancient interpretation, with occasional striking parallels in Christian exegetes—most especially Origen of Alexandria, but also others like Ephrem the Syrian and Maximus the Confessor.

Origen saw in the "letter" the veil by which the Holy Spirit concealed God's "intent" or "purpose" (skopos). Thus, the Alexandrian interpreter accorded a great deal of attention to the "letter" as it hid and revealed the intended meaning. Searching for the divine "intent" dressed in human wording was a preeminent task of Alexandrian interpreters. The validity of this search is based on the assumption mentioned above, namely, that Scripture is a perfectly harmonious document. Against any apparent contradiction or inconsistency, there is a skopos, a divine "intent" that has to be discovered by interpreter's hard and prayerful work.

The Bible Is Divinely Inspired

The Scripture itself asserts that it is inspired. "Thus says the Lord" is a running introductory phrase in prophetic and legal texts of the Bible.

It might be added here that when church fathers refer to "inspiration," they always accentuate the spiritual experience, the dynamic dialogue between God and the human author.[15] Their view is in harmony with the scriptural evidence itself. One may note that the Hebrew language has no specialized terms for "inspiration," "inspired," "to inspire." Andrew Louth is quite right when he notices with regard to the Eastern Orthodox view on biblical inspiration that "the authority of the Scriptures we now call the Old Testament rests, not so much on their inspiration, as on their reception by the Church as prophetic witness to Christ."[16] The "theology of inspiration" and the "inerrancy" or "infallibility" of the Bible are late concepts used by Protestant theologians in support of the Reformers' dictum sola scriptura, defining the self-sufficiency of the Bible as means of God's revelation.[17]

Unlike Eastern Orthodoxy and Roman Catholicism rooted in the tradition of the church fathers, Protestantism developed a whole theology of inspiration understood primarily as "dictation." The words of Scriptures are God's utterances dictated by him to the human author whose only task was to accept being God's scribe or recorder. Worth mentioning here is John Webster's observation, which reflects a new trend in present day Protestantism, marked by a certain return to the patristic approach: "Faith's certainty is grounded in God alone, not in inspiration; faith is 'founded' on Scripture, not because of its formal property as inspired but because Scripture is the instrument of divine teaching which proceeds from God. Within such a context, talk of inspiration will have its place; detached from that context, it goes awry. . . . Inspiration is not primarily a textual property but a divine movement and therefore a divine moving."[18]

Speaking of scriptural inspiration, Georges Florovsky insists on its dialogical aspect: "What is the inspiration can never be properly defined—there is a mystery therein. It is a mystery of the divine-human encounter."[19] In this encounter, the Word of God does not replace the word of man, but to contrary the latter is "transfigured," made fit to its divine counterpart.[20] This is in keeping with the "Chalcedonian" pattern that marks the whole mystery of redemptive history and the Church, in which human freedom is rehabilitated, creatively actualized, and included in God's design. In Florovsky's view, what makes Scripture unique is that crisscrossing between God's word and human response, in which the human response is taken up, assumed into the very fabric and medium of God's own Word. Other components of Tradition (e.g., creeds, patristic writings, liturgy, etc.) represent man's reflection on the Word. True theology—human speech about God—is only possible on the basis of the fact that God first spoke to man in the act of revelation and through the means of inspiration. Hence, the centrality and preeminence of Scripture over all the other human endeavors that came to shape the Holy Tradition.[21]

The seven rules or principles of rabbinic interpretation (Heb. *middoth,* "measures") attributed to Rabbi Hillel the Elder (ca. 60 B.C.E.–10 C.E.) are similar in their basic scope and idea to the four assumptions observed by the patristic interpreters.[22] Whether or not these middoth have in fact been always applied, one may infer the belief of those ancient Jewish interpreters that, by making use of a set of rules and through topical associations between texts (i.e., intertextuality), Scripture could be explained by itself.[23] Both sets of hermeneutical rules point to Scripture as a perfectly harmonious document, hence the synchronic reading practiced by both ancient Jewish and Christian interpreters.

The general consensus among scholars is that Jewish exegetical traditions had an influence on Christian exegesis and probably the obvious commonality between the Jewish and Christian hermeneutical rules or assumptions should be explained as a result of this early influence.[24] Even in their polemical interaction with the Jews, when the Septuagint text was not clear enough or when they needed access to the Hebrew text, patristic authors (e.g., Origen, Jerome) paradoxically resorted to and paid tribute to the rabbinic literature.[25]

No matter how important these rules of ancient Jewish or Christian interpreters might appear, assumptions alone cannot generate meaning. The interpreting community had an important say in shaping the meaning of a text. For instance, the Old Testament texts cited in the New Testament were selected in order to support the emerging beliefs of the first followers of Christ who were Jews looking at the old Scriptures as to a source of authority. The Old Testament texts that came to be used in the New Testament were considered by these Jewish Christians as scriptural "proofs" of their belief in Jesus as Messiah and Lord.[26]

The church fathers apparently observed these assumptions, discussed above, in conjunction with their basic belief that Jesus, the exalted Lord, is the master-key that can open any locked room in the Scriptures. Christ is the only one who can take away the "veil" and allow the listeners of the

Law to understand its ultimate meaning (2 Cor 3:15–16). In other words, Christ is not only the Savior, the exalted Lord, but he is also the hermeneutical key that opens the Scriptures for understanding the decisive message hidden in them.

For the ancient Christian interpreter observing these four assumptions, there was no inconsistency or insignificance in the Bible. Each detail up to the minutest was worth analyzing.

As James L. Kugel well notices,[27] the ancient interpreters are often misjudged for being quite loose when dealing with the biblical text. Yet while no one would contest that they could be quite fanciful at times in their interpretations, this does not mean that they were not doing exegesis. Their apparently "fanciful" interpretations were well anchored in minute analysis of the biblical text, even though the details chosen by them were not always significant, from a modern reader's point of view, I might add. No matter how creative and imaginative their assertions might be, they are in fact a type of exegesis. For instance, Jesus's crucifixion was predicted in Gen 22 by the "binding of Isaac," even up to the detail of the "crown of thorns" foreshadowed in Gen 22:13 by a "ticket" on Mount Moriah. Kugel terms these assertions "ideologically motivated interpretations," wherein the ancient interpreter asks the text to say something that would fit well with his own ideology. However, more often the ancient interpreter is not guided by his ideology, but rather by a genuine desire to find the meaning of a particular text. To distinguish between a "pure" versus agenda-driven exegesis is difficult, first of all because there is no such "pure" or entirely "objective" exegesis. One thing is sure, and that is the honest desire of ancient interpreters to clarify the text by observing closely the four assumptions discussed above. To say that ancient interpreters "abused" the biblical text by forcing it to speak according to their own ideologies is a misrepresentation of reality. Assuming that the Bible was a relevant document, the ancient interpreter always sought to go beyond the surface text in an ongoing effort to reach the deep significance of the text that would be true in any time, including his own age.

Elements of Patristic Interpretation
Working on the Septuagint

Unlike Jewish rabbinic interpreters who used Hebrew in their interpretations and worked on a Hebrew text (e.g., Midrashim), the New Testament authors[28] and the church fathers had to work on the Septuagint text. The first great challenge for ancient Christian interpreters was to render the Septuagint text into the "vernacular" Greek language of their readers. This is why, patristic interpretations are often mere paraphrases to the Greek text of the Septuagint, explicative glosses. The modern reader should not be harsh on patristic interpreters, who had to wear two hats at the same time: to "translate" a text written in a language different from the one spoken by their readers; and to interpret the sacred text following a set of theological assumptions.

The second challenge for patristic authors was to work with a text reflecting a religious system not entirely appropriated by the apostolic Church, if one takes into account the almost exclusively Christological use of the Jewish Scriptures by the New Testament authors.[29] With an Old Testament well-embedded within the Christian Bible, patristic writers felt their own duty to extend the list of Old Testament texts as well as the array of interpretations going far beyond the common Christological import. In addition, the ideas gleaned by patristic authors from the Old Testament were quite different from, even in conflict with, the religious-cultural fabric of Late Antique society where the hearers and readers of these patristic productions were located. This made the ancient interpreters' task even more difficult.

Regarding the use of Old Testament texts in the New Testament, a few remarks are warranted at this point. On the one hand, the authors of Hebrews, Matthew and to a certain extent the Johannine writings deal with the Old Testament material, primarily prophetic, according to the pattern of prophecy-fulfillment,[30] showing that what the ancient prophets proclaimed was fulfilled in Jesus's life and his salvific work. On the other hand, Luke and the pastoral epistles tried to show the universal character of the old Scriptures, how these Scriptures were addressing both groups, Jews and Gentiles, united within a growing Church moving away from its Jewish ties and roots. As for Paul, the "apostle of nations" downplayed somewhat the old Scriptures in light of the revelation of Jesus, so that the Gentiles might be attracted by and become members of the new religious entity, the apostolic Church. Using one of the Jewish middoth (i.e., deductive argument), Paul declared the end of the old Law and the emergence of a new covenant mediated by Jesus the Lord. However, such a categorical attitude against the Law did not obstruct the way of using sapiential material (e.g., Proverbs, Psalms) for paraenetical purposes. The novelty here does not lie with the hermeneutical maneuvers attested in the New Testament, which are encountered also in ancient Jewish interpretation.

Rather, what is truly new is the emphasis on Jesus, the exalted Lord, as the hermeneutical principle in light of which everything, old or new, should be (re-) evaluated.[31]

The use of the Old Testament in patristic writings can be of two types: compositional and expositional. The church fathers used the Scripture either as intertwining with their own theological ideas (in treatises) or in an expositional way (in biblical commentaries). These two types, however, are really inseparable. Frances M. Young suggested that patristic exegesis emerged from creed-like formulations. This creedal provenance may be detected in the emphasis placed by ancient Christian interpreters on the unity of Scripture. For the fathers, creedal formulations helped especially to build a framework within which the scriptural message was configured as a history of salvation from creation to eschaton.[32]

The Senses of Scripture

The patristic exegesis is defined by various types of interpretation, namely, "literal," "allegorical," and "typological."[33] The church fathers are considered the precursors of the medieval fourfold sense.[34] More simply, for ancient Christian interpreters, there were two basic levels of meaning: the literal sense and the spiritual (or, more-than-literal) sense of Scripture.

The tripartite sense division followed by Origen (literal, moral, allegorical) seems to have been first supplemented with the fourth, the anagogic (Gk. *anagō*, "to lead up") sense by John Cassian (ca. 360–435 c.e.). In order to illustrate the fourfold layer of meanings, Cassian takes the city of Jerusalem as an illustration: "One and the same Jerusalem can be taken in four senses: historically as the city of the Jews; allegorically as Church of Christ, anagogically as the heavenly city of God, 'which is the mother of us all,' tropologically, as the soul of man, which is frequently subject to praise or blame from the Lord under this title" (*The Conference of Abbot Nesteros* 8).[35] By the medieval period, biblical interpreters (especially in the West) were distinguishing four senses of Scripture: (1) the historical or literal, (2) the allegorical (including the typological) or Christological, (3) the tropological (anthropological) or moral, and (4) the anagogic or eschatological.

The literal (historical or grammatical) sense is the one the biblical author had in his mind at the time of writing. The interpreter comes upon the literal sense through a careful analysis of the historical and literary context of the biblical passage. However, due to the twofold nature of scriptural inspiration, even the literal sense cannot be exclusively human in its origin. Moreover, in certain cases, the literal sense has also a dynamic aspect because texts can be open for re-readings even when the literal sense is concerned. This is the case, for instance, with the royal psalms (e.g., Ps 2) which, following the cessation of the monarchic system and the Babylonian deportation, were reread as foundational texts-charters of an ideal kingdom and king (Messiah).

The spiritual sense may be detected when one reads the Scripture prayerfully under the guidance of the Spirit and in light of Christ. The spiritual sense should be always based on the literal sense. In fact, the spiritual sense equates mostly the Christological sense, with Jesus having fulfilled the Old Testament Scriptures. Detecting the spiritual sense is not a sort of eisegesis, a mere reading into the text. Based on the literal sense or the "letter" of the Scripture, the spiritual sense is a way through which old Scriptures are open to newer Scriptures. Typology is an aspect of the spiritual sense, the most significant one in ancient Christian interpretation. The spiritual sense is discovered by the interpreter who looks at the Christian Bible as to a perfectly harmonious document. In light of this assumption, each text is regarded as an integral unit or part of a whole whose hypothesis (perspective) or skopos (unifying purpose) is to be found in Christ, the incarnate Word. An example of spiritual sense obtains with 2 Sam 7:12–13, more precisely, Nathan's prophecy to David regarding one of his successors to the throne. From a historical perspective, this text is a royal *laudatio*. However, in light of the Christ-event, the same text gains a spiritual sense concerning the eternal "dynasty" or kingship of Christ.[36]

The "fuller sense" (*sensus plenior*) witnesses to the mysterious role of the Spirit who could move the biblical author to use words, expressions, and images whose deep meaning the latter would not be able to fully understand at the time of writing. The reality of the fuller sense becomes obvious when the interpreter analyses a text in light of other biblical passages and the doctrinal guidelines of the Church's living Tradition. Raymond E. Brown defines the sensus plenior thus: "That additional, deeper meaning, intended by God but not clearly intended by the human author, which is seen to exist in the words of a biblical text (or group of texts, or even a whole book) when they are studied in the light of further revelation or development in the understanding of revelation."[37]

An illustration of the fuller sense is Isa 7:14, originally a prophecy delivered by Isaiah to king Ahaz of Judah in the second half of the eighth century B.C.E. regarding the birth of a male child whose symbolic name *Immanuel,* "God with us," indicates a new act of salvation God will intervene and work for his people. The text is used by Matt 2:22–23 with reference to Jesus's birth from a virgin, Mary. By using this old Scripture in the Septuagint rendition, Matthew suggests that Isa 7:14 conceals a sense deeper and fuller than the one Isaiah was aware of. In other words, God intended to say through Isaiah more than the prophet could grasp at the moment of writing. It was an interpreter, centuries later, by the name of Matthew, who found the deep, fuller sense of that prophecy. Another example of the fuller sense is the frequent use of Gen 3:15 as referring to Messiah's victory over evil as well as the role of the mother of Messiah in this victory. The literal (plain) meaning of this text is about struggle, a continuous conflict with the harassment of evil, and an ambiguous outcome. Nevertheless, the sensus plenior goes beyond the literal meaning of the text by pointing to the final victory of the good over the evil.

As one can see, any spiritual (typological, allegorical) interpretation relies on such a fuller meaning. Even though the term sensus plenior was coined relatively late (by Andrea Fernández in 1925), the assumption regarding a hidden sense fuller than the literal one was embraced by all the ancient practitioners of typological interpretation.

There are apparently two ways of reaching the sensus plenior. One way is to look in Psalms and Prophets. For instance, Ps 21(22), a lament of a suffering person, was read as a prophecy hinting at the last moments of Jesus's life. The sensus plenior here is alluded at by Jesus's recitation of the first words (if not of the entire Ps 21[22]) on the cross as he was dying (Matt 27:46). The other way is to read a text within the context of the entire book, or a book within the context of the entire Bible: in other words, to do "biblical theology." By definition, discovery of the sensus plenior is contingent upon such exercise in biblical theology and intertextuality.

Is the sensus plenior a fuller meaning seeded in the depth of the text or simply a fuller understanding of God's revelation? The greatest hurdle that this question has to face is the view on inspiration. If divine inspiration does not put away man's liberty and his personality, how would be possible for God to hide a fuller meaning of which the human author would not be aware? Those who support a view on inspiration where man is a mere "instrument" will have no problem accepting the concept of sensus plenior; others may find more difficulty. Yet in spite of all difficulties that this concept of sensus plenior might raise, there is something positive in it—the realization that finding the meaning of a text by historical-critical exegesis is not the end but the beginning of a long, endless search for further and deeper meanings.

Typology and Allegory

The word "allegory" originates from Gk. *allēgoria,* a noun deriving from verb *allēgoreō* (*allos* plus *agoreuō*), "to speak in public so to imply something other than what is said." Thus "allegory" is a kind of speech intended to mean something else than what one literally says. It is a *trope* (turn), a figure of speech, close to metaphor and irony in its deceiving appearance. In fact, allegory is a uninterrupted, extended metaphor.

"Typology"[38] comes from Gk. *typos,* meaning the impress or print of a seal. The word *typos* appears in John 20:25 with reference to the "mark" of the nails on Jesus's resurrected body. Hermeneutically speaking, typos (type) points to a certain correspondence between two narrative elements. "Typology" means "figurative composition" or "figural interpretation." It is not an exegetical method, but rather a hermeneutical key.[39] Philo of Alexandria was the first ancient author who applied the term typos to the interpretation of Scripture. A similar use of *typos* can be detected in the New Testament, more precisely in Rom 5:14, where Paul calls Adam "a type of the one to come" (*typos tou mellontos*)—a prefiguration of Christ, "the last Adam" (*ho eschatos Adam* in 1 Cor 15:45). Frances M. Young identifies four kinds of *types* in patristic exegesis, "all of which in some sense create intersections of time and eternity, particular and universal: (1) exemplary (or biographical—potentially 'universal'); (2) prophetic (or 'historical'—narrative prefiguration); (3) spatial or geographical; (4) recapitulative (cosmological/eschatological)."[40] Unlike "allegory,"[41] however, the term "typology" does not belong to the patristic lexicon; it is rather a modern coinage.[42]

The scholarly cliché of clear-cut distinction between typology and allegory has had a powerful shelf life in recent decades. The modern assertion that typology is different from allegory was first launched by Jean Daniélou in the 1950s.[43] This distinction, immediately accepted by the scholarly community,[44] presented typology as rooted in history, while allegory in contrast had no sense of history at all. As Frances M. Young summarizes, "the Alexandrians were credited with having confused historical with symbolic typology—that is, with allegory. . . . Typology, it was suggested, had biblical roots and was reclaimed (or indeed formally developed) by the Antiochenes as an acceptable method that did not evacuate biblical history."[45]

If at the theoretical level this distinction sounds fair, in practice, it is impossible to draw a clear-cut line between allegory and typology when dealing with early Christian literature. The supposed inseparable relation with history in case of typology is discarded by the use of typology in Hebrews and Barnabas where the relationship is between Jesus and rituals rather than historical events.

It has been long thought that the linkage of typology with the historical reality makes it distinct from an allegory that has no connection with historical events. Nevertheless, according to Frances M. Young, "It is not its character as historical event which makes a 'type'; what matters is its mimetic quality."[46] The prefigurative symbols of the Old Testament ("types") were fulfilled by the "reality" of the "antitypes" in the New Testament. Strictly speaking, typology is a relation between two narrative events, institutions, figures, and not between a narrative block and a historical event. Thus, typology is a form of intertextuality. There is no difference between the texts entering into a typological relation. Both texts are "real," and the "reality" or "fulfillment" of a "type" is a *textual*, rather than a historical category.

Charles Kannengiesser is right when he suggests that Christian typology derived from the "crucible of the gospel event . . . a hermeneutical event of radical interpretation. . . . The *Christian* reception of Old Testament 'types' is one of the many side effects of the gospel event."[47] The gospel event conferred upon the Jewish biblical history a climactic point, and a sense of fulfillment. Something similar, though not identical, with Christian typology obtains with classical historiography where past figures are seen as ideal *exempla* to be followed. In ancient Jewish interpretation (e.g., Philo), Adam, Abraham, and other people mentioned in the old Scriptures are simply allegorized as symbols of virtues, but never considered types. Unlike the *exemplum* that turns the reader's mind toward the past with a certain nostalgic feeling, the typos moves the reader's attention toward future, to the event or figure to come.[48] The first precursors of typology, long before the patristic interpreters made use of it extensively, are to be found in the Old Testament. For instance, Deutero-Isaiah announces a new exodus (Isa 43:18–21) preceded by the old exodus. If in the Old Testament, the old figures or events *precede* new figures or events, starting with the New Testament, new figures or events are not only preceded but also *anticipated* (*prefigured* or *foreshadowed*) by the old figures or events. Thus, typology is a specifically Christian hermeneutical maneuver underscoring the continuous and harmonious unity between the Old and the New Testament.

Harold P. Scanlin connects patristic typology to the goal of *theoria* (inspired vision): "The hermeneutical method of the Fathers was typology and the aim was *theoria* 'an inspired vision of the presence and purpose of God within history and within the Church.' The patristic concept of *theoria* holds that Scripture contains both a literal and a spiritual sense."[49] According to Frances M. Young, theoria (spiritual vision or contemplative insight) is half way between a Hellenism that emphasized "allegory" and a Judaism concentrating on "wording." This is what the fathers actually did—they bridged the gap between two extremes, and it is why the classical division between "allegory" (school of Alexandria) and "literalism" (school of Antioch) does not do justice to patristic interpreters that are actually moving between extremes.[50]

John Breck notices that theoria, as a hermeneutic goal characteristic of patristic exegesis, refers to the "divine Truth as revealed in the person of Jesus Christ and in the biblical witness to him."[51] Theoria is a God-given gift that enables the ancient Christian interpreter to see the "hidden" meaning of the text. Breck writes: "To identify either the Emmanuel born of a virgin (Isa 7:14) or the Suffering Servant (Isa 52–53) with the person of Jesus requires an insight into the 'hidden' sense of the text, a meaning that was not apparent to the prophet himself." Before building any typological relation the interpreter has to find the hidden meaning. So, concludes Breck, "It is this vision that unites typology and a certain allegorical perspective in a single hermeneutic program."[52]

Speaking of typology, Georges Florovsky notices first that "allegorical" interpretation is not interested in historical concreteness but rather in the hidden meaning or in the eternal Word of God concealed in the depth of the text. The allegorist is always on quest for eternal meanings that surpass history. The Bible, Florovsky notes critically, is for an allegorist a mere collection of "edifying examples." Nevertheless, Florovsky stresses, the Bible is history—though not simply human history. It is about God's mighty deeds in man's history that altogether constitute the "history of salvation." The "typological" interpretation takes into account the historical character or more precisely the continuity of this mega-historical narrative called the Bible. In fact, any typological relation lies on this historical narrative unfolded over two separate collections of books, the Old and New Testaments. Florovsky reiterates the older view when he suggests that "'typology' was not an exegesis of the texts themselves, but rather an interpretation of the events." The mistake the proponents of this older view make is that they confound historical narratives with historical events when they define "typology" as correspondence between historical events. So for Florovsky: "A 'type' is no more than a 'shadow' or image. In the New Testament we have the very fact." Florovsky notices, "Typology is thus an historical method, more than a philological one," as would be the allegorical interpretation. Yet there is no "pure" historical event in the Bible. Everything in the Bible, as in any other literary production, is an *interpreted* historical event. Thus, typology lies on correspondence between narratives—the only access one has to the historical events behind them. For Florovsky, "typology" is a relation between a prophetic text and its fulfillment that is either Christ or the Church. "It is only in the light of Christ that the Old Testament can be properly understood."[53] As much as Florovsky underscores the historical character of this fulfillment one should not forget that it is the Christ of the New Testament or of the apostolic kērygma that is considered the fulfillment of the Old Testament prophecies. This holds true when dealing with "typologies" attested in the New Testament (e.g., Israel-Jesus upon his return from Egypt, Matt 2:15; cf. Hos 11:1) or in the patristic literature. The correspondence is between Old Testament "texts" and either apostolic oral proclamation or New Testament evidence on Jesus the exalted Lord, both being theological interpretations of the historical Jesus.

Typology is commonly seen unilaterally as a move from the past to the future patterned by a prophecy-fulfillment hermeneutical scheme. Nevertheless, typology has also a direction moving from future to the past. As John Breck points out, "a type is not merely a sign that points toward a future or transcendent reality—it is also a historical locus in which that reality is proleptically realized."[54] As illustration, Breck chooses 1 Cor 10, where Paul speaks of the ancient Israelites during their wondering through the wilderness after crossing the Red Sea. The Israelites, Paul asserts, were all "baptized" in the cloud, they ate "spiritual food" and drank "spiritual drink." And Paul concludes with a rather enigmatic remark: "For they drank of that spiritual rock that followed them: and that rock was Christ" (1 Cor 10:4). The rock of which the apostle speaks here is the "traveling" rock—an ancient interpretation due to the same symbolic name *Meribah* (Heb. "strife") qualifying two places (i.e., Refidim [Exod 17:7] and Kadesh [Num 20:13, 24]) and apparently one gushing rock which miraculously traveled with the Israelites from Refidim to Kadesh.[55] As

Breck comments, "to the apostle's mind, Christ was present among the people of Israel in preincarnate form. A virtual identification is established between the rock and Christ, between the prototype and its antitype, such that the eschatological antitype is conceived as being present to or existing in the historical prototype . . . the rock as a prototype serves as the locus at which the future saving work of Christ is proleptically realized in Israel's history."[56]

This move from future to the past confers the history of Old Testament more than an anticipatory value. In light of typology thus construed, the Old Testament is not only a step toward fulfillment of all its types. It is a locus where the fulfillment was already proleptically given and foretasted. "This means that the perspective of typology is that of an authentic 'salvation history.' Events of the past are fulfilled by future realities; but that future or eschatological fulfillment is already manifest in the event itself."[57] On this token, Georges A. Barrois speaks of "an ontological relationship between the type and the typified mystery, by reason of the gradual realization, within time, of God's eternal design."[58]

With Byzantine theological and historical works, typology switched dramatically from a "textual" correspondence between the Old and the New Testament, as attested in patristic interpretations, to a "textual"-"nontextual" relation. According to various Byzantine authors who supported the imperial ideology, typology connected "the present with the biblical past of the Old Testament" and "the extension of Old Testament time reached only partial fulfillment with the coming of Christ into the world, and it continues on into the present until the Second Coming and the end of the world."[59] Thus, Moses, David and other royal figures of the Old Testament became *typoi* of or models for the Byzantine emperors.[60]

The application of Old Testament figures to emperors began with Constantine and Eusebius. Thus, the battle between Constantine and Maxentius at the Milvian Bridge over the river Tiber (October 28, 312 C.E.) is described with images and phrases borrowed from Exodus's depiction of the confrontation between Moses and Pharaoh at the Red Sea. Constantine parallels Moses who led his people to freedom, while Maxentius who drowned in Tiber represents the Egyptian Pharaoh who found his end in the waters of the Red Sea (cf. *Church History* [8–10], published in 325 C.E.; and *Life of Constantine* [passim], written in 337 C.E.). In the absence of further authorial qualifications, one may consider the correspondence between Eusebius's "present" and the Old Testament past event more than a *comparatio* (*synkrisis*). It is seemingly an example of typology. If typos

"shapes its imprint," and exemplum "invites imitation," as Rapp points
out,[61] then the confrontation at the Red Sea does not invite imitation; it
rather shapes its counterpart at Milvian Bridge; hence, the typological relation between the two events and their protagonists.[62]

The debate over how to interpret the Scripture was very early spread
among Christians, Jews and pagans. For Philo, Clement, Origen, and
Didymus the Blind, all living in Alexandria, Scripture was inspired;
hence its codified character and the interpreter's quest to find the hidden
sense. The method chosen by these Alexandrians was the allegorical interpretation employed for centuries by Greek scholars in order to explicate
their poets. Pagan philosophers such as Celsus and Porphyry of Tyre are
known for their criticism against Christian use of allegorism. The issue
was not allegory as an exegetical method but rather the appropriateness
of the Christian Bible for this exegetical method.[63] In Porphyry's view,
Christians resorted to allegorical interpretation to covert the contradictions and deficiencies of the Bible. Christians should rather have rejected
the Jewish Scriptures altogether. Porphyry chides Origen for applying the
allegorical interpretation in order to find hidden, deep meanings to texts
that are not suited for this method, as for example Old Testament texts
seemingly promoting immorality, such as Gen 19 where Lot sleeps with
his own daughters.[64]

Christological Interpretation

Distinguishing between Christological and rabbinic interpretations,
Jon D. Levenson asserts:

> I make no claim that Rabbinic Judaism offers the correct under-
> standing of the Hebrew Bible. One needs not subscribe to the reg-
> nant prejudice to see that Talmudic religion is different from its
> biblical ancestor, one of the major differences being the presence in
> it of a Bible. But the change seems more evolutionary than revolu-
> tionary; it lacks the 'quantum leap' apparent in the Christian claim
> of a new Israel and, ultimately, a New Testament. . . . My claim is
> that because Judaism lacks an overwhelming motivation to deny
> the pluriform character of the Hebrew Bible in behalf of a uni-
> form reading—such as the christological reading—Jewish exegesis
> evidences a certain breadth and a certain relaxed posture, both of
> which are necessary if the Hebrew Bible is to receive a fair hearing.[65]

For Levenson, moving from the religion of the Jewish Bible to rabbinic Judaism in spite of all changes inherent of any evolutionary process is not the same with moving from the old Scriptures to Christianity. The latter took a "quantum leap" by considering Jesus as the "new Israel," and bringing forth a "new" testament. This "quantum leap" required finding a way to tie a nascent faith based on a person (not a book), Jesus of Nazareth, to old Scriptures, thus providing the religious context for the revolutionary move. And there is another difference between rabbinic Judaism and Christianity: while the latter has in Christological interpretation of the Jewish Bible a motivation for uniformity, the former, lacking such a motivation, revels in pluriformity.[66]

Christological interpretation is perhaps the most known and pervasive Christian example of typological interpretation that in its turn is based on one of the ancient Christian and Jewish hermeneutical assumptions, namely, the Bible is a perfectly harmonious document. Beginning with the New Testament, this type of interpretation has a long tradition among the church fathers. It originated in apostolic times when the first eyewitnesses of Jesus used in their proclamation (kērygma) the Jewish Scriptures as "proof-text" or "proof from prophecy" to support Jesus's claim to messiahship revealed in the midst of history.[67] As one may infer from the New Testament itself, Christological interpretation of the Jewish Scripture among the apostles was initiated by Jesus's conversation with Luke and Cleopas on the way to Emmaus, when he explained to them all the messianic prophecies: "Then beginning with Moses and all the prophets, he interpreted to them the things about himself in all the scriptures" (Luke 24:27; cf. v. 44).

The second century c.e. was a key point in the development of this hermeneutical approach, in the form of Justin Martyr's Christological reading of the Jewish Scriptures. According to Justin, the apostolic proclamation (kērygma), so infused with Christological overtones, was delivered upon Jesus's instruction to the apostles. "For if the prophets declared obscurely that Christ would suffer, and thereafter be Lord of all, yet that [declaration] could not be understood by any man until he himself persuaded the apostles that such statements were expressly related in the Scriptures" (*Dialogue with Trypho* 76).[68] However, the same Justin states that Christ, after his resurrection, urged his apostles to check the Scriptures that prophesied about him: "Accordingly, after he was crucified, even all his acquaintances forsook him, having denied him; and afterwards, when he had risen from the dead and appeared to them, and had taught them to read the prophecies in which all these things were foretold as coming to pass, and when they had seen him ascending into heaven, and had believed, and had received power sent thence by him upon them, and went to every race of men, they taught these things, and were called apostles" (*First Apology* 50).[69]

Regarding the modus operandi of Justin's Christological exegesis, one may assume that he used in *Apology* and *Dialogue* a sort of Christian testimony book, a "Christianizing targum," with text and exegesis pointing to Jesus as the fulfillment of the old prophetic material. Key texts were gathered in these text-books that had the pattern and authority of creedal formulations. The selection of these essential texts was done based on a widely accepted hypothesis of Scripture. Justin could have resorted to the full scriptural text, but apparently preferred this testimony book due to its brevity, high authority and wide popularity among his hearers (or readers). Unlike the New Testament proof-texts, Justin's collection is quite Jewish: the messianic texts used by Justin appear as such in the Talmuds (Isa 11:1–4; Mic 5:1–4; Ps 72:5–17). Texts like Gen 49:10 and Num 24:17, unattested in the New Testament, are considered messianic both by Targum of Onqelos and by Justin. This discrepancy between Justin and the New Testament regarding the messianic texts can be explained by the need of the eyewitnesses of Jesus to support the unexpected aspects of Jesus's life (the cross, death, resurrection, ascension), leading to certain peculiarities in the New Testament selection of messianic texts. This process continued in Justin's days; yet a new need emerged among second-century Christians to show that the Jewish traditional messianic texts were fulfilled in Christ. This was the main goal of Justin's quoting the Jewish Scriptures.[70]

The *Dialogue with Trypho* 33 can be adduced as a sample of Justin's Old Testament Christological interpretation. Here, the apologist exegetes Ps 109(110):4 by relating "Melchizedek," the (non-Hebrew) high-priest and king of Salem (Jerusalem), to Christ. This typological correspondence between Melchizedek and Christ was already employed by the author of Hebrews (5:6, 10; 6:20; 7:1, 10, 11, 15, 17, 21). Unlike the typological use of Melchizedek in Hebrews, where Jesus represents the *antitype* of the Old Testament *type* (as the new high priest of a new covenant meant to replace the old), Justin's Christological interpretation of Melchizedek focuses rather on the fact that Christ is the high priest of the uncircumcised who would believe in him.

Another peculiarity of Justin's interpretation of Melchizedek is the way this interpretation is conditioned by a polemic with his interlocutor, Trypho the Jew, who asserted that Melchizedek prefigured the good king Hezekiah of Judah (ca. 715–687 B.C.E.). Justin rejects Trypho's explanation. This brief biblical episode (Gen 14:18–20) was in anticipation of the Jews' unbelief, he suggests, that the Gentile Melchizedek foreshadowed Christ. Hezekiah was a king, but not a priest; hence, he could not typologically match Melchizedek who was both king and high-priest. In order to preempt Trypho's further critique of Jesus's humble life, which did not look so royal, Justin proffers the end of Ps 109(110):7, "He will drink from the stream by the path; therefore he will lift up his head"—for Justin, a reference to Christ's two comings, first in humiliation, second in glory.

Debunking an Old Cliché: Alexandria versus Antioch

The old, long-lived and repeatedly embraced view that the school of Antioch promoted a literal interpretation of Scripture, while the school of Alexandria followed an allegorical type of interpretation, is gradually fading away.

Patristic interpretation is usually described in terms of polarity, "literal" versus "allegorical" (or "typological"). Frances M. Young argues that terms like "literal" or "typological" are inadequate tools to describe the patristic interpretation. Stating that the Alexandrians eschewed the "literal" meaning of the text by their proclivity toward the "allegoric" sense is demonstrably an overgeneralization. As a philologist, Origen of Alexandria gave painstaking attention and labor to the "letter" of the text. Origen's preoccupation with the letter resulted in his monumental Hexapla, with catenae of texts identifying the "idioms" of the Bible, comments on various readings, and etymological explications.[71]

Speaking of patristic interpretation of the Old Testament, Demetrios Trakatellis justifiably notes: "This unique body of literature, though highly appreciated, seems somehow to have suffered from stereotyped and oversimplified classifications. Biblical patristic exegesis of the first five centuries, for instance, has been conveniently divided into schools of exegesis, basically the Alexandrian and the Antiochene. Such a division and classification, justifiable to a certain degree, is, nonetheless, inadequate if not misleading."[72] Hence Trakatellis's inspired coinage "synthesis of exegetical tradition" to describe the work of interpreters of either school. The difference between these two schools or rather between the representatives of these schools is not about "senses" or "meanings" of the text (literal [historical] versus allegorical [typological]), but rather about the "activities" of individual exegetes and their concrete objectives. This is why, patristic interpreters, regardless to which school of interpretation they belong (Antioch or Alexandria), tend to be synthetic in their approach to Scripture by mixing literal explanations with allegorical readings of the sacred text. For this token, a more appropriate and nuanced characterization of these famous exegetical schools should be adopted.

From the onset, one may mention that *historikon* does not equal our modern "historical," at least as understood in light of historical criticism. In classical antiquity there was little interest in "historicity" in this narrow sense. The term historikon designates not an "objective" reality, but an investigation of a story defined by Thucydides as *ktēma eis aei*, "a possession forever." "The critical question about narrative was whether it was probable or persuasive, and the methods of assessment were *anaskeue* (refutation) and *kataskeue* (confirmation). Three types of narrative were distinguished: true history, or an accurate account of real events; fiction, or what could have happened but did not; and myth, what could not have taken place, a 'false account portraying truth,' as Theon described it."[73] In the same vein, Diodore of Tarsus, preeminent representative of School of Antioch, defines "history" as "'a pure account of something that happened,' 'pure' because it is not interrupted by authorial comments or dramatisations, the absence of which was one of the recognized stylistic devices for creating 'objectivity' in history-writing."[74]

According to Northrop Frye, the difference between Antiochene and Alexandrine does not lie with the literal (grammatical, historical) versus spiritual (allegorical) types of exegesis, but rather with two different modes of looking at the text: as a whole (i.e., iconic—Antioch) or in terms of individual pieces (i.e., symbolic—Alexandria). Alternatively, Frye describes these two modes as the "mirror" (the text provides a kind of mirror which images the true understanding) versus the "code" (the text provides a code to be cracked—what Frances M. Young calls, "a tokenist exegesis"). Antiochenes were emphasizing the coherence of the narrative while the Alexandrians were focusing on words. Thus, for instance, the objection of Eustathius of Antioch against Origen regarded a method that "fastened on words and ignored the sequence of the story and the coherence of the narrative, both with itself and with the rest of scripture."[75]

Speaking of exegetical schools, Demetrios Trakatellis begins with Theodoret's commentary on Isaiah, where he detects four major "facets" or "methods" deriving from various interpretative traditions: (1) interest in the textual-philological aspect of exegesis; (2) a strong adherence to historical facts of the text; (3) metaphorical-allegorical interpretation; and (4) a Christocentric principle of exegesis. This situation obtains with an Antiochene interpreter who according to the old "Alexandria-Antioch" dichotomy should have been an exclusive literalist focusing on the letter of the text, with no interest whatsoever in its allegorical openness. On the contrary, Trakatellis finds in Theodoret a certain preoccupation with metaphorical-allegorical exegetical approach—even though he, as a good "Antiochene," also works with literal, textual and historical aspects of the biblical text.

Referring to ancient interpreters who read Isa 1:22 allegorically, Trakatellis cites John Chrysostom's pastoral comment: "I am not dishonoring such an interpretation (*ouk atimazō tautēn tēn exēgēsin*)," says Chrysostom, "but I think that the other one that I propose is more true, namely that the prophet here speaks about greed and fraudulence in transactions." In the case of Chrysostom, Trakatellis notes that his emphasis on the literal aspects of the text could be explained not simply resorting to the long-prevailing view of Antioch's literalism, but rather with reference to the interpreter's "intense social-ethical sensitivities" vis-à-vis the moral decay of the wealthy layer of society at that time. Similarly, regarding the Alexandrines, Trakatellis takes Cyril as a case in point to challenge the old specious dichotomy: Cyril's exegetical program is a mix of historical-literal and spiritual interpretation. Examining Cyril's own commentary on Isaiah, Trakatellis writes: "In his prologue, he [Cyril] explains that the prophetic word is obscure and filled with hidden concepts. Therefore the task of the interpreter is to find out the precise historical facts and, at the same time, the interpretation or application of the spiritual theoria (PG 70:9)."[76]

As Trakatellis points out, a special feature of Cyril's exegesis is precisely his emphasis on historical meaning of the text. "Cyril opens his exegesis of Isaiah 7 with a very interesting statement about the importance of the historical exegesis of the biblical text. He says that the spiritual theoria (*theōria pneumatikē*) is good and useful, but when Scripture offers to us historical accounts (*historikōs pepragmena*) we must gather from them whatever is profitable, so that we take every salvific and edifying element provided by the God-inspired text [on Isa 7:1; PG 70:192]." Trakatellis concludes: "This statement coming from an Alexandrian exegete is significant indeed."[77]

Returning from Alexandria to "the East," Diodore of Tarsus, preeminent representative of the school of Antioch, wrote his commentary on Psalms[78] with special emphasis on *historia* (history) and the *lexis* (wording) of the text, while also searching for *anagoge* (ascent) and theoria (vision). In Diodore's view, historia is not opposed to theoria; rather, the former constitutes the foundation for the latter.[79]

On the same line of deconstructing the old Antioch-versus-Alexandria cliché with regard to biblical interpretation, Bradley Nassif suggests that the Antiochene biblical exegetes were interested not only in the letter but also in the spirit of the Scripture. Nassif insists programmatically on the centrality of theoria in the approach of Antiochene interpreters of the Bible. "To write about 'spiritual exegesis' in the School of Antioch," notices Nassif, "will appear to many readers as a historical curiosity. Understandably, this curiosity stems from the prevailing caricature of Antiochene exegesis."[80]

For Frances M. Young, the difference between the Antiochene and the Alexandrian approaches to exegesis finds an interesting parallel in the tension between philosophers and sophists in classical tradition, or between philosophy and rhetoric as ways of education. Young's point is that philosophy and rhetoric represent two different yet interacting approaches to text. One may look at the differing approaches of the two great exegetical schools in a similar way.[81]

Samples of Patristic Exegesis

To illustrate the patristic exegesis of the two famous schools, I am going to choose one of the most debated Old Testament texts, Hosea 1–3, along with three ancient interpreters who produced quite valuable commentaries on the Minor Prophets: Cyril of Alexandria, Theodoret of Cyrus, and Theodore of Mopsuestia.[82]

This case study focusing on the complexity of patristic exegesis and its quest for various senses implied by the sacred text makes the old clear-cut division between the "literalism" of Antioch and "allegorism" of Alexandria appear as an artificial construal. The following is a brief parade of various interpretations on a controversial *locus scripturae* that typify the use of the Old Testament by the church fathers irrespective of their modern matriculation into literalists and allegorists.

Hosea 1–3 is a *crux interpretum* due to the unusual command of God, unique in the entire Bible, demanding a saintly person, a prophet, to marry a prostitute (Heb. *'ēšet zənûnîm*, literally, "a woman of fornications"). At God's behest, Hosea marries Gomer bat Diblayim. Three children are born, to whom, following God's command, Hosea gives symbolic names: Izreel, Lo-Ruhamah, and Lo-Ami. Eventually, Gomer leaves Hosea with his children at home while attaching herself to a place of worship, probably, a Canaanite sanctuary promoting "sacred prostitution." After a poetical-prophetic section paralleling the two couples, Hosea-Gomer and God-Israel (chapter 2), comes another, even more unusual divine command (chapter 3). This time, God pushes his prophet to do something against the Law: to re-marry his adulteress wife (cf. Deut 24:2–4). And as if transgressing the Law at God's instigation would have not been weird enough, Hosea is asked by the same God to love, not simply to accept, but rather to treat his adulterous wife as a new wife worthy of love and respect. Hosea pays a redemption price to get Gomer out of her slavelike situation. The intricate calculation of the payment, a mix of cash and produce (Hos 3:2), testifies to Hosea's poor social status and his great love for his lascivious wife, love that determines Hosea to sacrifice everything even up to the basic commodities. Back home, Gomer is nevertheless required to spend a period of abstinence as a disciplinary measure to a better marital relationship. The end of chapter 3 compares again the two couples, pointing to the imminent Assyrian conquest of kingdom of Israel and the following deportation (721 B.C.E.) as God's disciplinary measure imposed on an obstinate nation.[83]

Explaining the divine command as well as the marriage between a prophet and a prostitute was a difficult task for many ancient interpreters, Jewish and Christian alike. How could a God whose main attribute is holiness (transcendence) ask a prophet, his spokesperson, a holy man (put aside or called for a special mission) to marry a woman of such low morals?

To resolve this scriptural conundrum, some of the ancient interpreters, especially on Jewish side of the interpretive range, merely negated the reality of this episode altogether, resorting to a visionary or dreamlike, allegorical interpretation. Nevertheless, Christian interpreters saw in this uncommon command and its realization a type, foreshadowing the real, flesh and bone incarnation of the Logos. Similar to Hosea who married a prostitute, God himself assumed our fallen human nature in the act of incarnation. As is quite plain here, historical, tropological, and typological do coexist within a single interpretation; there is nothing like modern lines of demarcation between senses and ways of interpretation.

Speaking of Hosea's marriage to a prostitute, Theodoret of Cyrus[84] accepts the "historicity" of this episode, but focuses more on Hosea's

virtues than on his wife's promiscuous inclinations: "The remarkable
Hosea, then, took the prostitute, not in thrall to lust but in obedience to
divine wishes, and that relation was holier than any marriage, not only
because it was done in accord with a divine wish, but because it also represented a type of God and the way the holy one reposing in the holy ones
was styled a bridegroom of the licentious mass of the Israelites" (*Commentary on the Twelve Prophets: On Hos 1:2*).[85] In this short comment, Theodoret, a representative of so-called "historical" school of Antioch, makes use
of the *historical* sense (he accepts this marriage as real), the tropological
(moral) sense (underscoring Hosea's obedience toward God's word), and
the typological sense (seeing in Hosea a foreshadowing or type of God's
covenantal relationship with an unworthy Israel). Loaded with anti-Judaic
overtones, Theodoret explains why Hosea did not get defiled by marrying
a prostitute: "If the God of all put up with the loose and adulterous synagogue, however, and the fount of holiness was not defiled by that loathsome and abominable thing, neither did the prophet incur any defilement
from that licentious woman." He goes on to say that a deed should be
judged according to its first purpose. Hosea did not marry a prostitute
out of lust but with a good intention: to obey God's will. For this token,
his deed should be labeled good. It is a similar situation as obtains with
killing, reasons Theodoret: "The murderer takes life, and the judge takes
life; while the latter does so lawfully, however, the former does it lawlessly,
and while the action is the same, it differs in purpose" (*Commentary on
the Twelve Prophets: On Hos 1:2*).[86] And the historical and typological in-
tertwine again in Theodoret's remark on the second divine command
to Hosea (Hos 3:1): "After these promises of good things [Hos 2], God
again bids the prophet be fond of an adulteress wife living a wicked life so
as once more to portray in reality the divine affection for the unworthy"
(*Commentary on the Twelve Prophets: On Hos 3:1*).[87]

In order that the hermeneutical tableau offered by Theodoret of Cyrus
might be complete, I will adduce here a brief Christological comment
that the Antiochene interpreter makes with regard to the betrothal between God and Israel after its return from exile (Hos 2): "While this happened as a type under Zerubbabel, in reality it was after the Incarnation
of Christ the Lord, when he also betrothed the Church forever; then it was
also that those believing in him were truly styled a faithful people, and
he was really called God of those believing in him" (*Commentary on the
Twelve Prophets: On Hos 2:21–22*).[88] As one can see, the typological sense
even predominates in this fragment.

Next to Diodore of Tarsus, Theodore of Mopsuestia (350–428 C.E.)[89] has been always considered the most significant representative of the Antiochene School founded by Lucian of Antioch. Theodore is known for placing a great deal of emphasis on the historical circumstances in which a biblical book took its shape. In terms of Christological interpretation, Theodore does not accept even the use of those classical texts adopted by the Church for this purpose from her early days (e.g., Mic 4:1–3; Zech 3:8; Mal 4:2 [3:20 LXX]).[90]

Theodore explains Hosea's marriage to a prostitute as a wake-up call rousing Israel to greater attentiveness to the will of God:

> The fact that God has the prophets do a number of things that to the general run of people seemed unseemly, like ordering Isaiah to appear naked and barefoot in the midst of everyone, clearly has the following explanation. Since we general run of people normally listen to words idly, but are startled at the novelty of what happens and comes to our attention, especially if it is at variance with the normal behavior of the one doing it, it made sense for God, with the Jews' disobedience in mind, to have the prophets frequently perform such things so that the people might in some fashion be converted by the novelty of what happened, and come to learn the reason and be instructed in their duty.
>
> *Commentary on the Twelve Prophets: On Hos 1:2*[91]

Where the more moderate Antiochene, provides a Christological explication (Hos 2:21–22—the betrothal between God and the restored Israel), Theodore of Cyrus eschews such an inference. He does the same with Hos 3:5, where "David" is usually interpreted as a reference to Christ. Theodore's literalism is further shown in glosses such as the following:"[T]he sky will provide rain for the earth according to my intention (by heaven referring to the sky, just as when he speaks of birds of heaven he means those crossing the sky). Normally when the earth is watered, it will provide its crops in abundance, and from these Israel will have enjoyment of the good things of the earth" (*Commentary on the Twelve Prophets: On Hos 2:21–22*).[92]

Nonetheless, Theodore cannot escape the universal compulsion any ancient interpreter had to face: allegorizing. Thus, when mentioning the price of redemption paid by Hosea in order to get his wife back, Theodore explains, "There was also need of the demonstration I bought since God had also attached the Jews to himself with great gifts as well as payments" (*Commentary on the Twelve Prophets. On Hos 3:2*).[93] The meaning of the price goes beyond the literal historical sense, pointing toward another reality: God acquiring Israel through various gifts.

Theodore's literalism is seen in his proclivity for details and historical explanations. The mere mention of the name of Gomer's father (Hos 1:2) is for this Antiochene interpreter an indication that the prophetic account is not a fiction but rather the record of a historical fact. Here is Theodore's gloss on "raisin cakes" (Hos 3:1): "The phrase *raisin cakes* suggests as much implying bread variously prepared and mixed with raisins and dried fruits, which according to a custom of those so disposed they offered to the idols, the phrase *fond of raisin cakes* meaning taking pleasure in doing this out of respect for the idols" (*Commentary on the Twelve Prophets: On Hos 3:1*).[94]

Cyril of Alexandria,[95] one of the most famous representatives of the Alexandrian School, is known for his typological (Christological) interpretations of the Old Testament. Interestingly enough, Cyril defends at length the historicity of Hosea's marriage to prostitute Gomer. One expects from Cyril an exclusively typological (allegorical) interpretation. However, Cyril's literalist way of interpreting Hos 1:2 shows one more time that there is no clear-cut distinction between allegorists and literalists. In fact, their interpretations are configured not by school affiliation but by theological intentions. Here is Cyril's explanation of Hosea's marriage: "No argument would persuade us to repudiate the text, to condemn the unlikelihood of the facts, to dismiss the tastelessness of the event itself, or even to think (as some commentators do) that there was no marriage or marital intercourse with Gomer, when the sacred text says that the conception took place and the birth as well, cites also the child's name, and mentions the woman's father and in addition to that the woman's actual name" (*Commentary on the Twelve Prophets: On Hos 1:2*).[96] Hosea is not to be condemned for his deed, but, as Theodoret interpreted above, the prophet's act of marrying Gomer is laudable because he followed God's command. Writes Cyril: "My view is that those under orders should without delay concede the dictates from on high to be correct and faultless, and hasten to execute the command, even if it is not altogether to their satisfaction" (*Commentary on the Twelve Prophets: On Hos 1:2*).[97]

But Cyril also employs the other two ways of interpreting Hosea's marriage—namely, bringing to light the typological and tropological meanings hidden in God's command. On the one hand, Hosea's marriage speaks of Christ embracing the entire humanity, including sinners: "Our Lord Jesus Christ dined with tax collectors and sinners. . . . [Hosea] very beautifully describes for us the divine Word's bestowing on us spiritual communion with himself while we were still loathsome and unclean" (*Commentary on the Twelve Prophets: On Hos 1:2*).[98] The prophet's marriage should be read as a type: "He takes Gomer, not acting out of lustful passion, but discharging a task of obedience and service, and acting as an instrument of the type, as we shall class him by giving as far as possible a spiritual character to fleshly and earthly things" (*Commentary on the Twelve Prophets: On Hos 1:2*).[99] On the other hand, Hosea's marriage speaks tropologically of the sanctity of marriage in all its aspects: "Now no one in my view would in the future find anything shameful in the goal of the prophet; the word of the divinely inspired Scripture does not exclude marriage, sexual relations, and having children" (*Commentary on the Twelve Prophets: On Hos 1:2*).[100]

Unlike Theodore and to a lesser degree Theodoret, Cyril as a proper Alexandrine offers a lavishly Christological exegesis of Hos 2—the eternal betrothal between God and Israel is fulfilled in Christ and God's eternal kingdom that is to come:

> *I shall betroth you to myself in faith, and you will know the Lord.* Faith made its entrance in advance, therefore, and we were enriched also in this way by knowing Christ—and this in my view, is the meaning of what is said to some: "If you will not believe, neither will you understand." Now the fact that the clear understanding of the mystery of Christ achieves a share in eternal life for those worthy of it the Son himself confirms in speaking to God the Father in heaven: "Now this is eternal life, that they may know you, the one true God, and Jesus Christ, whom you have sent."
>
> *Commentary on the Twelve Prophets: On Hos 2:20*[101]

Cyril also resorts to allegorical interpretation when dealing with the price paid by Hosea:

> [T]he number fifteen includes eight and seven, and almost always in the inspired Scripture there is a reference in seven to the whole time of the Law up to the holy prophets and to the Sabbath on the seventh, and likewise in eight to the new covenant by which the

resurrection of our Savior Jesus Christ happened on the eighth. This, in my view, is the indirect reference in the verse. "Divide them seven ways, or even eight" [Eccl 9:2], that is, let them have a place among you, the Law and the Prophets after them out of respect for the Sabbath on the seventh, and let the eight have a place, that is, the apostles and evangelists after the Savior's resurrection day.

Commentary on the Twelve Prophets: On Hos 3:2[102]

As a distinctive mark, Cyril's vigorous typological and anagogical exegesis is especially well rooted in the literal meaning of the text.

As one may see from the examples above, none of these three interpreters of Hosea allows himself to be boxed into either side of the schematic division between the two famous schools. The work of each interpreter should be labeled, to reiterate Trakatellis's phrase, a "synthesis of exegetical tradition," where literal and spiritual explanations come together under one and the same pen, whether Alexandrine or Antiochene.

This patristic interpretive synthesis corresponds to the wide array of meanings with which each text is charged. Here is Ephrem the Syrian:

If there only existed a single sense for the words of Scripture, then the first commentator who came along would discover it, and other hearers would experience neither the labor of searching, nor the joy of finding. Rather each word of our Lord has its own form, and each form has its own members, and each member has its own character. Each individual understands according to his capacity and interprets as it is granted him.

Commentary on the Diatessaron 7.22[103]

Themes found in patristic exegesis reappear in the aural and visual modes of interpretation so characteristic of Eastern Orthodox tradition, which make up the object of the final chapters of this work. The typology so popular among the church fathers will have a long life throughout the Byzantine period. As we shall see, it can be detected in liturgical productions (hymnography, homilies) and in iconographic imagination, both media used to interpret the Scriptures by adorning phonically and visually the sanctuary in which the Word of God is proclaimed, heard, and mystically appropriated.

6

Aural

> *It is the kingdom of heaven we are entering, after all; we are going to places where lightning flashes. Inside, it is all silence and mysteries beyond telling. Pay precise attention, however: the reading out of the Scriptures is the opening of the heavens. It is a theology of the Word with implications, of course, also for our age's liturgies: public reading of the lectionary is the congregation's key to heaven.*
>
> JOHN CHRYSOSTOM, Six Homilies on Isaiah 6

THE CURRENT CHAPTER aims to illustrate in bare outlines just how imaginative and creative the Eastern Orthodox Church tradition has been in selecting, interpreting, and decanting biblical texts, images, and themes into the liturgical imagery and theology. Given the enormous wealth of liturgical material belonging to the Orthodox Church, much of it yet untouched by scholarly hands, the present chapter offers but a sketch. If ancient Jewish interpretation of the Bible has received a fair amount of attention from the part of modern biblical scholars, the situation in Eastern Orthodox studies is quite modest. Apart from the number of fine works on patristic biblical exegesis, the remainder of the *fontes* of Eastern Orthodox tradition, such as liturgical aural expression of scriptural interpretation, has been often underestimated or entirely overlooked. This neglect comes often from a hasty reading and a shallow understanding of the liturgical and theological context in which the biblical material was embedded. However, with an attentive reading of the biblical material in its liturgical, patristic, and theological intertextuality, the Orthodox liturgical use and interpretation of Scripture will be well appreciated by any student of the Bible. These liturgical productions are as creative and rich as the Jewish Midrashim, to employ one of the handy terms of comparison. Yet, alas, precious little ink has been spilled to bring forth these interpretive gems to the frontline of today's reevaluation of ancient Jewish and Christian interpretations of the Old Testament.

Speaking of biblical authority, Paul D. Hanson notices: "All efforts to comprehend the meaning of Scripture and to grasp the significance of biblical authority are doomed if the interpretive enterprise does not locate its ultimate aim in doxology. For doxology alone acknowledges that when humans open themselves to the message of Scripture they are encountered by God, leading to a sense of gratitude, humility, and awe that finds its most fitting expression in praise."[1] It is quite refreshing to see such remarks on the import of liturgical experience for understanding the Bible coming not from a liturgist but from a biblical scholar. And indeed, the Eastern Orthodox liturgical life is about just that: "gratitude, humility, and awe," ushering in doxology. The preeminently doxological character of the Eastern Orthodox liturgy is deeply rooted in its historical development. As early as the gospel accounts, one may infer that the Eucharist instituted at the Last Supper was concluded by hymns: "And after they sang hymns (hymnēsantes), they went out to the mountain of Olives" (Matt 26:30, author's translation). "Psalms and hymns and spiritual songs" were part of the early Church's liturgical practice (Col 3:16). This early Christian tradition can be traced back to ancient Israel's liturgical experience. Psalms were always an important component of Israelite worship, and psalms and hymns were composed and sung at Qumran even before Jesus's time.

Since the first Christians were of Jewish origin or faith and thus quite familiar with the Temple and synagogue worship, it was the Jewish Scripture before the New Testament that received the attention of the modern scholars studying the relation of Scripture to worship. Scholars are divided as regards the import of Jewish worship on early church liturgy, with some stressing the importance of the Temple and others the synagogue.[2]

In what follows, we investigate in general lines the relation between the Old Testament and the worship of the early Church and its further developments in Eastern Orthodox liturgy. The investigation will show how the Church interpreted the Bible by integrating it into her liturgical life. We begin with a brisk parade of ancient literary fontes delineating the liturgy in its main historical avatars. After this brief survey, we consider the interpretative use of the Old Testament in various liturgical forms or "genres," such as, readings, hymns, catecheses, homilies, prayers, and synaxaria.

Scriptural Readings in Early Christian Liturgy

One of the earliest sources of information is the New Testament. Here is a passing glance at the communal and liturgical life of the apostolic Church.

> They devoted themselves to the apostles' teaching (*didachē*) and fellowship (*kinōnia*), to the breaking of bread (*klasei tou artou*) and the prayers (*proseuchais*). Awe came upon everyone, because many wonders and signs were being done by the apostles. All who believed were together and had all things in common; they would sell their possessions and goods and distribute the proceeds to all, as any had need. Day by day, as they spent much time together in the temple (*hierō*), they broke bread at home (*oikon*) and ate their food with glad and generous hearts, praising God and having the goodwill of all the people. And day by day the Lord added to their number those who were being saved.
>
> Acts 2:42–47

Obviously, the text from Acts 2 refers to the Jerusalem Church immediately after Christ's ascension. Unity in teaching and fellowship, and equal distribution of goods characterize the early Christian community. The text allows one to cast a quick glimpse into the earliest liturgy, which consisted of two parts: "prayers" and "breaking of bread" (Eucharist). The author is silent on scriptural readings. There were two places where earliest followers of Christ worshipped: the "Temple" (not the synagogue!) and various "houses."

Christian catechetical instruction and traditional scholarship place the roots of the "breaking of bread" in the Last Supper account found in synoptic Gospels (Matt 26:26–29; Mark 14:22–25; Luke 22:14–20). The event itself occurred during the Jewish annual festival of Passover. The traditional view on the origin of Eucharist is emblematically associated with Gregory Dix's classic, *The Shape of the Liturgy* (London, 1945). According to Dix,[3] the earliest evidence on the "seven-action shape" of the Eucharistic meal is found in 1 Cor 11:23–26:

> For I received from the Lord what I also handed on to you, that the
> Lord Jesus on the night when he was betrayed took a loaf of bread,
> and when he had given thanks, he broke it and said, "This is my
> body that is for you. Do this in remembrance of me." In the same
> way he took the cup also, after supper, saying, "This cup is the new
> covenant in my blood. Do this, as often as you drink it, in remem-
> brance of me." For as often as you eat this bread and drink the cup,
> you proclaim the Lord's death until he comes.

These are the seven actions listed in the text above:[4] (1) Jesus took bread,
(2) blessed it (cf. the Jewish *berakah*, "blessing"), (3) broke it, (4) gave it to
the apostles by revealing the meaning of the bread that it was his body.
Then, after the meal, (5) he took the cup of wine, (6) said a prayer of
thanksgiving (*eucharistia*), and (7) gave it to his apostles revealing the
meaning of the wine that it was his blood, of the new covenant.

At the end of the first century or the beginning of the second century
C.E., the Eucharistic meal disappeared, surviving sometimes under the
form of the agape of Christian community. A "four-action shape" of the
Eucharist was at that time configured: (1) taking, (2) blessing and thanking, (3) breaking, (4) giving both the bread and the cup to the community.
This fourfold Eucharistic structure along with the Jewish synagogue's
"liturgy of the word" formed the basis of the two-part liturgy attested in
both East and West. The first action, "taking," turned into the preparatory
service (*proskomidē*). The second step, "blessing" and "thanking," became
the Eucharistic prayer (*anaphora*). The "breaking" turned into the fraction
rites, while "giving" became the distribution of the Eucharist.

Regarding the twofold structure of the early liturgy ("liturgy of the
Word" and "liturgy of the Eucharist"), it was understood by earlier liturgical scholarship as a combination of the Jewish synagogue scriptural reading and an early Christian Eucharistic meal. However, there is no way of
knowing what the structure of the synagogue worship before 70 C.E. was.
Was it based exclusively on readings? Did it contain a communal meal of
sorts? Steven Fine argues that early Jewish synagogue was more than a
"house of study" (*beyt ha-midrash*) as commonly perceived. It was in fact
a house of prayer in imitation of the Jerusalem Temple. Fine coined the
term "templization" to describe this phenomenon by which the synagogue
began to be regarded as sacred place of worship. Texts from Qumran, New
Testament, and Tannaim testify to this hermeneutical process.[5] Nevertheless it remains true that the early synagogue rituals were more didactic

than liturgical in purpose. Among the first evidenced Jewish liturgical readings are those from the tannaitic period (70–200 c.e.).[6]

Lawrence H. Schiffman notices that after the destruction of the Jerusalem Temple, in late first century to early second century c.e., a system of Torah and Prophets readings was already functional in institutionalized tannaitic circles. This can be seen in the lively debates between Rabbi Ishmael and Rabbi Aqiba ben Joseph with respect to the number of Torah lessons for Sabbath and festivals. The official setting for reading of the Torah was the synagogue as attested by *t. Megillah* 3(4):12–13. A three-year cycle of Torah readings is mentioned by the anonymous *gemara* in *b. Megillah* 29b. Besides the Torah readings allotted for the Sabbath of a whole year, there were ascribed lessons for special occasions and festivals. Schiffman rightly concludes, "Because these [*tannaitic*] prescriptions seem to match the descriptions in the New Testament, we can assume that the synagogues described there would have followed similar patterns."[7]

The notice in Luke 4:16–21 on Jesus's reading from the Book of Isaiah (i.e., Isa 61:1–2) corresponds to the Jewish liturgical reading of *haftara* (a lesson from a prophetic book). The haftara was usually read by the same person who read the Torah lesson prescribed for that Sabbath. For this token, one may assume that Jesus read both the Torah and haftara portions prescribed for that Sabbath.

The "traditional" view regarding Jewish influence on the early Christian Eucharist and the latter's relation to the Last Supper, as represented by Gregory Dix, has been gradually abandoned. Nevertheless, there are at least two points that should be underscored. First, the early Christian Church and her worship emerged within the Jewish religious context. However, there is no concrete evidence to identify the precise points of intersection between the Jewish worship and that of the nascent Church. Second, there are clearly detectable similarities between the two worship structures. A good illustration is found in *Didache* 9 and 10. The Eucharistic prayers found here are very similar to the Jewish *berakoth* (blessings) prayers, primarily the *birkat ha-mazon* (blessing over food).

Proceeding from a very different angle, several scholars relate the Eucharistic meal to the ancient symposia so popular among Jews, Romans, and Greeks in the Mediterranean world. It has been suggested that the Christian Eucharist was modeled on these meetings.[8] The proponents of the symposium theory emphasize on the social dimension of the early Eucharist, while the adherents of Jewish origin hypothesis insist on the religious and liturgical character of the "breaking of bread."[9] A strong argument in favor of the former is the communal character of the early Christian liturgy that survived in all future liturgical revisions in both East and West. This communal aspect led the Church to create a set of rules of inclusion and exclusion of her members. The weak side of this theory lies with the broad area and diversity of ancient Hellenistic symposia, which makes the collection of data and the comparative analysis a quite difficult task. One may ask: What could a philosophical symposium have to do with such an anamnetic (recollecting, reminiscing) and sacrificial meal, or, widening the field, with the Jewish *havuroth*, "fellowships, groups," and those religious meals held by Qumran community?

In fact, both theories run the risk of insisting too much on one or the other of two foundational aspects of the Eucharist and Christian liturgy at large. Gerard Rouwhorst well noticed, "Whereas scholars in search of Jewish roots run the risk of focusing exclusively on the religious significance of texts, adherents of the symposium theory are in danger of going to the other extreme, emphasizing social practices and related social codes at the expense of religious meanings."[10] A more balanced, inclusive and nonreductionist, approach is needed to explain the sources of Christian liturgy—an approach that would have to take into account both Jewish and non-Jewish, and textual and nontextual, pieces of evidence.

According to the earliest evidence as found in 1 Cor 11 and *Didache* 9–10, the first-century Eucharist was a true meal, taking place in a house-church. Sometime in the second century the meal was reduced to distribution of consecrated bread and wine within a worship setting made of hymns, prayers, and readings. The proponents of the traditional hypothesis (the Eucharist modeled on the Last Supper) commonly select two ancient sources that legitimize their view: Justin Martyr and the *Apostolic Tradition*. In what follows below, we consider these and several other early sources describing the early liturgy and the place of Old Testament readings within it.

Justin Martyr

From the second century comes one of the earliest evidences regarding the scriptural readings in conjunction with the Eucharist. Justin Martyr in his *First Apology*, written about the year 150 C.E., gives a detailed description of a Sunday worship service centered on Eucharist:

And on the day called Sunday (*tē tou Ēliou legomenē ēmera*), all who live in cities or in the country gather together to one place, and the memoirs of the apostles or the writings of the prophets are read, as long as time permits; then, when the reader has ceased, the president verbally instructs, and exhorts to the imitation of these good things. Then we all rise together and pray, and, as we before said, when our prayer is ended, bread and wine and water are brought, and the president in like manner offers prayers and thanksgivings, according to his ability (*hosē dynamis autō*), and the people assent, saying Amen; and there is a distribution to each, and a participation of that over which thanks have been given [or: "of the eucharistic elements"], and to those who are absent a portion is sent by the deacons. And they who are well to do, and willing, give what each thinks fit; and what is collected is deposited with the president, who succors the orphans and widows and those who, through sickness or any other cause, are in want, and those who are in bonds and the strangers sojourning among us, and in a word takes care of all who are in need. But Sunday is the day on which we all hold our common assembly, because it is the first day on which God, having wrought a change in the darkness and matter, made the world; and Jesus Christ our Savior on the same day rose from the dead. For he was crucified on the day before that of Saturn (Saturday); and on the day after that of Saturn, which is the day of the Sun, having appeared to his apostles and disciples, he taught them these things, which we have submitted to you also for your consideration.

First Apology 67[11]

Here is the structure of the second-century Sunday Eucharist service as reflected in Justin's testimony: (1) scriptural readings; (2) exhortation; (3) prayers offered by assembly; (4) bread, wine and water are brought in; (5) prayers and thanksgivings offered by president over the eucharistic elements; (6) distribution of the Eucharistic elements (a portion is sent to those absent through the deacons); (7) offerings by those willing and able to share with the needy (orphans, widows, poor, those in bonds, strangers), given in the custody of the president who had the duty to distribute them to the needy.

The Eucharist as described by Justin has seven sections. These sections point to the religious and social aspects of the Christian liturgy and to its possible precursors, the Jewish ritual meal and the Hellenistic symposium. As one may notice, the Eucharistic service concludes with distribution of the offerings to the needy. Everything up to that point—scriptural readings, exhortation, distribution of Eucharistic elements—was aimed to build up the momentum for social implementation of the religious message and ritual. The later dual structure of the Christian liturgy ("liturgy of the word" and "liturgy of the sacrament") may also be intuitively gleaned from the above description.

One may notice from Justin's description that the Eucharistic elements were dissociated by then from the initial meal held prior to Justin's time in the evening. Moreover, scriptural readings following the Jewish synagogue custom were brought into the structure of the Eucharistic service. This emerging dual structure of the Eucharistic liturgy is the most characteristic perennial form of Christian liturgies in both East and West up to the present times. The important role of scriptural readings in the second-century Christian worship is attested by their opening position in Justin's Eucharistic service.

The scriptural readings used to go on "as long as time permits," as Justin tells us. From this phrase one may infer that there was no fixed lectionary (order of readings) by the mid-second century c.e. Whether or not the text actually speaks of the practice of *lectio continua* (continuous reading) one cannot say. One thing is sure: the length was not prescribed.

The lessons were selected from "the memoirs of the apostles or the writings of the prophets," as Justin remarks. The "or" perhaps indicates that there was no fixed dual reading from both the Old *and* New Testament, but that the reader could choose to read from either collection.

Unlike the Jewish synagogue, where the scriptural lessons were read in descending order, beginning with the most important division of the Hebrew Bible, the Law, and continuing with a lesson from the Prophets, in Christian worship the ascending order is characteristic, with the apostle followed by the gospel reading. Finally, after the readings were completed, the president gave an explanation of what was read, urging his hearers to put in practice what was read—the basic form of the homily which, according to proper Orthodox order, is still supposed to precede the Eucharistic prayers.

Apostolic Constitutions

The *Apostolic Constitutions* is a late fourth-century c.e. composite work consisting of catechesis and liturgical regulations. Written in a hortatory tone, it purports to have been compiled by Clement of Rome. However, the Church never considered this work as apostolic in origin.

Apostolic Constitutions 2.7.57[12] offers a bird's-eye view of the church as a gathering hall with a definite architectural form. We are introduced to a solemn assembly seated on chairs in an oval pattern. On the one end, there is the clergy flanking the bishop in the center, the deacons standing next to the seated presbyters. On the other end are seated the laity: first the men, then the women behind them. In the middle of this shiplike church there is a high place with a lectern, whence the scriptural lessons are read and the exhortations are offered. The sequential structure of the Eucharistic service proceeds as follows: (1) readings (two from the Old Testament, followed by Acts, an epistle, and a gospel); (2) exhortations (the presbyters with the bishop at the end, as a "commander" of the ship, deliver exhortations); (3) catechumens and penitents now leave the church—the second part of the liturgy, the Eucharist proper, is about to begin; (4) the whole assembly is praying eastwards, facing the place of the lost paradise; (5) the bishop's first deacon urges the people to get rid of any grudge and quarrel and to prepare themselves for the Eucharist; (6) the kiss of peace is offered (men with men, women with women); (7) the deacon's prayer follows, offered for the whole world, the Church, the presbyters and rulers, for the high priest, and for the fruits of the earth; (8) the bishop prays for and blesses the people; (9) the oblation is offered; (10) the whole assembly partakes of the consecrated Eucharistic elements.

As regards scriptural readings, the Old Testament lessons are called "the Prophet" or "the Prophecy," probably because these lessons were not read for themselves alone but rather in conjunction with the New Testament lessons. After the Old Testament came the New Testament lessons. There was a reading from any text of the New Testament, except the Gospels, called "the Apostle," because most of the lessons under this title were chosen from the Pauline epistles. At the reading of "the gospel" following the epistle lesson, the congregation was summoned to stand—a sign of the special honor given, not to the reader, but rather to the one speaking through him. Unlike the other lessons, that were read by a reader or a lector out of the congregation, the gospel was read by either a deacon or presbyter; this added to the solemnity of the reading.

The bipartite structure of the liturgy intimated in Justin Martyr and clearly attested by the *Apostolic Constitutions* is found again and again in every historical development of the liturgy. According to Robert F. Taft, there were three important watershed moments in the development of the Byzantine liturgy: the late sixth century, after Justinian; the struggle and victory over iconoclasm (726–75; 815–43 C.E.); and the Paleaologan dynasty (1261–1543). The last period is called "Byzantine synthesis." To each of these three watersheds corresponds a mystagogy, which, in Taft's view, is to liturgy what exegesis is to Scripture.[13] There are four important commentaries (mystagogies) on the Divine Liturgy: those of the pseudonymous author Dionysios the Areopagite (sixth century),[14] Maximos the Confessor (d. 622),[15] Germanos of Constantinople (d. 730)[16] and Nicholas Cabasilas (d. 1350).[17] Cabasilas's commentary brings forth a liturgy in the final form of its "Byzantine synthesis."

Itinerarium Egeriae

The Spanish nun Egeria (or Etheria) made a pilgrimage to Egypt, the Holy Land, Edessa, Asia Minor, and Constantinople, shortly before 400 C.E. She describes in her narrated itinerary how the Eucharist was celebrated in the Church of the *Anastasis* (Resurrection) built by Constantine in 335 C.E. in Jerusalem on the traditional site of Jesus's tomb. According to the *Itinerarium*, the usual time of the service was the third hour (9 a.m.) on Saturdays and Sundays. The liturgical language of the Jerusalem Church was Greek, but interpretations of scriptural lessons and various instructions were conducted also in Syriac for those who did not know Greek. Exhortations by presbyters and finally by the bishop were offered at the end of the service. The preacher would sit while the audience was standing, after the Jewish synagogue model. Applause was not only permitted, but even invited by the speaker.[18]

On Good Friday, from the sixth (12 p.m.) to ninth hour (3 p.m.), the assembly gathered in the open space between the Anastasis and the Cross. A chair is placed for the bishop in front of the Cross and lessons are read: first lessons from those Prophets and "hymns" (Psalms) alluding to the Lord's passion, then lessons from the apostles (epistles or Acts) suitable to the commemoration and passages from the Gospels. Here is a fragment from Etheria's lively description:

> Then the readings from the Prophets where they foretold that the
> Lord should suffer, then from the Gospels where he mentions his
> Passion. Thus from the sixth to the ninth hours the lessons are so
> read and the hymns said, that it may be shown to all the people that
> whatsoever the prophets foretold of the Lord's Passion is proved

from the Gospels and from the writings of the apostles to have been fulfilled. And so through all those three hours the people are taught that nothing was done which had not been foretold, and that nothing was foretold which was not wholly fulfilled.[19]

There is a common assumption that the readings from different parts of the Christian Bible were already fixed in the pre-Nicene period even though there is no consensus on the exact number of scriptural lessons used in the liturgy. Toward the end of the fourth century, the readings were reduced to three due to the increasing elements added to the *synaxis* or so-called liturgy of the word. The threefold scriptural reading consisted of the lesson from the Old Testament, the apostolic writings, and the gospel.

Among the church fathers, Basil the Great (*Homily* 13) mentions the number of lessons read at a specific worship service: three lessons (one from Isaiah, one from Acts and one from Matthew). In *Homilia dicta in Lacizis,* Basil lists three lessons: from Proverbs, epistles, and Gospels.[20] It looks like a pattern for the fourth century Church to have three lessons: one from the Old Testament (Law, Prophets, wisdom books) and two from the New Testament (Acts or epistle and gospel).[21] This situation, at least regarding the New Testament lessons, will continue to be emblematic for Christian liturgies in both East and West. Augustine (*Sermo 176: De tribus lectionibus*) numbers among the scriptural lessons the epistles and the gospel, sometimes adding also the Prophets. As additional sources of information on liturgy, one may mention the *Catechetical Letters* of Cyril of Jerusalem (347 C.E.) and the *Sacramentary* of Serapion, bishop of Thmuis (about 350 C.E.).[22]

As early as the seventh century, the Old Testament lessons that were read in the church at various liturgical services were collected in a single book called *Prophetologion.*[23] While the *Euangelion* and *Praxapostolos* represent the "liturgical" New Testament, the *Prophetologion* or *Paroimiarion*[24] is the Old Testament lectionary.[25] According to James Miller, the *Prophetologion* was for Byzantines what the Old Testament is for the moderns.[26] The influence of the *Prophetologion* decreased, however, in the twelfth century, when its contents were inserted in various liturgical books such as Triodion and Menaion.[27]

Throughout the seventh and eighth centuries, the main literary genres (the Akathist, canons, Triodion, Octoechos, etc.) of liturgical poetry were fully developed. By the ninth century, the worship was divided in two forms: cathedral and monastic, each one with its own *typikon* (a liturgical manual regulating the services during the ecclesiastical year). The cathedral rite lasted until the fourteenth century in some areas, but was eventually overtaken by the monastic typikon. As Anatoly Alexeev notes, the seventh through eighth centuries is the ad quem point of liturgical experiment. If one wants to go to earlier periods, one should examine the liturgical lectionaries of Syrian, Armenian, and Georgian origin. All these go back to Jerusalemite archetypes supported by the late fourth-century testimony of Etheria (Egeria).[28] It can be said that the basic form of public worship in Byzantium received its last major revisions by the end of the first millennium and has been preserved in great lines up to the present in Eastern Orthodox Churches.

The Old Testament in Eastern Orthodox Worship

I should begin by deconstructing an old cliché. Teaching Old Testament classes at an Orthodox seminary, I have been often confronted with a rather defensive attitude on the part of some of my students. Why do we need to learn all these modern steps of exegesis (i.e., textual, form, literary, and redaction criticism) when we have a valuable trove of patristic interpretations? First, I would reply, the ancient Christian (patristic) interpretations cover just a few letters—let us say, A, B, C, D, and E—of the rich alphabet of biblical interpretation. There are so many other letters to be deciphered by modern readers, approaching the text with a new, fresh look and different assumptions than those held up by the ancient interpreters. Second, I detect in this reputed question a misconception, widespread among even educated readers within my tradition, namely, that earlier patristic interpretations are the climax and the endpoint of the exegetical work to be done within the confines of this tradition.

In fact, it may be argued that the greatest exegetical work in the Eastern Orthodox tradition does not lie so much with the specific (discursive) interpretations penned by the church fathers, but rather with the imaginative creativity found in the liturgical productions of this tradition. Each hymn is overflooded with daring metaphors gleaned from various books of the Bible. To reconstruct the creative mind beyond this metaphoric and imagistic artistry is an exegetical exercise in itself, for a cavalcade of succeeding metaphors mirrors an extraordinary familiarity of the hymnographers with the Holy Writ, as well as their ability to interpret the sacred text within a different *Sitz im Leben,* the liturgy, that is. Biblical metaphors, liturgical embellishments, and kerygmatic framework all together create a holistic unity—so much, that some prefer to call the Byzantine hymnography a "rewritten Bible."[29] Yet I would not go so far to label this treasure as "rewritten Bible," as there is still a great difference between these dispersed hymns and, for instance, the Book of Jubilees—a perfect candidate for the "rewritten Bible" status. I would rather call it "a compendium of biblical metaphors in liturgical garb."

Eastern Orthodox worship is profoundly scriptural. The Second Council of Nicaea in 787 c.e. decreed: "Every one who is raised to the rank of the episcopate shall know the Psalter by heart, so that from it he may admonish and instruct all the clergy who are subject to him" (*Canon Two*).[30] One may assume that other parts of Scripture were also memorized. Thus, it is only with a slight hyperbole that John McGuckin asserts: "If ever all the bibles in the world were lost, sacred Scripture could be rewritten by reference to the service books of the Orthodox Church. The monks would single-handedly be able to recite the entire Psalter by heart. The ordinary faithful would reconstitute the Gospels verse by verse; and what was left lacking from the other apostolic and prophetic literature would be readily discoverable in the liturgies and offices of prayer."[31] But the wealth of Scripture found in the Orthodox services does not come to us naked. Rather, it is clothed and framed, interpreted and celebrated by a treasure of hymnographic "liturgical exegesis." Etheria during her pilgrimage to the Holy Land was fascinated with the way Psalms, hymns, prayers and scriptural lessons were interwoven by the Jerusalem Church into a beautiful liturgical synthesis. Pertaining to the "Procession with Palms on the Mount of Olives," she noted: "Hymns and antiphones suitable to the day and to the place are said, interspersed with lections and prayers."[32] The synthesis hinted at by Etheria is still present today in Eastern Orthodox services as recorded in diverse service books such as the Menaion, Octoechos, Triodion, and Pentecostarion.[33]

Unlike the patristic exegesis found in commentaries, which is quite descriptive or discursive[34] and often tamed by theological inferences, the "liturgical exegesis" is more flexible in its flow of ideas, and multivalent through its accelerating use of metaphors. For this reason of metaphoric polivalence, Orthodox liturgical exegesis, I would say, is close in spirit to the Hebrew Bible, even though the Septuagint has always been the default Scripture of the Byzantine Orthodox Church.

I find Byzantine hymnography to be one of the most insightful and condensed types of exegesis one could think of. Here is the zenith of the Eastern Orthodox contribution to biblical hermeneutics. Byzantine hymnography is rich, creative, integrative, poignant, and imaginative. It challenges the reader's familiarity with the written Word of God, in all its vast and densely thicketed historical, symbolic and metaphorical landscape. Those who say that Scripture is to be found and heard within the liturgy are right; but if their statement makes them stay away from reading the Bible, they are mistaken. On the contrary, the hymnographers did not want to replace the Bible with their poetic productions. Rather, like the patristic interpreters musing over and sermonizing the Scriptures, they invite the listeners to a continuous and imaginative reading of the Bible. The condensed liturgical exegesis is again a challenge to hearers and readers to locate the texts, events, images, and figures woven into the hymnography.

Below is a selection of examples under the rubric of the aural mode of interpretation of the Old Testament. Hymns, Psalms, scriptural lessons, homilies, and synaxaria are all analyzed in their intertextuality throughout the Byzantine liturgical year, with its festal days dedicated to the Theotokos, Christ, events in the history of salvation, and saints.

Liturgical Year

The Byzantine liturgical year is configured by two basic overarching cycles: the annual Menaion cycle (Gk. *mēnaion*, "moon"—the monthly cycle) of feasts with fix dates, and the dominical cycle determined by the date of Easter Sunday. At the center of the liturgical year lies the great feast of Pascha (Easter) commemorating the passion, death, and resurrection of Christ.[35] One may add that the dominical cycle further configures the Triodion, the Pentecostarion, as well as all Sundays from Pentecost to the Sunday of Zacchaeus.

The Christian liturgical year imitates in principal the Jewish liturgical year. The latter commences in autumn with the month of *Tishri* (September-October), indicating the beginning of a new agricultural year after the late harvest. In spring, the month of *Nisan* (March-April) heralds the *Pesach* (Passover), originally a festival of farmers and shepherds, but later a religious celebration commemorating Israel's exodus out of Egypt.

Similarly, the Byzantine liturgical year begins in autumn, on September 1, with its multicolor bouquet of festal days. However, as Georges

Barrois rightly observes, the festal cycle is intrinsically linked to the dominical cycle: "The festal cycle does not run separately from the paschal or dominical cycle, but concurrently. The sanctification of the historical time of the Menaion must not be opposed to the eschatological time of the Triodion and the Pentecostarion. They combine with each other, and we are not permitted to drift aimlessly from day to day, from saint to saint, from feast to feast, and forget the goal that is set before us, the kingdom which Christ ushered in and which he will consummate on the last day."[36]

Worship in Eastern Orthodox tradition has a twofold goal. First, it has a Eucharistic, mnemonic function, commemorating the multifaceted salvific work of Christ: his life, passion, crucifixion, death, burial, resurrection, ascension, sitting at the right hand of the Father and sending of the Holy Spirit. Second, worship has a formative and sanctifying function. Both goals are at the core of Eastern Orthodox ethos. Attending worship in Eastern Orthodoxy is not only a mere memorial of what Jesus of Nazareth performed long time ago or a disembodied symbol of his presence in the Church. Worship for Orthodox believers is also a laboratory room where the formative power of the gospel is implemented, tested, realized, and rehearsed repeatedly in a lively personal-communal relationship with the exalted Lord Jesus. This formative dimension determines the specific structure, selection, and direction of the Orthodox liturgical experience.

Psalmody

The most common creative use of Scripture in the worship for both Judaism and Christianity is the psalmody: the recitation and chanting of Psalms[37] during liturgical services.[38] The Book of Psalms was the liturgical trove of the Jerusalem Temple, inherited by both the Jewish synagogue and nascent Christian Church.

Presumably, the Book of Psalms, containing 150 canonical Psalms, was divided in so many songs to cover a three-year liturgical cycle, according to the model of the five-volume Torah (*Pentateuchos*)—but there is no concrete evidence to support this supposition. There are no traces of a such a division in the Masoretic Text, nor is there any such practice in today synagogue's worship.

The continuous reading[39] of the Psalter in Eastern Orthodox worship is still detectable in two different periods of the liturgical year, before the feast of Nativity and during the Holy Week (Triodion). In theory, in every monastery, all 150 canonical Psalms are read as lectio continua each week.⁴⁰ During the Great Lent, the Psalter is read twice a week. The reading of Psalms is suspended in the last three days of the Holy Week and during the Bright Week (i.e., the week between Easter and the Sunday of St. Thomas).⁴¹

Vespers

The selection of Psalms tends to be topical as much as this criterion works with poetical material. There are a few exceptions where the topical selection is clearly notable at this point in the development of liturgical services. For instance, the Vespers opens with the reading of Ps 103(104):1, "Bless the Lord, O my soul; O Lord my God, you are greatly magnified" (NETS), lauding God for his providence to the entire creation. This theme is appropriate as one ends a day and is about to begin a new day. In the liturgical cycle, the day begins with the sunset, which is the usual time to perform the Vespers service. Ps 103(104) is a poetical insight into creation as God's first work of his unfolding self-disclosure (revelation). It invites us to look at God's creation as an artist's masterpiece. The doxological aspect of the Vespers ("Bless the Lord, O my soul") which opens and ends Ps 103(104): 1, 35, is found in the Orthros service (Ps 102[103]:1, 22). Out of the entire Psalter, this sentence appears only in these two Psalms, making the selection of Ps 102(103) and 103(104) for the Orthros and Vespers respectively even more interesting. If Ps 102(103) blesses God for his saving forgiveness, Ps 103(104) blesses God for his creative providence.

Ps 103(104) has sometimes been considered by modern biblical scholars as the "poetical version" of the priestly creation account of Gen 1.⁴² The central idea found in both texts is that creation cannot be separated from the Creator. On the one hand, creation is different than the Creator. On the other hand, creation cannot exist without God the Creator, so that even his providence itself is but a consequence of his creative work. "You will send forth your spirit, and they will be created, and you will renew the face of the ground" (Ps 103[104]:30, NETS). Sending forth the Spirit equals re-creating creation. Ps 103(104) reaches its climax with an exclamation that links God's providence to his creative work. God's wisdom is apparently the bridge between these two important divine works, "How magnified were your works, O Lord! In wisdom you made them all" (v. 24, NETS).

Ps 103(104) is primarily about God's providence toward his creation. Unlike Ps 8, which is quite anthropocentric in its scope, Ps 103(104) regards the human being as any other creature with no special qualification.

Dissimilar to our modern tendency of speaking about world in a quite fragmentary way, Ps 103(104) provides a holistic, integrative view on the world by re-locating the human being within the creation.[43] "You set darkness, and it became night; in it all the animals of the forest will pass through, the whelps roaring to seize and to seek their food from God. The sun rose, and they gathered, and in their dens they will lie down. A person will go out to his work and to his labor until the evening" (vv. 20–23, NETS). God's providence keeps everything under control. The primordial waters are defeated by God's establishing of the earth and his rebuking the waters (vv. 5, 7). Even the "dragon," symbolizing chaos and malefic forces, is domesticated and reduced to a mere object of amusement, "this dragon (*drakōn houtos*)[44] that you formed to mock at him" (v. 26, NETS). In a nutshell, God's providence is a quite appropriate theme for those gathered in worship at the Vespers, the end of one day and the beginning of another, recounting God's acts of providence and strengthening their faith and hope in God, the providing Creator, who will carry them throughout the upcoming night. Both God's creation and providence determine the psalmist to doxologize the Lord, "I will sing to the Lord in my life; I will make music to my God while I have being" (v. 33, NETS).

Other Psalms (Ps 129[130], 140[141], 141[142]) read at the Vespers are supplications triggered by various needs—physical, social, moral, and religious. "My soul hoped in the Lord from morning watch until night; from morning watch, let Israel hope in the Lord" (Ps 129[130]:6, NETS): waiting in hope for God's mercy for as long as it takes to reach the supplicant. "O Lord, I cried to you; listen to me; pay attention to the voice of my petition when I cry to you. Let my prayer succeed as incense before you, a lifting up of my hands be an evening sacrifice" (Ps 140[141]:1–2, NETS). The mention of "incense" and "evening sacrifice" is meant to bring in an almost archaic liturgical flavor, while transposing the Christian audience liturgically back into the days of Solomon's Temple in Jerusalem, with the burnt offerings on the altar every evening. Ps 141(142) continues the theme of "crying" to the Lord from preceding Psalm: "With my voice I cried to the Lord; with my voice I petitioned the Lord. I will pour out my petition before him; my affliction I will announce before him" (vv. 2[1]–3[2], NETS). The same theme is found in Ps 129(130):[1]–2: "Out of depths I cried to you, O Lord. Lord, listen to my voice! Let your ears become attentive to the voice of my petition!" (NETS). Here, lamenting is accompanied by a great deal of hope: "My soul hoped in the Lord from morning watch until night; from morning watch, let Israel hope in the Lord" (v. 6, NETS).

As one may infer, the "morning" / "night" motif was perhaps one of the main reasons why this Psalm was selected for the Vespers service.

Matins

The "six Psalms at Orthros (Matins)" (Ps 3, 37[38], 62[63], 87[88], 102[103], 142[143]) depict the human predicament in sober tones with a few orange-white sparks coming forth from the dark-brown-to-black backdrop of the Matins's psalmody—as in a painting by Rembrandt, where glimmers of ardent light timidly yet buoyantly struggle to emerge out of the shining blackness of the canvas.

According to the superscript ("A Psalm. Pertaining to Dauid. When he was running away from his son Abessalom," v. 1, NETS), Ps 3 was composed by David when his son Absalom rebelled against him (2 Sam 15). One can easily visualize a barefoot David fleeing Jerusalem, crossing the Kidron brook, and eventually climbing the Mount of Olivet. On the top of Olivet, the fugitive king worships God (2 Sam 15:32) and spends the night, heading out through Bethany for the wilderness of Judaea the next day. With a similar itinerary and in a resembling stressful situation, a "deeply grieved" (perilypos) Jesus (Mark 14:34) accompanied by his disciples leaves the room of the Last Supper on Thursday night, crosses the Kidron brook and stations in a private garden, Gethsemane, at the bottom of the same Mount of Olivet.

Those responsible with composing and revising the Orthros service made a discriminating choice by selecting and placing Ps 3 at the beginning of the service. As any lament in the Psalter, Ps 3 interweaves fear with hope. Faith does not come easy. Faith cohabitates often with grief. Faith is always tested.

The morning encounters us with a double perspective: fear and hope. Night just ended, a new day ushers in with a mixture of hope and apprehension. The psalmist in Ps 3 assures his hearers that God is on the side of those who put all their hope in him. Enemies are always lurking in the dark. They can take different forms: figures within our daily experiences, emotions or realities from a spiritual realm.

> O Lord, why did those who afflict me multiply? Many are rising against me; many are saying to me, "There is no deliverance for him in his God." Interlude on strings (diapsalma). But you, O Lord, you are my supporter, my glory, and the one who lifts up my head. With my voice I cried to the Lord, and he hearkened to me from his

holy mountain. Interlude on strings (*diapsalma*). I lay down and slept; I woke again, because the Lord will support me. I shall not be afraid of ten thousands of people who are setting themselves against me all around.

Ps 3:2[1]–7[6], NETS

One can imagine a lonely and sorrowful king David awaking from his sleep on Mount Olivet or in the morning of his battle with Absalom (2 Sam 17:27–29). In spite of the emerging gloomy reality, the king puts his hope in God who helped him in the past and during the night of fear and agony that has just passed.

The term *Selah* (Gk. *diapsalma*, "musical interlude, break," in the LXX), whatever it meant in Hebrew, creates a pause in liturgical recitation. That was probably the moment when those attending the worship would have responded, so sharing in the psalmist's experience of fear and hope.

What is the relation between Ps 3 and the remainder of Psalms prescribed for the service of Orthros (Matins)? Ps 37(38) continues the lamentation of Ps 3 by bringing more examples of a man attacked by enemies within and without. The pain is even greater as the fear generated by the increasing number of enemies is now accompanied by deep feelings of abandonment. Friends and siblings leave the man under assault completely alone: "My heart was troubled, my strength failed me, and as for the light of my eyes—it too is not with me. My friends and my fellows approached opposite me and stood, and my next of kin stood far off" (Ps 37[38]:11[10]–12[11], NETS). Nevertheless, the psalmist still hopes in God's mercy: "Because in you, O Lord, I hoped; it is you, O Lord, my God, who will listen" (Ps 37[38]:16[15], NETS). Ps 37(38) ends up in a cry for help: "Do not forsake me, O Lord; O my God, do not stand far from me; attend to helping me, O Lord of my deliverance" (Ps 37[38]:22[21]–23[22], NETS).

Through its superscription ("Pertaining to David. When he was in the wilderness of Judea"), Ps 62(63) situates the lamenting psalmist in the middle of the wilderness at dawn: "O God, my God, early I approach you (*orthrizō*); my soul thirsted for you. How many times did my flesh thirst for you in a land, desolate and trackless and waterless?" (Ps 62[63]:2[1], NETS). The verb *orthrizō*, "to rise, seek, approaching early" (LXX), apparently contributed to the selection of this Psalm for the Orthros (Gk. *orthros*, "day-break, dawn") service. I say contributed, and not exclusively dictated, because the theme of complete abandonment of the sufferer was probably the first reason for this selection. In Ps 62(63), the one attacked by his enemies (Ps 3) and abandoned by his friends and relatives (Ps 37[38]) is now left alone in the middle of nowhere with no means of survival. There is a crescendo in intensity of pain, fear, and abandonment. However, the psalmist's hope in God is also growing stronger in proportion with his struggle.

Ps 87(88) is the first non-Davidic Psalm in the six-Psalm sequence opening the Orthros service. This is the last Psalm in the Psalter attributed to the sons of Kore (Korah). The superscription of this Psalm reads: "An Ode. Of a Psalm. Pertaining to the sons of Kore. Regarding completion. Over Maeleth in order that he be answered. Of understanding. Pertaining to Haiman the Israelite" (v. 1, NETS). According to 1 Chr 6:33, Haiman (Heman) was one of the singers appointed by king David to be in the service of Lord's House. In 1 Chr 16:41–42, he is granted a high position among the musicians at the Jerusalem Temple.

The dramatic crescendo, initiated with Ps 3 and worked through in Ps 37(38) and 62(63), continues with Ps 87(88). Truly, the psalmist allows us to cast a glimpse into the darkness reigning in his soul: "Because my soul was full of troubles and my life drew near to Hades, I was counted among those who go down into a pit; I became like a helpless person, free among corpses, like casualties lying asleep in a grave, whom you remembered no more, and they were thrust away from your hand. They put me in a very deep pit, in dark places and in death's shadow. Upon me your anger was fixed, and all your billows you brought upon me. Interlude on strings (*diapsalma*)" (Psa 87[88]:4[3]–8[7], NETS). The sufferer is abandoned by his relatives and friends. But far more difficult to understand and accept is the fact that God himself is the cause of this misery. "You distanced my acquaintances from me" (v. 9[8], NETS) is echoed in the last lines of this Psalm, "You distanced from me friend and fellow and my acquaintances due to misery" (v. 19[18], NETS). The greatest abandonment the speaker faces is from God himself, who leaves his servant lonely among the dead, in a godforsaken watery netherworld (v. 18[17]).

Ps 87(88) continues the idea of Ps 37(38), further interpreting the abandonment of the siblings and friends as being determined by God's wrath (*thymos*) against the suffering psalmist (v. 8[7]). But in this circumstance with no foreseen resolution, the psalmist does not lose his faith and hope in God, even though the psalmist's hope is now but a mere recognition of God's relentlessly terrifying actions against him: "I cried out to you, O Lord, all day long; I spread out my hands to you" (Ps 87[88]:10[9], NETS). The psalmist's praying attitude as the only means of survival made Ps 87(88) a good candidate for the six-Psalm series which opens the Orthros service: "In the morning (*prōi*) my prayer will anticipate (*prophthasei*) you" (v. 14[13], NETS). "All day long (*holēn tēn hēmeran*)" (v. 10[9]) is a reminder for the faithful that Matins is only the beginning of a daylong prayerful disposition. Verses 11(10)–13(12) raise a tough question: If God wants to destroy his servant utterly by bringing him down to the "grave" (or netherworld), then who will praise God? The answer to the question is expected to come from the choir of worshippers: Surely, not the dead, but the living are those who will praise God.

With Ps 102(103), however, there is dramatic change in tone, from lament to doxology. The psalmist recounts all the blessings God has poured upon him. One of the first divine acts in this roster of marvels is that God "redeems your life from corruption, crowns you with mercy and compassion, satisfies your desire with good, and your youth will be renewed like an eagle's" (Ps 102[103]:4–5, NETS). This is in sharp contrast with what was heard in the preceding Psalm: "I was counted among those who go down into a pit"—Ps 87[88]:5[4], NETS). God's intervention is depicted as a resurrection from the dead. Psalm 102(103) has an intricate structure. It contains twenty-two verses corresponding to the twenty-two letters of the Hebrew alphabet, an indirect hint at this text's compendiousness. The Psalm begins and ends with the same words, "Bless the Lord, O my soul," as a genuine doxology. The negative imperative, "Do not forget all his repayments" (v. 2, NETS), shows the way in which the worshipper can stay in the same mode of praise and thanksgiving: he must continually remember God's dealings with Israel. These dealings are rehearsed in the Psalm itself. This liturgical rehearsal of the *magnalia Dei* can be divided in four parts delineated by the use of the key Hebrew term *ḥesed*, "long-suffering love, kindness" (Gk. *eleos*, "mercy"), found in verses 4, 8, 11, and 17. In verses 4 and 8, *ḥesed* appears along with r-ḥ-m, "to be compassionate" (e.g., Heb. *raḥămîm* corresponding to Gk. *oiktirmos* "compassion").

God's two main attributes, steadfast, longsuffering love (Heb. *ḥesed* and Gk. *eleos*) and compassion (Heb. *raḥămîm* and Gk. *oiktirmos*), are found in God's proclamation to Moses in the wilderness—a self-revelation centered on God's personal name, Yahweh, and its character, after the faithless manufacture and worship of the golden calf by Aaron and the people (Exod 34:6–7). In fact, the assertion in Ps 102 [103]:8, "Compassionate and merciful is the Lord, slow to anger and abounding in mercy" (NETS), is quoted from this divine proclamation in the wilderness, one of the most important theological statements in the entire Old Testament. Longsuffering love (*ḥesed*) is God's personal attribute, portraying him as a father who loves his children unconditionally. The attribution of compassion (*raḥămîm*, related to *reḥem,* "mother's womb") depicts God as a mother who feels viscerally her children's suffering and pain. The psalmist declares three times that God's longsuffering love and compassion are for those "who fear the Lord" (vv. 11, 13, 17), namely, those who place God as the center of their lives. The faithful attending the Orthros (Matins) service and listening to this Psalm are urged to follow this ideal.

Unlike the preceding Psalms in the Orthros service, all prayers of a seemingly isolated individual, Ps 102(103) links the psalmist to the worshipping community: "As a father has compassion for sons, the Lord has had compassion for those who fear him, because he knew our makeup. Remember that we are dust!" (vv. 13–14, NETS). The emphasis moves from an individual sufferer to all human beings made of dust (cf. Gen 2:7). The Psalm ends by summoning the celestial hosts of angels and dominions to join the earthly worshipping community in giving thanks to God who forgives, redeems, and restores those who put their hope in him (vv. 19–22).

Ps 142(143) returns to the more common "I" of the Psalms. It is an individual prayer for help. The psalmist begins his prayer by asking God to forgive him without bringing his case to judgment. The reason for such a daring petition is that no one is righteous according to God's high standards: "And do not enter into judgment with your slave, because no one living will be counted righteous before you" (v. 2, NETS).

Thematically, Ps 142(143) is close to Ps 87(88); it is the same grave-like, depressing setting. This time, the psalmist complains against a certain "enemy" who makes his life unbearable: "Because the enemy (*echthros*) pursued my soul, he humbled my life to the ground; he made me sit in dark places like those long dead. And my spirit became weary in me; within me my heart was troubled. . . . Do not turn your face from me, and I shall be like those who go down into a pit" (142[143]:3–4, 7b, NETS). The theme of remembering God's past interventions connects this Psalm to the preceding one. This liturgical rehearsal helps the psalmist to put his hope in God: "I spread out my hands to you; my soul was like a parched land. Interlude on strings (*diapsalma*). Listen to me quickly, O Lord; my spirit failed" (vv. 6–7a, NETS). "I spread out my hands to you" is found in Ps 87[88]:10[9] mentioned above. The leitmotif of "morning" used several times in the six-Psalm series of Orthros reappears in v. 8 side by side with "hope": "Make me hear your mercy in the morning (*prōi*), because in you I hoped (*ēlpisa*). Make known to me, O Lord, a way in which I should go, because to you I lifted up my soul." All the petitions for forgiveness, mercy, deliverance, guidance, redemption, and justice are anchored in the psalmist's strong belief that in spite of all adversities he is God's servant, "Because your slave (*doulos*) I am" (v. 12, NETS).

Criteria for Psalm Selection

Typology. According to Georges Barrois,[45] typology was the main criterion in Psalm selection for various liturgical services. Whereas the sixteenth century Reformers, the Enlightenment and nineteenth- and twentieth-century historical criticism all sought either to underplay or entirely debunk typology as a hermeneutical approach with its own merit, those responsible with the configuration of the Byzantine liturgical services gave typology a preeminent place when they decided what Psalms were to be used, especially on festal commemorations. This typological criterion was further reinforced by an interest in elements from the Psalms that could be related to the themes and motifs of specific feast days.

As an illustration for the role of typology in Psalm selection, one may adduce the feast of the "Exaltation of the Precious Cross" held on September 14.

The first part of the "small entrance"[46] hymn (Ps 98[99]:5) prescribed for this festal day speaks of the "footstool" of Lord's feet: "Exalt the Lord our God, and do obeisance at the footstool of his feet, because holy is he!" (v. 5, NETS; slightly modified wording in v. 9).[47] The second part of the entrance hymn insists on the crucifixion of none other than the Son of God, "O Son of God, who was crucified in the flesh, save us who chant to you: Alleluia."

In biblical metaphorical language, "footstool" (Heb.: *hădōm*; Gk.: *hypopodion*) is the sign of royalty or kingship (e.g., the golden footstool of Solomon's throne, 2 Chr 9:18). The same term was used as a metaphor for the "ark of covenant" found in the Holy of Holies. The ark of covenant was considered the footstool of God's throne (1 Chr 28:2; Ps 131[132]:7). In the same token, Jerusalem or Zion is described as the footstool of the invisible God (Lam 2:1). In a more cosmic setting, Isa 66:1 asserts that the heaven is the "throne" of God while the earth is his "footstool" (cf. Matt 5:35; Acts 7:49). Theodoret of Cyrus applies the "footstool" typology intimated in Ps 98(99):5 to the Christian Church where the same God is worshipped: "His footstool is to be taken in reference to olden times as the

Temple in Jerusalem, and in reference to present times as the churches throughout all land and sea, in which we offer worship to the all-holy God" (*Commentary on Psalm* 98[99]).[48]

The "footstool" serves as a key term in the liturgical services held on September 14, functioning as a bridge between the two sides of the Lord's profile: king and sufferer. The footstool refers to both throne (or ark of covenant) and the cross. The paradoxical juxtaposition of exaltation (throne or ark) and extreme humility (cross) is the very theme of the feast of the "Exaltation of the Precious Cross." Through scriptural lessons read at the Vespers and Liturgy, and through hymns and antiphons, we are introduced to the mood of Good Friday and to the postresurrection times—the liturgical life of the Church as advancement toward the eschaton.

Theme. Sometimes the theme of the festal day dictates the Psalm selection for a specific liturgical service. For instance, on the feast of Ascension, at the epistle *prokeimenon* during the Liturgy, Ps 56(57):12(11) is intonated: "Be exalted to the heavens, O God, and to all the earth be your glory" (NETS). The *kontakion* preceding the epistle reading and the thrice-holy hymn puts forward the main theme of this day, the ascension, that is: "When you had fulfilled your dispensation for our sakes, uniting things on earth with the heavens, you did ascend in glory, O Christ our God, departing not hence, but remaining inseparable from us and crying to them that love you: I am with you, and no one can be against you." As a rule, throughout the whole liturgical panoply, Psalm recitation, scriptural reading (Acts 1:1–12) and hymnody are tightly interrelated around the single theme of the ascension.

Literary Motif. Often, Psalm selection is triggered by a simple literary motif or key word. Let us look again at the feast of Ascension. At the Liturgy, the "small entrance" hymn is taken from Ps 46(47):6(5): "God went up with shouting, the Lord with a sound of trumpet" (NETS). The selection of this Psalm verse was probably dictated by the motif of God's going up ("God went up") encountered in the second part of the entrance hymn, "O Son of God, who has ascended from us in glory into the heavens, save us who chant to you: Alleluia," and intimated by the epistle lesson (Acts 1:10). The patristic interpretation has always seen in Ps 46(47) an Old Testament prophecy of Christ's ascension. Here is Augustine: "'God is gone up with jubilation.' Even he, our God, the Lord Christ, is gone up with jubilation; 'the Lord with the sound of a trumpet. . . .' What is jubilation, but admiration of joy that cannot be expressed in words? As the disciples in joy admired, seeing him go into heaven, whom they had mourned dead;

truly for the joy, words sufficed not: remained to jubilate what none could express. There was also the voice of the trumpet, the voice of angels" (*Expositions on the Book of Psalms*).[49]

Scriptural Readings, Hymns, Homilies, Prayers, and Synaxaria

At the beginning of his fine monograph on Scripture readings in Orthodox worship, Georges Barrois warns: "We ought to be reminded here that Scripture readings are only one element of the total liturgical complex, the hymns and prayers of the Church being the others. Obviously none of these elements should be given precedence over the others. Our concentrating on the biblical element does not mean at all that we regard the hymnody and the liturgical prayers as secondary or negligible."[50] One cannot but agree with Barrois on the holistic character of Eastern Byzantine worship, where all its components (scriptural lessons, hymns, prayers, Psalms, homilies, synaxaria) are vibrating in unison. For this reason, it would be a futile exercise to speak of each component separately. Having said this, however, Barrois's caveat needs further qualification. In Orthodox worship, as we saw already in the case of the relationship between Scripture and Tradition itself, the unity of genres or media of expression has its center in Scripture.

Eastern Orthodox liturgical life is enticingly imbued with Scripture. The challenge comes when one wants to pin down the scriptural provenance of a series of metaphors within a particular hymn. There are no footnote references, no indexes to assist. It is if the hymnographer's intention was to challenge the biblical literacy of the worshippers or, even better, to make them curious and eager to discover the whole biblical story beyond that hymn. The intricate way in which the liturgists interweave biblical material with standardized liturgical elements makes this task even more difficult, yet quite exciting. These hymns, homilies and prayers can be considered midrash-like interpretations of Scripture, a type of "liturgical exegesis," sometimes more insightful in its conciseness and depth than the patristic exegesis found in commentaries and theological writings. Due to its rich, ambiguous, and highly poetical interface, Eastern Orthodox liturgy invites one to "faithful imagination," a phrase used by Walter Brueggemann with respect to Hebrew Bible's counterreality projections in times of crisis.[51]

Eastern Orthodox worship functioned as a "Bible Study" class where those attending church services could be instructed in and fashioned by

God's living word. If someone wants to be versed in Scripture, urges John Chrysostom, let him come to church and listen carefully to the readings from "Prophets and Apostles" (Old and New Testaments). Nevertheless, mundane distractions, notices Chrysostom, keep many people away from church, hence from Scripture:

> For if one should come in here [i.e., church] regularly, even though he read not at home, if he attends to what is said here, one year even is sufficient to make him well versed in them; because we do not today read one kind of Scriptures, and tomorrow another, but always and continually the same. Still such is the wretched disposition of the many, that after so much reading, they do not even know the names of the books, and are not ashamed nor tremble at entering so carelessly into a place where they may hear God's word. Yet if a harper, or dancer, or stage-player call the city, they all run eagerly, and feel obliged to him for the call, and spend the half of an entire day in attending to him alone; but when God speaks to us by Prophets and Apostles, we yawn, we scratch ourselves, we are drowsy. And in summer, the heat seems too great, and we betake ourselves to the market place; and again, in winter, the rain and mire are a hindrance, and we sit at home; yet at horse races, though there is no roof over them to keep off the wet, the greater number, while heavy rains are falling, and the wind is dashing the water into their faces, stand like madmen, caring not for cold, and wet, and mud, and length of way, and nothing either keeps them at home, or prevents their going thither. But here, where there are roofs over head, and where the warmth is admirable, they hold back instead of running together; and this too, when the gain is that of their own souls.
>
> *On John: Homily 58*[52]

In spite of these obvious benefits, the Byzantine Orthodoxy removed Old Testament lessons from the Eucharist service (Liturgy) some time after the seventh century.[53] Already in the fifth century C.E., the Church of Constantinople began to shorten the list of scriptural readings by eliminating the Old Testament lessons. Rome followed this example and did the same some time near the end of the fifth or beginning of the sixth century. In the traditional Roman rite, however, the process of excluding the Old Testament readings from the Mass was never fully completed. In the Roman missal, there were always a few Old Testament readings each Wednesday and Saturday Ember Days.[54] Following the Second Vatican Council, the Latin Church restored the usage of Old Testament readings to Mass lectionary for all Sundays and major feast days outside of Paschal Tide (from Easter Sunday to Pentecost). In the Byzantine Orthodox order of services, the Old Testament readings are now restricted to a number of liturgical days and periods. For instance, Old Testament lessons are found in vesperal liturgies (i.e., Vespers combined with the Liturgy of St. Basil) on Thursday and Saturday of Holy Week. Pericopies from Genesis, Isaiah and Proverbs are also read throughout the vesperal services during the Great Lent or Triodion.[55] Other Old Testament lessons can be found in the services of Holy Week, in the Vespers of great feasts throughout the year, and in the services of Royal Hours on certain major solemnities (Christmas, Theophany, Holy Friday). However, apart from the use of certain fixed Psalms, there are at present no Old Testament readings in the Byzantine Orthodox Eucharistic service.[56] This is in contrast to the older practice that is still attested in so-called Oriental or non-Chalcedonian Orthodox Churches (Syriac, Indian Malankara, Armenian, Coptic, and Ethiopian), all of which have retained a lectionary of readings from the Old Testament in their Eucharistic services.

In today's Greek Orthodox Church, the Old Testament readings are prescribed according to two rules. First, there are lessons following a continuous sequence, similar to the lectio continua of the Psalter. The continuous reading of Old Testament lessons occurs during the week following the Sunday of the Last Judgment, and the Holy Week. During the Holy Week, prophecies pertaining to the passion and crucifixion are read in continuous sequence. Second, Old Testament lessons are selected thematically in relation to a specific liturgical day. For instance, thematic lessons are prescribed for the feasts of the Lord, of the Theotokos, the Holy Cross, and major festal services of the saints.

One may notice at this juncture that some of the Old Testament books are totally absent from the liturgical readings. Books not employed in Eastern Orthodox worship include the following: historical: Ruth, Samuel, Chronicles, Ezra and Neemiah, Tobith, Macabees; poetical: Ecclesiastes, Song of Songs, Ecclesiasticus; and prophetical: Lamentations, Hosea, Amos, Obadiah, Nahum, Haggai. This situation can be explained by the primacy role of hymnody within the liturgical services. The hymnody determined the selection of Old Testament books and passages. Georges Barrois notices that while the Latin liturgy makes a good use of historical books in its lectionary, the Eastern Byzantine liturgy omits these books from Joshua onward, except for Kings. This has something to do with the scope and perspective of each liturgical system. Whereas the Latin liturgy is predominantly retrospective, looking backward at the events and figures of the past, the Eastern Orthodox worship is preeminently prospective, gazing at the eschatological fulfillment. As Barrois notes, "John D. Zizoulas compared this sublimation of historical, 'linear' time in Eastern Orthodox liturgy with the 'epicletical' change of the bread and wine in the Eucharistic liturgy."[57]

The Old Testament lessons of the Byzantine cycle, usually gathered in threes and currently distributed over services other than the Divine Liturgy, were selected to cover the three sections of the Old Testament, the Pentateuch (MT: Torah, "Instruction, Law"), the Prophets (MT: Nebiim), and the Wisdom (MT: Kethubim, "Writings").[58] Interestingly, the Byzantine liturgists followed the classical threefold division of the Jewish Bible. Christian Bibles are often divided in four sections: Law, historical, prophetical, and wisdom books. There is good Christological reason, however, for the Church accepting the Jewish tripartite division. In Luke 24:44, the risen Lord on his way to Emmaus mentions to Luke and Clopas that everything written about him in "the Law of Moses (*nomō Mōyseōs*), and Prophets (*prophētais*), and Psalms (*psalmois*) was to be fulfilled." "Psalms" refer here to the third section (Kethubim). Since Luke 24:44 has always been regarded as a main scriptural support for early and later typologies, predominantly Christological, the tripartite division followed by the liturgists in selecting the Old Testament lessons for worship underscores the typological (Christological and Mariological) direction of Byzantine liturgical synthesis. On this specific aspect of liturgical selection of scriptural lessons, as in so many other respects, Eastern Orthodox tradition maintains a strong continuity with Judaism.

Below, the Old Testament lessons are discussed along with hymns, prayers, and homilies in an effort to understand this peculiar form of exegesis within the Orthodox liturgical synthesis. The scriptural lessons are selected from the Festal Menaion.

The Menaion cycle is divided into (a) feasts of the Lord, (b) feasts of the Theotokos (Birthgiver of God), and (c) feasts of the Saints. It should be mentioned here that the feasts of the Theotokos are always related in a way or another to some aspects of Christ's life, hence their interconnectedness with the feasts of the Lord.

Nativity and Dormition of the Theotokos

A theologically significant design may be detected in the Byzantine ecclesiastical year that begins on September 1 and is flanked by two feasts
dedicated to the Theotokos, the Nativity (September 8) and the Dormition (*Koimēsis*, "sleeping in") (August 15). The Theotokos, always related
to Christ, represents the central profile within the life of the Church. In
essence, the liturgical year begins and ends with Mary. As John of Damascus (*On the Orthodox Faith*, 3:12) remarks, the name of the Theotokos
encapsulates the whole history of the divine economy of salvation.

In Eastern Orthodox tradition, the liturgy is the locus par excellence
of Mariology. Specific to the Orthodox liturgical and hymnographic ethos,
Mary is always depicted and addressed along with her Son. Mariology in
the Orthodox tradition is a preamble to Christology. The icon of Mary
with the Child on the iconostasis on the one side of the royal doors reflects
the Byzantine way of understanding the role of Mary in the history of
salvation and Church's life. She is central yet always as pointing to Christ
her Son as the one Savior.

There are a significant number of liturgical commemorations honoring Mary, the Theotokos or the Mother of God. Four of these festal
days are part of the twelve-feast series titled the "Royal Feasts": Nativity
(September 8), Dormition (August 15), Entrance of the Theotokos into the
Temple (November 21), and Annunciation (March 25). Other minor feasts
dedicated to the Theotokos are the Protection of the Virgin (October 1),
Synaxis of the Theotokos (December 26), and Conception of the Theotokos (December 9).

Interestingly, the Old Testament lessons prescribed for Great Vespers on the Nativity of the Theotokos (September 8) are identical with
the lessons for the Great Vespers of Dormition (August 15), namely, Gen
28:10–17; Ezek 43:27–44:4; and Prov 9:1–11. Apart from the conception
and nativity of her Son, Mary's birth and falling asleep are seen as the
main moments in her earthly journey along with the followers of Christ.
The reading from Ezekiel is also used at the vigil of the Entrance of the
Theotokos into the Temple.

The first reading, Gen 28:10–17, narrates Jacob's dream at Bethel
during his flight from Beersheba (southern Palestine) to Haran (northern Mesopotamia). "And he dreamed, and see, a ladder (*klimax*)[59] set
firmly in the earth, whose top was reaching into heaven, and the angels
of God were ascending and descending on it. And the Lord leaned on it

(*epestērikto ep'autēs*)"[60] (Gen 28:12–13, NETS). The Lord promises Jacob that he will be with him on his trip. When Jacob awakes, he is afraid and says, "'How awesome is this place! This is nothing other than the house of God (*oikos theou*), and this is the gate of heaven (*pylē tou ouranou*)'" (Gen 28:17, NETS).

God's first promise ("I will be with you") is related to the ladder Jacob saw in his dream. The Lord leaning on the ladder assures the frightened fugitive that he will not abandon him. This promise refers to the living presence of God on earth, or rather to God's willingness to descend on a mysterious ladder and become a support for those living like Jacob in fear, need, and unresolved trials. In fact, the proper name God reveals later to Moses (Exod 3:14–15), the *tetragrammaton* YHWH (*Yahweh*, "He Is . . . "), and the prophetic name *Immanuel* ("God with us") unveiled by Isaiah to the unbelieving king Ahaz (Isa 7:14) and applied by Matthean Church to Jesus of Nazareth (Matt 1:23), both point in the same direction: God's concrete dwelling among men. Walter Brueggemann comments on Jacob's ladder: "Now it is asserted that earth is a place of possibility because it has not been and will not be cut off from the sustaining role of God. In this image are the seeds of incarnational faith, of the power of God being embodied in a historical man. Thus our text points to the statement of Jesus (John 1:51)."[61]

As incarnation requires a vehicle or receptacle, for Byzantine liturgists this role was designed to be played by the Theotokos. Thus, key words such as "ladder," "gate of heaven," and "house of God," which in Jacob's dream suggest the possibility of divine indwelling on earth, were used by the hymnographers to portray the Theotokos, the facilitator of incarnation and the bridge linking heaven and earth.

The focus of the second Old Testament reading (Ezek 43:27–44:4) prescribed for both Marian festal days is placed on the eastern "outer gate" of the Jerusalem Temple.

> And he turned me [Ezekiel] by the way of the outer gate of the holies (*pylēs tōn hagiōn exōteras*) that looks to the east (*anatolas*), and it was shut (*kekleismenē*). And the Lord said to me: "This gate shall be shut; it shall not be opened, and no one shall go through it, because the Lord (*Kyrios*), the God of Israel, shall enter through it, and it shall be shut. Therefore, the leader (*hēgoumenos*)—he shall sit in it to eat bread before the Lord; he shall enter by the way of the *ailam*[62] of the gate, and he shall go out by his way." And he brought

me in by way of the gate to the north, opposite the house, and I
looked, and behold, the house of the Lord (*oikos Kyriou*) was full of
glory (*doxēs*), and I fell upon my face.

Ezek 44:1–4, NETS

The prophet Ezekiel, member of a leading family in Jerusalem, was
brought to exile in Babylon in the year 597 B.C.E. He lived among other
deportees in a settlement called Tel-abib, not far from Nippur. After the
destruction of the Jerusalem Temple in 586 B.C.E., Ezekiel was transported miraculously by the power of the Spirit to Jerusalem where an
anonymous person (Heb. ʾîš, "man") led him to the sanctuary. The text
just quoted narrates Ezekiel's trip to the outer gate on the east side of the
sanctuary.

The text is completely silent as to the identity of the guiding "man" (ʾîš)
who led the prophet to the outer gate of the sanctuary. We are not told who
shut the gate and how was it done, whether by walling up or barring the
entrance. The text is also mute on the significance of this shutting of the
gate. Walther Zimmerli comments:

> With regard to men a clear ruling has been given: No human foot
> shall in the future cross the threshold over which Yahweh passed
> to his sanctuary. The closed gate proclaims the majesty of the one
> who came. One may ask, over and above however, whether it does
> not testify to a second aspect, namely the finality of Yahweh's entry
> into his sanctuary, an entry which has been referred to in 43:7, 9 as
> *lʿwlm* ("for all time"). Yahweh closes behind him the doors which
> he no longer intends to open for a new departure of the nature of
> that in 11:23. Thus, in addition, the closed gate could proclaim also
> Yahweh's fidelity.[63]

Zimmerli's question is whether or not this shutting refers to God's final
entry into his sanctuary and his eternal dwelling in midst of his people.
Interestingly enough, this comment by a modern exegete concords well
with the interpretation given by the Byzantine liturgists who explained
Ezek 44:1–4 typologically in relation to Nativity and Dormition of the Theotokos. The hymnody of the Dormition insists on the continuous dwelling of the Theotokos in the midst of her people, even after her falling
asleep. Here is the Dismissal Hymn sung on the day of Dormition: "In
giving birth, you did preserve your virginity; in your dormition, you did

not forsake the world, O Theotokos. You were translated to life, since you are the Mother of Life; and by your intercessions do you redeem our souls from death." The hymn speaks of the Theotokos's falling asleep in terms of a transition from life to life while she still remains somehow present in this world, the same way God in Ezekiel's vision remains in this world even after the outer gate has been shut.

Proverbs 9:1–11 is the third Old Testament lesson assigned for both Marian feasts:

> Wisdom built herself a house (*oikon*) and supported it with seven pillars. She slaughtered her own sacrificial victims; she mixed her own wine in a mixing bowl, and she prepared her own table. She sent out her slaves, summoning with a stately proclamation to the drinking feast, saying, "He who is a fool, let him turn aside to me," and to those lacking sense she said: "Come, eat of my bread, and drink wine, which I have mixed for you. Abandon folly, and you will live, and seek prudence in order that you may live, and erect understanding with knowledge."
>
> Prov 9:1–6, NETS

The opposition between the Woman Wisdom and the Woman Folly represents the central theme of Prov 9:1–18. Written in Deuteronomistic style and centered on the theme of regard or disregard of the Torah (cf. Deut 6:1–3; Jer 7:1–15), this passage mirrors the two alternatives with which Jewish youth were confronted with during the precarious Persian period (539–331 B.C.E.): wisdom or frivolousness. The opposition between two deities disputing the control over the cosmos and human life is a recurring theme in ancient Israel and in Syria-Palestine region. Yahweh versus Baal and Baal versus Mot (or Lotar) are other two examples of an endless disputation on narrative and worshipping levels. However, during Persian period, the opposition took the form of the antagonism between Wisdom and Folly. Prov 9 depicts Wisdom as the queen of heaven who builds a house and invites the simpleton and unlearned to a banquet of life. Folly is introduced as a goddess of fertility who invites the fool to have intimate relationship with her. Those who are lying with her are heading for the underworld (v. 18). The difference between the two goddesses is the difference between life and death.

What is the function of the house that Wisdom built? According to Leo G. Perdue, Wisdom's house should be understood as a sacred building, a temple of sorts, whence Wisdom exercises her power over creation and human life. Yahweh's dwelling in the Jerusalem Temple (cf. Ps 46[47], 48[49], 76[77]; 1 Kgs 5–8) and Baal's presence in his palace are two parallels to Prov 9's imagery. Both temple/palace building narratives (1 Kgs 5–8 and the Cannanite *Baal Cycle*) end up with a banquet where the lordship of the deity is publically acknowledged. Thus, building of the house, as well as the invitation to a banquet, in Prov 9:1–2 conveys the idea that Wisdom, by whose "suitable" mediation (Prov 8:30)[64] God created a harmonious universe, dwells among and entertains with human beings while maintaining the primordial structure and order of God's great creation.[65]

The House. If one looks at the three Old Testament texts (Gen 28; Ezek 44; Prov 9) assigned for the Vespers of the Nativity and Dormition of the Theotokos, one notices that the common image-denominator linking them together as a scriptural continuum is the term "house" (oikos): house of God (*theou*), of the Lord (*kyriou*), and of Wisdom (*sophias*). If one considers "God," "Lord," and "Wisdom" from these phrases as epithets of the Son of God, then the term "house" may be a metaphor for Theotokos, the recipient or sanctuary of Wisdom's incarnation and dwelling among men. The Theotokos as the "house" of God's Wisdom, the incarnate Logos, is a central theme in hymnody of the days neighboring the two Marian feasts.

On the day of the Holy Hieromartyr Phocas of Sinope (September 22), at the Matins, one chants: "The Wisdom of God has built himself a house (*oikon*) of your pure blood, O Lady Theotokos, even as it seemed good to him" (Ode Five, *theotokion*). This hymn is a liturgical interpretation of Prov 9:1. Wisdom has a preeminent role in building his own house out of the pure blood of the Theotokos in the incarnation by which the Logos assumed the human nature from her body.

On the eve of the Exaltation of the Precious Cross (September 13), at the Matins: "Beyond nature you became the undefiled dwelling place (*endiaitēma*) of the Father's Wisdom, O pure Virgin, whereby we have now been delivered from the evil of the wily deceiver" (Ode Four, theotokion). In this hymn, the Theotokos is described as the dwelling place of the Father's Wisdom, the Son of God. This is a good example of Mariology juxtaposed with Christology. Note the peculiar term *endiaitēma*, "dwelling place" (cf. oikos, "house," Prov 9:1), which underlines the idea of incarnation as God's "dwelling" among men.

On the day of the Holy Martyr Andrew the Commander (August 19), at the Vespers: "The boundless Wisdom (*apeiros sophia*) of our God has built himself a house (*oikon*) from you in the Holy Spirit, passing mind and speech, O all-hymned Theotokos; and now he has translated you to immaterial tabernacles (*aylous skēnas*) on high" (Second sticheron of the Feast). This hymn is not only Christological ("boundless Wisdom"),[66] but also Trinitarian. The Wisdom of God builds a house for his incarnation, from within the Theotokos (*ek sou*), with the cooperation of the Holy Spirit (*en Pneumati hagiō*). Note the subtle interplay between Wisdom's "house" (oikon) and "immaterial tabernacles" (*aylous skēnas*) to which the Wisdom "translated" (*metethēke*) the Theotokos upon her Dormition.

On the day of the Holy Righteous Martyr Dometius (August 7), at the Matins: "Wisdom built himself a divine house (*oikon . . . theion*), O all-hymned Virgin, when beyond understanding and speech he made his dwelling (*skēnōsasa*) in your chaste and venerable womb, which was purified in the Spirit" (Ode Three, theotokion). The accent is placed here on the womb of the Theotokos wherein Wisdom built a "divine house" as his "dwelling."

On the Forefeast of the Dormition (August 14), at Matins, this hymn is chanted: "The all-pure dove, the house (*oikos*) that held him who upholds all things, passes over to the heavens to dwell, having been shown to be a heaven (*ouranos*) and throne (*thronos*) and great palace (*mega palation*) of Christ; let us praise her divine Dormition" (Ode Six, troparion). The metaphors for the Theotokos flow one after the other. She is the "house," "heaven," "throne," "great palace" of Christ, the One who upholds the universe. The "throne" and "house" metaphors appear again together in the next hymn reminiscing the Theotokos's birth:

> We who are vain and vile, with what lips shall we praise now the newly-born Maiden? Greater than creation in holiness, she is more honored and venerable above the dread Cherubim and all Saints; the firm and unshaken throne (*thronon . . . asaleuton*) of the one King of all; the house (*oikon*) in which the Most High has made his dwelling-place; she is the whole world's salvation, God's own sanctuary (*to Theou hagiasma*), she who grants to the faithful great mercy abundantly upon her divine nativity.
>
> The Holy Martyrs Menodora, Metrodora, and Nymphodora
> [September 10], Vespers, sticheron

On the day of the Deposition of the Venerable Sash of the Theotokos (August 31), at Matins, one chants, "You were named (*echrēmatisas*) house (*oikos*), because the Word was incarnate (*sarkōthentos*) of you, O very beautiful spotless one (*perikallēs achrante*); and in your holy house (*en hagiō sou oikō*) you have deigned to place your sash, which as we venerate, we are sanctified" (Ode Third, second *canon*). The "house" metaphor is plainly related to the Word's incarnation. Note also the interesting poetic parallel drawn between the Theotokos as "house" of the Logos and her "house" where the sash was preserved.

We will wrap up this brief parade of samples with a hymn showing the limitless creativity of Byzantine hymnographers in accommodating and extending classical metaphors such as "house" also to persons other than the Theotokos. Here is the application of "house" metaphor to the seven Maccabees brothers: "The Wisdom of God has built a temple (*naon*) and has supported it upon seven rational pillars (*hepta stylois logikois*), manifestly showing these youths to be keepers of the Law" (The Seven Holy Maccabees [August 1], Ode Six, sticheron). Here the identity of the temple (not house) built by Wisdom is not revealed. However, the seven Maccabees are compared to the seven pillars of the Wisdom's house (Prov 9:1-6).

Other metaphors used in the Old Testament lessons read for the Marian feasts are "gate" (*pylē*) (Gen 28; Ezek 44) and "ladder" (*klimax*) (Gen 28). Both metaphors are reworked in the festal hymnody.

The Gate. On the Nativity of the Theotokos (September 8), at the Matins, one chants, "O immaculate Virgin, in your birth are fulfilled the prophecies of the God-proclaimers, who faithfully called you a tabernacle (*skēnēn*) and gate (*pylēn*), a spiritual mountain (*oros noēton*), a bush (*baton*), and the rod (*rhabdon*) of Aaron that sprang from the root (*rizēs*) of David" (Ode Four, troparion). This is a good illustration of the typological interpretation employed by both patristic writers and the largely anonymous liturgists. Since "gate" appears in both texts prescribed for the Nativity (Gen 28 and Ezek 44), it is difficult to say which biblical text should be considered the source of inspiration for this troparion.

The answer comes from another feast in honor of the Theotokos, the Entry into the Temple (November 21) and its prescribed Old Testament lessons (Exod 40; 1 Kgs 8; Ezek 43–44), which speak of Israel's sanctuary. Exod 40:2 refers to the movable sanctuary in Moses' days, called the "tabernacle of the testimony" (LXX: *skēnēn tou martyriou*). Note that the same term *skēnē*, "tent, tabernacle," also appears in the above-cited troparion. John 1:14 could be adduced in support for the use of this imagery: the Logos' incarnation and dwelling among humans is depicted as "tabernacling" (*eskēnōsen*).[67] This leads one to the conclusion that all metaphors

but the last one (i.e., "root of David")[68] in the troparion were taken from
the Book of Exodus. Using these metaphors, the liturgist who compiled
the troparion connected the Theotokos to sacred places and objects during
Israel's wandering through the wilderness. Thus, the answer to the aforementioned question is that the "gate" in the troparion has to be related
to the "eastern outer gate" of the Temple (Ezek 44). Note the association
between the "gate" and the "noetic mountain" in the following *heirmos* at
the Matins of the Entry into the Temple: "O you faithful, let us truly honor
the Virgin and the Mother of God (*Parthenon kai Mētera Theou*) who is
blessed by the hands of the priests as the saving gate (*pylēn sōtērion*), the
noetic mountain (*oros noēton*), and the animate ladder (*klimaka empsy-
chon*)" (Ode Eight).

The Ladder. Another series of metaphors, even more daring and sophisticated, is encountered on the Dormition of the Theotokos, at the
Great Vespers, "O strange wonder (*tou paradoxou thaumatos*), great and
marvelous! For the fount of life (*hē pēgē tēs zōēs*) is laid within a sepulcher;
a ladder (*klimax*) to heaven's heights does the small grave become. Be
glad, O Gethsemane, the sacred precinct (*to hagion temenos*) of her that
gave birth to God. You faithful, let us cry out, possessing as our commander great Gabriel: Maiden full of grace, rejoice, with you is the Lord
our God, who abundantly grants his great mercy to the world through
you" (sticheron). The hymnographer warns his hearers and readers that
this description of the Theotokos is "wonder of the paradox"—the greatest paradox of all: Having been laid in the tomb, the Theotokos becomes
"the fountain of life" in a lifeless place! Consequently, her tomb in Gethsemane turns into a "ladder toward heaven." Gethsemane itself becomes
"the sacred precinct," with Mary's tomb as a sanctuary containing nothing less than the fountain of life.

The "ladder" metaphor appears in a Greek prayer to the Theotokos attributed to Ephraem the Syrian, where Mary is called the "throne of the
King (*kathedra Basileōs*) who is on the Cherubim, heavenly ladder (*klimax
epouranie*), through whom we, the earthlings, are running up to heaven,
bride of God (*nymphē Theou*), through whom we were reconciled with
him. . . . <elevated> ladder through which the heavenly angels came down
to us. . . . " (*Precationes ad dei matrem* 4).[69]

In his famous sermons on the Dormition, John of Damascus corre-
lates Jacob's ladder with the Theotokos, in whom he sees a bridge uniting
heaven and earth. The "descent" (*katabasis*) of God (i.e., Logos-incarnation) occurred through the Theotokos. Through her, angels descended to

minister to the incarnate God, and men following the angelic example are carried up to heaven:

> I had nearly forgotten Jacob's ladder. Is it not evident to every one that it prefigured you, and is not the type easily recognized? Just as Jacob saw the ladder bringing together heaven and earth, and on it angels coming down and going up, and the truly strong and invulnerable God wrestling mystically with himself, so are you placed between us, and are become the ladder of God's descent (*katabaseōs*) toward us, of him who took upon himself our weakness, uniting us to himself, and enabling man to see God. You have brought together what was parted. Hence angels descended to him, ministering to him as their God and Lord, and men, adopting the life of angels, are carried up to heaven.
>
> *Sermon I: On Dormition*[70]

There is a notable difference between patristic exegesis proper and so-called liturgical exegesis with respect to the Old Testament lessons selected for the Marian feasts. If the patristic interpretation tends to be Christological in its hermeneutical direction, the liturgical exegesis is more Mariological (see examples above).

The ancient Christian (patristic) interpretations of Gen 28 are almost exclusively Christological. The fathers saw Christ in the "gate of heaven," the "ladder" or the top of it, and in the "stone" used as pillow. Yet while largely absent among the discursive writings of church fathers, Mariological interpretation of this passage is well attested, as we have already seen, in the liturgical hymnody.

The Christological interpretation of Jacob's ladder began with the New Testament's explanation in John 1:51 where Jesus compares himself with the ladder. Among the church fathers, Aphrahat and Chromatius interpret the ladder as symbolizing the cross of Christ. For Cyril of Alexandria, Christ is at the top of the ladder. According to Caesarius of Arles, both Jacob and the top of the ladder represent Christ.[71] Didymus the Blind interprets: "The ladder foreshadows the cross by which the believers are going up to the heavenly tabernacles; on this ladder God himself was leaning (*epestērigmenos*), the one who for us was voluntarily nailed on the cross" (*De trinitate* 1.15.103).[72] This is a quite imaginative interpretation. Didymus relies on the LXX reading. His interesting interpretation of Christ being nailed voluntarily on the cross was triggered by the LXX's lexical choice, *epestērikto ep'autēs*, "[God] leaned on it [ladder]" (Gen 28:13). Didymus uses the same verb found in the LXX, *epistērizō* (in passive), "to lean on," to speak metaphorically of Christ being nailed on the cross. In the same Christological vein, Aphrahat writes:

> Our father Jacob too prayed at Bethel and saw the gate of heaven opened, with a ladder going up on high. This is a symbol of our Savior that Jacob saw; the gate of heaven is Christ, in accordance with what he said, "I am the gate of life; every one who enters by me shall live for ever" [John 10:7]. David too said, "This is the gate of the Lord, by which the righteous enter" [Ps 117:20 LXX]. Again, the ladder that Jacob saw is a symbol of our Savior, in that by means of him the just ascend from the lower to the upper realm. The ladder is also a symbol of our Savior's cross, which was raised up like a ladder, with the Lord standing above it.
>
> On Prayer 5[73]

Nativity of the Lord

In Phil 2:7-8, Paul wrote some of the most poetical lines in honor of the divine *kenosis*. The second person of the Trinity, the eternal Logos (or Wisdom) emptied himself (*heauton ekenōsen*) of the glory (*doxa*) he had before the world was created. In the same vein with the Pauline thought, the Nicene-Constantinopolitan Creed states with regard to the Son of God that, "He, for us men and for our salvation, came down (*katheltonta*) from heaven, and was incarnate (*sarkōthenta*) of the Holy Spirit (*Pneumatos Hagiou*) and the Virgin (*Parthenou*) Mary and was made man (*enanthrōpēsanta*)." The incarnation of the Logos took place as a synergy between the "Holy Spirit" and the "Virgin Mary"—a historical event remembered on the feast day of Annunciation.

The mystery of incarnation or God's kenosis is liturgically reenacted by a series of five festal days arranged after the Menaion cycle beginning with September 1: Nativity (December 25), Circumcision (January 1), Epiphany or Baptism (January 6), Meeting or Presentation (February 2), and Annunciation (March 25). One may mention that the Eastern Byzantine liturgy has held since its beginnings the middle way between triumphalism and defeatism. This liturgy is joyful, colorful, and vivid, yet not triumphalist. Five festal days "celebrating" the kenosis of the Logos speak volumes of the Eastern Orthodox way of combining doxological and realistic aspects into a "liturgical synthesis" marked by a high level of artistry and spirituality. In a nutshell, the Eastern Orthodox liturgy is characterized by both *theologia crucis* and *theologia gloriae,* and there is no other liturgical locus where this distinct feature is more obvious than in the feast days of the Lord's kenosis.

As in the case of Marian feasts, we are going to survey briefly the Old Testament lessons prescribed for two of these five feasts in their conjunction with appropriate liturgical hymns.

ROYAL HOURS

The liturgical service for the Nativity of the Lord begins with the previous day (The Holy Martyr Eugenia), more precisely with the Royal Hours that follow immediately after the Matins.

There are a few rounds of scriptural readings. The Old Testament lessons read throughout the service of the Royal Hours are as follows: Mic 5:2(1)–4(3) along with Heb 1:1–12 and Matt 1:18–25 (First Hour); Bar 3:35–4:4 along with Gal 3:23–29; Luke 2:1-20 (Third Hour); Isa 7:10–16; 8:1–4, 8–10 along with Heb 1:10–2:3; Matt 2:1–12 (Sixth Hour); Isa 9:6–7 along with Heb 2:11–18; Matt 2:13–23 (Ninth Hour).

At the First Hour, the first Old Testament lesson, Mic 5:2(1)–4(3), locates the central event, the birth of an ideal ruler, in Bethlehem of Judah: "And you, O Bethleem, house of Ephratha, are very few in number to be among the thousands of Ioudas; one from you shall come forth for me to become a ruler (*archonta*) in Israel, and his goings forth (*exodoi*) are of old (*archēs*), from days of yore (*hēmerōn aiōnos*)" (Mic 5:2[1], NETS).

An *idiomelon* written by Patriarch Sophronius of Jerusalem (560–638 C.E.) functions as a midrash actualizing and expanding the biblical text: "Now the prophecy does press forward to fulfillment, which mystically says: And you, Bethlehem in the land of Judah, who prepares in advance the cave (*proeutrepizousa to spēlaion*), are not the least among the princes (*hēgemosi*); for out of you shall come to me through flesh a ruler of the nations (*hēgoumenos tōn ethnōn dia sarkos*), even Christ our God, from a Virgin Maiden (*Parthenou Korēs*); he shall shepherd his people, the new Israel (*ton neon Israēl*). Let us all render majesty to him" (First Hour). Sophronius inserts an explicative gloss, "who prepares in advance the cave," which is not found in the Septuagint reading of Micah. But that is fine, as the hymnographer warns us to read this prophecy "mystically" (*mystikōs*). Bethlehem is depicted here as preparing "the cave." Which cave and for what purpose? One may infer that the "ruler" will be born in a cave of

Bethlehem. The New Testament accounts of Jesus's birth (i.e., Matthew and Luke) that use the text of Micah are conspicuously silent with regard to a birth-cave. In fact, Luke 2:7 reports that the newborn Jesus was laid in a "manger" (*phatnē*) because there was no place for Joseph and Mary in the "guest room" (*katalyma*). The word *katalyma* should not be taken in a technical sense as inn or hotel. Luke uses a different term (*pandocheion*) for a proper "inn" (Luke 10:34). The word *katalyma*, as François Bovon suggests, designates "a room in a private house in which travelers could usually spend the night."[74] The word *phatnē* in Luke's account indicates a (stone?) manger in a stall or feeding place that was usually located in the living room or in any annex of a house.[75]

The earliest evidence of such a tradition that Jesus was born in a "cave" (*spēlaion*) may be found in Justin Martyr: "But when the child was born in Bethlehem, since Joseph could not find a lodging in that village, he took up his quarters in a certain cave near the village; and while they were there Mary brought forth the Christ and placed him in a manger, and here the Magi who came from Arabia found him" (*Dialogue with Trypho* 78).[76] The same tradition is attested by the second-century *Protoevangelium of James* 18[77] and third-century Origen's *Against Celsus* 1.51.[78] Jerome mentions the cave where Jesus was born which was close to his own cave-cell where he worked on Vulgate: "After this, she [Paula] came to Bethlehem and entered into the cave where the Savior was born" (*Letter 108: To Eustochia* 10).[79] Jerome came to Bethlehem in 384 C.E. and was later joined by Paula and her daughter Eustochia. The first church built on the traditional site of Jesus's birth in Bethlehem was dedicated on May 31, 339 C.E. Eusebius mentioned the construction of this church by the empress Helena: "The pious empress honored with rare memorials the scene of her [Mary's] travail who bore this heavenly child, and beautified the sacred cave with all possible splendor." (*Life of Constantine* 3.43).[80] This church would be later demolished and rebuilt as a bigger edifice by the emperor Justinian after 529 C.E., following the Samaritan uprising. Remarkably, the church escaped the destruction of the Persians in 614 C.E. because of the mosaic on the façade representing the Magi in oriental dresses.

Returning now to the First Royal Hour, one may note the wise selection of Psalms. The first Psalm prescribed for this service, Ps 44(45), is a nice complement to Mic 5. Psalm 44(45) is an *epithalamion* (wedding song) praising the king and his wife on the day of their marriage.[81] It is clearly divided into two parts. Verses 3–10 describe the qualities of the king, while verses 11–16 laud the queen's genuine obedience toward the king as well as her exquisite wardrobe.[82]

"Your throne, O God, is forever and ever. A rod of equity is of your rule; you loved righteousness and hated lawlessness. Therefore God, your God, anointed (*echrisen*) you with oil of rejoicing beyond your partners (*metochous*)" (Ps 44[45]:7[6]–8[7], NETS). This is a unique ruler anointed by God to be with no parity among his royal peers; hence the king is called "God" and his reign will last forever. Verse 7[6]a is a *crux interpretum* that has divided the interpreters of this Psalm into two distinct camps. On the one hand, the modern biblical scholars try to emend the Hebrew text by resorting to different vocalizations than the one offered by the Masoretes, or they try to come up with new renditions by more or less ingenious syntactical permutations.[83] On the other hand, the ancient Christian interpreters saw in this difficult text a prophecy pertaining to the incarnate Logos and his relationship with the Church. Quite interestingly, the Septuagint supports the difficult MT, reading *ho thronos sou ho Theos eis ton aiōna tou aiōnos*, "Your throne, O God, is forever and ever," with "God" in vocative.[84] One may note here the flurry of Christological interpretations generated by these lines. As a brief illustration, here is John Chrysostom's comment: "Hence God, your God anointed you. After all, the Father is by no means the Christ, nor has he been anointed. Whence it is clear that the verse is about the Only-begotten, about whom also the previous remarks were made. Isaiah said this, too, that there will be no end to his kingdom" (*Commentary on Psalms: Psalm 44[45]*).[85]

Psalm 44(45) speaks also of a "queen" (LXX: *basilissa*), interpreted by ancient Christian commentators as typifying the Church or the Theotokos in her dual role, maiden and queen: "Daughters of kings are in your honor; the queen stood at your right in gold-woven clothing, decked out in many colors. Hear, O daughter, and see, and incline your ear, and forget your people and the house of your father, because the king desired your beauty, because he is your lord" (vv. 10[9]–12[11], NETS).

The first troparion after the first three Psalms of the Orthros reads, "As the fruit of David's seed, Mary (*Mariam*) was registered of old with the Elder Joseph in Bethlehem, when she conceived with a seedless conception (*asporon kyophorian*). Behold, the time of birthing came, but no place was found within the lodging place (*katalymati*) for them; yet the cave appeared (*edeiknyto*) to the Queen (*tē Basilidi*) as a delightful palace. Christ is born to raise the image that had fallen aforetime."

The liturgical exegesis proves again to be innovative. The "queen" in Ps 44(45) is not the Church, as, for instance, in Chrysostom's commentary, but rather the Theotokos. Mary is described in this troparion as a "queen." The term *basilis*, "queen," used in this hymn for the Septuagint lexical choice *basilissa*, appears in the patristic literature with reference to the Virgin Mary, the Church, the soul united to Christ, the "queen" of virtues. By underscoring the queen's Davidic lineage, the hymnographer offers an intricate interpretation of Ps 44(45). On the one hand, the queen is not the spouse of the king but rather his mother. On the other hand, the "divine" king of Ps 44(45) is in fact the ideal "ruler" of Mic 5 (with dual provenance, wrapped-in-mystery "days of yore" and a precise location, "Bethlehem"). Hence, the qualification "from the seed of David" (*ek spermatos Dauid*) for the "queen" is well warranted. Note though that both Matthew (1:20) and Luke (1:27) mention Joseph, not Mary, as "of the house of David." Calling Mary "of the seed of David," the hymnographer seeks to create a parallel between the divine king and the queen (his mother) while relating both to Bethlehem, the place of origin for the Davidic dynasty. The "cave" (*spēlaion*) of Bethlehem "appears" (*edeiknyto*) to the Queen Theotokos as a "delightful palace" (*terpnon palation*) where "God" the King, the ruler of old, will be born. Both prophecies speaking of a divine king/ruler with reference to a remote past or wrapped in mystery future are made actual in liturgical time. "Christ is born" (*Christos gennatai*) "now," while chanting these hymns, the liturgists would say.

Note that the prokeimenon announcing the reading of Micah prophecy is taken from Ps 2:7: "The Lord said to me: 'My son you are; today I have begotten you'" (NETS). This verse may function as a hermeneutical bridge between Ps 44(45) accenting the "divinity" of the ideal king and Micah's prophecy pointing to the ruler of old born to tend his flock. Ps 2:7 also aims at taming the exuberant language of Ps 44(45):7(6) that calls the king "God." Ps 2:7 seeks to dissipate any misreading of this difficult description by stating that Israel's king is just the adopted (not natural) son of God, and the divine adoption occurs on the day of his coronation.

The central theme of the First Hour is to proclaim the "royalties" involved in the Nativity: God the Father, the Logos (Wisdom, Torah, Ruler) and Mary as maiden and queen. It is a celebration of royalties fitting quite well the generic name of this liturgical service, the Royal Hours. But this celebration cannot be done in a triumphalistic mode because the incarnation event in its uniqueness threw those outside this royal circle into utter confusion. This was especially the case of Joseph. Here is his genuine confession in poetical garb crafted by the same gifted Sophronius of Jerusalem. The *Protoevangelium of James* as tone and wording is easily detectable in the following liturgical hymn:[86]

> Thus says Joseph to the Virgin: O Mary, what is this spectacle (*drama*) that I behold in you? I am at a loss and sore amazed (*aporō kai existamai*), and my mind is stricken with dismay; wherefore depart from my sight straightway. O Mary, what is this spectacle that I behold in you? In the stead of honor, you have brought me shame; in the stead of gladness, sorrow; in the stead of praise, condemnation. No longer, therefore, shall I bear the reproach of men; for I received you from the priests of the temple as one blameless before the Lord (*amempton Kyriou*). And what is this that I now behold?
>
> First Hour, idiomelon

And the answer to Joseph's puzzlement, which also expressed the questioning of those in the liturgical gathering, comes from Joseph himself: "'Tell us, O Joseph, how did you bring the Maiden (*Korēn*) whom you received from the temple, now pregnant (*enkyon*), to Bethlehem'? 'I have searched the Prophets,' says he, 'and have been instructed by an Angel, and I am persuaded that Mary shall give birth to God in a manner past interpretation.' In homage to him, Magi shall come from the East, worshipping him with precious gifts. O you who were incarnate for our sakes, Lord, glory be to you" (Third Hour, idiomelon).

GREAT VESPERS

The Great Vespers for the Nativity are combined with the Liturgy of Basil the Great.

Eight Old Testament lessons are assigned for the Great Vespers of the Nativity: Gen 1:1–13; Num 24:2–3, 5–9, 17–18; Mic 4:6–7; 5:2–4; Isa 11:1–10; Bar 3:35–4:4; Dan 2:31–36, 44–45; Isa 9:6–7; Isa 7:10–16; 8:1–4, 8–10. These lessons cover all the three divisions of the Hebrew Bible, plus a reading from an *anaginōskomenon* book (Baruch).

The first Old Testament lesson, Gen 1:1–13, refers to the first three days of creation and their corresponding creatures: light, firmament separating heaven from earth, and vegetation. In the following hymn all these things God created through his Word (Logos) are bringing their tokens of appreciation to their Creator who appeared as man on earth: "What shall we offer you, O Christ? For you have appeared on earth as man for our sakes. Of all the creatures made by you, each offers you thanksgiving. The angels offer you the hymn; the heavens, the star; the Magi, their gifts; the shepherds, their wonder; the earth, her cave; the wilderness, the manger; and we offer you a Virgin Mother. O God, who were before the ages, have mercy on us" (idiomelon).

The main function of the liturgy is to make the history of salvation (in this particular case, its climax—the incarnation of the Logos) actual and personal. The birth of Christ is "the present mystery" and it is the all-embracing and omnipresent "I" who experiences the blessings of this mysterious and salvific event. Note the use of present tense actions and first-person statements in the following idiomelon. Through liturgy, the Scripture—companion and record of, and witness to the history of salvation—becomes what the media (printed, audio-visual, digital) is for modern man, namely, a way of tuning in an immediate and concrete reality. The liturgized Scripture is not a mere artifact kept on a library shelf. It is rather a media outlet spreading continuously the same good news, thus enabling the faithful to tune in the reality of salvation.

> Come, let us rejoice in the Lord as we declare this present mystery (*to paron mystērion*). The middle wall of partition [Eph 2:14] is broken asunder; the flaming sword is turned back, the Cherub steps aside (*parachōrei*) out of the Tree of Life, and I partake of the Paradise of Delight (*paradeisou tēs tryphēs*), whence I was cast out before through disobedience (*parakoēs*).[87] For the identical image (*aparallaktos eikōn*) of the Father, the distinctive mark (*charaktēr*) of his eternity, takes the form of a servant (*doulou*), and without undergoing change he comes forth from a mother with no experience of marriage (*apeirogamos*). For that which he was, he has remained, even true God; and that which he was not, he has taken upon himself, becoming man out of love for man. To him let us cry: O God, who are born of a virgin, have mercy on us.
>
> idiomelon by Germanos of Constantinople.

As for the relation between this hymn and the first reading, the only thing detectable is the detail of "taking hold" (*metalambanō*) again of the primordial paradise of delight. "Vegetation" (*botanē*) produced by earth (Gen 1:12) could be a hint at the Garden of Eden (Gk. *paradeisos*),[88] where the divinely allowed diet for the first man and woman was vegetarian (Gen 2:16).

The bridge between Gen 1:1–13 and the following hymn is quite evident. The word "light" appears several times. Christ, the "Light of Light," through his birth, made the entire creation radiant:

> Your Kingdom, O Christ God, is the Kingdom of all the ages, and your sovereignty is in every generation and generation. Incarnate of the Holy Spirit and become man of the Ever-virgin Mary, you have shined light upon us by your coming, O Christ God. O Light of Light, Effulgence of the Father, you have made all creation radiant. Every breath praises you, the express Image of the Father's glory. O you who are, and have ever been, and have shone forth from a virgin, O God, have mercy on us.
>
> idiomelon

The second Old Testament lesson, Num 24:2–3, 5–9, 17–18, is a cento of lines from the so-termed "Balaam's Third Oracle." Balaam, a non-Israelite seer, is chosen by God to speak on his behalf for the good fortune of Israel while wandering after the exodus. This is a singular case in the Hebrew Bible that shows that central notions of "election" and "prophetic call" are more flexible than one might think. After few introductory words (vv. 2–3), v. 4, relating the modus operandi of Balaam's oracle, is cautiously skipped from the liturgical reading. The following lines, vv. 5–9, describe how God took Israel out of Egypt and poured his blessing upon him, so the one who blesses Israel will be blessed and the one who curses him will be cursed. The last three verses of this scriptural lesson are the most important for the history of ancient Christian interpretation: "I will point to him, and not now; I deem him happy (*makarizō*),[89] but he is not at hand. A star (*astron*) shall dawn (*anatelei*) out of Iakob, and a person (*anthrōpos*) shall rise up (*anastēsetai*) out of Israel, and he shall crush the chiefs of Moab, and he shall plunder all Seth's sons. And Edom will be an inheritance, and Esau, his enemy, will be an inheritance, and Israel acted with strength" (Num 24:17–18, NETS). "Star" (*astron*) is a symbol for a king in ancient Near East (e.g., in Isa 14:12 [LXX], the king of Babylon is called *heōsphoros*, "morning star," literally, "bringer of the first rays of the dawn"). The Jewish messianic interpretation of Balaam's oracle is discernable as early as the making of the Septuagint: the Hebrew word šēbeṭ, "scepter," is rendered by the Greek Bible with *anthrōpos*, "person, man."[90]

Oddly enough, Matthew does not cite Num 24:17–18 in his account on the star of Bethlehem (Matt 2:1–2, 7, 9, 10). Nevertheless, ancient Christian interpreters saw in Balaam's oracle the hermeneutical key to Matthew's account (e.g., Justin Martyr, *Dialogue with Trypho* 106; Irenaeus *Against Heresies* 3.9.3; Origen, *Against Celsus* 1.60; Eusebius, *Proof of the Gospel* 9.1).[91]

The first clear evidence of the use of the second Old Testament lesson in connection with Matthew's account on the star of Bethlehem is found not during the office of the Great Vespers, but rather at the Matins of the Nativity. In the following hymn, the Magi, the "star-gazers," are described as "wise initiates" who studied the words of Balaam's divination and were led to Christ, the star of Jacob, as the "first-fruits of the nations": "When you did rise as the Star out of Jacob, O Master, you did fill the star-gazers with joy, those wise initiates (*myētas sophous*) of the words of Balaam, the ancient diviner (*manteōs*), who were led to you as the nations' first offering (*ethnōn aparchēn*); and as they brought you acceptable gifts, you did openly receive them" (Matins, Ode Four, troparion). The following hymn mentions the word "scepter" (*rhabdos*), though the Septuagint of Num 24:17 reads *anthrōpos*, "person, man." Is this a sufficient proof that the hymnographer knew about a reading with "scepter" (e.g., Hebrew reading) or is this novel reading a simple hint at Ps 45(44):7(6) which speaks of both "scepter" (*rhabdos*) and "throne" (*thronos*) as royal insignia. Apparently, the lexical duet ("scepters" and "thrones") in the following hymn leads one toward the latter explanation: "In calling the Magi by a star, heaven brought the first-fruits of the nations to you, a babe lying in a manger; and they were astonished that there was neither scepters (*skēptra*) nor thrones (*thronoi*), but only the uttermost poverty. For what is meaner than a cave? And what is lowlier than swaddling clothes? Yet in them the riches of your Divinity shone forth. O Lord, glory be to you" (The Nativity, Matins, Ode Three, *hypakoi*).

The sixth scriptural lesson is a cento of verses from Dan 2, "Nebuchadnezzar's Dream" (i.e., vv. 31–36, 44–45). The Babylonian king asks his sages to reproduce his dream and give the right interpretation. The sages are unable to deliver what the king has asked of them. Daniel, one of the Jewish exiles, receives from his God both the revelation of king's dream and its interpretation. The dream can be summed up this way: A stone cut (not by human hands) from a mountain strikes a composite statue (head of god, breast and arms of silver, thighs of bronze, and feet of iron and clay), turning it into utter dust. Then the stone becomes a great mountain filling the entire earth. Daniel's interpretation follows:

> And in the days of those kings the God of heaven will establish a kingdom that will not be destroyed forever, and his kingdom will not be left to another people. And it will pulverize and scatter all the kingdoms, and it will stand up forever; as you saw, a stone (*lithos*) was cut from a mountain (*orous*),[92] not by hands, and it pulverized the earthenware, the iron, the bronze, the silver, the gold. The great God has made known to the king what must happen after this, and the dream is true, and its interpretation trustworthy.
>
> Dan 2:44–45, Theodotion recension, NETS

John J. Collins underscores that whereas dreams of giant statues were quite common in ancient Near East, the statue in Daniel representing history rather than cosmos is a characteristic of the biblical account.[93] The four kingdoms are: Babylon, Media, Persia, and Greece. Daniel mentions in his interpretation of a fifth (eschatological) kingdom that this will replace all other four previous kingdoms. The last kingdom "will never be destroyed" (v. 44)—close as idea to 2 Sam 7 on David's dynasty in perpetuity.

Although the stone motif applying to Christ is well attested in the New Testament (Mark 12:10-11; Matt 12:42; Luke 20:17 with reference to Ps 118:22; and Rom 9:33 with reference to Isa 8:14), the only application of the same motif in Dan 2 is Luke 20:18. It was the common opinion among ancient Jewish and Christian interpreters that the stone quarried out of the mountain with no human agency ("not cut by hands") refers to the Messiah. Among Christian interpreters, one may mention: Irenaeus, Hippolytus, Tertullian, Ephrem, Eusebius, Athanasius, Cyril of Jerusalem, Jerome who saw in the stone a type of Christ or the Church.[94]

Theodoret of Cyrus interprets "not cut by hands" as an indication of the virgin birth: "Therefore we are taught both by the Old and the New Testament that our Lord Jesus Christ has been designated by the stone. For he was cut out of the mountain without hands, being born of a virgin apart from any nuptial intercourse, and the divine Scripture had always been accustomed to name him as having had his origin contrary to nature, the cutting out of a stone (*Commentary on the Visions of the Prophet*

Daniel 2.34–35).[95] The iconographic expression of this typological relation between the stone and Christ will be dealt with in the following chapter.

What is the "liturgical exegesis" of the stone motif found in the scriptural lesson above summarized? In the following hymn, the composer combines two scriptural lessons, Isa 11:1–10 and Dan 2:31–36, 44–45, from the vesperal service, with Luke 1:35 where the angel tells Mary that the "power of the Most High will overshadow (*episkiasei*) you." There are four key words linking these biblical texts together in depicting Logos-incarnation, namely, "rod," "blossom," "mountain," and "overshadowed." Mary is portrayed as a "densely overshadowed mountain" and Christ appears in this hymn as both "rod" and "blossom" from the root of Jesse: "Rod (*rhabdos*) of the root of Jesse, and blossom (*anthos*) that blossomed from it, O Christ, you have sprung from the Virgin; from the mountain (*orous*) densely overshadowed (*kataskiou daseos*) have you come, O Praised One, made flesh of her that knew not wedlock. O you who are immaterial (*aylos*) and God, glory to your power, O Lord" (The Nativity, Matins, Ode Four, heirmos).

Unlike the patristic interpreters, mostly Christological in their exegesis of Dan 2:44, the liturgists tilt to a Mariological interpretation of the mountain-stone motif. In the following heirmos the emphasis falls on the "mountain of the Virgin" bringing the Word forth: "For as a young babe (*neon brephos*) from the mountain of the Virgin (*orous tēs Parthenou*) did the Word (*Logos*) come forth to refashion (*anaplasin*) the peoples" (The Nativity, Matins, Ode Four, heirmos).

The last Old Testament reading for the Nativity's Vespers is a cento of lines from the first part of the Book of Isaiah (7:10–16; 8:1–4, 8–10).

On the backdrop of an imminent foreign invasion during the so-called Syro-Ephraimite War (735–32 B.C.E.), Isaiah offers king Ahaz of Judah the hope-giving sign of Immanuel (7:10–25).

Upon his first intervention in Judean policy, Isaiah asks Ahaz to choose any sign he wants and God will perform it as warranty of his protection. Ahaz refuses to ask for a sign because he would not put God to test. For a Christian reader, Isaiah's reply to Ahaz's refusal is probably one of the most known prophecies of the Old Testament: "Therefore the Lord himself will give you a sign. Look, the virgin (*hē parthenos*) shall be with child and bear a son, and you shall name him Emmanouel" (Isa 7:14, NETS).

Within the wider context of Semitic mindset, a "sign" is more than a mere indicator pointing to a destination. It is rather a symbol or pledge of a reality that is here and there, now and then. A sign or symbol will keep a community in a state of permanent tension between a current time—the time of the sign, and its final consummation (eschaton).

Identifying the Hebrew key terms of this prophecy, *ha-ʿalmāh*, "the young (unmarried) woman" and *Immanuel*, "God is with us," remains an open, complex question, amplified by Septuagint's rendition of *ha-ʿalmāh* as *hē parthenos*, "the virgin."[96] Ibn Ezra and Rashi, a long time prior to the dawn of modern historical criticism, sought to find the *peshat*, the plain, literal sense of Isa 7:14 while rejecting Immanuel's identification with Jesus and Hezekiah (king Ahaz's son) on the grounds of historical improbability. Today, after the rise and demise of historical critical approaches, readers of the Bible come to accept what Martin Buber called its "infinite interpretability": a text can have a plurality of meanings contingent on interpretative communities.[97] This is the case with the Christian Church that from her early days (Matt 1:23) identified, via the Septuagint reading, Emmanouel (Immanuel) with Jesus of Nazareth and *hē parthenos* with the Virgin Mary.[98] The Byzantine liturgist's choice for Isa 7:14 as part of the scriptural lessons for the feast of the Nativity (Vespers service) needs no further comment.

In the following hymn the name of Isaiah was replaced with that of David who is labeled "prophet." Was king David a prophet? In 2 Sam 23:2 David states, "The spirit of the Lord speaks through me, his word is upon my tongue" (NETS). Peter calls David a prophet (Acts 2:30) and many of David's Psalms are read by Christians as messianic prophecies referring to Christ. On the Sunday after the Nativity, at Matins, one chants: "As Prophet David said, 'A Virgin was found to hold (*chōrēsasa*) in her womb him that by nature is uncircumscribable (*physei aperigrapton*), even God Emmanouel (*Theon Emmanouēl*).' The divine and celebrated Joseph, because he understood it not, was instructed by an angel as he slept by night" (Ode Five, theotokion). Here, the idiomatic expression used already by the Septuagint, *en gastri hexei*, "[the Virgin] will have in [her] womb" for the Hebrew verbal root *h-r-h* "to be(come) pregnant" leads to an interesting contrast between the Theotokos' "womb" and the inherent uncircumscribability of Immanuel, the incarnate Logos.

In the next hymn, Immanuel is not a sign of the powerful intervention of God in the unfolding tumults of Judah at the crisscrossing of military powers of the time, as in Isa 7:14. Rather, Immanuel is a sign of the paradoxical kenosis (Phil 2:7) or "great poverty" on the part of God made man aiming at man's enrichment in "divine things":

Whence is your great poverty (*pollē ptōcheia*), which nothing can equal, whereby fallen Adam is made rich in divine things (*ta theia*)? So cried the Virgin, holding in her arms the Emmanouel, God and Creator (*Emmanouēl Theon kai Ktistēn*), who had received from her his body; to him we all shout: Blessed are you who have been born, our God, glory be to you.

> The Holy Twenty Thousand Martyrs Burned in Nicomedia
> [December 28], Matins, sticheron

Theophany of the Lord

"Wishing to save man who was gone astray, you did not disdain (*ouk apēxiōsas*) to clothe yourself in the form of a servant (*doulon morphēn endysasthai*); for it befitted you, as Master and God, to take upon yourself our nature for our sakes. For when you were baptized in the flesh, O Redeemer, you did count us worthy of forgiveness. Wherefore, we cry to you: O Benefactor, Christ our God, glory be to you" (Great Vespers, sticheron).

"The Holy Theophanies of our Lord Jesus Christ" (*Ta Hagia Theophaneia tou Kyriou hēmōn Iēsou Christou*), "Feast of Lights" (*Heortē tōn Phōtōn*), or simply "Theophany"—is another festal day (January 6) honoring the divine *synkatabasis* ("condescension"), or the willingness of the Logos to "clothe himself in the form of a servant." Like the Nativity, Circumcision, and Presentation into the Temple, the Theophany is part of the kenotic process outlined by Paul in Phil 2:7 (cf. John 17:5). As Georges Barrois remarks, "In the eyes of the Church, the mystery of the Incarnation, through the Theophany, enters into the reality of historical events."[99]

The plural *ta theophaneia* ("the divine manifestations") hints at either the revelation of the Trinity (i.e., Father's voice from heaven, incarnate Logos, and the Spirit in the form of a dove—Luke 3:21–22) or the beginning of Christ's series of divine manifestations, culminating with his resurrection and ascension to heaven. In any event, the accent in Eastern Orthodox tradition falls on the divine manifestation of Christ on the day of his baptism by John, when the entire world was enlightened by the Lord's light.

The order of services on Theophany is similar to the one followed on the Nativity, but with the important addition of a special service, the "Sanctification" (*Hagiasmos*) of waters.

GREAT VESPERS

What is peculiar for the Vespers service on this festal day is the significant number of scriptural lessons (thirteen passages from the Old Testament followed by the epistle and gospel lessons) that leave almost no room for hymns.

The Old Testament lessons are as follows: (1) Gen 1:1–13; (2) Exod 14:15–18, 21–23, 27–29; (3) Exod 15:22–16:1; (4) Josh 3:7–8, 15–17; (5) 2 Kgs 2:6–14; (6) 2 Kgs 5:9–14; (7) Isa 1:16–20; (8) Gen 32:1–10; (9) Exod 2:5–10; (10) Judg 6:36–40; (11) 1 Kgs 18:30–39; (12) 2 Kgs 2:19–22; (13) Isa 49:8–15; and the New Testament lessons: 1 Cor 9:19–27; Luke 3:1–18. The Old Testament lessons are taken from the Law, historical books (or Former Prophets, according to the Jewish nomenclature), and Prophets.

The central theme of the scriptural lessons is summed up by the following hymn sung immediately before the readings: "You have bowed your head before the Forerunner; you have crushed (*synethlasas*) the heads of the dragons (*karas tōn drakontōn*). You have descended into the running waters (*reithrois*); you have enlightened (*ephōtisas*) all things, that they might glorify you, O Savior, the enlightenment (*phōtismon*) of our souls." The Theophany or the Baptism of Christ is about water, dragons, and enlightenment! The first lesson, Gen 1:1–13, read also on the Nativity of the Lord, shows how the first three days of creation are organized. The climax of this reading is actually in v. 2 where one reads, "However, the earth was invisible and unwrought, and darkness was over the abyss (*abyssou*), and the Spirit of God (*pneuma theou*) rushed (*epephereto*)[100] upon the water" (LXX, author's translation). Primordial realities such as water, darkness, and abyss are mysteriously juxtaposed with the Spirit of God rushing upon the water. Interestingly, as chaotic and dark as this watery deep might have been, it is the starting point of God's creative actions, the source whence earth and life will emerge at God's powerful commands. In Gen 1, water stands for both chaos and order, death and life, hence the controlling, protective, life-giving role of the Spirit of God moving over the primordial watery deep.

The two imageries, creation and baptism, are interwoven by juxtaposing the "streams of Jordan" with the divine "fountain," and identifying the Christ to be baptized with the "Fashioner" of the old days of creation: "The streams of the Jordan received you, the Fountain (*pēgēn*); and the Comforter (*paraklētos*) came down (*katērcheto*) in the form of a dove. He that bowed the heavens bows his head, and the clay does shout and cry to the Fashioner (*plastourgō*): Why do you enjoin upon me what is beyond me? I have need to be baptized of you. O you who are without sin, Christ our God, glory be to you" (Theophany, Great Vespers, sticheron).

The second lesson is a selection of verses from the Book of Exodus narrating the miracle of crossing the Red Sea (Exod 14:15–18, 21–23, 27–29).

Here water is a boundary between slavery and freedom, death and life. At God's command, Moses stretched his hand lifting up his rod and the sea parted so that the Israelites were walking as if on the dry ground. Another stretch and the water returned to its place, killing all the Egyptians. Through God's guidance and intervention, Moses comes to control the dangerous waters. The idea of the Spirit of God rushing upon the primordial water (Gen 1:2) parallels Moses' hand gesture over the waters of the Red Sea. Both actions are foundational, leading to life and freedom out of such an ambivalent, danger-charged reality—water, that is.

The third lesson is taken from Exod 15:22–16:1, describing the sweetening of the bitter waters of Merra (Marah). This lesson is also read on the day of the Elevation of the Cross. Instructed by God, Moses succeeds controlling the dangerous water by turning it into something harmless. This lesson is echoed by one of the lines of Sophronius's prayers at the service of "Sanctification" (*Hagiasmos*) of the waters: "Today the bitter water, which was in the time of Moses, is changed into sweetness for the people by the presence of the Lord." A set of *troparia* separates these lessons from the following scriptural readings.

The fourth lesson is a cento from the Book of Joshua (3:7–8, 15–17). The miracle at the Red Sea is repeated at the Jordan River. God's instruction is closely followed. The Israelites were crossing Jordan while the priests carrying the ark of covenant were standing in the midst of Jordan. The water is again controlled, this time by Joshua and the priests, and again upon God's instruction.

The fifth lesson is taken from 2 Kgs 2:6–14. Elijah (Elias) and Elisha (Elisseus). Elijah separates the waters of Jordan using his mantle. In the midst of Jordan, Elijah is taken up to heaven into a chariot of fire. The scriptural pericope is silent as to God's instruction. Elijah's gesture brings the water of Jordan to utter submission.

The sixth lesson, 2 Kgs 5:9–14, narrates the healing of Neeman, a captain in the Assyrian army. Upon Elisha's instruction, Neeman immerses himself in the Jordan River seven times and his leper disappears. This is another way of controlling water, by turning it into a special, healing reality.

The seventh lesson, Isa 1:16–20, is an urgent call to repentance: "Wash yourselves; become clean; remove the evil deeds from your souls before my eyes; cease from your evil deeds; learn to do good; seek judgment; rescue the one who is wronged; defend the orphan, and do justice to the widow" (vv. 16–17, NETS). The cleansing aspect of the water is underscored.

The eighth lesson is from Gen 32:1–10 narrating Jacob's return to Canaan. The fugitive patriarch is about to ford Jordan leaving behind his shaky Aramaean relatives and getting ready to encounter his brother Essau whom he cheated long time ago. The water serves here as a buffer preventing hostility between these three parties.

The ninth lesson, Exod 2:5–10, is about the rescue of the infant Moses from the waters of the Nile and his adoption by the Pharaoh's daughter. This event foreshadows the great miracle at the Red Sea, decades later, when the Israelites will get out safe from the dangerous waters.

The tenth lesson is from Judg 6:36–40. Gideon moves from fear to faith, testing God two times (Judg 6:17–24, 36–40) until he is sure of God's support. The two parts of the second test make Gideon look faithless. He is almost redundant and quite ridiculous in his request.[101] If the dew will fall only on the fleece while the ground will remain dry, this will be a sign for Gideon that God chose him. But it is so. Gideon then asks God to confirm this sign by allowing the dew to fall a second time, on the ground and not on the fleece. And again it is so. The meaning of the story concerns God's condescension. Instead of being indignant at Gideon's nagging tests, God responds without hesitation.

Proclus of Constantinople (d. 446/7 C.E.), responsible for crafting the rhetoric and rationale for the Byzantine *cultus* of Mary, uses the fleece motif with reference to the Theotokos: "She who called us here today is the Holy Mary; . . . the purest fleece [Judg 6:37–38] drenched with the rain which came down from heaven, whereby the shepherd clothed himself with the sheep [Jn 10:11]" (*Homily* 1.1, 18–19).[102]

For the compiler of the following hymn, the fleece refers to the Virgin Mary and the dew (rain) to the Logos about to become man: "Descending into your womb like rain upon a fleece, the River of Peace, the Fountain of Goodness, he who numbers the drops of rain, became flesh, even he, the blessed God of our Fathers" (Feast of St. Gregory Theologian [January 25], Matins, Ode Seven, theotokion). Inspired by the patristic Marian interpretation of Judg 6:36–40, the Byzantine iconographers depicted the fleece as bearing the medallion icon of the Theotokos.[103]

The eleventh lesson is taken from 1 Kgs 18:30–39. On Mount Carmel Prophet Elijah challenges the prophets of Baal and Ashera to offer sacrifices and on which altar fire will descend from heaven that god may be acknowledged as the true god in Israel. Elijah's prayer is heard. Fire comes down from heaven and consumes the offering on Elijah's altar.

The twelfth lesson, 2 Kgs 2:19–22, reminding one of the miracle of Moses at Marah (Merra), narrates how Elisha turned the bad water into drinkable water by throwing some salt into the water-source of the city of Jericho.

The thirteenth and last lesson is Isa 49:8–15: "And they shall feed in all their ways; in all the paths shall be their pasture; they shall not hunger or thirst, neither shall burning heat nor sun strike them down, but he who has mercy on them will comfort them and through springs of water will lead them" (vv. 9b–10, NETS). In a new restored setting, marked by a dramatic transition from humiliation to glory, pointing to the early Christian apocalyptic switch from kenosis to *doxa*, Israel will be led "through springs of water." This image describing Israel's return to its homeland fits with the wandering through the wilderness after the exodus from Egypt as well as with the paradisiac ideal.[104]

Surveying all these scriptural lessons, Georges Barrois noted:

> Our twentieth-century minds may find some difficulty in relating these Bible stories and prophecies to the central theme of the feast. In fact, they have all a point in common. In addition to the recurring theme "waters," foreshadowing the baptism of regeneration, they imply a radical, "existential" change in the destiny of a people or of an individual, involving an agonizing decision to be taken, an issue of life or death. And so it is with us, for we were buried with Christ in baptism, in which we were also raised with him through faith in the operation of God. Col 2:12[105]

As one notices from this brief presentation, water can have various valences: a quite dangerous reality hiding in itself a strange mix of death and life, chaos and order; it can be a cleansing means, a saving buffer, a boundary between past and future, between slavery and freedom. What is the inner link between these almost contradictory aspects of water and Jesus's baptism, or to use the liturgical nomenclature of this festal day, between water and the Enlightenment (*Phōtismon*) or God's Manifestations (*Theophaneia*)? In order to reach a tentative answer to this difficult question, one may want to take a look at the Old Testament lessons within the liturgical setting of the special service called the "Sanctification" (*Hagiasmos*) of the waters, usually done at the end of the Liturgy on Theophany.

SANCTIFICATION OF THE WATERS

The "Sanctification" (*Hagiasmos*) service begins with a rather proclama-tory line from Sophronius, Patriarch of Jerusalem: "Today the nature of the waters is sanctified; and the Jordan is rent in two, and holds back the stream of its own waters, on seeing the Master being washed." Whatever was the mystery with the primordial waters (Gen 1:2), we are told from the onset that through Christ's baptism the "nature of the waters is sanc-tified" (*tōn hydatōn hagiazetai hē physis*), hence the natural inference that prior to this kenotic event, the waters had been in that ambiguous state described above. Seeing Jesus approaching to be baptized, the wild waters "were afraid" (*ephobēthēsan*) and John exclaimed, "How shall the lamp illuminate the Light? How shall the servant lay his hand upon the Master? Sanctify (*hagiason*) both me and the waters, O Savior." This implies a state of continuous enmity between the waters—reminiscent of the primor-dial watery deep—and God, the Creator of Life: "The waters saw you, O God, the waters saw you and were afraid" (Hagiasmos service, a prayer by Sophronius, Patriarch of Jerusalem).

The Old Testament lessons are all from the Book of Isaiah (35:1–10; 55:1–13; 12:3–6). The first lesson, Isa 35:1–10, describes the joy of Israel's restoration by evoking the picture of a second exodus. The New Testament understood the salvation through Christ as a new and final exodus (John 6:48–51; 1 Cor 10:1–4). In fact, the exodus under the leadership of Moses became a type for Israel's return from the exile and Christ's redemptive work. All this joy of the exiles is connected to the image of abundant water turning the wilderness in a *locus vitae*: "Water has broken forth in the wil-derness and a gully in a thirsty land; the dry place shall turn into marsh-lands, and in the thirsty land there shall be a spring of water; the joy of birds shall be there—bed of reed and marshlands" (Isa 35:6b–7, NETS).

The second lesson comes also from the Book of Isaiah (55:1–13). In this pericope, the exilic prophet invites his people to a banquet of exquisite joy. Everybody is invited to the eschatological banquet with only one prereq-uisite, having a genuine "thirst" (longing) for God: "You who thirst, go to water, and as many of you as have no money, go, buy, and drink wine and fat, without money and without price" (v. 1, NETS). Seeking God is a con-dition to be admitted to his banquet: "Seek God, and when you find him, call upon him" (v. 6, NETS). Nevertheless, God's ways are always hard to understand: "For my plans are not like your plans, nor are your ways like my ways, says the Lord. But as heaven is far from the earth, so is my way far from your ways and your notions from my thought" (vv. 8–9, NETS).

The banquet image evokes God's love: Passover out of Egypt (Exod 12) and Sinai covenant (Exod 24) are celebrated with a banquet; the eschatological age will be marked with a banquet (Isa 25:6; Matt 5:6). The entire creation participates into the people's everlasting joy: "For you shall go out with joy and be taught with happiness; for the mountains and the hills shall leap forth as they welcome you with happiness, and all the trees of the field shall clap with their branches" (Isa 55:12, NETS).

The third lesson, Isa 12:3–6, is a hymn of gratitude for salvation: "And with joy you will draw water out of the springs of salvation. And you will say in that day: Sing hymns to the Lord; call his name out loud; declare his glorious deeds among the nations; remember them, because his name has been exalted" (vv. 3–4, NETS). The well was the common place where people were coming together to share the joy of an important event. Thus, a new exodus will make Israel to outburst in a song of thanksgiving.

The epistle lesson, 1 Cor 10:1–4, links these three Old Testament lessons, centered on the theme of exodus and the life-giving water, to Christ's baptism. Paul interprets typologically the parting of the Red Sea and the march of the Israelites as on the dry land (Exod 14:15–16). In Christian baptism, through incorporation in Christ, the believers are experiencing the deliverance from sin, corruption, and death: "I do not want you to be unaware, brothers and sisters, that our ancestors were all under the cloud, and all passed through the sea, and all were baptized into Moses in the cloud and in the sea" (1 Cor 10:1-2).

The following hymn explains Paul's typology in relation to the Christian baptism: "The cloud and the sea, in which the people were once baptized by the lawgiver as he led them out of Egypt, prefigured the wonder of divine Baptism. The sea was a figure of the water, and the cloud was a figure of the Spirit, whereby we are perfected and cry out: Blessed are you, the God of our Fathers" (Matins, Ode Seven, troparion). Gennadius of Constantinople (d. 471 C.E.) goes even further by underscoring the protective power of the Spirit along with the saving water of baptism, typified in the days of old by the cloud and the Red Sea, respectively:

> The cloud was a figure standing for the grace of the Spirit. For just as the cloud covered the Israelites and protected them from the Egyptians [Exod 14:19], so the Spirit's grace shields us from the wiles of the devil. Likewise, just as the crossing of the sea protected them from their enemies and gave them real freedom, so baptism protects us from our enemies. That was how the Israelites came

to live under the Law of Moses. This is how we, in baptism, are clothed with the Spirit of adoption and inherit the covenants and confessions made in accordance with the commands of Christ.[106]

The Great Litany following the scriptural lessons in the Hagiasmos service aims to interconnect the past, present and eternity as a single purifying stream of water. The priest prays that the water may "be sanctified by the power and working and descent of the Holy Spirit" (as it was on the day of Jesus's baptism), "be a gift of sanctification" for the faithful, and "be water springing up to everlasting life" (linking the liturgical present to the eschaton ushering in eternity).

In a prayer after the litany, Christ is addressed as the "Well-spring of life and immortality (*hē pēgē tēs zōēs kai tēs athanasias*), the Light of Light (*to phōs to ek phōtos*)." Both metaphors, Christ the "well-spring of life" and "the light," set a contrast between the dark, disorderly watery deep and the first among God's creatures—the light, that is (Gen 1:2–3). Sophronius's exclamation at the service of Hagiasmos, "The abysses shudder before you (*se prittousin abyssoi*)," may be a subtle hint at the "deep" (*abyssos*) in Gen 1:2. "For you, O Master, because of your mercy, could not endure to behold the race of man oppressed by the tyranny of the devil, but you came and did save us." On the day of Christ's baptism, Jordan became the embodiment, or perhaps the actual recapitulation, of the primordial ambiguous "deep" populated with dragons: "You did also sanctify the streams of the Jordan, sending down from heaven your All-Holy Spirit, and did crush (*synetripsas*) the heads of the dragons (*drakontōn*) that were lurking therein."

But it is not only about the Lord who crushed the dragons. In the same "deep" of the water of the Jordan River, the same Lord also "fashions Adam anew": "In the streams of the Jordan, the Lord, the King of the ages, fashions (*anaplattei*) corrupted Adam anew, and crushes the heads of lurking dragons (*drakontōn emphōleuontōn*); for he is glorified" (Hagiasmos, First Canon, Ode One, troparion). According to Eastern Orthodox hymnody, Baptism as a sacrament of the Church (Gk. *mystērion*, "mystery"), patterned on Christ's own baptism, is not simply a cleansing from corruption. It is actually an act of courage of someone willing to immerge along with the Lord into the primordial watery deep to experience both his refashioning and the defeat of hostile powers lurking in the water. Thus, Basil writes: "If Israel had not crossed the sea, they would not have escaped from Pharoah; so you, if you do not go through the water, you will not escape from the cruel tyranny of the demon" (*Homily XIII on the Holy Baptism* 1.3.7).[107] The Iambic Canon composed by John of Damascus echoes the same idea of the old, corrupted man, buried with Christ in the streams of Jordan: "To snatch (*harpasai*) our Ancestor (*Genarchēn*) from the land of darkness (*chōrou zophōdous*), and from every stain to cleanse the whole creation, him that by error was ruined, you renewed; buried with you (*syntaphenta soi*) in the streams, O Word without beginning."

The wound Christ inflicted on the evil one occurs on the day of Lord's baptism.[108] With the help of two Old Testament images, the hymnographer depicts this odd wrestling in terms of "deceiving the deceiver" theme associated by church fathers with Christ's descent to the Hades.[109] "He that once grafted (*emphyteusas*) deadness (*nekrōsin*) into all creation, wearing the form (*schēmatistheis*) of a beast that works evil [Gen 3:1], is seized with darkness at the incarnate Advent (*sarkikē parousia*). Striking against the Master, the Shining Daybreak (*Orthrō phananti*)[110] [Isa 14:12], he does break his own malicious head asunder" (Matins, Ode Three, Second Canon, troparion).

Exaltation of the Cross

This feast, held on September 14, should be distinguished from the Veneration of the Holy Cross (Gk. *Stavroproskynēsis*) held on the third Sunday of the Great Lent.

The main difference between the two commemorations of Christ's cross is that while the Veneration gazes forward to the Holy Week, anticipating Christ's victory over death, the Exaltation looks back at the cross through the lens of the resurrection event, while projecting the hopes and prayers of the faithful upon the eschaton, when the true and complete defeat of suffering and death will shine forth (1 Cor 15:26).

The Universal Exaltation of the Cross takes the faithful to the postresurrection times, to the Church's history: first, to the year 335 C.E. when the Church of the *Anastasis* (Resurrection—today Holy Sepulchre) built by Constantine on the traditional site of Christ's tomb in Jerusalem was consecrated; and secondly, to the year 629 C.E. when Byzantine emperor Heraclius recovered the relic of the true Cross from the Persians, who had looted the sacred object from the Anastasis in the year 614 C.E. Heraclius brings the Cross into the Church of *Hagia Sophia* (Holy Wisdom) in Constantinople and elevates it in sign of triumph. The serendipitously paradoxical juxtaposition of "exaltation" and "cross" for the September 14 commemoration takes its proper place within the scope of Christ's resurrection and the eschatological hermeneutics of Eastern Orthodox worship.

> Today the Tree of Life, raised up from the hidden recesses of the earth, confirms the Resurrection of Christ, who was nailed upon it. And raised on high by priestly hands, it declares his Ascension into the heavens, whereby our nature, lifted from its fall to earth, becomes a citizen of the heavens. Wherefore, let us cry in thanksgiving: O Lord, who was lifted up on the Cross, and through it has lifted us up with yourself, vouchsafe the joy of heaven to us who sing your praise.
>
> Exaltation of the Cross, Matins, idiomelon

The Old Testament lessons prescribed for the Great Vespers of the Exaltation of the Cross are as follows: Exod 15:22–16:1, Prov 3:11–18, and Isa 60:11–15, according to the tripartite division of the Jewish Bible: Law, Prophets, and the Writings (Hagiographa).

The first lesson, Exod 15:22–16:1, comes immediately after the songs of Moses and Miriam. This is the first experience with the harshness of the wilderness (of Sour) after the crossing of the Red Sea and defeat of the Egyptian army. After a three-day trip, the Israelites came upon a source of water, at Marah (LXX: Merra), but they could not drink for the water was bitter.[111] People complain against Moses for the lack of drinkable water. The center of this pericope is occupied by Exod 15:25–26, "Then Moyses cried to the Lord, and the Lord showed him wood (*xylon*),[112] and he threw it into the water, and the water became sweet. There he set for him statutes and judgments, and there he tested him. And he said, 'If you by paying attention listen to the voice of the Lord, your God, and do before him pleasing things, and give ear to his commandments, and keep all his statutes, every disease which I brought upon the Egyptians, I will not bring upon you. For I am the Lord who heals you'" (NETS). The saving warrior at the Red Sea (Exod 15:3) turns into the protecting healer during Israel's sojourn in the wilderness.

The second Old Testament lesson, Prov 3:11–18, urges the hearers not to reject the Lord's discipline (*paideia*), for this is another form of divine love toward those he accepts and loves (vv. 11–12). Wisdom is praised as the most precious treasure carrying with her longevity, riches, fame, righteousness, mercy, goodness, and peace (vv. 14–17). The focus of this lesson, in the Septuagint reading, is on the identification of wisdom with the tree of life and the Lord. "She is a tree of life (*xylon zōēs*) to all those who lay claim to her, and she is steadfast (*asphalēs*) to those who lean (*epereidomenois*) upon her, as on the Lord" (v. 18, NETS).

The third Old Testament lesson for this festal day is taken from Isa 60:11–15. The prophet proclaims a change in fortune for the Babylonian Jews, envisioning the reconstruction of Jerusalem, which had been destroyed in 586 B.C.E. Those who once were hated and forsaken are now saved by the Lord and brought back to their homeland. The Babylonian Jewry enjoyed the Persian king Cyrus's edict of release issued in 539 B.C.E. Zion became once again the City of the Lord and all the nations start bringing their wealth to the city whose gates will never be shut (a sign of perfect security). Among the presents brought by these nations is the famous timber from the forests of Lebanon: "And the glory (*doxa*) of Lebanon shall come to you, with cypress (*kyparissō*) and pine (*peukē*) and cedar (*kedrō*) together, to glorify (*doxasai*) my holy place" (v. 13, NETS).

Below there a few examples of hymnody interconnected with the scriptural lessons mentioned above. The golden warp holding this literary fabric (lessons and hymns) together can be encapsulated in one sentence: Christ's saving Cross is the genuine tree of life able to heal humans of corruption, suffering and mortality.

Source of Healing. Targum of Pseudo-Jonathan equates the tree mentioned in Exod 15 with the bitter oleander plant. Jewish lore refers to oleander as a plant with both healing and toxic powers having also the ability to desalinize water.[113] In 2 Kgs 2:19–22, Elisha "heals" a salty river by throwing salt into it. The paradox of healing by using harmful objects, substances is well spread in the Bible as well as in ancient Jewish and Christian interpretations. "God's way of healing is not man's way. In human healing, that which is used for hurting is not used for healing— one strikes with a knife and heals with a bandage. Not so with God: The very means by which he strikes he also heals" (*Mekhilta Wayhi* 5).[114]

Similarly, John Chrysostom speaks of Christ's cross that sweetens the embittered world: "Solomon says, 'Blessed is the wood through which the righteousness comes' [Wis 14:7]. And Isaiah, 'Whence and of what wood was the cross'? says, 'Of cypress and pine and cedar, to glorify my holy place.' And Moses throwing a piece of wood into Merra, the bitter waters became sweet as a type of Christ's Cross that sweetens the world from the demons' bitterness" (*De adoratione pretiosae crucis* 3).[115]

On the Exaltation of the Cross, at the Great Vespers, one chants:

Come, all you nations, let us worship the blessed Tree, through
which was wrought the everlasting righteousness. For he, who by
a tree beguiled our forefather Adam, is himself ensnared by the
Cross; and he, who by tyranny gained dominion over the creation
of the King, is by faith overthrown in utter ruin. By the blood of
God, the serpent's poison is washed away; and the curse of a just
condemnation is loosed by the unjust judgment passed against the
Just One. For it was fitting that the wood should be healed by wood;
and that the sufferings of him who was condemned because of the
tree should be done away through the Passion of him who is pas-
sionless. But, O Christ our King, glory to your dread dispensation
toward us, whereby you have saved us all, since you are good and
the friend of man.

sticheron

Guiding Wisdom. Similar language (*asphaleia*, "steadfastness," and *en-
teuthen zōēs to xylon*, "the tree of most precious life") defining the Wisdom
links subtly Prov 3:18 to this hymn at the end of Matins for the Exaltation
of the Cross: "Disobedience brake the commandment of God, and the
tree partaken of untimely brought death to mortals. Henceforward the
tree of the most precious life (*tēs eritimou zōēs to xylon*) was steadfastly (*en
asphaleia*) enclosed, till the one lying in wait by night (*nyktilochos*), dying
a lingering death (*dysthanous*), opened the way to it again as he cried with
gratitude: O You supremely praised God of our Fathers and our God, for
ever are you blessed" (Ode Seven, troparion).

In the following hymn, the cross is depicted as the guiding Wisdom.
She gives hope, guides, protects, steadfasts, heals and restores the dead
to life: "O Cross of Christ, you, hope (*elpēs*) of Christians, guide (*hodēge*)
of them that are gone astray, haven (*limēn*) of the storm-tossed, victory
(*nikos*) in wars, steadfastness (*asphaleia*) of the whole world, physician
(*iatre*) of the sick, and resurrection (*anastasis*) of the dead: Have mercy on
us" (Matins, idiomelon).

Tree of Life. Ancient interpreters identified the tree mentioned in Exod
15:25 with the Edenic "tree of life" (Gen 2:9): "And there he commanded
him many things and showed him the tree of life, from which he cut off
and took and threw into Marah, and the water of Marah became sweet"
(Pseudo-Philo, *Biblical Antiquities* 11:15).[116]

On the Exaltation of the Cross, at Vespers, one chants: "The tree of
true life (*xylon tēs ontōs zōēs*), which was planted in the Place of the Skull,

whereon the King of the ages wrought salvation in the midst of the earth, sanctifies the ends of the world as it is exalted today, and the Church of the Resurrection (*Anastasis*) is consecrated" (idiomelon). The cross as the new tree of life brings forth the immortal fruit: "O you unsullied tree (*xylon achranton*)! through which, as we send up glory to Christ, we partake of Eden's comely and immortal fruit (*athanatou brōseōs*)" (sticheron).

One may conclude this brief survey on the feast of Exaltation of the Cross by noticing that Eastern Byzantine liturgy with all its emphasis on jubilation, exaltation of the cross as source of healing, life and restoration, and as a banner of victory, is not at all triumphalistic. The cross that was exalted in the majestic Church of Hagia Sophia in Constantinople is the same cross of Golgotha on which the Lord was nailed. Moreover, the gospel reading at the Divine Liturgy is a cento of verses from John 19:6–11, 13–20, 25–28, 30, which narrates the passion with the trial before Pilate, the crucifixion on the Golgotha, and the death of Jesus. The joy the cross may theologically generate is liturgically tamed by references and hints at that terrifying Friday afternoon when the gates of heaven seemed to have been forever shut. Exquisite Old Testament texts (Job, Psalms, Proverbs, Prophets) used in the Byzantine liturgy remind us that, until the shining eschaton, "hope" (*elpis*) is our only trustworthy companion.

As we have seen, Eastern Orthodox worship is replete with Old Testament scriptural material. Psalmody, scriptural lessons, hymns, prayers, homilies, synaxaria are all shaped by the Scriptures. The Eastern Orthodox Church is a scriptural Church per excellence.[117] In his statistical study of three liturgies and four sacraments, Demetrios Constantelos counted over a thousand scriptural verses or parts of verses. This indicates that more than a quarter of the services are made of scriptural material.[118]

Liturgy is an innovative, almost subversive form of religious experience when compared with more discursive modes such as patristic exegesis or theology. A similar contrast obtains between Scripture and Tradition. Liturgy makes extensive use of art. Like poetry versus prose, liturgy through aural and visual arts is subversive—working beneath, and sometimes at odds with, theology. Speaking of Orthodox liturgical theology, Robert F. Taft underscores the power of metaphors used by the Byzantine liturgists: "The genius of metaphorical language is to hold in dynamic tension several levels of meaning simultaneously. In this sense, one and the same eucharistic table must be at once Holy of Holies, Golgotha, tomb of the resurrection, cenacle, and heavenly sanctuary of the Letter to the Hebrews. So it is not the multiplicity of meanings but the

attempt to parcel them out that can lead to an artificial literalism destruc-
tive of symbol and metaphor."[119] Similarly, Georges Florovsky suggests
that the experience of the Orthodox Church is best reflected not so much
in dogmas as in liturgical symbolical acts and texts. "The concreteness of
symbols," observes Florovsky, "is sometimes even more vivid, clear, and
expressive than any logical conceptions can be, as witness the image of
the Lamb taking upon himself the sins of the world."[120]

The "liturgical exegesis" of the Scriptures is quite untamed as compared to patristic interpretation. If the latter goes parallel to or in support
of towering theological discourse, the former, along with iconography,
often represents the folk level theology or people's piety. Michael Prokurat
remarks: "For the Bible to be 'alive' in the Tradition, it must be heard and
experienced liturgically—it is the Word which dwells in the heart of the
people of God."[121] It would be a great benefit if someone were to examine
critically and thoroughly the interesting interplay between the two levels
of theology in Eastern Orthodox tradition, namely, the folk and the more
erudite or scholarly one.

In addition to its hermeneutical value, liturgy has a formative function. In Eastern Orthodox tradition, the entire Christian life is liturgical. Scripture and Tradition meet together on the fertile ground of liturgy
whose ultimate purpose is to shape the life of worshippers in the image
and likeness of Christ. Alexander Rentel writes: "This complex structure
[of Liturgy] also forms the faithful; it gives them a way of understanding
above all the Orthodox faith and also how they should live their lives being
united with Christ. Even beyond deeds and works, the liturgical rites provide the faithful with suitable words, metaphors, and symbols, which they
can use to understand and communicate their faith to the world around
them."[122] The Great Canon of Andrew of Crete (d. 740 C.E.), prescribed
for the Great Lent, is a good example of reading the Scripture in a creative
way aimed at spiritual renewal. Doru Costache notices that Andrew's goal

> was not to "master" the Bible but rather to extract from it the
> required wisdom for the readers' renewal. To reach this goal, he
> made the effort to transfigure Scripture by personalising, interior-
> ising and subjectifying all biblical events and characters evoked in
> the poem (except Christ and the Theotokos). Integrated into this
> new and personalised metanarrative, the scriptural figures, typi-
> fying general human attitudes, become pretexts to speak of, and
> speak to, oneself. Consequently, there is no longer Adam or David

who have done such and such— it is "you, my soul" who did all
these and more, and for whom the Lord "has made compassionate
salvation in the midst of the earth."

Wednesday, Ode Four, troparion 3[123]

Liturgy creates an arch over time linking past events, that is, the history
of salvation in its many and varied moments, with a perpetual present
time experienced by worshipers in a personalized way within and outside church's confines. Listening to the "liturgized" Scripture, worshippers become gradually part of the history of salvation with all its valleys
and peaks. In their struggles and trials, Scripture provides them not only
with radiant models to follow but also converging points of human frailty.
Paradoxically, these examples of weakness, confusion, and apparent
defeat may contribute to the strengthening of their own spiritual warfare.
Wrapped in hymns of high poetry, the unreachable scriptural models
become reachable and the scandalizing negative examples are turned pas-
torally with steady effort into a springboard for renewal.

7

Visual

But now when God is seen in the flesh conversing with men, I make an image of the God whom I see. I do not worship matter; I worship the Creator of matter who became matter for my sake, who willed to take his abode in matter; who worked out my salvation through matter. Never will I cease honoring the matter that wrought my salvation.

JOHN OF DAMASCUS, On the Divine Images

"ANATHEMA TO THE calumniators of the Christians, that is to the image breakers. Anathema to those who apply the words of Holy Scripture that were spoken against idols, to the venerable images. Anathema to those who do not salute the holy and venerable images" (*Extracts from the Acts of the Seventh Ecumenical Council: Session 1*).[1] These are three of the ten anathemas composed by bishop Basil of Ancyra (a former iconoclast) as part of his confession of faith at the Seventh Ecumenical Council.

The Seventh Ecumenical Council held at Nicaea in 787 C.E. was a preview of the victorious restoration of icons that would occur some fifty years later at the "Home Synod" convened by the Empress Theodora in 842–43 C.E. After that, a public celebration followed inside the Church of Hagia Sophia where the *Synodikon of Orthodoxy*[2] was for the first time read. The Sunday of March 4, 843 C.E. marks the so-called Triumph of Orthodoxy, and the inception of an ongoing liturgical tradition—the reading of the *Synodikon*, considerably expanded throughout the time, in all churches on the First Sunday of the Great Lent (called the "Sunday of Orthodoxy"), in order to commemorate the end of the torturous iconoclastic controversy (726–843 C.E.).

Some hundred years later after the "Triumph of Orthodoxy," an old Russian chronicle recorded the words filled with awe of the messengers of prince Vladimir of Kiev (d. 1015) upon their return from Constantinople: "We knew not whether we were in heaven or on earth, for on earth there is no such splendor or such beauty, and we are at a loss to describe it. We know only that God dwells there among men, and their service is finer than the ceremonies of other nations."[3] The messengers could not express the experience they had inside the Church of Hagia Sophia ("Holy Wisdom") in Constantinople. This well-known and much-cited story shows how closely the aesthetic and the spiritual have been intertwined in the Eastern Orthodox Church. Here, the untouchable can be well nigh touched by senses as in Michelangelo's fresco *The Creation of Adam* in the Sistine Chapel, where Adam's finger approaches daringly the Creator's finger. Through icons and liturgical hymns, the ontological gap between Creator and creation decreases, so to speak, and the experience of God becomes quite personal and appealing.[4]

In Dostoevsky's *The Idiot*, Ippolit Terentiev asks Myshkin, "Is it true, prince, that you once said that beauty will save the world? And what kind of beauty will save the world?" The answer came from Dostoevsky himself in another novel, *The Devils*: "The world will become the beauty of Christ." Paraphrasing, one may say that, "Christ's beauty will save the world." Yet another question arises, "Which beauty of Christ?" The one hinted at by the Christological interpretation of Ps 44(45):3(2), "Youthful in beauty you are, beyond the sons of men; grace was poured on your lips" (NETS)? But what about Isa 53:2, which speaks plainly of a suffering Messiah, "he has no form or glory, and we saw him, and he had no form or beauty" (NETS)—a text applied by church fathers to Christ's passion?

The comments of Joseph Ratzinger (now resigned Pope Benedict XVI) on this scriptural-exegetical conundrum are quite interesting and insightful.[5] Ratzinger appeals to Augustine's *De pulchro et apto* in order to show that the two biblical texts are not in contradiction, but they present rather a dynamic contrast that conveys the "true Beauty, or Truth itself." True beauty is not strange to suffering. Whether it be Plato's original perfection conceived in aesthetic terms or Nicholas Cabasilas's Christic beauty, man will always experience nostalgia or longing after what is more than himself. And unavoidably a continuous, yet to be quenched longing translates into suffering. In the words of Cabasilas, to whose theological aesthetic Ratzinger draws our attention: "When men have a longing so great that it surpasses human nature and eagerly desire and are able to accomplish things beyond human thought, it is the Bridegroom who has smitten them with this longing. It is he who has sent a ray of his beauty into their eyes. The greatness of the wound already shows the arrow that has struck home, the longing indicates who has inflicted the wound" (*The Life in Christ* 2.15).[6] Icons and hymns do facilitate such an intimate realization of God who personifies beauty and truth. The only thing needed to reach this personal experience is allowing oneself to be moved by seeing and hearing these magnificent pieces of art.[7]

Nevertheless, criticism may arise from an existential perspective suggesting that the power of falsehood, violence, and evil pervades into every single pore of reality, thus rendering aesthetic perfection—most especially of the religious kind—a lure toward escapism and moral or political indifference. What is real and true, the beauty of a hidden and peace promising world or the ugliness of a visible and violent world?

As Ratzinger notices, after Auschwitz and the questions raised in post-Holocaust thought about "the silence of God" to the atrocities of history, beauty alone is no longer a sufficient ideal. Nevertheless, the paradoxical juxtaposition between "beauty" and "no beauty" found in the two above-cited messianic texts (i.e., Ps 44 [45] and Isa 53) suggests that in Christ's passion the ideal beauty is not corroded or expunged by ugliness and violence of this world. Instead, the beauty is overcome and transformed by the truth and love conjoined in the one who did "lay down his life for his friends" (John 15:13). Through Christ's suffering, beauty becomes more real and profound. Having allowed himself to be slapped, spat upon, and crowned with thorns, Christ testifies that beauty can coexist with suffering and violence. And the true, perfect beauty is the beauty of love as self-offering for others. This beauty is stronger than the violence it suffers in this world, precisely because it offers itself as a gift in the midst of unsettling rampage. For this reason, Christ's followers should not be disheartened by life's trials. While embracing the Lord's irresistible beauty they are urged to take courage in their search for beauty, love, and truth (John 14:27; 16:33).

If the true beauty born of self-offering and long-suffering love frees the beholder, nevertheless there is also a dazzling and deceptive beauty that can lock the viewer into himself. If the goal of the former beauty is to create or elicit a desire for self-offering, the aim of the latter is to enforce the will for possession and self-indulgence. Christian art has two enemies: the ugliness of a violent world that tempts us with the slogan "Beauty is unreal," and the seductive art that makes the human being prisoner of its basic instincts and desires.

Throughout church history there were attempts to stifle figurative visual art as an affront to the invisibility and unknowability of God. This can be seen equally in the eighth–ninth century iconoclasts and the sixteenth-century Zürich Reformers. For a long period the West, not only Protestant but also Roman Catholic, was deprived of the richness of Christian iconography. However, in the wake of World War II, a number of prominent theologians and philosophers (e.g., Paul Tillich, Jacques Maritain, Nikolai Berdyaev) began to talk about the interrelationship between theology, arts, and contemporary culture.[8] The immediate conclusion of this discussion was that icons, as nondiscursive, nonverbal but rather symbolic modes of expression, are "necessary to balance and even to challenge the limits of the verbal."[9]

Icon Manufacture and Worship
Aniconic or Anti-iconic?

The early Christian attitude toward images was modeled on Jewish views. With respect to representing God in images, early Judaism took a trenchant position against it. The second commandment of the Decalogue (Exod 20:4) was the scriptural basis for both early Christian and Jewish positions against figurative representation of the invisible God.

However, the "prohibition of images" found in the Hebrew Bible can be understood in two different ways: (a) an interdict on all images, religious and nonreligious in character (cf. Exod 20:4; Deut 4:15–18) or (b) a ban on representing God and venerating his image (or using the image as an idol) (Deut 27:15). The former interpretation, the absolute prohibition of any image, was soon discarded from the common Israelite memory, as evidenced for instance by the cherubs in the Temple (1 Kgs 6:23–29). The latter interpretation—a ban on the production and worship of all images depicting the invisible God—has nonetheless been always carefully observed. In fact, the avoidance of any depiction of God is one of the most important tenets of Jewish iconography throughout its history.

One may mention here an early eighth-century B.C.E. Israelite jar discovered in a fortresslike structure at Kuntillet Ajrud in the northern Sinai. The image inscribed on this jar contains two figures borrowing traits of the Egyptian dwarf-god Bes (feather crown, phallus, crooked legs),

who could take both male and female form. The accompanying inscription reads, "Utterance of Amaryaw. Say to my lord, Is it well with you? I
bless you by Yahweh . . . and by his *asherah*. May he bless and keep you
and be with my lord."[10]

The debate continues: Who is depicted on this jar? What is the relation between these drawings and the inscription above? And if Yahweh
is figuratively represented, could this be due to a narrow interpretation of
the prohibition in Exod 20:4 as referring to a cult statue (idol) or graven
image (Heb. *pesel*; Gk. *eidōlon*) and not to a pictorial depiction?

Whatever the historical reality, one thing is sure. The First Temple
period (1000–586 B.C.E.) seems to have been permissive with regard to art
and figurative imagery in general. This permissiveness even continued
throughout Persian and early Hellenistic periods until the Hasmoneans
(165–63 B.C.E.), when the prohibition of images became stricter. This rigid
interpretation of Exod 20:4 lasted until the amoraic period (200–500 C.E.)
when developed synagogues,[11] decorated with mosaics, made their appearance. In Gamaliel II's view, art is generally permitted unless idolatry
is involved (*Avodah Zarah* 3–4).[12]

These remarks bring us to a much-debated question: Is Judaism an
"aniconic" or "anti-iconic" religion? In other words, is it artless or iconoclast? Franz Kafka once wrote, "We Jews are not painters; we are story-
tellers." Yet this statement is more rhetoric than reality. Lexical tropes
found in the Bible are often complemented by the figurative metaphors
encountered in Jewish art. One may mention here the decorated synagogues during the compilation of the Mishnah and Talmud (second
through sixth century C.E.) where the figurative art ranges between
human figures to objects with symbolic ritual value (*menorah, shophar*).[13]
More elaborate Jewish imagery may be found in thirteenth through fifteenth century manuscript illuminations produced in Italy, Germany, or
Spain.

The end of the twentieth century represents a great turn in Jewish
scholarship; old clichés introduced by Christian scholarship that Judaism
is artless or aniconic are now being debunked. In the middle of the twentieth century, Jewish scholar Erwin R. Goodenough[14] suggested that it
was a mystical, nonrabbinical Judaism that created Jewish figurative art.
Recent Jewish scholars, such as Steven Fine,[15] argue that Goodenough's
analysis of Jewish art was done against the backdrop of Western thought.
As a reaction to such a Christian (especially Protestant) contextualized
analysis that presents Judaism as aniconic or iconophobic, Jewish scholars

have embarked on a long and tedious journey of discovery and publication of artifacts of Jewish art and archeology proving the contrary.[16]

The early Christian Church emerged against the backdrop of an anti-iconic, yet not aniconic, Judaism. This situation explains on the one hand Church's hostile attitude against idolatry since the time of persecutions when Christians were forced to bring sacrifices in front of the imperial images. On the other hand, the Church has always made use of figurative art in spreading the gospel. As in the case of Judaism, the Christian Church was never aniconic.

Pro-Icon Apology

Quite interestingly, the debate over the legitimacy of icons was carried on along with the discussion regarding the validity of Mosaic Law for Christians. In the mid-eighth-century pro-icon writing entitled *Admonition of the Elder Concerning the Holy Images* (*Nouthesia Gerontos*), there is a dialogue between an iconophile monk and an iconoclast bishop. To the latter's claim that Christians should not venerate icons because doing so they transgress the second commandment (Exod 20:4), the former responds that Moses and the Prophets addressed only the world before Christ; hence, there is no need that the old injunctions be followed by Christians. Further, the Old Testament prohibition of visual representation of God was lifted by and for Jesus Christ, the incarnate Logos, and for all those participating or sharing in his deified body: his Holy Mother, the apostles, and saints. The bishop replies that except for certain rules lifted by Christ, the Law of Moses is eternal; thus, Christians should observe the injunctions of the Old Testament, including the second commandment of the Decalogue.[17]

The arguments adduced by iconophiles in support of icon production and veneration were scriptural and creedal. In other words, both the production and the veneration of icons had to be supported by Scripture and Tradition.

Scripture

In the iconophiles' view, the incarnation of the Logos was the main scriptural argument justifying religious visual art. According to Col 1:15, Christ is not only the Word of God but also his "icon" (*eikōn*). In the words of Photios: "Christ came to us in the flesh. This is seen and confirmed and proclaimed in pictures, the teaching made manifest by means of personal eyewitness and impelling the spectators to unhesitating assent" (*Homily* 17.5).[18] The incarnation supports the icon and the icon witnesses to the incarnation. For this reason, the iconoclasts' denial of icons was considered a denial of incarnation.

Another scriptural argument mustered by iconophiles was the concept of the "image and likeness" in man's creation. In his fine study, Gerhardt B. Ladner[19] examines Gregory of Nyssa's exegesis of Gen 1:26–27 and its follow-up in the wake of iconoclast controversy. Gregory observes: "As painters transfer the human forms to their pictures by means of certain colors, applying to their work of imitation (*mimēma*) the proper and corresponding tints, so that the archetypal beauty may be transferred exactly to the likeness (*homoiōsis*), thus it would seem to me that our Maker also, with certain tints as it were, by putting on virtues, paints the image [man's image] with various colors according to his own beauty" (*De opificio hominis* 5).[20]

The earliest explicit use of this patristic interpretation as support for icon veneration may be found in a seventh–eighth-century Byzantine writer, Stephen of Bostra (Bosra in Syria), who wrote a treatise against the Jews containing many anti-iconoclastic passages. First, Stephen distinguishes between image (*eikōn*) and idol (*agalma* or *zōdion*). Then he quotes Genesis 1:26, and continues: "Now is it idolatry and impiety that man is an image of God? Far from it. If Adam were an image of demons, he would be abject and unacceptable; but because he is an image of God, he is honorable and acceptable. . . . And what is the honor rendered to the image if not just honor, as also we sinners do reverence (*proskynoumen*) one another in accordance with honor and love?"[21]

Combining the two scriptural touchstones, the incarnation of the Lord and the creation of man, John of Damascus argues that the icons fit quite well with the bidimensionality of the human person: "Since we are fashioned of soul and body, and our souls are not naked spirits, but are covered, as it were, with a fleshly veil, it is impossible for us to think without using physical images. Just as we physically listen to perceptible words in order to understand spiritual things, so also by using bodily sight we reach spiritual contemplation. For this reason Christ assumed both soul and body, since man is fashioned from both."[22]

Tradition

The iconoclast controversy revolved tacitly around the question of "authentic" tradition. To the iconophiles, the "breakers of icons" (iconoclasts)

distanced themselves from church tradition. Likewise, from the iconoclasts' stance, the iconophiles were not standing within the mainstream
of the Tradition. Both groups tried hard to find authoritative texts to support their respective charges.

The iconoclasts brought as evidence from Tradition passages penned
by Athanasius of Alexandria, Gregory of Nazianzus, Basil of Caesarea,
John Chrysostom, Theodotus of Ancyra, Amphilochius of Iconium.
However, as Ambrosius Giakalis noted, "Most of these witnesses seem
colorless and irrelevant—detached phrases taken out of their original
context."[23] The most important supposedly patristic testimony against
the veneration of icons was a series of statements attributed to Epiphanius's *Testament*.[24] Here, the author urges his fellow Christians, "My
beloved children, keep it in mind not to set up icons in churches, or in
the cemeteries of the saints, but always have God in your hearts through
remembrance. Do not even have icons in private houses. For it is not
permissible for the Christian to let his eyes wander or indulge in rev-
eries."[25] Responding to the iconoclasts, John of Damascus judged these
statements of Epiphanius as "spurious and forged."[26] Other writers from
Nicephoros of Constantinople to the present have cast similar doubt on
their authenticity.[27]

In spite of all these quasi-iconoclast statements, which, as noted
above, precede in time the eighth–ninth century iconoclast controversy,
and which were often triggered by excesses on the part of the iconodules,
the Eastern Church has managed to steer clear of a rigorous aniconic
attitude.

The iconophiles used the Tradition as platform for their icon worship.
The Seventh Ecumenical Council decreed: "The making of images is not
an invention of the painters but an accepted institution and tradition of the
catholic church; and that which excels in antiquity is worthy of respect."[28]
The term "tradition" here is wide enough to include Old Testament examples: the cherubs on the ark of covenant (Exod 25:18–20) and the visions
of divinity recorded in the prophetic books (e.g., Isa 6; Ezek 1; Dan 7)—
now expanded through the incarnation to all humanity. Appeal to Old
Testament images as foundational for the veneration of icons is seen also
in the proliferation of Old Testament scenes in the marginal Psalters of
the ninth century. The interest in tabernacle furnishings attested in the
ninth-century *Christian Topography* by Cosmas Indicopleustes testifies to
the continuity in liturgical and iconographic tradition between Judaism
and the Byzantine Church.[29]

Iconoclastic Rebuttal

The iconoclasts had their own objections against the veneration of icons. First, the icons were considered the mere products of the painter's fanciful imagination. Second, the icons were not even consecrated objects.

To the iconoclasts' first objection, the iconophiles responded that the sacred images do not derive from the iconographer's imagination but rather from the Church's tradition, transmitted from one artist to another: "The making of icons is not an invention of the painters but an accepted institution and tradition of the catholic church" (*Nicaea II, Session 7*).[30] The very fact that the icons are placed in the church means that they are an expression of the Church's life (Tradition) and within the "mind" of the church fathers, "who, having built venerable churches, set up icons in them and offered inside them prayers to God and bloodless sacrifices which are accepted by him, the Master of all. The idea, therefore, and the tradition are theirs [that is, the Fathers'], not the painters.' Only the art is the painters', whereas the disposition is certainly that of the Holy Fathers who built the churches" (*Nicaea II, Session 6*).[31]

Thus, according to the Seventh Ecumenical Council (Nicaea II, 787 c.e.), it was not the artist's imagination that spoke through the icons, but rather the apostolic spirit, conveyed by church fathers to the iconographers who were working with the liturgical tradition of the Church. Leonid Ouspensky underscores the same truth when he writes,

> This art reflects a general ecclesiastical guidance and a tight control over the artists' work. Nothing was left to chance or to the whim of the artist. Everything is concentrated on the expression of the Church's teaching. From its first steps, the Church begins to develop an artistic language which expresses the same truth as the sacred word . . . this language, just like the theological expression of the Christian teaching, will become more and more specific throughout the Church's history, and will become a most perfect and exact instrument of teaching.[32]

One concrete way to confine the painter's fanciful imagination was the spiritual preparation for painting, which consisted of prayer and fasting. Another way of softening the painter's free imagination by placing it under the guidance of church tradition was the so-called skills-tradition. The skills-tradition, handed down from artist to artist, may be defined as a set of conventions regarding the way scenes and figures should be depicted, the technical procedures involved in icon production. There is an obvious link between skills-tradition and Church's theological tradition, since the final product of the iconographer is destined for use in liturgy and prayer, which are part of church tradition. These skills-conventions were for centuries transmitted orally; only in relatively modern times was this iconographic tradition fixed in writing, in the so-called painter's manuals (in singular, *hermeneia*, "interpretation"). There are three great painter's manuals compiled by Dionysios of Fourna (early 1730's), Fotis Kontoglou (1895–1965), and Leonid Ouspensky (1902–87).

Regarding the second objection raised by the iconoclasts, namely, the lack of consecration, Andrew Louth[33] shows that the participants at the Second Nicaea Council (787 C.E.) did not have any problem with icons not being formally consecrated.[34] Only later did the Orthodox Church—most especially the Russian Church—come up with an assemblage of prayers for icon consecration.

Icon's Nature and Functions

Nature

In Eastern Orthodox view, icons represent a bridge between this world and the kingdom of God, proclaimed by Christ, to have "come near" (*ēngiken*) (Matt 3:2). Neither divine nor profane in nature, they are rather "sacred images," connecting their beholders with the unseen yet still "coming" kingdom of God (cf. Matt 6:10). John of Damascus makes a clear distinction between "worship" (*latreia*) offered to God, and "veneration" (*proskynēsis*) given to the saints, the cross, relics, and icons. This distinction became determinative for the entire following tradition.[35]

The veneration given to an icon is transferred to the prototype depicted on that icon, asserts Basil the Great: "The sovereignty and authority over us is one, and so the doxology ascribed by us is not plural but one; because the honor paid to the image passes on to the prototype" (*On the Holy Spirit* 18.45).[36] Centuries later, Theodore of Studios argues that through the incarnation of the Logos the prototype may be detected in the image: "Whoever does not confess that our Lord Jesus Christ is represented in a picture does not confess that he lived in the flesh. For to have lived in the flesh and to have been represented in a picture is the same thing. Whoever does not venerate his holy image does not venerate the Lord (*hostis ou proskynei tēn hagian autou eikona ou proskynei ton Kyrion*); in the image, in effect, is the prototype, and the image is exposed and venerated according to the prototype of whoever is represented" (*Parva catechesis* 51.142).[37] The image reveals the prototype transforming the veneration of the icon into a worship of its prototype, Jesus Christ.

Functions

Icons have two aims: aesthetic and functional. However, even the aesthetic aim is functional. The aesthetic beauty of the icons does not remain closed in itself, only to be admired. This beauty sanctifies the sight, keeping it away from any mundane distraction, so that believer's mind may focus on hearing the gospel message.

LITURGICAL

From an Eastern Orthodox perspective, not just any religious pictorial representation is an icon. The main function of icons is to help establishing the liturgical setting as the actualizing *locus* and *tempus* of the unfolding history of salvation.

In San Vitale Church in Ravenna, there is a mosaic depicting Abel and Melchizedek as they bring their offerings (a lamb and a loaf of bread) over an altar table (Figure 7.1). God's hand points from heaven toward the table adorned with a fringed cloth decorated with an eight-pointed star. On the table—patterned after an altar table from Justinian's time—are two

FIGURE 7.1 Offerings of Abel and Melchizedek, presbyterium mosaic, San Vitale, Ravenna

(Photo: Ioan Popa.)

patens (Gk. *diskos* [singular]) and a double-handled chalice (Gk. *potērion*). Bread and wine were the offerings Melchizedek, priest of the Most High and king of Salem, brought to Abraham and his servants as they were returning from a victorious campaign against a coalition of foreign kings. The biblical account of the encounter between Melchizedek and Abraham is quite brief (Gen 14:18–20) and totally unrelated to the remainder of Gen 14, itself an enigmatic chapter of international politics standing alone within a book whose primary focus is on patriarchs and their families. In spite of its brevity and apparent singleness, Gen 14:18–20 seeks to contrast the self-offering of Melchizedek, the ideal king and priest, ready to serve unconditionally, and the king of Sodom, symbolizing the worldly rulers eager to dominate and exploit their subjects.[38] The innocent Abel, whose sacrifice was favored by God over Cain's offering (Gen 4), is depicted in this mosaic as a shepherd, raising a sacrificial lamb heavenwards. Interestingly, the mosaic of Abel and Melchizedek is placed in the sanctuary on the south wall (*diakonikon*)[39] in the proximity of the altar table where the Eucharist, the bloodless sacrifice, has been offered since the consecration of San Vitale basilica on April 19, 548 c.e. Through its theme and location, San Vitale mosaic bridges visually the Scripture to the liturgy, emphasizing the latter's actualizing function.[40]

As Leonid Ouspensky well noted, "It is absolutely impossible to imagine the smallest liturgical rite in the Orthodox Church without icons. The liturgical and sacramental life of the Church is inseparable from the image."[41] To the present time, the Orthodox Church relies heavily on iconography in her worship. And this close relation between icon and worship distinguishes the Eastern Orthodox Church from the Western Church. Patriarch Germanos of Constantinople (715–30 c.e.) wrote the following lines with the famous Church of Hagia Sophia in mind, but his insightful remarks can be extended to apply to any Orthodox Church: "The church is an earthly heaven in which the super-celestial God dwells and walks about. It represents the Crucifixion, Burial, and Resurrection of Christ; it is glorified more than the tabernacle of the witness of Moses, in which are the mercy-seat and the Holy of Holies. It is prefigured in the patriarchs, foretold by the prophets, founded in the apostles, adorned by the clergy, and fulfilled in the martyrs."[42]

ANAGOGICAL

Another function of the icon, closely related to liturgical tradition, is the anagogical (spiritual). In Eastern Orthodox tradition more than in its Western counterparts, spirituality is a part of the liturgical life of the Church. The icons are "vehicles of holiness" through which the believer can have access to God. In the Eastern Orthodox Church, this access, the believer's participation in the life of Christ, is called deification (*theosis*).[43] Ambrosios Giakalis is right when he notices, "On the deepest theological level the iconoclast controversy was about deification. Much of the debate was centered on the person of Christ, on whether his portrayal in colors on wooden boards did equal justice both to his human and to his divine natures."[44]

Further, in the Orthodox understanding, spiritual life is to be pursued within the ecclesial community, interacting with one another for the salvation of all. This is what one calls *koinonia*, "communal" experience in sharing and participating to the life of Christ. In Eastern Orthodox tradition, icons serve this koinonia through their "mediatory role in conveying sacred realities, manifesting the experience of timeless communion with the saints and angels in the Kingdom of God, whether one is standing in communal worship or carrying out domestic responsibilities within the home."[45]

This anagogical dimension is reflected in "distortions" (e.g., long figures) or "demateralization" (e.g., lack of perspective, specific coloristic)—a "fasting of sight," to use Paul Evdokimov's inspired description of the icon. These "distortions" discourage the beholder from finding delight in the aesthetic beauty of the icon, while reminding one of a "hidden" beauty to be fully revealed at the eschaton and now given only as a foretaste within the liturgical setting. Moreover, the figures in Byzantine iconography are depicted in two dimensions, thus creating a visionlike ambience. The physiognomy of the figures follows a number of established conventions (e.g., slender and elongated fingers, small mouth, thin nose, almond-shaped eyes). This refinement of bodily features is meant to reflect the transfigured state of the saintly figures. The perspective and physical light with shades and illuminated areas are intentionally suppressed. The décor is restricted to a few, essential elements, which are significantly schematized. The iconographer does not struggle to imitate the colors of nature but rather employs a non-natural chromatic, which exudes a mystical air.[46]

Yet in spite of so many conventions, the Byzantine sacred art is marked by a sort of strange naturalness (e.g., the thirteenth century *Deesis*[47] mosaic in Hagia Sophia Church in Constantinople). However, this naturalness should not be confounded with the realism of Western religious art, which reached its climax in Mathias Grünewald's triptych, where the crucified Christ is depicted as a decomposing corpse. In Byzantine iconography, the same Christ would evoke a calm dignity in the midst of his passion. It is not as if Christ were impassible or ignorant of his real suffering, but rather that he undertook this suffering voluntarily, and in so doing, overcame it. Christ's face in the Byzantine icon of Crucifixion conveys both profound sorrowfulness and forgiving sereneness.

PEDAGOGICAL

The church fathers repeatedly underscore the pedagogical function of the icon. John of Damascus states rather emphatically that the sacred image is the Bible for the illiterate: "I say that everywhere we use our senses to produce an image of the incarnate God himself, we sanctify the first of the senses (sight being the first of the senses), just as by words hearing is sanctified. For the image is a memorial. What the book does for those who understand letters, the image does for the illiterate; the word appeals to hearing, the image appeals to sight; it conveys understanding" (*On Holy Images* 1.17).[48] This didactic dimension of the icon was especially appreciated in the preschism Latin Church. In the famous words of Honorius of Autun, spoken at the Synod of Arras in 1025, *pictura est laicorum litteratura*, "pictures are the literature of the laity." For the East, though, the main function of the icon has been and remained liturgical and anagogical. More importantly than being a Bible for the illiterate,[49] the icon is a means through which God's word becomes alive and colorful. Along with its aural counterpart, the visual interpretation of the Scripture seeks to form and transform (more than merely inform) the faithful while participating in Church's liturgical life.

Periodization of the Byzantine Art

According to Kurt Weitzmann, Christian iconography of the Old Testament derived from Jewish illuminated manuscripts. Weitzmann's thesis, dubbed the "lost-manuscript theory," suggests that now lost illustrated copies of Hebrew Scriptures (e.g., the Septuagint, the Pentateuch, or the Octateuch) were the springboard of Christian art. Weitzmann placed these lost manuscripts in the pre-Christian world of Hellenized Jews living in Alexandria and Antioch. Attempting to trace the origins of Old Testament illustration, Kurt Weitzmann and Herbert L. Kessler[50] consider the third century Dura Europos synagogue the missing link between a hypothesized Jewish tradition of manuscript illumination and Christian sacred art.

Whether Jewish illuminated manuscripts were really the main source of inspiration for Christian art remains to be proven. Yet one thing is certain. As Robin M. Jensen suggests, the implicit assumption that images must be connected to texts undermines the intrinsic value of the former, thus subverting "religious iconography's important function as an independent vehicle for theological expression."[51]

Early Byzantine (Fourth–Ninth Century C.E.)

Early Christian art[52] began to flourish by the middle of the third century. The paintings in the Dura Europos mud-brick house-church (ca. 240 C.E.) and the third-century Christian catacombs outside the city walls of Rome testify to this fact. Christians begin now to appropriate and adapt the art forms of the Greco-Roman world to convey the core of the apostolic kērygma, namely, the belief in resurrection and life after death through the work of Jesus Christ. Salvation scenes gleaned from the Old and New Testaments decorate the walls of these catacombs. The most popular depictions in the pre-Constantinian period, coming from Asia Minor (marble sculptures) and Roman catacombs (wall painting), are Jonah and the Good Shepherd.

By the year 311/2 C.E. when the Christian Church became a legal religion, the images were universally accepted besides the sacred texts. The Christian art of Constantinople continued this early tradition after the dedication of the city on May 11, 330 C.E.

Byzantine art really begins to make its glorious entrance during the reign of Justinian I (527–65 C.E.) in various territories: Asia Minor, Syria, Palestine, Sinai, Egypt and North of Africa, Italy, Balkans, and Greece. At the apogee of this artistic flourishing was the Church of Hagia Sophia (Holy Wisdom) in Constantinople. Initially dedicated in 360 C.E. and rebuilt by Justinian after the Nika riots of January 532 C.E., Hagia Sophia was rededicated on Christmas of 537 C.E. Interestingly, Justinian's temple to Holy Wisdom lacked in figurative mosaics; the only image was that of the cross embedded in the gold mosaics of the vaults. In contrast, other churches built by the same emperor, such as St. Catherine's at Sinai and San Vitale at Ravenna, were filled sumptuously with figurative mosaics. The explanation for this peculiarity of Hagia Sophia was in all likelihood either practical (to finish the decoration quickly) or technical (the surfaces were thought to be too high for figurative imagery).[53]

The Council in Trullo, called Quinisext (Fifth-Sixth) on account of the fact that its canons were appended to the Acts of the Fifth and Sixth Ecumenical Councils, is emblematic for this period. Held in the imperial palace in 692 c.e., the council produced 102 canons. Though most of these canons are disciplinary in nature, a few pertain to the arts. For instance, canon 73 forbids the representation of the cross on the floors of churches. Canon 100 suggests artistic censorship: everything impure defiling the beholder should be avoided in figurative art; and the penalty for making such defiled art is excommunication. Best known of all the canons dealing with art, however, is canon 82, which directs that henceforth Christ should not be depicted in the form of a lamb, as in the past, but rather in his own incarnate human image.

The council differentiates between past and future practices in an attempt to revise and amend the mistakes of the past. This is the first significant "filtering" or "revisionist" move attested in the Byzantine history, with the goal to define "orthodoxy." One may note here that the Western Latin Church has never accepted canon 82. By adopting this canon, the Eastern Orthodox Church went further on the path of excluding symbolism so characteristic of the early days of the catacomb art.

The most crucial yet formative period in Byzantine sacred art was the iconoclastic controversy, which lasted over one hundred twenty years (i.e., 726/30–843 c.e.). The most important facts and dates pertaining to iconoclasm are succinctly mentioned below.

Around 700 c.e. a special emphasis was placed on the pedagogical or catechetical function of iconography. This is the time when the Church of the Nativity in Bethlehem was adorned with scenes depicting the ecumenical councils. The understanding was that art could and should teach the faith established at these councils. The beginning of iconoclasm is dated for 726/30 c.e. Emperor Leo III the Isaurian (717–41 c.e.) saw the eruption of the volcano Thera (today Santorini) in the Aegean Sea in 726 c.e. as a sign that God was angry with him regarding the worship of icons. Thus, in 730 c.e., Leo issued a decree against icons. As an immediate consequence, the icon of Christ on the Chalke Gate of the Great Palace in Constantinople was destroyed, and a public riot broke out. Figural art was henceforth banned from the Christian Church.

The first iconoclast council, dubbed the "Headless Council" due to the absence of the Pope of Rome and the Eastern Patriarchs, was held at Hiereia at Chalcedon near Constantinople in 754 c.e. The council focused on the "allowable functions of religious art," in a way continuing the trend initiated by the Quinisext Council at Trullo in 692 c.e. when the arts were for the first time explicitly related to the Church's theological agenda.[54] At Hiereia, the three great iconophiles, Germanos of Constantinople, George of Cyprus, and John of Damascus, were excommunicated. The iconophiles (especially monks) were henceforth harshly persecuted.

The Seventh Ecumenical Council held at Nicaea in 787 c.e. revisited the issue discussed at Hiereia but the conclusions were quite contrary to those drawn in 754 c.e. The argument raised by the iconoclasts at Hiereia was that the Eucharist is the only correct "image" of Christ. The iconophiles gathered at Nicaea in 787 c.e. responded to the iconoclasts' accusations with the argument that Christ's historical incarnation validates the Lord's representation in paint. The ecumenical council distinguished between "veneration" (*proskynēsis*) given to the icons, and the adoration or absolute "worship" (*latreia*) given to God alone. Later, another iconoclast council, held in 815 c.e. in Hagia Sophia, rejected the resolutions of Nicaea II by reaffirming the decisions of the first iconoclast council of 754 c.e.

During the iconoclastic controversy, a number of important documents in support of iconography were produced. One may mention here especially the following: John of Damascus's *Three Apologies against Those who Attack the Divine Images*, extensively used at the Council of Nicaea in 787 c.e.; Theodore of Studios's (758–826 c.e.) *Refutations of the Iconoclasts*; and Patriarch Nikephoros's (806–815 c.e.) *Apologeticus minor* (814 c.e.)

Middle Byzantine (843–1204)

The period of Middle Byzantine Art begins with the Constantinopolitan council of 843 c.e., which upheld Nicaea II as the Seventh Ecumenical Council and celebrated the triumph of Orthodoxy over all past heresies, including the iconoclasm.

After the defeat of iconoclasm, the decoration of Byzantine churches was significantly restricted to New Testament scenes and saintly figures. Churches built in middle and late Byzantine times lack in long naves embellished with cycles of Old Testament narratives. This situation could be a consequence of canon 82 of Trullo forbidding the use of symbolism in the sacred art and of the exclusion of Old Testament reading from the Byzantine liturgy.[55] Nevertheless, beginning with the twelfth century, Old Testament representation and exegesis played a major role in western Europe.[56]

The Middle Byzantine period is called in art history the "Second Golden Age" (Justinian I's was the first) or the "Macedonian Renaissance" (ca. 870–1025). Characteristic of this period are the Byzantine illuminated manuscripts of the ninth through the eleventh centuries.

Byzantine mosaic makers, possibly from Constantinople, also worked during this period in Kiev (Saint Sophia), and Venice (San Marco).

Late Byzantine (1204–1453)

The first part of this period was marked by the Latin Kingdom of Constantinople (1204–61) and the beginning of a long process of westernization of Byzantine art. During the Latin occupation of Constantinople, much of the city's art was transported to Italy and France. In order to recreate the Byzantine art at this juncture in time, one may want to examine the decorations of San Marco in Venice or Santa Maria Maggiore in Rome, to give only two examples.

The Latin occupation of Hagia Sophia in Constantinople led to the deterioration of the church building. Similarly, the Holy Sepulchre Church in Jerusalem was remodeled for the Latin use. The church's dedication occurred on July 15, 1149—the fiftieth anniversary of the city's capture by the Latins.

The most representative monument of Late Byzantine Art remains the Chora (Greek "countryside") monastery built in the sixth century, outside of Constantinople, and adorned with both mosaics and paintings between 1316 and 1321. The Early Palaeologan Renaissance (1261–1360) represents perhaps the peak of Byzantine visual art.

A sample of the Palaeologan Renaissance is the mosaic of the *Deesis* added to the Hagia Sophia Church after 1261. This mosaic strikes the sight by its majesty, fine colors, and the delicate softness of the faces of the Virgin and Christ. The thirteenth century artist Manuel Panselinos, surnamed the "Giotto of the Byzantine school" (Didron), is for all accounts the most representative iconographer of the Early Palaeologan Renaissance. The main locus of his frescoes is the Protaton Church at Karyes on Mount Athos. Panselinos's mastery is reflected in compositional monumentality, chromatic refinement, and minute facial expressionism.[57]

Byzantine art spread in the fourteenth century to Rus' as well as to the new empires of Serbia and Bulgaria. In fact, Serbia and Bulgaria used Byzantine artists for their church decorations (e.g., the Dečani monastery in Serbia, built and decorated between 1327–47). A similar situation obtained in Rus' when Theophanes the Greek, originally from Constantinople, came to work at the Church of Transfiguration in Novgorod in 1378. Theophanes's cooperation with Russian artists such as Andrei Rublev (1360–1427) is well established. This dissemination of Byzantine art outside the confines of the empire would continue after the fall of Constantinople in 1453, including other Orthodox lands such as the Romanian principalities of Moldavia and Walachia. Romanian historian Nicolae Iorga famously dubbed this cultural continuum as "Byzance après Byzance" (Bucharest, 1935).

With this expansion of Byzantine art outside the boundaries of the once great empire, a tendency toward "folklorization" of Byzantine iconography may be detected in some fifteenth through seventeenth century frescoes in Moldavian churches.[58] An example of "folklorization" obtains with the legend of the *Cheirograph* between Adam and Satan by which humans became Satan's slaves until Christ's Baptism, and which was represented among the exterior frescoes (1547) of the Moldovian Voroneţ Monastery (Figure 7.2). From a hermeneutical point of view, this "folklorization" of the sacred art, attested in composition and techniques

FIGURE 7.2 Adam and Satan, exterior fresco, north side, Voroneţ Monastery, Suceava, Romania

(Photo: Ioan Bratiloveanu.)

(e.g., exterior frescoes easily accessible to villagers) testifies to a continuous interest in the Eastern Orthodox tradition to make the Bible a book for everyone by bringing the biblical figures, such as Adam, Elijah, or Elisha, into the cultural-social milieu of the beholders.

Media of Visual Art

Manuscript Illuminations

Significant use of Old Testament in literature, art, and institutions of the Roman world really originated in the fourth century and reached its climax with the sixth century C.E. The evidence of such a cultural appropriation of the Old Testament is offered by the two isolated "deluxe illustrated manuscripts" of the Book of Genesis, namely the fifth century *Cotton Genesis* and the sixth century *Vienna Genesis*. One may notice that these are isolated and maverick illustrated manuscripts. They do not represent the norm nor do they have successors.[59]

The most interesting illustrated manuscripts Byzantium ever produced are the ninth to eleventh century marginal (illuminated) Psalters: Khludov (ca. 850), Pantokrator (ninth-century), Paris (ca. 950–70), Theodore (1066), and Barberini (ca. 1095).[60] To these one may add the Joshua Roll (950) and the Bible of Leo Sakellarios (ca. 940).

Portable Devotional Icons

Compared to metal and mosaic icons, the painted wooden icon is perhaps the longest lived subcategory of the Byzantine artistic medium of portable devotional icons. The earliest collection of wooden painted icons is found at St. Catherine Monastery in Sinai: some twenty-seven pieces dated to the sixth through seventh centuries. They are all painted in encaustic (pigment and wax) and tempera (pigment and egg yolk).

In terms of style, the portable icons follow the Late Antique commemorative portraits and imperial *lavrata*. Thematically, they employ scenes and figures from the Old and New Testaments. These icons were introduced into church as votive donations and remained in use for extra-liturgical or individual devotional purposes.

During the tenth and eleventh centuries, when art was well linked to a more standardized liturgy, the portable icons begin to reflect the new trend by depicting various subjects of liturgical feasts. The liturgical appropriation of the portable icons may be detected in their moving from being stored in the aisles unto the emerging *templon* (the screen separating the altar from the nave) and *proskynētarion* (the icon stand in front of the templon). The eleventh through twelfth century portable icons are characterized by a high degree of creativity within the liturgical framework.[61] The climactic point for the proliferation of portable icons occurred in the fourteenth century during the Palaeologan period.[62] This is the time when the templon becomes the high iconostasis found in most Eastern Orthodox Churches today. The distribution of portable icons on the iconostasis follows a certain set of iconographic rules. On the upper level, the patriarchs are succeeded by the prophets holding scrolls with inscribed messianic prophecies; then, in the midsection, the main liturgical feasts with scenes from the New Testament, and the *Deesis* in the center. On the lower level are to be found the icons of Theotokos, Christ, and the patronymic saint or feast of that church.[63]

Monumental Art

Unlike the miniatures found in the illuminated manuscripts, which were mostly the production of individual patrons and seen only by a small number of people, the monumental art reflects the teaching of the Church and was widespread and seen by large masses.

Mosaics

Mosaic (Gk. *psēphidōton, mousaikon*) is the most expensive and complex medium used by Byzantine artists. Beginning with the fourth century C.E., mosaics consisting of small cubes (tesserae) were used, not for floor decoration as in the pre-Constantinopolitan period, but rather in wall and ceiling decoration. The tesserae, initially multicolored stone and marble, became gradually more sophisticated in materials (brick, terra cotta, semiprecious stones, colored glass, silver, gold). The mosaicists used to place these tesserae into a setting bed prepared with plaster. The apex of this medium was reached during the reign of Justinian I. Among the sixth century masterpieces are Hagia Sophia in Constantinople, St. Catherine at Sinai, Poreč, and Ravenna. By the eighth century, mosaic became the common medium employed in sacred decoration. This was also the favorite technique employed by Byzantine artists for the imperial portraits in Hagia Sophia dating to the ninth through eleventh centuries.[64]

Frescoes

This technique, for which Byzantine artists had no special term, consists of application of lime-binding natural pigments to a wet plaster added over an initial plaster coat. Fresco technique has been always used as a less costly alternative to mosaic decoration. Nevertheless, beginning with the thirteenth century, which marks the decline of mosaic technique, frescoes become quite popular.[65]

The Old Testament in Eastern Orthodox Iconography

The Byzantines adopted from the pre-Constantinopolitan period a number of Old Testament scenes, figures, and themes. Jonah and the sea beast and the crossing of the Red Sea are resiliently the most popular depictions throughout the Byzantine art history. The early typological interpretation of these two biblical stories alluding to survival and resurrection over against chaotic powers at work are the main trigger in their quick adoption and copious use in visual arts. The theme of deliverance is at the center of apostolic kērygma and continues to be central in pre- and post-Nicene periods.

A list of favorite Old Testament themes used in pre-Constantinopolitan art can be reproduced with the help of the *Commendatio animae*, "Recommendation of the [departed] soul [to God]," a Western prayer ritual for the dead dated to the third century C.E. Consisting of thirteen petitions patterned after the formula, "Deliver his soul, O Lord, as you freed Daniel from the lions' den," the *Commendatio animae* recollects a number of figures and events from the Old Testament, all centered on the deliverance theme: Noah and the Deluge, the binding of Isaac, Job's suffering, Jonah and the sea beast, Daniel in the lions' den, the three Hebrew youths in the furnace, and Susannah and the elders. Scenes mentioned in the *Commendatio animae* appear also on the walls of catacombs.[66]

In his informative study on the ninth century Constantinopolitan copy of the *Homilies* of Gregory of Nazianzus (*Paris.gr.510*), Leslie Brubaker enumerates the most popular Old Testament books, themes, and figures attested in manuscript illustration beginning with the ninth century.[67] The books selected by the illuminators are primarily Genesis, Exodus, Joshua, Judges, Kings, Job, Prophets, and Maccabees. As for the themes and figures, the most employed are as follows: the story of Adam and Eve in Paradise, the tower of Babel, Noah and the Deluge, the binding of Isaac, Joseph and his brothers; Moses receiving the Law, the burning bush, the water from the rock, the crossing of the Red Sea and the dancing of Miriam, Moses supported by Aaron and Hur while praying; Joshua stopping the sun, meeting the angel, the fall of Jericho, scenes from the life of Samson and Gideon; the anointing of David, the penitence of David, the judgment of Solomon, the ascension of Elijah; Job on the "dung heap" (Job 2:8 [LXX: *koprias*] vs. MT: *'ēper,* "dust"); the vision of Isaiah, Hezekiah and Isaiah, the martyrdom of Isaiah (cf. the apocryphon *Martyrdom of Isaiah*), Jeremiah raised from the pit, Ezekiel in the valley of dry bones, Daniel in the lions' den, the three youths in the furnace; and the martyrdom of the Maccabees.

Besides the main uses (liturgical, anagogical, didactic) mentioned above, icons also function hermeneutically. As the name indicates, iconography (literally, "image-writing") is a visual, figurative interpretation of Scripture.

Whereas patristic exegesis is discursive in nature, the sacred visual art, as a mode of interpretation, is essentially intuitive. To the tedious process of passing from premise to conclusions by reasoning characteristic of patristic exegesis, the Byzantine visual artists respond with a more direct, spontaneous, intuition-driven way of reading the Scripture. Nevertheless, as noted above, the artistic spontaneity of the iconographers does not clash with the Church's tradition whose confines are quite flexible in their inclusiveness.

If patristic exegesis, and to a certain degree the liturgical hymnography, is sequential in its unfolding, iconography has the communicative power of being simultaneous. In other words, when one reads a patristic commentary, this can be understood only as a sequence of various frames. One needs to read the whole passage as a sequence of observations and arguments in order to have a good grasp of it. The result of such a sequential reading is an analytical, more schematic understanding of the scriptural pericope. As for icons, they can convey many things in a flash. Icons are open leafless "books." Figures and scenes are depicted in a concurrent, interactive way.[68] Moreover, the "reading" of an icon is reduced in terms of time, and the immediate result is a synthetic, more inclusive, holistic appreciation of the scriptural text and its unsolved ambiguities.

Story in a Flash

The Binding of Isaac and the Faithfulness of Abraham (Gen 22:1–19)

To illustrate this simultaneous and interactive way of reading, interpreting and appropriating a scriptural passage, I would like to begin with a

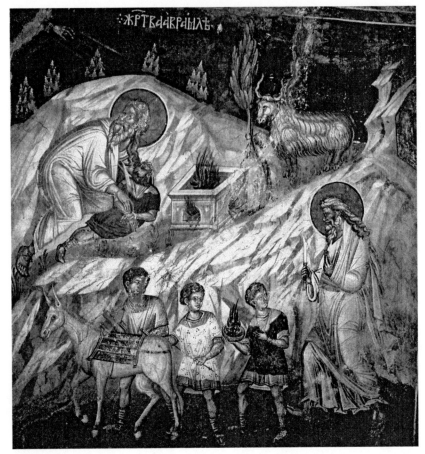

FIGURE 7.3 Abraham's Sacrifice, fresco, Gračanica Church, Gračanica, Kosovo
(Photo: Courtesy of BLAGO Fund Inc. [www.srpskoblago.org].)

much-debated text, Genesis 22, and its pictorial rendition in a fresco from
the Gračanica church (Figure 7.3).[69]

Genesis 22:1–19, the account of the near-sacrifice of Isaac, is a foundational text where Jewish and Christian interpreters alike struggle and
interact in search for answers to questions raised by one of most terrifying stories of the Bible.[70] It is the story of a father caught between his
unshaking faithfulness toward God and his love for his son, a father ready
to suppress his paternal love for his faithfulness. It is the story of a son
whose obedience to his father is majestic in its silent promptness.

In the Gračanica two-register fresco, both titles given to Gen 22
throughout the history of interpretation, the Christian "Sacrifice of

Isaac" or "Abraham's Offering of Isaac," and the Jewish *Aqedah* or "Binding of Isaac,"[71] find their meeting place. The Gračanica fresco combines
the Jewish and Christian interpretations within a single pictorial frame.
Within this interesting marriage between Jewish and Christian hermeneutic overtones there are various temporal sequences united in one
single artistic tableau, offering a simultaneous "reading" of one of the
most intricate and puzzling stories of the Old Testament.

In the lower register, Abraham is depicted as an agonizing yet reso-
lute father, holding a knife in his right hand while his left hand is placed
on his breast, in a gesture of speechless but full obedience toward God's
commandment to bring Isaac, his unique son, as a "whole burnt offering"
(LXX: *holokarpōsin*; MT: *'ōlāh*, "burnt offering, holocaust"; Gen 22:1–3).
Abraham's right foot, almost pushing Isaac forward, suggests a sort of
urgency. On the one hand, this rush could betray Abraham's struggle
to overcome fear and hesitation by fully observing God's order. On the
other hand, it could evoke the patriarch's eagerness to see the divine de-
nouement of such a terrifying mystery. The two servants and Isaac have
their faces turned half way toward Abraham, as if their listening to his
commands; all the eyes are on him, the tried, obedient, and faithful man.
Abraham's unhesitating obedience is matched only by the three youths'
collective attentiveness. The fresco's lower register could be rightly titled
"Abraham's Obedience"—a Christian variant to the Jewish *Aqedah*. Paradoxically, through obedience, Abraham binds himself to God's sovereign
will so that in the end the physically bound Isaac is offered not to fire on
the altar but rather to the God of life.[72] The Gračanica visual rendition is
in harmony with the liturgical interpretation of this story's twist of faith
due to Abraham's sheer obeisance: "Abraham, prefiguring your slaughter,
O Christ, ascended the mountain out of faith and in obedience to you,
O Master, to sacrifice like a sheep the son he had begotten. But they returned rejoicing, Isaac and the old man, supremely exalting you to all the
endless ages" (Sunday Before the Nativity of Christ, Ode Eight, troparion).

Conspicuously, the wood Abraham split at the dawn on the day of his
departure (Gen 22:3) is missing in the lower register of this fresco; it can
be barely seen inside of the stone altar in the upper register. Gen 22:6
informs us that on the third day of their journey, at the bottom of the
mountain, Abraham took the wood from the back of a donkey and laid
it on Isaac's back. However, the fresco does not reflect these details. As
a matter of fact, the saddled donkey does not carry any wood. Neither
does Isaac. The presence of the donkey in the fresco is utterly pointless.

Another difference: the biblical narrative makes Abraham hold the fire, whereas in the fresco Isaac is the one who holds it. The noticeable absence of the wood in the lower register excludes the possibility of any typological association between Isaac carrying the wood and Christ bearing the cross, as it obtained with many patristic interpretations of this text. Moreover, the towering profile of Abraham with the three youths looking at him points primarily to Abraham as a model of genuine obedience and perfect faithfulness. It is noteworthy that in the New Testament there are only a few references to Isaac's sacrifice. There the story was used not as a typology between Isaac and Christ but rather to underline Abraham's obedience and faithfulness (Heb 11:17–19; cf. Jas 2:21).[73] Nevertheless, Abraham's obedience is not blind. His obedience flows from his strong faith in God's promise (Gen 21:12, ". . . for in Isaac an offspring will be called for you") that his son in a way or another will outlive that ordeal.

In the upper register of the Gračanica fresco, the emphasis falls on Isaac with bound hands behind his back and bound feet, while his father is about to slaughter him. Abraham's face is turned toward heaven, whence the hand of God reaches out toward the three earthly foci: the statuary duo of Abraham and Isaac, the altar, and the ram tied to a tree. The ram is looking invitingly and intently to Abraham. The beholder's eye is automatically attracted by Isaac's binding. His curbed body and head bent backward create a dramatic effect in which the other pictorial elements (i.e., the heavenly hand, Abraham, the altar, the ram) fade out in importance. In Gen 22:9, Abraham takes the wood and places it on the altar and then sets the bound Isaac on the altar. In the fresco, Isaac is on the ground, next to the altar. The upper register of the fresco deserves to be titled the "Binding of Isaac": a son's complete surrender to his father's will—a Jewish variant of the Christian "Abraham's Obeisance," depicted in the lower register. The Byzantine liturgist sought to underscore the idea of Isaac's obedience to his father in a Christological setting when he wrote: "When you were led to be sacrificed in obedience to your father, O most blessed Isaac, you plainly became a type of Christ's Passion; wherefore, you are counted blessed, and are truly a genuine friend of God, dwelling with all the righteous" (Sunday of the Holy Forefathers of Christ, Matins, Ode Six, troparion).

Such an obvious lack of interest in typology manifested in this fresco is matched by the early Christian depictions of the same episode (e.g., catacomb and funeral art) where the theme of deliverance takes preeminence. Thus in a painting found in the Callixtus catacomb in Rome, Abraham and Isaac are depicted as *orantes*, their hands gesturing upward in thanksgiving to God for the happy end of that unique testing. The theme of deliverance found in this catacomb painting had a long life, being used by later Byzantine liturgists, as the following hymn attests: "We have reached the middle of the course of the fast that leads to your precious cross. Grant that we may see your day that Abraham saw [John 8:56] and rejoiced when he received Isaac back alive on the mountain as from the tomb! Delivered by faith from the enemy may we share in your mystical supper, calling out to you in peace: Our Light and our Savior, glory to you!" (Wednesday of the Fourth Week of the Great Lent, Matins, *aposticha*).

The depiction of Isaac's sacrifice was quite popular in early Christian times, as Gregory of Nyssa's *Oratio de deitate Filii et Spiritus Sancti* indicates: "Many times I have seen this tragic event depicted in pictures and I could not pass by the sight without shedding tears so clearly and evidently did the art present it to my eyes."[74]

In pre-Constantinian art, Isaac is never depicted as bound on the altar, as he is, for instance, in the sixth century San Vitale mosaic. Isaac carrying the wood thus foreshadowing Christ bearing his cross can be detected as early as late third century c.e. painting in the catacomb of Priscilla, in Rome. These differing details show that the iconographers, though depending on the same biblical material, were free in treating this material in an imaginative way, sometimes going outside the better established interpretations launched by church fathers and liturgists. Edward Kessler rightly notices that artistic interpretation should first be examined in its own right and not, as was done in the past, through the lenses of literary tradition.[75]

Typological textual (not pictorial) interpretations of Gen 22 begin to appear at the end of the first century. As Jon D. Levenson rightly suggests,[76] the Christological interpretation of Isaac's sacrifice was facilitated by the connection between *Aqedah* and the origin of Passover found in the second-century b.c.e. Jubilees. Moreover, Jesus's death is compared with the slaughtering of the paschal lamb (John 19:36, with reference to Exod 12:46; cf. 1 Cor 5:7). Hence the typological relationship between Isaac's sacrifice and Christ's passion attested among the early Christian writers such as the author of the Epistle of Barnabas, Melito of Sardis, and Origen.[77] The carrying of the wood was considered among the main similarities connecting the two stories. In addition, the reading of Gen 22 occupied an important place in the late fourth-century c.e. lectionary, as one can deduce from Egeria's pilgrimage to Jerusalem; the Book of Genesis used to be read on Thursday before Easter.

In those few instances where the binding of Isaac is mentioned in Eastern Orthodox liturgical texts, this detail typifies Christ's passion: "Isaac was taken up into the mountain, Jonas was taken down into the deep, and both depicted your Passion, O Savior: The first, the bonds and the slaughter; the other, the grave and the life that ensued from your dread arising. O Lord, glory be to you" (Wednesday Second Week after Pascha, Matins, *katavasia*) or, "Bound for slaughter, O Isaac, you are a figure of the Word Most High, who shall come to be slaughtered" (Sunday Before the Nativity of Christ, Matins, synaxarion).

Below there are several examples of visual interpretations of Old Testament, which continue to fascinate the beholder by untiring creativity and exuberant imagination. The guiding principle for the following selection was the interpretive value and interplay between image and text found in these "precritical" pictorial renditions.

Leslie Brubaker notices that the nexus between image and text can be basic (i.e., fusion) or more complex (i.e., intertextual and intervisual commentaries). Perhaps unlike the modern reader, the Byzantine was used to thinking of images as the best way to memorize and preserve the feats of the past. Images, more than texts, were considered memory-aids in recording history. They were seen as an alternative way of communication. Nevertheless, images and texts can be more than two ways of saying almost the same story (e.g., fusion). They can also stand in a dialectical relationship. In this case, images have the propensity to become meta-texts or springboards for new images that would make an old text and its visual commentary relevant to a modern audience.[78]

Fusion of Text and Image

In manuscript illuminations (e.g., marginal Psalters), the image is verbally linked to the text. A phrase or even a word may trigger a whole depiction or visual interpretation of the text. This marrying together of image and text based on "relevant vocabulary"[79] proves that visual interpretation is less rigorous than the aural and purely textual (discursive) modes, hence its high degree of creativity.[80]

"O Lord, you brought up my soul from Hades" (Ps 29[30]:4[3], NETS)
Let us see now how a single biblical text, actually a sentence, may generate two distinct visual interpretations.

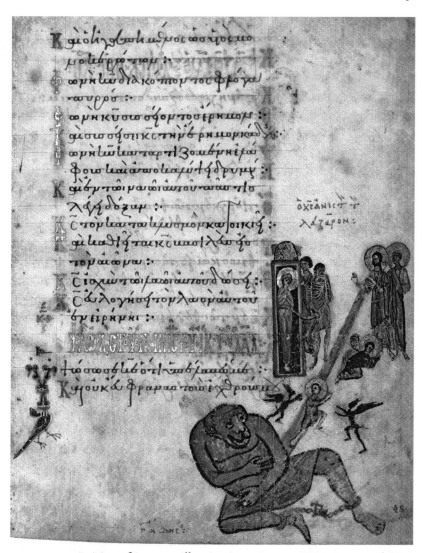

FIGURE 7.4 Raising of Lazarus, illumination—Ps 30:3 [LXX: 29:4], Barberini. gr.372, f. 48r, Vatican Apostolic Library
(Photo: Vatican Apostolic Library.)

In the Barberini Psalter,[81] on folio 48r (Figure 7.4), there is an interesting depiction of the story of raising Lazarus (John 11:1–46). The image was added to the Psalter margin as a pictorial commentary on Ps 29(30):4(3): "O Lord, you brought up my soul from Hades. You saved me from among those that go down into a pit (*lakkon*)" (NETS). Obviously, Ps 29(30):4(3) does not say anything about Lazarus's resurrection. This is an example of typological interpretation: an Old Testament text read in light of New Testament events. Nevertheless, it is not merely a direct linkage between an old text and its New Testament "realization." Rather it is an intricate typology with an incursion into biblical theology. If one reads the New Testament account of "raising Lazarus," one may notice that there is no mention of the "Hades"-"pit" parallel attested in this Psalm. The Johannine pericope speaks only of the physical resurrection of a man dead for four days. At Jesus's three-word command, *Lazare deuro exō*, "Lazarus, come here, outside" (John 11:43), the miracle happens effortlessly and instantly: "The dead man came out, his hands and feet bound with strips of cloth, and his face wrapped in a cloth" (John 11:44)—no mention of "Hades," no mention of "pit," only sheer action.

The image in the Barberini Psalter is more complex than its textual basis (John 11:1–46) in the way that it tries to go beyond the words and deeds, in quest of a deeper explication. One may distinguish two registers of this illustration. In the upper register, there are two foci. On the one hand, there is Jesus, elbow to elbow with another apostle (probably Thomas, mentioned in John 11:16). Kneeling in front of Jesus there is Mary, with a halo and her face turned to the Lord in sign of complete trust and surrender, and her sister Martha, with no halo and her face turned half way toward the tomb in a slight expression of doubt or concern. Christ's right hand blesses and empowers Lazarus's rising. The other focus is on the tomb from which the bound Lazarus is now coming out, in sight of two men overcome by the heavy odor exuded by the opened tomb. One of the two men unbinds Lazarus, at Christ's behest (John 11:44). In the lower register, a lion(?)-headed creature occupies almost the entire space. His arms hold tightly his stomach as if struggling to grasp something. Apparently, this is the personification of Hades.[82] Between the hideous creature and Christ there is a river or jet of dark energy, upon which a naked infant endowed with a halo is floating toward Christ. The garmentless infant symbolizes the soul of Lazarus, until that moment a prisoner of a personified Hades. On both sides of the jet there are two black winged creatures with little tails and long horns. This is a typical representation of the evil angels or devils. They seek to stop Lazarus's soul from its ascension toward Christ. As one can see, Christ's right arm fulfills a double duty: it extricates Lazarus's soul from Hades while bringing his lifeless body out from the tomb and back to life.

The depiction of Hades as a lion(?)-headed monstrous creature in this illustration can be regarded as an example of intertextuality. The artist read

Ps 29(30):4(3) in conjunction with John 11:1–46 and probably other two texts, Luke 16:19–31 and 1 Pet 5:8, the result being this quite interesting and intricate depiction of Hades. On the one hand, the personified Hades is identified with Satan (i.e., "enemy" [*antidikos*], "slanderer, devil" [*diabolos*], or "roaring lion" [*leōn ōryomenos*] in Peter's epistle). On the other hand, Hades has a "bosom" in which all the souls are kept, in contrast with Abraham's "bosom" (*kolpois*) mentioned by Luke 16:23, where only the righteous souls reside.

Nevertheless, the main question is: Why did the artist connect John 11 with Ps 29(30):4(3)? The most probable hypothesis is that the miniaturist interpreted the miracle of raising Lazarus as Christ's demonstration of power per excellence. Unlike the other two resurrections recorded in the canonical Gospels (Jairus's daughter [Mark 5:22–43] and the son of the widow of Nain [Luke 7:11–15]) that occurred on the day of death, Lazarus's resurrection happened on the fourth day after death. This chronological detail made the miniaturist think of Lazarus's soul as being detached from the body and already situated in the underworld when Christ came to the tomb. By this token, the raising of Lazarus was different from the other two resurrections, which could have been easily interpreted as mere resuscitation. Raising Lazarus required something more than bringing a dead body back to life. It required Christ's power to liberate Lazarus's soul from Hades' "bosom." The name "Lazarus" could have been the relevant word that made the illustrator to link John 11 to Luke 16. This would explain the focus on Hades' "bosom," in the illustrated Psalter, as a contrast to Abraham's "bosom" in Luke 16:23.

One may mention here, as an additional step on this tentatively reconstructed hermeneutical track, the artist's own theological rumination that what Christ expressed in the parable of Lazarus and the rich man occurred after Christ's resurrection (i.e., the division between righteous and wretched souls with their corresponding "places" after death: Abraham's bosom versus Hades'). But as for the time of Lazarus' resurrection, at least in the artist's mind, there was only one place after death: the underworld (Heb. *šə'ôl*; Gk. *hadēs*) reserved for righteous and wretched without distinction. Hence, the bosom of Hades and not the bosom of Abraham held the soul of the righteous Lazarus—the friend of Christ from Bethany, whose righteousness is indicated by his halo.

Why Ps 29(30):4(3) came to be used in relation with Lazarus' resurrection and not with Christ's descent to Hades and his victory over Satan—as 1 Pet 3:19–20 alludes to, and church fathers as early as the beginning of the second century professed it—remains an open question. This question bears some value if one takes into account that Ps 29(30):4(3) was linked to a different depiction by another miniaturist, the one who illustrated the Kiev Psalter.[83] On folio 37v, the same Psalm is fused with the image of king David, the traditional author of the Psalter, as coming out of the bosom of a similar creature as the one in Barberini Psalter, a personified lion(?)-headed Hades. Again, his crossed hands are held against his breast. With an aureole around his head, David is pulled out from Hades' bosom by a winged angel. The miniaturist of the Kiev Psalter interpreted the words of Ps 29(30):4(3) as addressed by king David concerning his own person, in an individual prayer for help. If the visual interpretation of Barberini Psalter is typological in nature, engaging some biblical theological reflection and intertextual exegesis, the brief image-text fusion in the Kiev Psalter is an example of plain, literal, historical interpretation of Ps 29(30):4(3).

We may take now a quick look at the relationship between the unique iconography of the raising of Lazarus in the Barberini Psalter and patristic and liturgical interpretations.

The thematic association between the raising of Lazarus and Ps 29(30):4(3) is found outside the Barberini and Pantokrator Psalters (the folio is missing from Khludov Psalter) only in late patristic commentaries. The early patristic commentaries link Ps 29(30):4(3) to David (Eusebius; cf. Kiev Psalter), Hezekiah (Theodoret), and Christ (Didymus). The late eight century John of Euboea (*Homilia in Lazarum*),[84] a compatriot of John of Damascus, is the first patristic writer to relate this passage to the resurrection of Lazarus.[85]

According to Christopher Walter,[86] the miniatures found in the London and Barberini Psalters, and to a certain degree in the Pantokrator Psalter, could have a common parent: the lost miniature (and folio) in the ninth-century Khludov Psalter. The narrative source of inspiration for Khludov and its possible descendants is the *Homilia in Lazarum* composed by John of Euboea in 774 C.E.

While missing in early patristic writings, the thematic association mentioned above is paramount in liturgical hymns prescribed for the Saturday of Lazarus. Although the verbal linkage between the raising of Lazarus and Ps 29(30):4(3) is omitted, the theme of Christ's raising Lazarus' soul out of Hades appears in liturgical hymns, which could precede chronologically the *Homilia in Lazarum*.

In these hymns, the liturgist merges the visible act of raising Lazarus by Christ's all-powerful word, as recorded in John 11, with the invisible scene of "stealing" Lazarus' soul from the "jaws" of death and "darkness of Hades." As one may note, the liturgical interpretation matches closely the two-register depiction of "raising of Lazarus" found in the Barberini Psalter: "O Good Shepherd, you have come to Bethany to find your sheep. You have seized him from the fierce jaws of the wolf. You have brought him from corruption to life" (Saturday of Lazarus, Matins, Ode Eight, heirmos). Hades is compared here with a wolf, very close to Peter's description of the slanderer (cf. 1 Pet 5:8: "roaring lion") and Barberini's depiction of the personified Hades: "As soon as the Lord approached the tomb, his voice became life for the dead man. Hades groaned aloud, and released him in fear" (Saturday of Lazarus, Matins, Praises); and: "The gatekeepers of Hades tremble before you, O Christ, the bars of death are broken by your power, Lazarus rises from the grave at your command" (Saturday of Lazarus, Matins, Ode Four, heirmos).[87]

Maria Evangelatou[88] argues that between patristic and liturgical factors, the latter are more influential on manuscript illuminations. This can be seen in the fact that when a Psalm passage lacks in illustration, that Psalm passage is not used in liturgy either. The liturgical samples I quoted above support Evangelatou's point. In the particular case of the fusion between John 11 and Ps 29(30):4(3), it was the liturgy more than the patristic commentaries that had a great impact on the Barberini illustrator when he linked the raising of Lazarus to the psalmist's supplication. I might add that even John Euboea's late eighth-century sermon, *Homilia in Lazarum*, adduced as example of patristic evidence by Christopher Walter, does not belong precisely to the genre of "commentary" (patristic, in the narrow sense) but to the "homily" genre (liturgy).

"Tabor and Hermon will rejoice in your name" (Ps 88[89]:13[12], NETS)
Here is another example of "relevant vocabulary" fusing text and image into one whole. The Khludov Psalter[89] contains on folio 88v a depiction of Christ's transfiguration (Matt 17:1–9; Mark 9:2–10; Luke 9:28–36). It is a clichéd image. On the mountaintop, there is Christ flanked by Moses and Elijah,[90] all three figures being encompassed by a wide mandorla.[91] Midway up the mountain, there are the three apostles witnessing Christ's transfiguration. The theme of "sleepiness," found only in Luke 9:32 ("Peter and his companions were weighed down with sleep") and carefully rendered by most iconographic renditions of this episode, receives a special treatment in the Khludov Psalter. The young apostle John,

positioned in the middle, is sleeping, while James is half awake and Peter standing up addresses Christ.

The transfiguration miniature is found on the margin of folio 88v next to Ps 88(89):13(12) that reads: "The north and seas you created; Thabor and Hermon will rejoice in your name" (NETS). The New Testament accounts of Christ's transfiguration do not mention Hermon or Tabor. The place of transfiguration is briefly introduced as a "mountain" (Luke 9:28) or "high mountain" (Matt 17:1; Mark 9:2). The election of Tabor and Hermon as prime candidates for the transfiguration scene was suggested by the typological interpretation[92] of Ps 88(89):13(12) the traces of which are still visible in Eastern Orthodox liturgy.

There is a certain hesitation in early Byzantine sources regarding the identification of Hermon or Tabor as the spot of Christ's transfiguration.[93] For instance, the church historian Eusebius switches back and forth between the two. Moreover, the pilgrim of Bordeaux (ca. 333 C.E.) situates the scene on the Mount of Olives. The decisive moment is the year 348 C.E., when Cyril of Jerusalem (*Lecture 12* 16) speaks of Tabor as the historical place of the transfiguration. Cyril's statement is supported by Epiphanius of Salamis in the East and Jerome in the West, so that by the end of the fourth century a tradition was born: Tabor becomes the "(high) mountain" where Christ showed his glory to James, Peter, and John.

There is no evidence of the date when the first church was built on Mount Tabor. Yet the so-called Piacenza pilgrim informs that three "basilicas" marked the scene already by about 570 C.E. According to Jerome Murphy-O'Connor,[94] the apparent contradiction between Piacenza's testimony and that of Willibaldus, who in 723 C.E. saw only one church dedicated to Jesus, Moses, and Elijah, can be resolved by considering the three "basilicas" mentioned by Piacenza as three chapels within one church, as is still the case today.

Despite the importance of the transfiguration in Christ's life, this event was not commemorated among the earliest Christian festivals.[95] I might add though that the prokeimenon before the gospel reading at the Matins of Transfiguration (August 6) is Ps 88(89):13(12). This shows that the depiction of transfiguration in the Khludov Psalter on the same folio with Ps 88(89) had patristic and liturgical antecedents. In one of the festal hymns, king David, the traditional author of the Psalter, is imagined as summoning the entire creation to share into the joy of Christ's transfiguration:

David, the ancestor of God, foreseeing in the spirit your coming to men in the flesh, O Only-begotten Son, from afar calls creation together to make merry, and prophetically cries out: Tabor and Hermon shall rejoice in your name. For when you went up into this mountain with your disciples, O Savior, you were transfigured, making the nature that was darkened in Adam to shine like lightning once again, and transforming it into the glory and brightness of your divinity. Wherefore we cry to you: O Creator of all, Lord, glory be to you.

Transfiguration, Great Vespers, aposticha

"Many dogs encompassed me. . . . They pierced my hands and my feet. . . .
They parted my garments among themselves. . . ." (Ps 21[22]:17[16], 19
[18], author's translation)

Ps 21(22):17(16)c: "They pierced (*ōryxan*) my hands and my feet." The form *ōryxan*, aorist of *oryssō*, "to dig, make holes," occurs eleven times in the Septuagint with reference to the digging a well or a pit in the ground (e.g., Gen 26:15, 18, 19; Exod 7:24).[96] The rendering "pierced" or "gouged" (so NETS) is required by the context of Ps 21(22):17(16). The description offered by the Septuagint translator, hands and feet being drilled through or gouged, is quite graphic and dramatic.

Oddly enough, Ps 21(22):17(16)c was not employed by the gospel writers to describe the crucifixion scene, though this would have been a powerful Old Testament testimony according to the "prophecy-fulfillment" pattern so dear to early Christians. The first hint at crucifixion by "nailing" (and not binding) on the cross occurs in John 20: 20, "He [Christ] showed them his hands and his side" (on Sunday evening, the day of resurrection). The explicit reference to nailing or piercing is found in Thomas's reply to the disciples' claim that they saw the risen Christ: "Unless I see the mark of the nails (*typon tōn hēlōn*) in his hands, and put my finger in the mark of the nails and my hand in his side, I will not believe" (John 20:25).

The motif of "piercing the hands" found in Ps 21(22):17(16)c is also absent in Byzantine hymnography. Nevertheless, there are hymns hinting at this verse by depicting Christ as "nailed" to the cross: "O beloved Son, how is it that you are hanged on the tree of a wooden cross? How is it, O Word, O long-suffering Master, that your hands and feet are nailed (*prosēlōthēs*) by lawless people and you have poured out your precious blood?" (Righteous Nicon and His One Hundred Ninety-nine Disciples, Vespers, theotokion); and, ". . . the Light-bestower, pierced with nails (*proseloumenon*) . . ." (Holy Hieromartyr Gregory the Illuminator of Greater Armenia, Vespers, theotokion).

Among early Christian writers, Justin Martyr (*Dialogue with Thrypho* 104) is perhaps the first who cites Ps 21(22):17(16)c along with other verses of this Psalm as a "prediction" of Christ's death. The fact that Justin encounters no disproval from Trypho the Jew means that by the middle of the second century there was no textual difference between the understanding of Hebrew and Septuagint readings with respect to v. 17(16)c—a contrast to what will be the case later on due to the Masoretic vocalization. In the same vein as Justin, Theodoret of Cyrus (*Interpretatio in psalmos*) notices that Ps 21(22):17(16)c has never been disputed: "And this is clear and obvious even for the contenders. That is why, we hear the Lord in the holy Gospels saying to his holy disciples, 'Behold my hands and my feet, that I am.' Nevertheless, he showed to Thomas the marks of the nails as well as the lance wound."[97]

In contrast with the minimal and allusive hymnic evidence and sporadic patristic exegesis, Ps 21(22):17(16)c was well received by the illustrators of marginal Psalters (Khludov, Barberini, London, Bristol) in the ninth through twelve centuries. For instance, on the folio 20r of the Khludov Psalter, one finds the depiction of Christ being nailed to cross. The emphasis is not so much on crucifixion as a whole but rather on the "piercing" detail, and thus on the dramatic aspect of this episode. Large drops gush forth from Christ's pierced right hand, while his left hand is being nailed by a man suspended beside the cross. At the bottom, two other men transfix his feet to the wood. As customary with the Khludov Psalter, an arrow on top of the cross indicates that this scene is the visual replica to Ps 21(22):17(16)c, "They pierced my hands and my feet."

"The Lord said to me, 'My son you are; today I have begotten you'"
(Ps 2:7, NETS)

On the margin of folio 2v of the Khludov Psalter there are three illustrations accompanying Ps 2.

The image at the center represents the birth of Christ. It is a typical depiction of the Nativity, with the Theotokos next to a manger resembling the altar table on which lies the new-born Christ in swaddling cloths. Two animals flank the manger-turned-crib as rays come from heaven. At the bottom of the image, one can see a partial representation of Christ being washed after birth, a popular scene in Byzantine iconography.

Psalm 2 is a royal Psalm that was originally composed for the coronation of a king of the Davidic dynasty. According to v. 7, on the day of coronation, God has begotten the king of Israel as his son. The king became on that day the adopted son of God.

The Christian typological use of Ps 2:7 goes back to the apostolic times (Acts 13:33; Heb 1:5; 5:5). In Acts, Ps 2:7 is quoted in relation to Christ's resurrection. As he did in the past with the Israelite king on the day of coronation, God is doing now with Christ on the day of his resurrection: he has "begotten" him.[98] In Heb 1:5, Ps 2:7 is coupled with 2 Sam 7:14 (Nathan's prophecy on the perpetuity of Davidic dynasty) to underscore Christ's superiority to the angels. One may mention that early Christians understood Ps 2:7 in conjunction with Christ's baptism (Matt 3:16–17; Mark 1:10–11; Luke 3:21–22). Nevertheless, the former connection of Ps 2 to Christ's resurrection seems to be the earliest one.[99]

Among the patristic writers the most popular application of Ps 2:7 seems to be the incarnation or birth of Christ. Cyril of Alexandria interprets:

> The word today [Ps 2:7] indicates the present time in which he was made in the flesh—he who nevertheless in his own nature was the lord of everything. John testifies this [John 1:1], that he came among his own, calling the world his own. Having been called into a kingdom in accordance with his accustomed glory, he said, "I have been made king by him," that is, by God the Father. Furthermore, he fulfilled this by being made the Son in his humanity even if then he was the Son in his own nature. He smoothed the way for human nature to participate in adoption, and he called to himself people oppressed by the tyranny of sin.
>
> *Exposition of the Psalms 2.7*[100]

Nevertheless, according to Origen, Ps 2:7 is about the eternal generation of the Son: "There is no evening of God possible and, I think, no morning, but the time, if I may put it this way, which is coextensive with the unoriginated and eternal life, is today for him, the day in which the Son has been begotten. Consequently neither the beginning nor the day of his generation is to be found" (*Commentary on the Gospel of John* 1.204).[101]

In liturgical setting, Ps 2:7–8 is used as prokeimenon for the Royal Hours on the eve of the Nativity. Moreover, Hebrews 1:1–12 where Ps 2:7 is quoted represents one of the readings prescribed for this service.

Together with the upper and lower images, the icon of Nativity on folio 2v is more than a mere typological illustration of Ps 2:7 inspired by patristic and liturgical interpretations. The three images on folio 2v of the Khludov Psalter themselves frame a full visual commentary on Ps 2 in light of Christ's birth.

Folio 2v represents a case of visual *syncrisis* (comparison) so frequently employed by Byzantine writers and artists. As Henri Maguire points out, the rhetorical technique of syncrisis was used both for encomium and censure. In encomium, the subject was praised (e.g., a good emperor was compared to David), while in censure, the subject was blackened (e.g., a bad emperor was compared to Pharaoh).[102]

Here, the upper and lower images function as censure and encomium for two groups of people characterized by two attitudes toward the incarnation and birth of Christ as depicted in the median illustration. The upper image lies beneath a marred inscription that reads *legei hoti ouai ethnos hamartōlon*, "He says, 'Ah sinful nation!'"—a quotation from Isa 1:4.[103] The image depicts three men seated on lower thrones and symbolizing the rulers gathered to plot together against the Lord and his Messiah (LXX: *christou*) (Ps 2:2). The reader of the gospel accounts of Christ's birth could easily identify these plotters with Herod's council, the priests and scribes (Matt 2:3–4).[104] As with many other illustrations of the Khludov Psalter, this upper image could be a representation of the iconoclasts who by fighting against the icons reject the incarnation as the theological basis for icon veneration. This visual censure compares Herod and iconoclasts with the old rulers who conspire against God and his king, as stated in Ps 2:2.

The lower image depicting two shepherds with their flock is linked to Ps 2:9 (the last on folio 2v): "You shall shepherd (*poimaneis*) them with an iron rod; and like a potter's vessel you will shatter them" (NETS). Obviously, the verb "shepherd" in the LXX[105] triggered this illustration. Nevertheless, the image could be regarded as an encomium of the iconophiles who through their love for icons embrace the mystery of the incarnation. The iconophiles are compared here with the shepherds, the first to bring homage to the new-born king (Luke 2:8–20). Interestingly, the three-part illustration on folio 2v assimilates the iconoclasts with the ruling class, while the iconophiles are associated with the common folks.

The Hospitality of Abraham (Gen 18:1–8)

"Now let us see how each man receives his guests. 'Abraham saw', the text says, 'and ran to meet them'. Notice that Abraham immediately is energetic and eager in his duties. He runs to meet them, and when he had met them, 'he hastens back to the tent,' the text says, and says to his wife: 'Hasten to the tent'. [Gen 18:6] Behold in the individual matters how great is his eagerness to receive them. He makes haste in all things; all things are done urgently; nothing is done leisurely" (*Homilies on Genesis* 4.1).[106]

The picture painted here by Origen about Abraham's eagerness to welcome his heavenly guests (Gen 18:1–8) resembles in tone the two-register mosaic depicting the same story, which is found in the nave of Rome's Santa Maria Maggiore (Figure 7.5).[107] In the upper register, a running Abraham bows down in front of three beardless men seemingly floating

FIGURE 7.5 Hospitality of Abraham, nave mosaic, Santa Maria Maggiore, Rome (Photo: Santa Maria Maggiore.)

above the ground.[108] The floating detail can be explained by the Septuagint's use of the phrase *epanō autou*, "above him," with reference to the
three men's stationing in relation to Abraham (Gen 18:2). The Greek word
epanō, "above, on top of," renders the Hebrew preposition *'al*, "on, above;
by, next to, in front of." This lexical choice (*epanō*) of the Septuagint inspired the artist in the depiction of the three men as if floating above the
ground. Another interpretive particularity of this mosaic is that while all
three men have auras, only one, the central figure, is circumscribed by a
glowing mandorla. There is no other pictorial detail that would differentiate the central figure from the other two but his right hand, directed to
Abraham as a token of blessing or acceptance of the latter's welcome. This
distinction between the central figure and the other two men is supported
by the Septuagint reading of Gen 18:3 and chapter 19:1, where two of the
three visitors are called "angels" (*angeloi*). Although Abraham sees three
men, he addresses them with the singular "Lord" (LXX: *kyrie*) as directed
to one of them who is somehow more obviously central to the action than
the other two. In some contrast, the MT reads *'ădōnāy*, "my lords" with
reference to all three.[109]

In the lower register of this mosaic, Abraham is depicted twice. First,
he asks Sarah to bake three cakes (cf. Gen 18:6). The tent behind Sarah
resembles a basilica with a cross inscribed above the entrance. This
detail may have a midrashic overtone, as actualizing interpretation: the
Christian Church is thus invited to practice hospitality as Abraham did.
Moreover, the cakes have a triangle shape, a possible hint at the Trinity. Abraham approaches the three guests, now seated at a rectangular
table symbolizing the altar table. The patriarch offers the calf while the
central figure points his right hand toward the offering (Gen 18:8). The
three guests have auras but the mandorla from the upper register is
missing here.

With its two-register structure, this mosaic can be compared with the
raising Lazarus illumination from the Barberini Psalter and Gračanica
fresco depicting Abraham's sacrifice. All these three examples have something in common: the upper register is quite close to the biblical text,
while the lower register represents the subtext or the interpretive level
with special overtones. Thus, in the Barberini Psalter, the upper register
describes in images what John 11 conveys in words—the raising of Lazarus through Christ's word. In the lower register, there is the interpretation
of the miracle as the defeat of a personified Hades, now forced to release
Lazarus's soul. In Abraham's sacrifice, the upper level retells pictorially

the Gen 22 story, while the lower register insists on Abraham's commitment and the three youths' obedience, all four together determined to fulfill promptly God's order. In the mosaic of Abraham's hospitality, the upper register follows closely Gen 18, while the lower one places a special emphasis on Abraham's eagerness to serve his guests. More than in the other two examples, in the mosaic of Santa Maria Maggiore, the two registers are closely unified through the ubiquitous presence of Abraham who appears three times, always hastening to show his hospitality.

The sameness of the three guests depicted against a gold backdrop in the lower register may be a hint at the Trinity. If this is correct, the mosaic under discussion can be regarded as one of the earliest forerunners of Andrei Rublev's famous "Trinity" icon.

In fact, a trinitarian interpretation can be detected very early in the liturgical usage of Gen 18:1–8: "You beheld the Trinity as far as man may see him, and as a genuine friend, you did show him hospitality, O all-blessed Abraham. Wherefore, as the reward for your strange hospitality to strangers, you became through faith the father of innumerable nations" (Sunday of the Holy Forefathers, Matins, Ode Five, troparion). And in the following troparion, the three men are considered the hypostases of the triune God: "Of old God in three hypostases appeared to Abraham at the oak of Mambre, in his mercy giving him Isaac as a reward in return for his hospitality. Him do we also now glorify as the God of our Fathers" (Sunday of the Paralytic, Matins, Ode Seven, troparion).

The icon of Abraham's hospitality raises an important question regarding pictorial representation of God. As noted above, the incarnation has been the main argument for the production and veneration of icons. It is the visibility of Christ, the image of God, and then of those who are made in his image and deified through participation in him, that permits this representation. Nonetheless, it is the strict Eastern Orthodox understanding that pictorial depictions of the Father and the Holy Spirit are baseless and impermissible, for the simple reason that neither became incarnate: there is only one image of God, and only in Christ has God put on a human face.

Against the backdrop of Christological debates, the Old Testament *theophanies*, "appearances of God," were commonly interpreted as manifestations in human form of the second person of the Trinity. Nevertheless, Dan 7:9–10, 13–14 (Theodotion) contrasts *hōs huios tou anthrōpou*, "someone as the Son of man" (the preincarnate Logos, as the ancient Christian commentators would annotate) with *tou palaiou tōn hēmerōn*,

"Ancient of Days." The latter is described as an old man with grey hair. Could be this verbal description considered a scriptural basis for the pictorial representation of God the Father?

In her analysis of various interpretations given to "Ancient of Days" in Dan 7, Gretchen Kreahling McKay shows that according to Pseudo-Dionysius (*De divinis nominibus* 10), the Ancient of Days does not refer to a particular person of the Trinity but rather to the common nature of God that is above time and eternity. Dionysius explains that God is called in general terms the Ancient of Days because "he is the eternity and time of everything, and because he precedes days and eternity and time." Thus God is before and beyond time, before and beyond eternity.[110] Dionysius's insightful interpretation may be bolstered by philological analysis of the MT. The word *'attîq* in the Aramaic phrase *'attîq yômayyā'* of Dan 7:13 can be related to the Akkadian verb *etēqum* "to advance," hence the one who is ahead of days (time), the "everlasting" one.[111]

Nevertheless, church history shows that there were instances when artists influenced by Daniel's phrase, "Ancient of Days," and its more literal interpretation, depicted God the Father as an old man beside Christ and the Holy Spirit in shape of a dove. The "Trinity" icon by Andrei Rublev (1360–1430), however, represents a watershed and a model for later symbolic—though not strictly iconic—representations of Trinity.

Speaking of the relationship between icons and liturgical tradition, Andrew Louth notices that iconographers such as Andrei Rublev, while closely connected to the liturgical exegesis, were not fully aware of the patristic interpretation or, as he labels it, the "learned exegetical tradition." This can be seen in the development of the icon based on Gen 18–19: from an early phase, "Abraham's Hospitality" (the preincarnate Logos and two angels; cf. Eusebius, John Chrysostom) to a later phase, "The Trinity," represented by Rublev's masterpiece, where the three heavenly visitors come to symbolize "the three-in-oneness of the Godhead." The main point of Louth's study is that the liturgical tradition of Eastern Orthodox Church facilitated the interaction between the spiritual experience of the iconographers and the "learned exegetical tradition."[112]

The local "Council of the Hundred Chapters" (known in Russian as *Stoglavy Sobor*) convened by Ivan IV at Moscow in 1551 forbids painters to use their own imagination when they paint holy icons. With that occasion, Andrei Rublev's symbolic icon of Trinity was "canonized" as a model of Orthodox iconographic tradition. However, based on the fact that only the second person of the Trinity was manifest in the flesh, the Pan-Orthodox

Council of Moscow of 1666–67, following in the footsteps of the Seventh
Ecumenical Council, forbids the pictorial representation of the Trinity
with God the Father as an old man and the Holy Spirit as a dove.

Scenes from the Life of Cain and Abel (Gen 4)

Visoki Dečani Monastery[113] in Dečani, Kosovo, offers an interesting
series of pictorial variations on the life of the first pair of brothers, Cain
and Abel.

CAIN BORN AS AN ADULT

The biblical account of Cain's birth (Gen 4:1) raised a number of questions among ancient Jewish and Christian interpreters. Here is the Septuagint reading of this crux interpretum: "Adam knew Heua, his wife,
and after she has conceived she bore Kain and said, 'I have acquired a man
through God'" (NETS). This is not the customary way a woman would
address her husband after she gave birth to a child. Here are a few lexical
oddities deserving special attention: "I acquired" (*ektēsamēn*) instead of a
more common "I gave birth"; "human being, man" (*anthrōpon*) instead of
"(male) child" or "son"; and "through God" (*dia tou theou*), which places a
great emphasis on God and not at all on man.

The Hebrew word 'îš, "(adult) man" (cf. LXX: *anthrōpon*, "human
being, man"), led the ancient interpreters to think of Cain as being born
already as a grown up man, a calque of *hā-ʼādām* (LXX: *anthrōpon*), the
first human being created by God (Gen 2:7). Here is how the *Life of Adam
and Eve*, whose date of composition is set sometime between the third and
seventh century c.e., imagines the first actions of this prodigious child
immediately after birth. "And she bore a son and he was lustrous. And
at once the infant rose, ran, and brought in his hands a reed [in Hebrew,
qaneh] and gave it to his mother. And his name was called Cain [*qayin*]"
(*Life of Adam and Eve* 21:3). Cain's prodigy was possible due to the fact
that Eve gave him birth "with the help of the Lord" (LXX: *dia tou theou*,
"through God").[114]

A similar story to the one told in the *Life of Adam and Eve* may be
detected in a fresco from Visoki Dečani Monastery (Figure 7.6). The
painting depicts Adam and Eve in a tender embrace, while Cain, already
a lad, approaches his parents stealthily. The reed mentioned in the *Life* is
absent in the fresco, though Cain's swain-like resemblance may allude
to the adult-born motif found in the above cited text. Conspicuously, the
artist who painted this fresco found his source of inspiration outside

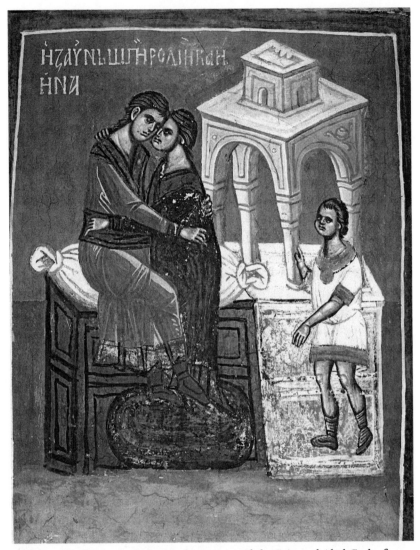

FIGURE 7.6 Cain and Abel: Cain born as an adult, Cain and Abel Cycle, fresco, Visoki Dečani Monastery, Dečani, Kosovo

(Photo: Courtesy of BLAGO Fund Inc. [www.srpskoblago.org].)

of Scripture, liturgy, and patristic interpretation, namely, in the area of pseudepigraphic literature.

CAIN MURDERS ABEL WITH A STONE

From Visoki Dečani Monastery comes another fresco whose theme is Cain killing Abel with a stone. One can see Cain raising a big stone while

FIGURE 7.7 Cain kills Abel with a stone, Cain and Abel Cycle, fresco, Visoki Dečani Monastery, Dečani, Kosovo
(Photo: Courtesy of BLAGO Fund Inc. [www.srpskoblago.org].)

Abel is lying down helplessly; another stone touches his bleeding head (Figure 7.7).

The Genesis account on Cain and Abel (4:1–16) is conspicuously laconic, almost reticent regarding the circumstances of Abel's death. The MT reads: "Cain said to his brother Abel . . . and when they were in the field, Cain rose against his brother Abel and killed him" (Gen 4:8, author's translation). The LXX fills in the blank of the Hebrew text as follows: "And Cain said to his brother Abel, 'Let us go through into the plain.' And it came about when they were in the plain, that then Cain rose up against his brother Abel and killed him" (Gen 4:8, NETS).

The detail "in the field (plain)" as the place of Cain's assault against his brother assisted the ancient interpreters in imaging the weapon

Cain used in killing Abel. Thus, the Jubilees states rather emphatically: "He [Cain] killed Abel with a stone" (*Jubilees* 4:31). Targum of Pseudo-Jonathan, after having filled in the odd lacuna of the Hebrew text ("Cain said to his brother Abel . . .") by reconstructing a possible conversation between the two brothers on the idea of justice in the world, concludes, ". . . and Cain arose against Abel his brother, and drove a stone into his forehead, and killed him." More imagistic elements are found in the following Midrash: "How did he kill him? He made many wounds and bruises with a stone on his arms and legs, because he did not know whence his soul would go forth, until he got to his neck" (*Midrash Tanhuma, Bereshit* 9).[115]

One might assume that the artist of the Dečani fresco was inspired by an ancient Jewish interpretation, similar to the ones cited above. Interestingly, the following liturgical hymn hints at stone as the possible murder's weapon: "My soul, truly you come to resemble those first two murderers, Cain and his descendent Lamech; for you have stoned your body with evil deeds and murdered your inward being with senseless passion" (The Fifth Week of the Great Lent, Thursday, Great Canon of St. Andrew of Crete, Ode Two, heirmos). This is the only allusion to the way Cain killed his brother in Eastern Orthodox hymnography. It is possible that a targum or a Jewish pseudepigraphon (e.g., Jubilees) may have inspired the liturgist and then the fresco artist would have borrowed this detail from a hymn as the heirmos quoted above. Although the question regarding the source of inspiration of this fresco remains open, and more detailed investigation is needed, one may conclude that pictorial interpretations are quite intricate and they often result from a rich and complex mix of aural and textual material.

EVE LAMENTING ABEL'S DEATH

Another fresco from the same fourteenth-century Visoki Dečani Monastery offers a fascinating case of intervisuality (Figure 7.8). "Eve lamenting Abel's death" fuses two visual interpretations into one whole. The image generated by a narrative elaboration of Gen 4:1–16 is artfully coupled with a late Byzantine iconographic composition within liturgical setting.

A woman is kneeling. She tenderly embraces and kisses dearly her dead son. Her face is marked by deep sadness and dignified sobriety. It is Eve lamenting her son Abel. Standing next to her, Adam raises his right hand to heaven in sign of suppressed anger. His left hand hesitantly seeks to grasp Eve from her falling. Abel, dressed in white, is stiff; his body is

FIGURE 7.8 Eve lamenting the death of Abel, Cain and Abel Cycle, fresco, Visoki Dečani Monastery, Dečani, Kosovo

(Photo: Courtesy of BLAGO Fund Inc. [www.srpskoblago.org].)

lifeless; his hands lie crossed over his breast. A winged angel tries to calm Adam and Eve. In the back, there is a vertical stone tomb topped by a cross. A little further, there is another scene with Christ questioning Cain about his brother Abel (cf. Gen 4:9). At the feet of Jesus, Abel's blood is coming out of the ground.

The Bible is silent regarding Eve's lamentation over her murdered son. Nonetheless, the *Apocalypse of Moses*, a work whose earliest manuscripts date to the eleventh century, contains an elaboration of the biblical account of Cain and Abel. According to this apocryphal work, Eve had a dream about Abel having been murdered by Cain. Both Adam and Eve decide to go and find out what happened with their younger son: "And they both went and found Abel murdered by the hand of Cain his brother. And God says to Michael the archangel: 'Say to Adam: 'Reveal not the secret that you know to Cain your son, for he is a son of wrath. But grieve not, for I will give you another son in his stead; he shall show to you all that you shall do. Do you tell him nothing,' Thus spoke the archangel to Adam. But he kept the word in his heart, and with him also Eve, though they grieved concerning Abel their son" (*Apocalypse of Moses* 3:1–3).[116] The parental grief dramatized in the *Apocalypse of Moses* is reflected in Dečani fresco.

The artist who painted this fresco is well aware of the typological relationship between Abel and Christ. In the New Testament, Abel is praised
for his faithfulness (Heb 11:4). His righteous blood, associated with the
pure worship of God, makes him comparable with any other martyr (Matt
23:35; Luke 11:51).[117] Abel's blood typifies the innocent victim crying for
vengeance; a parallel is suggested between the blood of innocent Abel
and the blood of innocent Christ. However, the author of Hebrews notices that Christ's blood is superior in comparison with the blood of Abel
(Heb 12:24). Unlike that of Abel, the blood of Christ brings mercy and
salvation.[118]

The Bible does not indicate whether Abel was good or evil. Nevertheless, the Jewish and Christian extra-biblical evidence turned Adam's
younger son into a model of righteousness. Christ mentions the "righteous blood" (haima dikaion) of the "righteous Abel" (Habel tou dikaiou)
(Matt 23:35). Similarly, Philo notices, "the righteous man [Abel] was
younger in time than the wicked one" (Questions in Genesis 1:59).[119]

Early Christian interpreters saw in Abel a foreshadowing of Christ.
Having connected the Aramaic word Pascha (cf. Heb. pesah, "Passover")
to the Greek verb pathein, "to suffer," the late second century Melito of
Sardis exclaims: "This is Jesus Christ, to whom be glory for ever and ever.
Amen. This is the mystery of the Pascha" (On Pascha 10–11). Among the
numerous prefigurements of Christ, Abel is the first, having been murdered in a similar manner to Christ—an innocent victim. Regrettably,
in the context of anti-Judaic polemic, Irenaeus and Tertullian argue that
Cain and his sacrifice typify the Jews, while Abel represents the Church
or Christ.[120]

From the hymnographic record, a subtle correlation between Christ's
death and resurrection, and Abel's death and salvation may be detected
in the following lines: "We commemorate the righteous Abel, the son of
Adam [among other forefathers of Christ]: Your blood cries to God, even
without your soul. You first among the dead, and first among the saved"
(Sunday Before the Nativity of Christ, Matins, synaxarion).

Inspired by the typology between Abel and Christ, the iconographer
intricately interweaves Eve's lamentation with that of Mary the Theotokos.
Mary's lamentation is richly embroidered on a cloth called the epitaphios,
still employed in Orthodox paschal services today. The emergence of the
epitaphios from the Late Byzantine aer[121] is related to the standardization
of the Holy Saturday service (called Lamentations and held by anticipation
on the evening of Good Friday) in the fourteenth century. Initially, the

epitaphios depicted the *amnos* (lamb), the dead Christ. By the fourteenth century, the epitaphios became the *epitaphios threnos* (burial lament). Instead of a solitary Christ lying dead as in the early epitaphios, the *epitaphios threnos*, depicting a funeral gathering of figures, includes the lamentation of the Theotokos over her dead Son.[122]

There is a striking resemblance between the Dečani fresco and the *epitaphios threnos* kept in the St. Catherine Monastery on Mount Sinai and dated to 1612/3. Eve's passionate expression in Dečani fresco reminds one of Mary's tender embrace on the *epithaphios*; Abel's lifeless body matches the dead Christ; Adam's dramatic posture imitates that of Joseph of Arimathea.

Although Abel is rarely mentioned in liturgical hymns and almost always with reference to his righteous blood, as a martyric model, through this fresco's wisely created intervisuality, the drama of Adam's murdered son is included within the most sacred time of the Eastern Orthodox calendar, the Holy Week. Abel is thus posed in typological relation to Christ during the Lamentations service of Holy Saturday around the epitaphios threnos.

"Prophets from above proclaimed you beforehand, O Maiden!"

SINAI ICON OF VIRGIN KYKKOTISSA (FIGURE 7.9)

Seated on a throne tapped with a red long pillow is the Lady Theotokos with the infant Christ in her arms. The bare legged child dressed in a soft sleeveless chiton is moving, twisting his legs tenderly against his mother's breast. With one hand, he grasps the fringe of the brown veil that rests over her *maphorion*;[123] with the other, he holds a scroll as a token of his authority. The Virgin's solemn face tilts gingerly toward the head of her Son. An inscription reads in red: "Mother of God." This is the center of the icon. Above the central panel reserved for the Virgin Mary is the adult Christ within a circular mandorla surrounded by seraphs and cherubs and the four symbols of the evangelists (lion, bull, angel, eagle). Beneath the central panel, there are five figures: Joseph surrounded by Joachim and Anna on his right side and Adam and Eve on his left. An inscription on the top of these figures reads: *Iōakeim k[ai]Anna eteknogonēsan k[ai] Adam k[ai] Eua ēleutherōthēsan*, "Joachim and Anna have begotten a child and Adam and Eve were freed." On both sides of the central panel there are ten frames containing nineteen figures. All of them hold scrolls with Greek, mostly biblical, inscriptions.[124] The following heirmos may be read as a gloss on this celebration of biblical figures pointing prophetically to

FIGURE 7.9 Enthroned Virgin Kykkotissa Surrounded by Christ in Glory, Prophets and Saints, portable icon, Monastery of St. Catherine, Mount Sinai (Photo: By permission of St. Catherine Monastery.)

the Virgin as vessel of Incarnation: "The words and dark sayings of the Prophets dimly foreshowed your Incarnation from a Virgin, O Christ, that splendor of your lightning which was to come forth as a light for the nations; and the deep calls to you in gladness: Glory to your power, O friend of man" (The Dormition, Matins, Ode Four).

Some of the figures in this icon stand next to the emblematic signs associated with them in the Old Testament, many of which were interpreted by church fathers and liturgists as Marian types or symbols. The list below containing these figures runs from left to right and downward, from the beholder's perspective.

In the first row Paul holds a scroll that reads, "Jesus Christ is the same yesterday and today and forever" (Heb 13:8). John the Theologian's scroll reads, "All things came into being through him, and without him not one thing came into being what has come into being" (John 1:3). That of John the Baptist proclaims: "This was he of whom I said, 'He who comes after me ranks ahead of me because he was before me'" (John 1:15). Finally, Apostle Peter confesses: "You are the Christ, the Son of the living God" (Matt 16:16).

The second row of two frames flanking the central panel consists of Aaron who holds a scroll with the inscription, "This is the rod that brought forth the virginal birth" (*Ē rhabdos autē hē blastēsasa parth[eniko]n tokon*). This inscription is a paraphrase on Num 17:5a: "And it shall be: the person, if I choose him, his rod shall sprout forth" (NETS). In the iconographer's view, the "rod" (*rhabdos*) points prophetically to the Virgin Mary. Moses stands next to a burning bush with a scroll that reads, "I will turn aside to see this great sight" (Exod 3:3). Patriarch Jacob is depicted twice in the same frame: as a sleeping young man and as an old man holding a scroll. Between these two depictions one can see the ladder spoken of on the inscription of his scroll: "And he [Jacob] dreamed, and see, a ladder set firmly in the earth, whose top was reaching into heaven, and the angels of God were ascending and descending on it" (cf. Gen 28:12, NETS).

The third row is occupied by two women and two men. Prophetess Anna holds a scroll that reads, "This child has established heaven and earth" (*Touto to brephos ourano[n] k[ai] gēn estereōsen*). This verse, though unattested in the New Testament, was associated with Prophetess Anna beginning with the twelfth century.[125] Symeon Theodochos ("God-Receiver") holds a scroll with the inscription, "Yes, a sword shall pierce through your own soul also, that the thoughts of many hearts may be revealed" (Luke 2:35). Zechariah's scroll reads, "Blessed be the Lord God of Israel, for he has looked favorably on his people and redeemed them" (Luke 1:68). Elisabeth has a scroll with the inscribed words, "For as soon as I heard the sound of your greeting, the child in my womb leaped for joy" (Luke 1:44).

The fourth row introduces four prophets. Ezekiel stands next to a gate while holding a scroll that reads, "And the Lord said to me: This gate shall be shut" (Ezek 44:2). David, close to a house-sanctuary, has a scroll with the inscription, "Rise up, O Lord, into your rest, you and the ark of your sanctity!" (Ps 131[132]:8, NETS). Isaiah, touching a seraph, brandishes a scroll with the words, "Then, one of the seraphim flew to me" (Isa 6:6). Daniel stands next to a mountain from which a rock came out; his scroll announces the prophecy, "And you saw until when a stone was cut from a mountain, without hands" (Dan 2:34).

The fifth row contains four male figures. Seer (*mantis*) Balaam, pointing to a star, holds a scroll with the promise, "A star will dawn out of Jacob, and a man shall rise up out of Israel" (Num 24:17). Habakkuk, close to a wooded mountain, carries a scroll bearing the inscription, "God will come out of Thaiman, and the Holy One from a shady, densely wooded mountain" (Hab 3:3). The scroll of Solomon reads, "Wisdom built herself a house and sup[ported it with seven pillars]" (Prov 9:1). Gideon holds a fleece and a scroll, "See, I am laying a fleece of wool on the threshing floor" (Judg 6:37).

One of the artistic treasures of St. Catherine Monastery in Sinai, the famous Virgin Kykkotissa of Sinai[126] was painted in tempera on wood between 1050 and 1100 (Kurt Weitzmann). The icon is known after the name of the monastery of Kykko in Cyprus, which received an icon of the Virgin as a gift from the Byzantine emperor Alexios I Komnenos (1081–1118).

The Sinai Kykkotissa is a variant of Virgin Eleousa type of Marian icons. The surname *Eleousa* ("Compassionate") has been affixed to the Virgin (Mary) since the eighth century onward. Today, Eleousa designates a specific iconographic depiction of the Virgin focusing on the compassionate mother's face that touches softly her child's face as the latter lays tenderly his arm around his mother's neck. This image goes back possibly to the seventh century, and was quite popular during the Komnenian dynasty (1081–1185) due to its association with the emerging passion liturgy.[127]

From an iconographic point of view, the Sinai icon represents a great turning point in Byzantine sacred visual art. Its uniqueness lies in the way it condenses the history of salvation by bringing together Old and New Testament illustrative characters that point toward the mystery of incarnation. The Old and New Testament men and women selected for this icon represent various guilds, such as patriarchs, seers, prophets, prophetesses, priests, judges, kings, and apostles. They are all, in one way or another, forerunners or witnesses of the incarnation accomplished through the Virgin Mary. Interestingly, the iconographer offers a special place to Joseph, Mary's fiancé, within God's plan of salvation. Joseph stands between Joachim and Anna, Mary's parents, and Adam and Eve, the forefathers of mankind. By her central position between Joseph at the bottom and Christ in glory at the top, the Virgin Mary becomes the bridge between earth (Joseph with all the Old and New Testament figures) and heaven (Christ surrounded by the heavenly beings). Given its theological intricacy in content and artistic distinctiveness, the common opinion is that the Sinai Virgin icon was painted either for a group of well-educated worshippers or else for the archbishop of Sinai.[128] The Sinai icon bespeaks the typological unity between Old and New Testaments by proclaiming Christ as the incarnate Logos and Mary as the chosen recipient of God's marvelous dealings with humanity.

THE DORMITION FRESCO OF STARO NAGORIČINO (FIGURE 7.10A)
A similar theological theme may be found in the Dormition fresco from St. George Church in Staro Nagoričino.[129] Most likely, the artists who painted this fresco were aware of the model of the Virgin Kykkotissa when working on their lavish Dormition scene.

FIGURE 7.10A Dormition of the Theotokos with Prophets and Saints (full image), fresco, Monastery of St. George, Staro Nagoričane, Republic of Macedonia (Photo: Darko Nikolovski.)

Serbian king Stefan Uroš II Milutin invited Michael Astrapas ("Light-ning"—an inspired nickname for a rapid painter) and Eutychios, origi-nally from Thessaloniki, to adorn his newly built church. The two artists were perhaps the disciples of the famous and legendary painter Manuel Panselinos,[130] who is thought to have painted the Protaton at Mount Athos around 1290. Michael and Eutychios finished their work in a relatively short time, from 1316 to 1318. All three of these icongraphers belong to the "Macedonian School" of the so-called Palaeologan Renaissance. The names of Michael and Eutychios were preserved in inscriptions in four churches, at Ohrid, Prizren, Banjani, and Staro Nagoričino. The style of their frescoes is characterized by "strong chiaroscuro and heavy drapery by hard folds."[131] The fresco cycle of the life of Mary including her Dormi-tion (koimēsis, "falling asleep") is found in the prothesis of the Church of St. George.

The depiction of Dormition of the Virgin Mary is the visual commen-tary of the feast with the same name, one of the twelve Byzantine great feasts, whose celebration on August 15 has been known since the sixth century.

The oldest preserved depictions of the Dormition date back to the tenth century, showing an already established iconographic development. The composition reached the highest degree of artistic and theological so-phistication by the twelfth century. In these icons, the Virgin lies on a bier surrounded by apostles and angels. Christ, standing behind the Virgin, holds her soul as a little swaddled infant in his arms. Two angels descend to receive the soul of the Virgin, while many colorless angels are peeping through a window open in heaven. In some icons, cloudborne apostles and the figure of Jephonias the Jew are added to the composition.[132]

What is original though with the Staro Nagoričino fresco is the fusion between the classical Dormition scene and the Virgin Kykkotissa icon. The monumental fresco of the Dormition covering half of the wall of the prothesis consists of two sections. The lower section depicts the full-fledged falling asleep of the Virgin. The upper section shows cloudborne apostles[133] and angels carrying the Virgin toward the window open in heaven. This widely opened window allows the beholder to glimpse the multitude of angels ready to welcome the Virgin.[134] One may hear in the following hymn a verbal echo of such a visual depiction:

When you did depart to him that was ineffably born of you, O Virgin Theotokos, James the Brother of God and first hierarch was present, together with Peter, the most honored chief disciple and summit of theologians, and the whole divine choir of the apostles, as with exalted hymns of praise and divine revelation they extolled the divine and astonishing mystery of Christ God's dispensation; and as they buried your life-originating and God-receiving body, they rejoiced, O all-praised Virgin. The all-holy and most venerable powers of the angels bowed down from above, and being so amazed at the marvel, they said one to another: "Lift up your gates and receive her that gave birth to the Maker of heaven and earth, and with hymns of glory let us praise her august and holy body, which held the Lord, whom we cannot gaze upon." Wherefore, we also, as we celebrate your memorial, cry out to you, O all-hymned one: Exalt the horn of Christians and save our souls.

The Dormition, Great Vespers, theotokion

The iconographic encounter of the Virgin Kykkotissa with the Dormition occurs in the upper section where Old Testament prophets along with scrolls and symbols already found in the Sinai icon are inserted among angels and apostles (Figure 7.10b).

In the Dormition fresco there are two rows of four figures ("prophets") each with their symbols (from left to right, up and down). The first row consists of Gideon (fleece), Isaiah (coal on a spoon), Daniel (rock), and Balaam (with the clypeate image of Theotokos on a star). The second row contains Ezekiel (gate), Moses (with the clypeate image of Theotokos on a burning bush), David (ark),[135] and Solomon (temple). Compared with the Old Testament cast of the Sinai icon, the fresco is missing Aaron, Jacob, and Habakkuk. Another difference consists of the clipeate with Theotokos image in Moses' bush and in Balaam's star both found only in the fresco (Figure 7.10c).[136]

All in all, what is really fascinating in the two depictions here discussed is the magisterial way the artists interpret the unity in diversity of the Old and New Testaments as foreshadowing and witnessing God's work of salvation wrought by Christ through the Theotokos for the benefit of the entire humanity. Here one cannot help but associate the Sinai icon and Staro Nagoričino fresco with the following hymn:

Prophets from above (*anōthen hoi prophētai*)[137] proclaimed you beforehand (*prokatēngeilan*), proclaimed you O Maiden (*korē*) beforehand, from above, O Maiden: jar (*stamnon*), rod (*rhabdon*),

FIGURE 7.10B Dormition of the Theotokos with Prophets and Saints (detail), fresco, Monastery of St. George, Staro Nagoričane, Republic of Macedonia
(Photo: Ioan Bratiloveanu.)

tablets (*plaka*), table (*trapezan*), lamp-stand (*lychnian*), ark (*kibōton*), unhewn mountain (*oros alatomēton*), golden censer (*chrysoun thymiatērion*) and tabernacle (*skēnē*), impassible gate (*pylēn adiodeuton*), palace (*palation*) and ladder (*klimaka*), and throne (*thronon*) of the King, did the prophets proclaim you, O Maiden. Prophets from above proclaimed you beforehand.[138]

The text of this hymn, a *mathima* ("lesson," a hymn used as a learning tool), is undatable. It was set to music by several composers, the most famous among whom being Ioannis Papadopoulos Koukouzelis (ca. 1270–1340). Although there is no clear prescription in any of the Eastern Orthodox *typika* (liturgical regulations) about such a use of the hymn, it is sung during the Orthros service when a bishop is vested outside the altar in preparation for the Divine Liturgy. What is the precise relation between this hymn and the visual depictions discussed above? The hymn's

FIGURE 7.10C Dormition of the Theotokos with Prophets and Saints (detail), fresco, Monastery of St. George, Staro Nagoričane, Republic of Macedonia (Photo: Ioan Bratiloveanu.)

metaphors, "rod," "ark," "unhewn mountain," "tabernacle," "impassible gate," "palace," and "ladder," may be effortlessly recognized in the two iconographic works celebrating the Theotokos and her prophetic "cloud of witnesses" (Heb 12:1–2). Nevertheless, the obvious discrepancy between the prophetic symbols used by *Anōthen hoi Prophētai* ("Prophets from Above") and those employed by the Sinai icon or the Staro Nagoričino fresco suggests that the two visual representations might have not been drawn on this liturgical hymn.

Summing up, we tried to underscore here the close relationship between aural and visual modes of interpretation. The iconographers seem to be inspired more by hymns of the Church than by patristic commentaries. This demonstrates once more that both iconography and hymnography belong to what one can label "folk theology," well rooted in the liturgical life of the Church. Iconography is both a Bible for the illiterate and a means of interpreting the sacred text. Pedagogical functions work in symbiosis with the anagogical. Worshippers are surrounded by visual interpretations of the Bible whose function is to direct their minds toward God and his salvific acts in human history, thus determining them to action in light of God's living Word. The icons at once inform, form and transform the beholders who participate in the Church's liturgical life. Further, since they are not strictly discursive modes of expression, the icons convey their message not sequentially but simultaneously. While verbal language must be understood gradually, as a sequence of bytes of information, the narrative world of meaning as mediated by the icons may be captured instantaneously and compendiously. As such, the visual medium of iconography forms an essential component of the Orthodox scriptural hermeneutic, mediating the persons and events of salvation history in a rich complementarity with the "verbal images" provided by the hymnography and by the Scriptures themselves.

Postscript

It is not possible, I say not possible, ever to exhaust the
mind of the Scriptures. It is a well that has no bottom.
JOHN CHRYSOSTOM, Homily 19: On Acts

THIS WORK HAS been concerned specifically with Eastern Orthodox ways
of reception and interpretation of the Old Testament. Given the scope and
the depth of such a project, the results are tentative and open ended for
further discussion and investigation.

As stated in the preface and throughout the entire text, this book is a
premier. Its topic has never been discussed at length or in as many aspects
as attempted herein. Nevertheless, the novelty exhibits both strength and
weakness. The reader is encouraged to approach this book as it was conceived and delivered: as a text that stirs the imagination, and a pure invitation to further, deeper analysis. I address here any reader eager to gather
more on a rich and luxurious, yet scarcely known tradition—the Eastern
Orthodox tradition. It remains my hope that someday, someone will find
the time, energy, and passion to build upon these initial soundings and
discover additional interesting data and solid conclusions.

But before then, I feel compelled to suspend this journey of more than
six years—this sojourn of searching and writing—and offer a few tentative concluding remarks from my own findings. What have I learned from
this study? The conclusion of a book is perhaps the most difficult task
confronting the writer. Readers may often be better oriented than authors
in drawing pertinent conclusions from the reading.

However, allow me to emphasize the hallmarks and those features
which distinguish the Eastern Orthodox reception and interpretation of

the Old Testament, apart from other ancient Christian or Jewish modes of appropriation and explanation of the Holy Writ. I will attempt to answer the following question: What is peculiar or characteristic of Eastern Orthodox tradition in approaching the biblical text—more precisely, the Old Testament?

General issues regarding the reception (unity in diversity of the Christian Bible, text, canon, and tradition) and the interpretation (discursive, aural and visual modes) have been discussed at length. There is no need to summarize the data here. The emphasis is placed here on the hallmarks of Eastern Orthodox reception and interpretation of the Old Testament.

Centrality of Scripture within Tradition

The hallmarks briefly considered in the following paragraphs derive from a working principle: the centrality of Scripture within the Tradition. Well-articulated by Gregory of Nyssa, this tenet has often remained underserved, even neglected at the discursive level in the East. Equally, the tenet has been substantially modified at the doctrinal level in the West, though untiringly operating at the intuitive level of Eastern Orthodox tradition. This last peculiar situation has much to do with the manner in which tradition is viewed in the East, primary as life and no mere depository of faith. Within such a flexible and nimble Tradition, the Scripture has always maintained a central place—a pulsating heart nurturing and permeating all facets of ecclesial life.

The centrality of Scripture within Tradition has determined and contoured the way the Eastern Orthodox Church perceives the Word of God. To the Orthodox, Scripture represents no simple transcript of God's self-disclosure, but—more significantly—a means of communication with the source of life. Since the Word of God has been perceived as more than detachable bites of information, the Eastern Orthodox tradition has had to develop corresponding ways of approaching and incorporating this living entity. These methods endure as the hallmarks of Eastern Orthodox reception and interpretation of the Old Testament.

Strictness and Flexibility

If one compares Eastern Orthodox tradition with Western counterparts, an interesting mix of flexibility and strictness at all levels of the faith community would be noticed. Regarding reception of the Old Testament, the textus receptus and canon are likely the best illustrations of this hallmark.

While considering Septuagint the default Bible of the Church, Eastern Church writers are also cognizant of the value of other text-witnesses, such as the Hebrew text. The strictness can be witnessed in the faithfulness the Eastern Orthodox Church shows toward the use of Septuagint as common basis for various translations, as well as for exegesis, hymnography and iconography. Flexibility is perceptible at the level of translating the Old Testament into vernacular languages. Moreover, a good number of ancient and modern Eastern interpreters have taken the effort to attempt to identify and solve lexical differences between Greek and Hebrew text-witnesses. Their exegetical endeavor can be offered as another example of ecclesial flexibility pertaining to the textus receptus.

The unrestrained use of other text-witnesses by church fathers supports the textual flexibility of the Eastern Orthodox Church. This use appears as early as Origen and his desire to revise the Septuagint by comparing it with the Hebrew text and utilizing the aid of other Greek recensions is a reminder that the LXX is only a translation depending on Hebrew text.

Knowledge of the Hebrew language, as scanty as the Eastern evidence may be, proves textual elasticity on the part of the biblical interpreters. In addition to Origen, Theodoret of Cyrus, Procopius of Gaza, and Photius provide an illustration of this learning preoccupation. Under this rubric, one may also mention the pertinent observations made by John Chrysostom and Photius on the "weaknesses" of the LXX due to the mere fact of being a translation. Chrysostom remarks that the "obscurities" of the Old Testament are the consequence of a deficient rendition of Hebrew idioms into Greek. These observations reveal a benevolent attitude of the Eastern church writers toward the Hebrew text.

The same blend of strictness and flexibility can be detected in the Eastern Orthodox stance on Old Testament canon. On the one hand, the Eastern Orthodox Church has always maintained a strict view of the thirty-nine books of the Jewish Bible by considering them "canonical" (normative) in matters of faith and morals. On the other hand, the Orthodox Church has crafted various opinions and terms for the so-called Septuagint additions—writings found only in the Septuagint manuscripts. From Athanasius's nomenclature ("canonical" versus "noncanonical"—anaginōskomena or "readable") to the seventeenth century councils and "confessions," the "additions" were regarded as noncanonical and/or good and useful for the spiritual growth of the faithful. The Eastern Orthodox flexible position ranges wide from Jewish-like lists excluding the anaginōskomena altogether (e.g., Amphilochius, Cyril Loukaris) to more embracing statements, calling them "canonical" (Confession of Dositheos and the Council of Jerusalem, 1672).

The Eastern Orthodox view of anaginōskomena books is quite different from Roman Catholic and Protestant views. The flexibility rests in the fact that the Eastern Orthodox never went so far as to officially include these books within the Old Testament canon for the sole reason that these were used in the liturgy, as occurred in the Roman Catholic Church following the Council of Trent. Moreover, the strictness of the Eastern Orthodox position stands in variance with the Reformers' point of view, labeling the anaginōskomena as apokrypha. Though remaining strict on the number of the books found in the Jewish Bible, this did not preclude the Eastern Orthodox Church from maintaining the Septuagint additions within their Bible editions. The presence of tension between a narrow (as in the case of the Reformers) and a broader canon (of the Roman Catholic Church) has been always the hallmark of the Eastern Orthodox Church. Interestingly and in spite of its high popularity, the use of the Septuagint in the Eastern Orthodox Church did not influence the ecclesiastical authorities to take a final step of adopting the Septuagint as official text and canon. The Eastern Church has always distinguished between text and canon. For this reason, there exists an interesting situation: frequently the text followed is Septuagint, while the biblical canon reflects the Jewish Bible canon with a notable consideration and use of the Septuagint additions (which have never been officially coined "canonical") in liturgical and pastoral settings.

Integrative and Holistic

Another hallmark of Eastern Orthodox reception and interpretation of the Old Testament is an integrative function and integrated or holistic use of the sacred text. By its vibrant ubiquitous presence, Scripture unifies all aspects of church life. The integrative function of Scripture springs from its centrality within the Tradition. In the Eastern Orthodox Church, Scripture does not occupy a mere compartment of church life, but lies at the very center of the unfolding life of a living Tradition. Nonetheless, this centrality does not imply Scripture is isolated at the center of Tradition.

On the contrary, Scripture is central primarily because it is present in the smallest, most remote parts of Tradition. In other words, Tradition is infused with Scripture and this precise situation grants Scripture centrality. Paradoxically, as important as Tradition might be in Eastern Orthodox modes of theological discourse, it is the centrality and ubiquity of Scripture that strengthens and unifies Tradition.

In the East, Scripture has no restricted place or use. Scripture is infused throughout—in the liturgy, iconography, patristic writings, homilies, synaxaria, and conciliar statements. The use of Scripture is not restricted to any educational level of audience. Neither does Scripture become an elitist experiment or an object of study in the hands of some illuminati—older or more recent. The gradual dissociative use of Scripture attested in the West along with the natural consequence—crafting new methodologies to cope with a compartmentalized view of religious life or life in general—led to an increasing number of biblical departments leaving the Church with a more reduced arsenal of ways and uses of Scripture in dialogue with her own faithful.

The Eastern Orthodox stance on Scripture is quite intricate. On the one hand, Scripture is central and preeminent; the untamed and untamable book; the pulsating heart feeding the mystical body of the Church. On the other hand, Scripture is always viewed within the Tradition. The latter represents the interpretative context of the former. Since its very appropriation, Scripture was interpreted within the Church, by the Church, and for the Church growth. Thus—though certainly central and preeminent—Scripture is symbiotically related to Tradition. It is central to and part of and found everywhere within Tradition.

Scripture's simultaneous centrality and ubiquity within and toward unifying the Tradition explains the inherent integrative function and integrated or holistic use. The Eastern Orthodox Church views her life as a whole. Consequently, the individual or compartmentalized use of Scripture in the West (e.g., in catechetical, liturgical, academic settings, to mention a few) contrasts sharply with the integrated or holistic use of Scripture in the East, where the Church has remained for centuries the efficient "Bible School."

Common assumption among outsiders is that the Eastern Orthodox Church reduces Scripture to the liturgical use, yielding biblical illiteracy among the Orthodox, a claim that parentheticallyis not entirely far from the truth, but for a host of different reasons. However, at a closer examination this assumption is faulty. First, the Eastern Orthodox liturgy is a rich construal that cannot be confined to liturgical terms and formulae. Liturgy also includes sacred images through iconography and through symbolical acts, involving both intellect and physical senses. Second, the use of Scripture in the Eastern Orthodox Church goes beyond the liturgical framework by addressing a variety of spiritual and intellectual inquiries. Scripture is used in various forms, such as, the liturgy, sacraments, sermons, catecheses and pastoral guidance, inside and outside of the church.

The holistic use of Scripture is quite resilient. It has outlived the Eastern importation of the Western seminaries by Peter the Great in the early 1700s and has continued up to the present time. Within American seminaries of the Eastern Orthodox Church, such as Holy Cross, St. Vladimir's, and St. Tikhon's, the teaching of Scripture—well positioned within the theological curriculum—is directly related to the liturgical and pastoral life of the Church in its complexity.

Although the Eastern Orthodox Church cannot compliment herself for a plethora of scholarly productions and academic achievements in the modern study of the Old Testament, a quite integrated use of Scripture is part of her ethos. Entering an Orthodox church in celebration is as if one entered the Holy Land of the prophets, apostles, Christ and his Mother, expanding to the *oikoumenē* "inhabited world" with their ascetics, martyrs, and saints. And Scripture has retained a central place within a rich and ongoing Tradition understood above all as the multifaceted life of the Church.

Discursive and Intuitive

The major Eastern Orthodox modes of interpretation may be classified under two headings: discursive and intuitive. The balance of tension and dynamics of these two complementary modes represent another hallmark of Eastern Orthodox tradition in addressing the Old Testament. On the one hand, the discursive mode reflected in the commentaries and theological works of the church fathers tends to be more informative and intellectual, representing a "conventional theology." On the other hand, the intuitive modes of interpretation, more poetic in content and tone of the aural (liturgy) and the visual (iconography) point to a "folk theology." The encounter of these two modes brings forth creativity and ingenuity at the level of scriptural interpretation. A more settled and well-defined patristic interpretation finds its counterpart in an intuitive and novel interpretation promoted by hymns and icons. Without contradiction, a rather tensed encounter exists between the two modes: a sort of duet arising from the same chorus—that is, the polyphonic guild of church interpreters.

Many authors dealing with ancient Christian interpretation have emphasized patristic exegesis. Still, ancient Christian interpretation—particularly, the Eastern Orthodox construal—has much to offer as intuitive modes of scriptural explication. The aural and visual interpretations often utilize themes and motifs other than those found in patristic commentaries. The roots of these outside influences can reach as far as the Pseudepigrapha or ancient Jewish writings. The outer boundaries of the intuitive modes are quite elastic, allowing such nonorthodox soundings to pervade the ecclesial space. To the intuitive flexibility of hymnographers and iconographers, the discursive mode reacts as a buffer against any excesses which might jeopardize the harmony of the parts within the unfolding Tradition. The exuberant ingenuity of the artists is mitigated by the halcyon heedfulness of the church fathers. The duet between discursive and intuitive modes of interpretation has protected the Eastern Orthodox tradition from yielding to either rationalism or emotionalism. The interplay of "conventional" and "folk" theologies, or the interaction between stabilizing and destabilizing tendencies at the hermeneutical level, sustains a continuous and dynamic tension promoting both originality and consistency.

Throughout this entire work, I have been attempting to discredit a well-established cliché, the common opinion spread at a grass-roots level even within educated Orthodox theological circles that the patristic exegesis is by far the most complete and satisfying expression of scriptural interpretation. Within such a construal, there is no room for modern interpreters to bring new insights alongside church fathers' ruminations over Scripture. This opinion is as counterproductive as the exaggerated optimism of some biblical scholars in the benefits of historical criticism. Metaphorically, patristic exegesis—far from offering a complete hermeneutic script—covers only a segment of the hermeneutic alphabet leaving the rest of this limitless alphabet to be deciphered by new cohorts of readers and interpreters of the Holy Writ.

Another cliché debunked in my book is the so-called mind of the fathers. Against an old assumption of a unified system of interpretation produced by church fathers, the textual evidence, partly discussed in this work, indicates to the contrary that there are many "minds of the fathers"—the polyphony of a diversified patristic chorus. By definition, even the discursive mode tends to be more harmonized, reflecting a conventional theology closer in reality than most could imagine to the elasticity of the intuitive modes. Thus, the delineation between discursive and intuitive is not as rigid as previously thought and suggested.

At this juncture, allow me to draw attention to the significance of preaching. Preaching is the hermeneutical locus where discursive and intuitive modes can meet in a creative dialogue. In preaching, the scholastic barrier between intuitive and discursive vanishes due to the prerequisite of assiduous preparation required to preach—a sort of preliminary theological discourse, coupled with a full personal and intuitive involvement within church life. In this area, Eastern Orthodoxy offers a significant contribution by blending the patristic, liturgical, and iconographic means of interpretation in a pastoral approach to Scripture.

Formative and Informative

The synergy between formative and informative as main goals of the use of Scripture is one of the most important hallmarks of Eastern Orthodox tradition. In the Eastern Orthodox Church, Scripture has been always used both for formative and informative purposes, to teach and correct the faithful—an apostolic desideratum (2 Tim 3:16–17). Nevertheless, the emphasis in this juxtaposition lies on the formative purpose. Information finds its foremost raison d'être in formation that—not only from a Christian point of view—should be the ultimate goal of any educational system. For patristic writers and their ancient role models, the goal of teaching using Scripture was twofold: to persuade and to instruct. The formative and informative aspects were present side-by-side. This quality remains the understanding and practice of the Eastern Orthodox Church from early times to the present.

The juxtaposition between formative and informative rests in harmony with other Eastern Orthodox hallmarks discussed above. For instance, the strictness and flexibility detected at the level of Old Testament canon in Eastern Orthodox tradition matches formative and informative functions of Scripture. The strict number of canonical books (39) reveals the informative function of the Old Testament—a storehouse of religious ideas and moral instructions. The liturgical use and flexible number of the anaginōskomena points to a formative function of Scripture—a means of shaping and modeling characters.

Yet the informative and formative functions of the Scripture become more evident on close analysis of the Eastern Orthodox liturgy. One may compare the Church to a school and the liturgy to a curriculum, with Old Testament classes taught in two intuitive modes: the aural and the visual.

Eastern Orthodox worship has a twofold goal: Eucharistic (mnemonic) to commemorate the life and salvific work of Christ; and, sanctifying or formative—to shape the lives of the faithful. While attending church services, the faithful may be recalling accounts of past acts accomplished by Christ and his Old Testament "types." But they are also introduced to Church as to a laboratory where the formative power of Scripture is tested, implemented, and rehearsed again and again in a personal, covenantal relationship between the faithful and their exalted Lord. This formative function defines the substance and the orientation of the worship.

In addition to their interpretive role, the aural and visual modes have a formative value, shaping the life of the faithful in the image and likeness of Christ. In the interpretation of the hymnographers and iconographers, Scripture becomes an efficient means of transformation.

Intuitive modes addressing the intellect and senses of one worshipping have been developed to facilitate the formative goal of worship. The symbiotic relationship between these intuitive modes of liturgical expression and scriptural interpretation contributes to the holistic reception and use of Scripture in Eastern Orthodox tradition. Within the Church and through aural and visual interpretations, the worshiper comes to encounter the transformative Word of God. The experience is both holistic by involving the entire person and formative via inquiry and decision-making.

Scripture is not simply to be memorized. Scripture is rather to be performed, thus sustaining interpersonal communication. Through aural and visual renditions, Scripture becomes personalized and internalized to a paramount degree. During the aural and visual performances of Scripture, the worshippers become part of the sacred history of ancient Israel, identifying themselves with the children of Abraham, travelling with a thirsty people through the wilderness or encountering Moses as he climbed Mount Sinai to receive the Law of God. This liturgical "incorporation" of the faithful into the narrative of the history of Israel brings a sense of urgency and collective responsibility to the faithful to live their lives at the level of their high calling.

At the end of these concluding observations on the hallmarks of the Eastern Orthodox tradition regarding Old Testament interpretation,

I would like to reiterate that I offer my work as an invitation to future Orthodox biblical scholars, encouraging others to identify further distinct characteristics of this rich tradition. It remains my hope that we be able to determine how this ongoing tradition, replete with church fathers, hymnography and holy icons, might enter the dialogue with post-Enlightenment approaches to the Scripture, overcoming the "hermeneutic of suspicion" that still overshadows the current conversation in biblical studies.

Notes

CHAPTER I. ONE BIBLE, TWO COVENANTS

1. For a detailed interpretation of Sinai icon of Christ, see Maximos of Simono-petra, *Art of Seeing*, chapter 1.
2. *ANF* 1:417.
3. "Johannine Christianity," 137.
4. Cf. Matt 17:2: "His face shone like the sun"; Mark 9:2 is silent on the appearance of Jesus's face.
5. For Levenson, *Hebrew Bible*, 28, both Judaism and Christianity are book reli-gions, "These religions," notices Levenson, "presuppose the coherence and self-referentiality of their foundational book." See the critique of Levenson's view by John C. Poirier, "Judaism," 531.
6. Klijn, "Baruch," 651. *Syriac Apocalypse of Baruch* (known as *2 Baruch*) composed around 100 C.E. in Palestine insists on the Torah (Law) as the only effective me-diator between God and his people.
7. Florovsky, *Bible, Church, Tradition*, 36, summarizes the unity between person and book in this way, "The Bible is closed just because the Word of God has been incarnate. Our ultimate term of reference is now not a book, but a living person. Yet the Bible still holds its authority—not only as a record of the past, but also as a prophetical book, full of hints, pointing to the future, to the very end."
8. Commenting on Revelation, Victorinus (d. ca. 303 C.E.) identifies the sealed book in the hand of Christ with the Old Testament which points to Jesus as eschato-logical judge: "'And I saw in the right hand of him that sat upon the throne, a book written within and without, sealed with seven seals.' This book signifies the Old Testament, which has been given into the hands of our Lord Jesus Christ, who received from the Father judgment" (*Commentary on the Apocalypse of the Blessed John. On the Fifth Chapter* [*ANF* 7: 349]).
9. *Sinai and Zion*, 216–17.

10. See Van Buren, *According to the Scriptures.*

11. *ANF* 1:414.

12. Holmes, *Apostolic Fathers,* 75. *Clement 1* (or *The Letter of the Romans to the Corinthians*) is perhaps the earliest extant Christian document outside the New Testament.

13. *ANF* 3:484.

14. The *Didache* (*Doctrine of the Twelve Apostles*), ca. 80–90 C.E., could be taken as a model of the gospel in its initial, oral form, the apostolic kērygma. The quotations in the *Didache* are too vague to be bridged to specific New Testament *loci*; this is an indication of oral kērygma prior to writing of the Gospels; see Henderson, "Didache and Orality," 283–306.

15. *ANF* 1:414.

16. Ibid., 1:428.

17. Victorinus, *Commentary on the Apocalypse of the Blessed John. On the Fourth Chapter* (*ANF* 7:347).

18. *ANF* 8:416.

19. Ibid., 8:764.

20. Eusebius, *Ecclesiastical History* 4.26.12 (*NPNF²* 1:206).

21. PG 9:1160A.

22. *Against Marcion* 3.14; 4.1.2; cf. *De Pudicitia* 12. Von Compenhausen, *The Formation of Christian Bible,* 276, notices that Tertullian who "attests the early spread of the loan-rendering 'vetus et novum testamentum,' himself uses it only infrequently, and prefers to speak of the 'vetus et novum instrumentum.'"

23. "Prelude," 14.

24. This common consciousness of the early Church in appropriating the Jewish Scriptures is evidenced in another process which goes hand in hand with the appropriation, namely, the reconfiguration of the ancient Scriptures seen in the contents and sequence of the Old Testament as part of the whole biblical canon of the Christian Bible. On reconfiguration of the Jewish Scriptures, see chapter 3.

25. *ANF* 4:588.

26. Hebrews 8 represents the longest Old Testament citation (i.e., Jer 31:31–34) in the New Testament. For general treatments of this topic, see Moyise, *Old Testament in the New;* Porter, *Hearing the Old Testament.*

27. Holmes, *Apostolic Fathers,* 181. In another passage, same Ignatius juxtaposes the Prophets and Gospels; yet the gospel has its preeminence in the fact that it proclaims clearly the passion and resurrection. "Do pay attention, however, to the prophets and especially to the gospel, in which the Passion has been made clear to us and the resurrection has been accomplished" (*Letter to Smyrnaeans* 7.2; Holmes, *Apostolic Fathers,* 189).

28. *Biblical Exegesis,* 16.

29. According to Pelikan, *Christian Tradition,* 1:14, the scriptural appropriation has been further facilitated by "the Christian adoption of Abraham as 'father of the

faithful' [Rom 4:11] and the Christian identification of the church, the city of God with the heritage of Abel [Augustine, Civ. 15.1]."

30. Jewett, Kotansky, and Epp, *Romans*, 563.

31. *ANF* 4:275.

32. *NPNF*¹ 10:436.

33. Pelikan, *Christian Tradition*, 1:34.

34. Tertullian, *Apology* 37 (*ANF* 3:45).

35. *ANF* 1:173.

36. Ibid., 4:576.

37. Williams, *Panarion*, 273.

38. *ANF* 3:257.

39. *Against the Donatist Schism* 4.5; see Edwards, *Optatus*, 88. Even though, almost unknown to the modern readers, Optatus was held in high repute by Augustine.

40. *ANF* 3:653.

41. Ibid., 3:310.

42. Pelikan, *Christian Tradition*, 1:75.

43. *ANF* 3:319.

44. *Christian Tradition*, 1:72.

45. *ANF* 3:285.

46. Ibid., 3:281.

47. Ibid., 3:324.

48. Here is a succinct list of those who wrote against Marcion's doctrine: Justin Martyr (*First Apology* and a lost work, *Syntagma pros Markiona*, from where a short passage is cited by Irenaeus [*Against Heresies*, 4.6.2]), Irenaeus (*Against Heresies*, especially books 3 and 4), Rhodon (a lost work, *Against Marcion*, cf. Eusebius, *Ecclesiastical History* 5.13), Tertullian (*Against Marcion* in five books, and elsewhere in his vast work, *The Prescription Against Heretics, On Christ's Incarnation, On Bodily Resurrection*, and *On the Soul*), Pseudo-Tertullian (a poem against Marcion, and a treatise against all heresies), Adamantius (*On the True Faith in God*), Hippolytus of Rome (*Refutation of All Heresies*, books 7 and 10), Epiphanius (*Panarion*, especially chapters 42–44), Ephrem (references to Marcion in *Commentary on the Diatessaron, Metrical Sermons*), and Eznic (*Refutation of the Sects*, book 4).

49. *Christian Tradition*, 1:80.

50. Clabeaux, "Marcion," 4:515, points to the effectiveness of Marcionite Church, which between 160–170 c.e. outnumbered the mainstream Church. Tertullian's declaration (*Against Marcion* 5.20) that "today" (his time) there were more those who accepted the Old Testament than those who rejected it shows that at an earlier time the number of the Marcionites was quite high; see Blackman, *Marcion and His Influence*.

51. *ANF* 1:352.

52. On Marcion's canon, see Gamble, "Marcion and the 'Canon'," 195–213.

53. Tertullian gives this piece of information on Marcion's desire to repent: "After-wards, it is true, Marcion professed repentance, and agreed to the conditions granted to him—that he should receive reconciliation if he restored to the church all the others whom he had been training for perdition: he was pre-vented, however, by death" (*On the Prescription of the Heretics* 30 [ANF 3:257]).

54. ANF 3:654.

55. "Marcion," 4:516.

56. Heine, *Reading the Old Testament*, 26–27.

57. Pelikan, *Christian Tradition*, 1:83.

58. ANF 1:346.

59. On the topic of Gnosticism and the Old Testament, see Painchaud, "Use of Scripture," 129–46; Wilson, "The Gnostics and the Old Testament," 164–68; Wintermute, "Gnostic Exegesis," 241–70.

60. See Attridge, "Gospel of Truth," 239–55; Jacqueline Williams, *Biblical Interpre-tation*.

61. See Frank Williams, *Panarion*, 198–204.

62. Thomassen, *Spiritual Seed*, 119.

63. Frank Williams, *Panarion*, 201–202.

64. The Manichean "scriptural" canon consisted of seven works written by him: (1) *The Living Gospel*, (2) *The Treasure of Life*, (3) *The Pragmateia*, (4) *The Book of Mysteries*, (5) *The Book of the Giants*, (6) *The Letters*, and (7) *The Psalms and Prayers*. Only fragments of these works outlived the test of time, being pre-served in the writings of Christian heresiologists and pagan historians. The writings of Augustine of Hippo (354–430 C.E.), a former Manichaean, repre-sent the most important source of evidence regarding Mani's doctrine.

65. Faustus of Milevis, a few years older than Augustine, left his wife and children behind to become a Manichean bishop, about 382 C.E. Faustus had a great in-fluence on Augustine. In 385 C.E., Faustus is exiled on an island due to his Manichean beliefs. Here he writes the treatises that will trigger Augustine to come up with his *Reply to Faustus the Manichean*. On Faustus's life and work, see Monceaux, *Le manichéen Faustus de Milève*.

66. NPNF¹ 4:212.

67. Ibid., 4:273–312.

68. Ibid., 4:274.

69. The Greek verb *ioudaïzō*, "to become a Jew, to Judaize," appears two times in the entire Christian Bible: once in Esth 8:17 (translating Heb. *mityahădîm*), with reference to those Gentiles in Persia who accepted circumcision and con-verted to Judaism to avoid the harsh measures stipulated in Esther's decree against all the former enemies of the Jews (Esth 8:13); and once in Gal 2:14, where it means "to live like Jews."

70. Jerome (*Letter* 112) has harsh words on the Jewish Christians: "But while they desire to be both Jews and Christians, they are neither the one nor the other";

see Boyarin, "Rethinking Jewish Christianity," 25, and note 75, for translation and discussion of this passage.

71. "Jewish Christianity," 89.

72. James, the spiritual father of the Jewish Christians, calls Torah "the perfect Law of liberty" (Jas 1:25). Christ is mentioned only twice tangentially (1:1; 2:1).

73. "Jewish Christianity," 94.

74. On Peshitta, see chapter 2.

75. *ANF* 1:218.

76. On patristic evidence of Jewish Christianity, see Klijn and Reinink, *Patristic Evidence.*

77. *ANF* 1:352.

78. Cf. Heb *'ebyōnîm*, meaning "needy, poor ones." Tantlevskij, "Ebionites," 225, suggests that the name may have been adopted by the Ebionites from the Beatitudes (i.e., "Blessed are the poor in spirit" [Matt 5:3; cf. Luke 6:20]), thus reflecting their low social status and spiritual humility (cf. Jas 2:1–7).

79. The Babylonian Talmud (*Shabbat* 116a) mentions the "house of the Ebionites" and the "house of the Nazarenes."

80. See Carleton, "Jewish Christianity," 755.

81. Pseudo-Clementine writings, though attributed to Clement (ca. 95 C.E.), originated and developed in Jewish Christian circles around third and fourth centuries.

82. *ANF* 8:87–88.

83. This gospel was known to Hegesippus (Eusebius, *Ecclesiastical History* 4.22.8) and Origen (Jerome, *Illustrious Men* 2). At a careful analysis of the quotations of this gospel in Epiphanius's *Panarion*, one may conclude that the *Gospel According to the Hebrews* is rather the product of a compilation between the three synoptic Gospels.

84. Mourant and Collinge, *Saint Augustine*, 12–13.

85. The word "supersessionism," derives from English "supersede," first noted in 1642 with the meaning "to replace." Previously, the same verb was used in Scottish legal English with the meaning "to restrain." Noteworthily, the term "supersessionism" was not used by the Latin church fathers to describe their views on the relationship between the two testaments or faiths; it was rather coined in modern times with regard to their views. The term "supersession" appears in the title of chapter three of Thelwall's translation of Tertullian's *Adversus Iudaeos* (ca. 198–208 C.E.), published in 1870.

86. On this topic, see Feinberg, *Continuity and Discontinuity.*

87. Note Florovsky's view on Scripture: "The Bible is *history,* not a system of belief, and should not be used as a *summa theologiae.* At the same time, it is not history of human belief, but the history of the divine revelation" (*Bible, Church, Tradition,* 29).

88. According to Soulen, *God of Israel,* 181 n. 6, "Structural supersessionism refers to the narrative logic of the standard model whereby it renders the Hebrew

Scriptures largely indecisive for shaping Christian convictions about how God's works as Consummator and as Redeemer engage humankind in universal and enduring ways."

89. *ANF* 4:111.

90. Ruether, *Faith and Fratricide*, detects a Patristic tendency to apply the Old Testament promises to the Church, and the curses to the Jews.

91. Phayer, *Catholic Church and the Holocaust*, 209.

92. *Christian Tradition*, 1:2.

93. Levenson, *Sinai and Zion*, 4; see Poirier, "Judaism," 525–36.

94. "Qumran and Supersessionism," 134.

95. *ANF* 3:431.

96. Hagner, *Matthew 1–13*, 105.

97. Simonetti, *Matthew 1–13*, 96.

98. Jon D. Levenson, personal communication, March 2013.

99. The same verb *pauō*, "to bring to an end, annul," connoting the same idea appears in Chrysostom's commentary on Isaiah. Trakatellis, "Theodoret's Commentary on Isaiah," 330, notices: "Chrysostom reads Isa. 6:4 as a prophecy announcing the end of the Temple and of the Old Testament: This was a sign of the desolation and of the destruction of the Temple; the Temple having been destroyed, all other things were destroyed too. The New Testament put an end [*epausen*] to the Old."

100. *ANF* 1:200.

101. Attridge, *Hebrews*, 225.

102. That the activity of this pedagogue was temporary can be seen from Jerome's explanation: "A custodian is given to infants to rein in an age full of passion and to restrain hearts prone to vice until tender infancy is refined by growth. . . . Yet the teacher is not a father, nor does the one being instructed look for the custodian's inheritance. The custodian guards another person's son and will depart from him when the lawful time of inheritance arrives" (*Epistle to the Galatians* 2.3.24; Edwards, *Galatians*, 49).

103. Betz, *Galatians*, 178.

104. Edwards, *Galatians*, 50.

105. Ibid., 91.

106. Ibid., 50.

107. *ANF* 6:216.

108. Jewett, *Romans*, 563.

109. Ibid., 574–77. See also Levenson, *Inheriting Abraham*, 28, 159–82.

110. Ibid., 563.

111. Bray, *Romans*, 246. On the same vein of continuity between covenants, Pelagius emphasizes the idea that the Israelites "had the old Law and the promise of the new Law" (*Commentary on Romans*).

112. Bray, *Romans*, 300.

113. Rogerson, "History of Interpretation," 427.
114. "Jewish Biblical Interpretation," 183.
115. See, for instance, Chrysostom's *Eight Homilies Against the Jews.*
116. Levering, *Jewish-Christian Dialogue,* 25.
117. Stendahl, "Qumran and Supersessionism," 136.
118. *Death and Resurrection,* 232. In his recent book, *Inheriting Abraham,* Levenson adds Islam to the mix.
119. St. Ephrem the Syrian, *Selected Prose Works,* 315.
120. "Can Roman Catholicism Validate Jewish Biblical Interpretation?" 170–85.
121. "Jewish Biblical Interpretation," 173.
122. Ibid., 184.
123. *New Testament: An Orthodox Perspective,* 31–32.
124. *Bible, Church, Tradition,* 19.
125. *ANF* 3:361.
126. "Qumran and Supersessionism," 135.
127. *NPNF*² 7:45.
128. Ibid., 10:100.
129. Ibid., 7:115.
130. Ibid., 9:89.
131. *PG* 50:796.
132. *NPNF*² 6:22. On the identity of God of the Old Testament, see Hofer, "Who is God in the Old Testament?" 439–58.
133. Holmes, *Apostolic Fathers,* 213.
134. Ibid., 289.
135. *NPNF*¹ 4:161.
136. Ibid., 4:227.
137. Charlesworth, "What Has the Old Testament to Do with the New?" 42–43.
138. The Commission referred to is the Pontifical Biblical Commission (PBC) and its document "The Interpretation of the Bible in the Church," published in 1994.
139. "Interpreting the Bible," 44.
140. *Biblical Theology,* 65.
141. *NPNF*² 3:226.
142. Holmes, *Apostolic Fathers,* 179.
143. *ANF* 4:252.
144. Ibid., 6:346.
145. *NPNF*¹ 9:204.
146. Ibid., 13:283.
147. Ibid., 1:419.
148. *ANF* 4:280.
149. See Pentiuc, *Long-Suffering Love,* 265–68.
150. *NPNF*¹ 3:287.

151. Ibid., 5:406.

152. *NPNF²* 4:224.

153. I hope that the recent publication of the first *Jewish Annotated New Testament*, edited by Amy-Jill Levine and Marc Z. Brettler (Oxford University Press, 2011), will stimulate Orthodox theologians and biblical scholars to start reading the Old Testament for its merit as Jewish Bible and not exclusively as proof-text for Christology. Such mutual readings in the other's scriptural corpus propelled by a genuine desire to understand each other's traditions will contribute to the betterment of Jewish-Christian relations.

CHAPTER 2. TEXT

1. The Old Slavonic Bible by Cyril and Methodius of 885 was based on Septuagint, but later Old Slavonic and Russian translations used also Hebrew and Latin texts. Thus, *Gennady Bible* of 1499 employed the Vulgate as translation basis for some books. The Old Testament in the *Russian Synodal Bible* by Filaret of Moscow of 1876 relies on the MT; see Negrov, *Biblical Interpretation*, 42–84.

2. On biblical inspiration from an Eastern Orthodox perspective, see Louth, "Inspiration," 29–44.

3. *Textual Criticism*, 29–34.

4. Ibid., 32–33.

5. "Pluriformity and Uniformity," 151–69.

6. The terms Masorete, Masoretic derive from Hebrew *masorah* or *masoret,* "tradition," hence the meaning "traditional, traditionalist."

7. *Textual Criticism*, 145–48; Würthwein, *Text*, 24.

8. On the Masoretic apparatus, see Barthélemy, *Critique textuelle*, 1:lxix–xcvii.

9. Tov, *Textual Criticism*, 58 n. 38.

10. The complete Masorah was published by Ginsburg, *Massorah.*

11. Traces of a similar division can be found as early as the Q scrolls; see Wurthwein, *Text*, 20 and n. 28.

12. On these liturgical divisions, see Ginsburg, *Introduction*, 32–65.

13. The text of first printed edition of the Hebrew Bible, Soncino 1488, was not yet divided into chapters. This will occur for the first time in the Rabbinic Bible published by Daniel Bomberg in Venice, in 1517.

14. "Traduire la Septante," 33–42. One may also note at this juncture that Marguerite Harl initiated and supported the French translation-interpretation project *La Bible grecque d'Alexandrie.*

15. See chapter 3.

16. Tov, *Textual Criticism*, 135; Jobes and Silva, *Invitation to the Septuagint*, 30–32.

17. For the Greek text of the *Letter of Aristeas*, see Swete, *Old Testament in Greek*, 533–606. An English translation may be found in Shutt, "Letter of Aristeas," 2:7–34. For a well-balanced analysis of the letter, see, Rajak, *Translation and Survival*, 24–63.

18. Würthwein, *Text*, 52–53.

19. Jobes and Silva. *Invitation to the Septuagint*, 35.
20. See Greenspoon, "Use and Abuse of the Term 'LXX'," 21–29.
21. According to the prologue of Wisdom of Jesus ben Sirach (Sirach), dated to 132–116 B.C.E., there was at that time a Greek translation "of the Law, the Prophets, and the rest of the books." Written in Hebrew around 180 B.C.E., the Book of Sirach was translated by his grandson into Greek and furnished with a prologue. Despite this information, the common assumption among scholars today is that the most of the Writings were translated into Greek probably during first century B.C.E.
22. Würthwein, *Text*, 53.
23. The literary sources, Jewish and Christians, regarding the *Letter of Aristeas* were gathered by Wendland, *Aristae ad Philocratem Epistula*.
24. Yonge, *Philo*, 494.
25. On inspiration of the Septuagint in patristic literature, see Benoit, "L'inspiration des Septante," 1:169–87.
26. "Septuagint," 18 and n. 95.
27. The evidence for pre-Christian Greco-Roman usage of the Septuagint is quite minimal. Some scholars suggest that pagan authors engaged with the text of the Old Testament as a result of Christian movement making inroads into paganism. This textual engagement of pagan authors may be placed under the heading of Late Antiquity "culture wars." See Cook, *Interpretation*, 1–54.
28. Hengel, *Septuagint*, 26–50.
29. "Septuagint," 20.
30. For such an interpretation regarding Matt 2:15 quoting Hos. 11:1, see Pentiuc, *Long-Suffering Love*, 260–61. Baumstark, "Zitate," 296–313, suggests that Hos. 11:1 in Matthew derives from a lost Tg. of the Prophets; for a different interpretation based on proto-Theodotion, see Menken, *Matthew's Bible*, 280–83.
31. For a detailed discussion on the use of the LXX and its revisions in the New Testament, see Tov, "Septuagint," 3–25.
32. Hengel, *Septuagint*, 39.
33. *Old Testament Homilies*, 3:30–31.
34. *NPNF²* 7:27.
35. *Biblia Sacra*, 3–4.
36. The Septuagint of Ps 87(88):11(10) reads, "Surely, you shall not work wonders for the dead? Or will physicians raise up, and they acknowledge you?" (NETS). One may wonder what have to do "physicians" with the netherworld. The parallel between "dead" (*nekrois*) and "physicians" (*iatroi*) in relation to the grave (v. 12[11]) seems odd. The second word "physicians" is apparently due to an erroneous etymology. The LXX translator of this Psalm related the Hebrew word *rəpā'îm* to the root *r-p-'*, "to heal," hence "physicians." However, given the context (grave, netherworld), the true derivation is from the root *r-p-h*, "to grow slak, to sink," the "sunk ones," namely the departed spirits or "shadows" of the netherworld.

37. *NPNF*[1] 6:4.

38. The first publication of the *Naḥal Ḥever* scroll by Barthélemy (*Devanciers*, 1963) has ever since revolutionized the field of textual criticism of the Hebrew Bible. Barthélemy's work is probably one of the clearest analyses of the transmission of the Hebrew Bible and its early Greek translations; see also Tov, Kraft, and Parsons, *Nahal Hever*.

39. Note that this group of papyri is of Christian origin and they are formatted after a codex pattern. Also *nomina sacra* (e.g., abbreviation KS, *Kyrios*, "Lord," for the *tetragrammaton*)—a distinguishing feature found in Christian Septuagint codices—are employed.

40. As, for instance, in the *Rylands Papyrus Greek 458* at Deut 26:17.

41. Either phonetically IAŌ, as in a Qumran fragment (Lev 2–4); or orthographically ΠΙΠΙ, imitating the four Hebrew consonants of YHWH; on the latter form and its misunderstanding by Greek readers, see Jerome, *Letter 25: Ad Marcellam* in Jellicoe, *Septuagint and Modern Study*, 272.

42. See Kahle, *The Cairo Geniza*.

43. Jellicoe, *Septuagint and Modern Study*, 271–72.

44. There have been preserved only nine fragments of Jewish biblical scrolls dated to second century B.C.E. to first century C.E., and coming from Egypt, Qumran, and Judaean desert, and fourteen Christian fragments dated to first century to third century C.E. and found in Egypt. The twofold cache from Egypt reflects the transition from scroll to codex and from synagogue to church with regards to the Septuagint textual transmission; see Hengel, *Septuagint*, 41.

45. "Bedeutung," 61.

46. Müller, *First Bible*, 118.

47. For a brief survey of these Greek translations, see Tov, *Textual Criticism*, 145–48; Würthwein, *Text*, 54–59.

48. Jobes and Silva, *Invitation to the Septuagint*, 38.

49. Tov, *Hebrew Bible*, 369.

50. Barthélemy, *Devanciers*, 81–88.

51. Tov, *Hebrew Bible*, 366 and n. 7.

52. It is known that the author of Hebrews relies extensively on the LXX while citing from the Old Testament. Nevertheless, Heb 11:33 quotes Dan 6:23 not from the LXX but rather from a recension very similar to the second century C.E. Theodotion. This quote and other places in the New Testament roster of Old Testament quotations postulate a proto-Theodotion recension that was in use during the first century C.E.; see Jobes and Silva, *Invitation to the Septuagint*, 42.

53. Tov, *Textual Criticism*, 145.

54. Hengel, *Septuagint*, 42–43 and n. 57.

55. In fact, the exceptions are two manuscripts, i.e., Ms. 88 (eleventh century) and Ms. 967 (a second-century ms. included in so called *Chester Beatty* collection); see Jobes and Silva, *Invitation to the Septuagint*, 41 and n. 30.

56. Friedmann (*Onkelos und Akylas*, 1896) was the first one to pose this identification.

57. See Barthélemy, *Devanciers*, 144; Grabbe, "Aquila's Translation," 527–36.

58. Tov, *Hebrew Bible*, 373.

59. SC 302:526.

60. See Parkes, *Conflict*, 392–93.

61. See Barthélemy, *Devanciers*, 144; "Qui est Symmaque?"451–65; Salvesen, *Symmachus in the Pentateuch*.

62. The oldest textual evidence regarding the three later translations is a sixth-century C.E. palimpsest found in 1897 in a Cairo *geniza* and containing two short fragments from 1–2 Kings according to Aquila version; see Kahle, *The Cairo Geniza*.

63. On these textual witnesses, see Marcos, *Septuagint in Context*, chapters 10–11.

64. *NPNF²* 3:373.

65. Tov, *Textual Criticism*, 147–48.

66. Young, *Biblical Exegesis*, 83.

67. *Septuagint*, 36.

68. *ANF* 4:386.

69. Ibid.

70. One of the surviving witnesses to the Syro-Hexapla is the ninth-century *Codex Ambrosianus Syrohexaplaris* in Milan. It comprises the Prophets and the Writings. This codex was photographed and published by Ceriani in *Monumenta Sacra et Profana 7*.

71. See Tov, "Lucian and Proto-Lucian," 101–113.

72. On the life and literary activity of Lucian of Antioch, see Metzger, "Lucianic Recension," 1–41.

73. Jobes and Silva, *Invitation to the Septuagint*, 52 and n. 21.

74. Würthwein, *Text*, 45.

75. According to Cross, *Library of Qumran*, 34, the Samaritan script developed from the paleo-Hebrew script of the Hasmonean period.

76. According to Tov, *Textual Criticism*, 98 n. 70, the best preserved pre-Sam. text is 4QpaleoExodm (Exod 6–37).

77. Data were collected and examined by Metal, *Samaritan Version*; see Tov, *Textual Criticism*, 84 n. 62.

78. Tov, *Textual Criticism*, 85–86.

79. Würthwein, *Text*, 78. The Sam. is also mentioned by Cyril of Alexandria, Eusebius, Jerome, Procopius of Gaza.

80. For more information on the Syriac textual witness, see Dirksen and Mulder, *Peshitta*.

81. In 1876, Antonio Maria Ceriani published a photolithographic edition of *Codex Ambrosianus*, i.e., *Translatio syra pescitto Veteris Testamenti*.

82. I.e., De Boer and Mulder, *Old Testament in Syriac*.

83. "*Vetus latina* de Jérémie," 51–82.

84. Jerome accomplished this Latin recension based on the OG between 383 and 390 C.E. Only the Psalter and Job survived.

85. *NPNF*² 6:153.

86. Ryan, "Place of the Septuagint in the Catholic Church," 16–17, notices that the recognition of the Vulgate as authentic did not entail the declaration of the other versions as inauthentic.

87. Lieu, *Christian Identity*, 27.

88. *Introduction*, 89.

89. Brock, "Translating the Old Testament," 90; "Phenomenon," 11–36.

90. On LXX-MT complementarity at the exegetical level, see Pentiuc's comments (*Jesus the Messiah*, 95–99) on Isa. 7:14.

91. *NPNF*¹ 2:385. Note Augustine's emphasis on prophecy as way of solving the textual difference between Hebrew and Greek scriptures: "But where the difference is not a mere copyist's error, and where the sense is agreeable to truth and illustrative of truth, we must believe that the divine Spirit prompted them to give a varying version, not in their function of translators, but in the liberty of prophesying. And therefore we find that the apostles justly sanction the Septuagint, by quoting it as well as the Hebrew when they adduce proofs from the Scriptures" (*City of God* 15.14 [*NPNF*¹ 2:295]).

92. *NPNF*² 6:112.

93. The *Pedalion* was published for the first time in Greece in 1800. The English version done by Denver Cummings was published by the Orthodox Christian Educational Society of Chicago in 1957, under the title *The Rudder*.

94. *Four Books on the LXX Interpretation*, Athens, 1844–49.

95. See Konstantinou, "Old Testament Canon," 53–54.

96. On the Pan-Orthodox Council, see Ware, "Toward the Great Council?" 162–68; Aghiorgoussis, "Towards the Great and Holy Council," 423–28; Damaskinos of Tranoupolis, "Towards the Great and Holy Council," 99–116.

97. The textual pluriformity, recognized and well implemented in Eastern Orthodox tradition, has its roots in Origen's ecclesiological principle outlined in the *Letter to Julius Affricanus* 8 (SC 302:533–34). According to Origen, the canonicity or authenticity of a particular biblical text relies primarily not on tradition but on God's "providence" (*pronoia*). If for instance, through God's providence, a community had access to the Word of God only through Septuagint, this version enjoys the status of authenticity; and the same with other versions (Peshitta, Vulgate, Coptic, Ethiopic) which through God's providence facilitated the access of various communities to the living Word of God, hence the authenticity and value for the entire Church; on Origen's ecclesiological principle and its impact on textual pluriformity, see Schenker, "Septuaginta und christliche Bibel," 459–64; Ryan, "Textual Pluriformity," 1–19.

98. For a complete list of biblical texts discovered at Qumran, see Glessmer, "Liste," 153–92.
99. Schenker, *Earliest Text*, vii.
100. Würthwein, *Text*, 53 and n. 7, 8.
101. "Large-Scale Differences," 139–44.
102. Ibid., 121–22.
103. *First Bible*, 99–104. Müller illustrates the textual fluidity during third-second century B.C.E. by resorting to Deut 32:8–9. In this passage, even the most passionate supporters of MT's preeminence among textual witnesses would accept the LXX reading as reflecting the earliest layer of the biblical wording. One may easily discern the LXX's universalist overtone (i.e., God "fixed the bounds of the peoples according to the number of the angels of God") versus the MT's particularistic outlook (i.e., God "fixed the bounds of the tribes according to the number of Israel's sons").
104. The rise of Jewish sectarianism is seemingly related to the rise of literacy and its democratization; see Lieu, *Christian Identity*, 36.
105. Brock, "Translating the Old Testament," 87.
106. My *Jesus the Messiah in the Hebrew Bible* is just an attempt to overcome the Eastern Orthodox oversight of the Hebrew text (pre- and MT), while also giving a hearing to patristic exegesis (both as methodology and selection of messianic texts) on the LXX, in order to redeem the Semitic undertones of the Christological interpretation of the Old Testament.
107. For a detailed survey of the use of Hebrew in the East, the reader is directed to De Lange, "Hebrew in Byzantium," 147–61; see also Oikonomos, "Hebrew Language," 29–47 and Elliott, "Hebrew Learning Among the Fathers," 2:841–72.
108. *ANF* 4:385.
109. *NPNF²* 6:22.
110. Ibid., 3:517.
111. "Theodoret's Commentary on Isaiah," 318.
112. *Handbook of Patristic Exegesis*, 195.
113. PG 87:1817–2718.
114. MT reads: "He was named 'wonderful counselor, mighty God, everlasting father, prince of peace.'"
115. I.e., Gk. transliteration of the Hebrew word *'ēl*, "God."
116. PG 87:2005B–C.
117. Ibid., 87:2008A.
118. Ibid., 56:178; see John Chrysostom, *Old Testament Homilies*, 29–30.
119. Ibid. 101:816. I thank Prof. Stamatia Dova of Hellenic College for her assistance with the rendition of this difficult text.
120. Ibid., 101:817–20.

CHAPTER 3. CANON

1. For general information on biblical, in particular Old Testament canon, the reader is directed to the excellent contributions found in McDonald and Sanders, *The Canon Debate.*

2. *ANF* 3:249.

3. *PG* 9:349A.

4. See Martens, *Origen and Scripture*, 130.

5. In early times there were various "charts" (handbooks), in Greek, *procheiroi kanones*, "handy guides." Eusebius composed a chart of gospel parallels. This chart known as "Eusebian sections and canons" bespeaks an increasing need for order and precision; see Dungan, *Constantine's Bible*, 30.

6. On the three-step making of the Jewish Bible, see the bibliography provided by Müller, *First Bible*; see also Sundberg, *Old Testament of the Early Church*; Ellis, *The Old Testament in Early Christianity.*

7. The Heb. word *tôrāh*, derives from the verbal root *y-r-h*, "to throw, shoot"; in Hiphil, "to teach," i.e., "to throw knowledge, wisdom"; hence the primary meaning of Torah is "instruction, teaching." The common designation "Law" comes from the Septuagint use of the Greek term *nomos*, "law" as a lexical match for Heb. *tôrāh*.

8. The *Laus partum* ("Praise of the Fathers") in Sir 44–49 represents the main textual evidence for the conclusion of this section (Prophets) by the second century B.C.E. Moreover, the Book of Daniel, written about mid second century B.C.E., was not apparently extant by 200 B.C.E.; otherwise, it would have been part of the second section, the Prophets. In fact, Daniel entered the last section of the Jewish Bible, the Writings, concluded by 100 C.E. The earliest evidence that the Book of Daniel as part of the Writings may be found in *b. Baba Bathra* 14b.

9. The completion of the third section, the Writings, is often placed in connection with the legendary Council of Jamnia. See Müller, *First Bible*, 25.

10. Yonge, *Philo*, 700.

11. Müller, *First Bible*, 29–30, argues that 4 Ezra accords to the seventy apocryphal writings the same inspiration as to the twenty-four "canonical" books.

12. Stone, *Fourth Ezra*, 437.

13. On the current discussion on this council, see Lewis, "Jamnia Revisited," 146–62.

14. See Schäfer, "Jabne," 54–64. On the differences between orthodox Christianity and rabbinic Judaism with regard to the notion of authority, see Boyarin, "Talmud and 'Fathers of the Church.'"

15. Prokurat, "Orthodox Interpretation of Scripture," 77, rightly noticed, "It is inappropriate to take late definitions of the scriptural canon (e.g., the Westminster Confession or the Council of Trent) and anachronistically retroject modern assumptions back onto any previous era, as with the 'Council' of Jamnia."

16. The expression "defile the hands" refers to the ritual of washing the hands after touching the scroll of a Scripture, and prior to performing a secular activity. Nevertheless, the meaning of such intricate expression is still debated. According to Lim, "Defilement of the Hands," 501–15, unlike other sacred objects, Holy Scriptures are not a source of holy contamination but rather they render those who touch them unclean. This idea is based on the assumption that no one is holier than the Holy Scriptures. Thus, even the holiest people are unclean by comparison with Holy Scriptures.

17. *First Bible*, 33.

18. On the formulae introducing citations in the New Testament, see Bratcher, *Old Testament Quotations* and Moyise, *Old Testament in the New.*

19. On the construal of the "Greek polis," see Morgen H. Hansen, *Polis.*

20. On corporate personality, see Robinson, *Corporate Personality* and Kaminsky, *Corporate Responsibility.*

21. The term "enculturation" related to the centrality of the text was borrowed from David M. Carr, *Writing on the Tablet.*

22. On Christian Church's struggle with pseudonymous and anonymous authorship in the scripture selection process, see Meade, *Pseudonymity and Canon.*

23. On the making of the Old Greek translation, see Chapter 2.

24. The Greek title "Pentateuch" for the Torah shows that the collection has been initially preserved in five distinct scrolls.

25. Evidence is provided by *Gemara* to b. Baba Bathra 14b, 15a.

26. Note though that in the fourth century c.e. Antioch there was a certain preoccupation with the number of canonical scriptures: "Is it not strange that those who sit by the market can tell the names, and families, and cities of charioteers, and dancers, and the kinds of power possessed by each, and can give exact account of the good or bad qualities of the very horses, but that those who come hither should know nothing of what is done here, but should be ignorant of the number even of the sacred Books?" (John Chrysostom, *Homily 32 on the Gospel of John* 3 [*NPNF*¹ 14:23]).

27. Dungan, *Constantine's Bible*, 78–85.

28. I would mention here one of the most recent and thorough treatments, McDonald and Sanders, *The Canon Debate.*

29. On the double canon hypothesis, see Sundberg, *Old Testament of the Early Church*, 3–4.

30. Similar to *tois exō* in Mark 4:11, designating Jesus's non-disciples; the term coheres with the later rabbinic language (*m. Sanh.* 10:1; *Num. Rab.* 14:4 on Num 7:48: h-ḥṣnym, "outsiders," indicating the Gentiles).

31. Yonge, *Philo*, 700.

32. *Against Apion* 1.38–42; see Whiston, *Josephus.*

33. This framework for divine inspiration from Moses to Ezra's time is paralleled by 4 Ezra 14:44–46 and *Baba Bathra* 14b–15a. Similarly, Tosefta's remark (*Yad.* 2.13,

ca. 250 C.E.) that "the book of Ben Sira and all other books written after the prophetic period do not defile the hands" (i.e., they are not canonical) reflects the rabbinic view of a closed canon with a well-defined number of books.

34. See *ANF* 1:278.

35. See *NPNF*² 1:206.

36. On the terminology of the two parts of the Christian Bible, see Chapter 1.

37. See *NPNF*² 1:272.

38. See Ibid., 4:551.

39. For a statistical study of patristic quotations of the anaginōskomena books, see Stuhlhofer, *Gebrauch*. The most quotations in church fathers are taken from the third section of the Jewish Bible (Kethubim). The quotations from the anaginōskomena run the lowest along with those from the canonical historical books; see Scanlin, "Old Testament Canon," 308.

40. Konstantinou, "Old Testament Canon," 89–107, mentions a similar discrepancy between practice and theory within the Judaism.

41. See *NPNF*² 4:26.

42. See Frank Williams, *Panarion*, 26.

43. See Bruce, *The Canon of Scripture*, 213.

44. Dean, *Weights and Measures*.

45. This is the Greek spelling of the Hebrew word ʾărôn, "chest, ark, coffin."

46. See *NPNF*² 14:158.

47. According to Prokurat, "Orthodox Interpretation of Scripture," 75, by canon 59, "the Church herself exercised authority to judge that which was to be read within her 'ecclesia.'"

48. Von Dobschütz, *Decretum Gelasianum* 5.

49. Clark, *History of the Councils*, 468.

50. *NPNF*¹ 2:760.

51. On Vulgate, see Chapter 2.

52. *NPNF*² 6:492.

53. Amphilochius's work *Iambics to Seleucus*, formerly attributed to Gregory Nazianzus, is found in PG 37:1590A (lines 194–98).

54. On the central position of Leviticus within the pentadic structure of the Torah, see Blenkinsopp, *Pentateuch*, 47.

55. PG 37:471–74.

56. *NPNF*² 9:752–53.

57. See Burke, "Deuterocanon as Scripture," 223–40.

58. Mowinckel, *Old Testament*, 112.

59. On the Tridentine Council, see Jedin, *Council of Trent*.

60. Even though the term "deuterocanonical" is employed by many Orthodox authors (e.g., Scanlin, Costantelos, Stylianopoulos) to define the additions to the Septuagint, I prefer the term "readable" (anaginōskomena) proposed by Athanasius because it points to the liturgical and catechetical functions of these books.

61. See Duncker, "Trent," 277–99.

62. As Ryan, "Textual Pluriformity," 1–19, rightly, notices, "a significant portion of the Old Testament has been transmitted in two or three different and irreducible versions." Ryan, a Dominican biblical scholar who has been working for years on various texts of the Old Testament, argues, based on church fathers and modern scholars such as Adrian Schenker and Maurice Gilbert, that the Catholic theological tradition is ideally situated to deal with the issue of textual pluriformity; see Schenker, "L'Ecriture sainte," 178–86; Gilbert, "Textes exclus," 51–70.

63. In January 1672 a synod was held at Jerusalem that ended with a confession signed by Dionysius, Patriarch of Constantinople. This confession, though shorter than Dositheos's Confession agrees with the latter in all theological points including the extension of the biblical canon.

64. *Acts and Decrees,* 155–56.

65. The Confession of Peter Mogila written in the form of a catechism in 1640 suffered substantial revisions up to its final form presented at the Synod of Jassy in 1643. It was sent out and received the approval of the four Eastern Orthodox Patriarchates. In 1672 it gained also the approval of the Synod of Jerusalem and thus it became the Creed of the Greek and Russian Churches and the basis for later Russian catechisms.

66. Metrophanes Kritopoulos was one of the students Patriarch Cyril Loukaris sent to Europe to be educated so that they may be able to counterattack the Jesuit proselytism.

67. "Old Testament Canon," 89–107.

68. *Byzantine Theology,* 7.

69. "Canon and Authority of Scripture," 260–61.

70. "Canon," 34.

71. The sequence and the names of those forty-nine books of the Eastern Orthodox scriptural corpus (i.e., "Sacred Scripture") are as follows: Genesis, Exodus, Leviticus, Numbers, Deuteronomy, Joshua, Judges, Ruth, 1–4 Kingdoms (= 1–2 Samuel and 1–2 Kings), 1–2 Paralipomena (= 1–2 Chronicles), 1 Esdras (anaginōskomenon), 2 Esdras and Nehemiah (both titles equate the canonical Ezra), Esther (along with the anaginōskomena additions), Judith (anaginōskomenon), Tobit (anaginōskomenon), 1–3 Maccabees (anaginōskomena), Psalms (in some editions along with Ps 151 and the 9 Odes and the Prayer of Manasse), Job, Proverbs, Ecclesiastes, Song of Songs, Wisdom of Solomon (anaginōskomenon), Wisdom of Siracides (= Sirach / Ecclesiasticus, anaginōskomenon), twelve Minor Prophets (beginning with Hosea and ending with Malachias), Isaiah, Jeremiah, Baruch (anaginōskomenon), Lamentations, Epistle of Jeremiah (anaginōskomenon), Ezekiel, Daniel (along with anaginōskomena additions, i.e., Susanna, the prayer of Azariah, and the Songs of the Three Youths, and the Story of Bel and Dragon). The Slavonic version contains also 2 Esdras (anaginōskomenon) perhaps under Roman-Catholic influence. Note that 4 Maccabees is found as an appendix in the Greek versions only.

72. *New Testament: An Orthodox Perspective*, 28.
73. Ibid., 25.
74. "Biblical Studies," 55.
75. "Old Testament Canon," 303.
76. Vassiliadis, "Orthodoxy and Ecumenism," 9.
77. "Canon and Authority of Scripture," 270.
78. Ibid., 262. Similarly, Constantelos, "Apocryphal / Deuterocanonical Books," xxix, notices: "It is perhaps this liturgical usage of the deuterocanonical books that has contributed to their canonical status in the Orthodox Church. The conscience and practice of the church in history counts more than theological opinion. But from as early as the fourth century the deuterocanonical books stand on a lower level than the rest of the Old Testament books."
79. "Old Testament Canon," 309–10.
80. "Holy Scriptures," 7–83; "Apocryphal / Deuterocanonical Books," xxviii.
81. Regarding the mention of Sirach in the Apostolic Canon 85 (pre-300 C.E. origin), Prokurat, "Orthodox Interpretation of Scripture," 73, remarks, "Besides these ['deuterocanonical books'] the Church recommends to teach the young people Ecclesiasticus (Wisdom of Sirach). With this admonition the Church recognizes the value of a certain book, although one not recommended for liturgical usage. Such a position is an important attitude to observe. A nonliturgical book has a marked, recognized value."
82. "Significance," 30.
83. See Chapter 2.
84. "Apocryphal / Deuterocanonical Books," xxx.
85. Ibid., xxvii.
86. See Florovsky, *The Ways of Russian Theology*.
87. Note that 2 Tim 3:16–17 may hint to the "formative" role of the scripture by linking this aspect to the notion of inspiration. Conventionally, *pasa graphē theopneustos* is rendered "the entire scripture is inspired by God" (v. 16). However, adjective *theopneustos* may have an active meaning, "inspiring, breathing." So, the whole phrase could be translated, "God is breathing (inspiring) through the entire scripture."

CHAPTER 4. TRADITION

1. "Tradition," 109.
2. Daniel H. Williams, *Tradition*, 17, note 7, mentions the new series of patristic commentaries on Scripture entitled the *Church's Bible*, edited by Wilken (Grand Rapids: Eerdmans, 2003–; four volumes are already out: Song of Songs, Isaiah, Romans, and 1 Corinthians). This series of commentaries is not the only sign of a postmodern reassessment of historical criticism vis-à-vis the traditional reading of the Bible might be it Christian or Jewish. The newly launched project "La Bible en ses traditions" (acronym B.E.S.T; English: "The Bible in Its

Traditions") under the tutelage of École biblique et archéologique française in Jerusalem (see Venard, "La Bible en ses traditions," 142–58 and http://www.bibest.org) is another example of reconsidering Church's tradition as interpretive context of the biblical text. I enthusiastically support École biblique's initiative by contributing with the Book of Hosea (translation, textual notes, and commentary) to the B.E.S.T. project.

3. "Perspectives in Orthodox Biblical Interpretation," 330.
4. "Biblical Authority Reconsidered," 76; see Lienhard, *Canon of the Christian Bible.*
5. *Bible, Theology, and Faith,* 6–7.
6. Ibid., 75–76.
7. Ibid., 26, 36.
8. "Scripture and Tradition," 25.
9. "Tradition of Orthodoxy," 306–307.
10. On *kērygma,* see below; see also Chapter 1.
11. This twofold structure is attested by Clement, a disciple of Paul and the third or fourth bishop of Rome. In the First Epistle of Clement to Corinthians, the ordination of bishops and deacons is simultaneous with the oral proclamation of the gospel. This epistle mirrors the situation in the Church of Rome during the last decades of the first century: "Having therefore received their commands, and being fully assured by the resurrection of our Lord Jesus Christ, and with faith confirmed by the Word of God, they went forth in the assurance of the Holy Spirit preaching the good news that the Kingdom of God is coming. They preached (*kērysontes*) from district to district, and from city to city, and they appointed (*kathistanon*) their first converts, testing them by the Spirit, to be bishops (*episkopous*) and deacons (*diakonous*) of the future believers" (*1 Clement* 42.3–4 [Holmes, *Apostolic Fathers,* 81]).
12. Theodoret of Cyrus tells that Ignatius was ordained bishop by the apostle Peter (PG 83:81A). In his *Ecclesiastical History* (3.36), Eusebius mentions that Ignatius, the third bishop of Antioch, was martyrized in Rome in the tenth year of Trajan, i.e., 108 C.E.
13. See Dibelius and Conzelmann, *Pastoral Epistles,* 54.
14. Holmes, *Apostolic Fathers,* 201–3.
15. See especially Ignatius, *Epistle to the Smyrnaeans* 8.1–2 in Holmes, *Apostolic Fathers,* 261.
16. ANF 7:397.
17. Robert Murray, "Tradition," 8.
18. The *Oxford English Dictionary* defines "tradent" (Latin *tradens, tradent-* from *tradere,* "to hand over, deliver") in legal use as "the person who delivers or hands over any property to another" (only one citation, 1880). Its use in reference to tradition is well established in written American English; e.g., the term is characteristic of Childs' vocabulary (see "Retrospective Reading," 362–77).

19. See Murray, "Tradition," 11. This move, persuasively argued by Congar (e.g., *Jalons*) is reflected in *Lumen gentium* and *Dei Verbum*.
20. *Orthodox Church*, 100.
21. See Florovsky, *Bible, Church, Tradition*, 53–54.
22. Ibid., 103.
23. *Being As Communion*, 123–42, 171–208.
24. *Bible, Church, Tradition*, 90.
25. "Tradition and Traditions," 141.
26. Florovsky, *Bible, Church, Tradition*, 46–47, notices: "The Church alone is the living witness of tradition; and only from inside, from within the Church, can tradition be felt and accepted as a certainty."
27. *Sabbath*, 101.
28. *Kerygma and Didache*, 1–2.
29. *NPNF*² 1:170.
30. On early Church's tradition as hermeneutical key to Jewish Scriptures, see Behr, "Scripture, the Gospel, and Orthodoxy," 223–48.
31. As Daniel H. Williams, *Tradition*, 23, notices, "The very concept of 'canon' was first applied to the church's profession of faith, not to a list of authoritative texts"; see Chapter 3.
32. On the phrase "rule of faith," see Chapter 3.
33. Boyarin, *Border Lines*, 2.
34. Ibid., 3–4.
35. Ibid., 17.
36. *Bible, Church, Tradition*, 79–80.
37. Young, *Biblical Exegesis*, 18; see the comprehensive treatment of this topic by Kelly, *Early Christian Creeds*.
38. PG 7:806C.
39. On Irenaeus and his views on Scripture, Tradition, and Church, see Behr's recent work, *Irenaeus of Lyons*. Unfortunately, I concluded my book when Behr's monograph was already at the press, so I was unable to use his excellent renditions of Irenaeus' texts.
40. *ANF* 1:330.
41. *Irenaeus of Lyons*, 105.
42. *Biblical Exegesis*, 21.
43. "Tradition," 59–99.
44. Here, the word "Gnostic" does not refer to the heretical groups of the same name, but rather to an orthodox believer with true knowledge of God.
45. *ANF* 2:554.
46. *Bible, Church, Tradition*, 106–7.
47. "Tradition," 131.
48. *Bible, Church, Tradition*, 49–50.
49. *Systematic Theology*, 1:11.

50. Scott, *Corpus Juris Civilis*, 12:125.

51. A similar situation obtains as early as the first half of the fifth century. Here's Theodoret of Cyrus, who places the Scripture on a par with the "teachers of the churches and luminaries of the world": "In our former discussions we have proved that God the Word is immutable, and became incarnate not by being changed into flesh, but by taking perfect human nature. The divine Scripture, and the teachers of the churches and luminaries of the world have clearly taught us that, after the union, he remained as he was, unmixed, impassible, unchanged, uncircumscribed; and that he preserved unimpaired the nature which he had taken" (Theodoret of Cyrus, *Dilaogue III: The Impassible* [*NPNF*² 3:216]).

52. *Systematic Theology*, 1:12.

53. Florovsky, *Bible, Church, Tradition*, 73–75, calls it "double 'ecumenicity' of Christian faith—in space and time." Vincent's formula echoes Irenaeus's own wording, *quae est ab apostolis, quae per successionem presbyterorum in ecclesiis custoditur*, "Which is being preserved in the church from the apostles through the succession of the presbyters." The two dimensions of this "ecumenicity" of Christian faith cannot be separated. *Antiquitas* "antiquity" and *consentio* "consensus" could be a warrant of truth as long as they are considered together. For instance, a doctrine going back to the time of the apostles is true only if it enjoys the consensus of the entire Church. Likewise, if a doctrine is embraced by the whole Church, yet its apostolic character cannot be demonstrated, this doctrine is not true part of Church's tradition.

54. *Systematic Theology*, 1:12.

55. "Biblical Authority in Eastern Orthodoxy," 1022.

56. Daniel H. Williams, *Tradition*, 24, notices: "Since the sixteenth century, one of the persistent conflicts between Protestants, Roman Catholics, and the Greek Orthodox involves discerning which aspects of traditions are normative and which are not."

57. See Chapter 3.

58. *The Confession of Dositheos of Jerusalem* (Council of Jerusalem, 1672), Decree 18: "Ought the Divine Scriptures to be read in the vulgar tongue by all Christians? No. For that all Scripture is divinely-inspired and profitable (cf. 2 Timothy 3:16) we know, and is of such necessity, that without the same it is impossible to be Orthodox at all. Nevertheless they should not be read by all, but only by those who with fitting research have inquired into the deep things of the Spirit, and who know in what manner the Divine Scriptures ought to be searched, and taught, and in fine read. But to such as are not so exercised, or who cannot distinguish, or who understand only literally, or in any other way contrary to Orthodoxy what is contained in the Scriptures, the Catholic Church, as knowing by experience the mischief arising therefrom, forbids the reading of the same. So that it is permitted to every Orthodox to hear indeed the Scriptures, that he may believe with the heart to righteousness, and confess with the

mouth to salvation; [Romans 10:10] but to read some parts of the Scriptures, and especially of the Old [Testament], is forbidden for the aforesaid reasons and others of the like sort. For it is the same thing thus to prohibit persons not exercised thereto reading all the Sacred Scriptures, as to require infants to abstain from strong meats" (*Acts and Decrees*, 152–53).

59. Pelikan, *Christian Tradition*, 2:288–89.

60. *Orthodox Church*, 100.

61. "Gospel of *Memra*," 246. Boyarin's view differs from the general stance that dates the "parting of the ways" sometime after the second Jewish revolt (132–35 C.E.) led by Simon Bar Kochba.

62. Boyarin, "Talmud," 69.

63. For a different view, pointing to the richness and diversity of patristic interpretations, see Constas, "To Sleep, Perchance to Dream," 91–124.

64. Boyarin, "Talmud," 69.

65. Ibid., 78.

66. Ibid., 77.

67. "*Begotten Not Made*," 78.

68. Boyarin, "Talmud," 78–79.

69. See Gray, "'Select Fathers'," 21–36.

70. As early as the late fourth century, Jerome reports that some of Ephraim's writings were read in church after the scriptural reading—so great was the popularity of this church father: "Ephraim, deacon of the church at Edessa, composed many works in the Syriac language, and became so distinguished that his writings are repeated publicly in some churches, after the reading of the Scriptures. I once read in Greek a volume by him *On the Holy Spirit*, which someone had translated from the Syriac, and recognized even in translation, the incisive power of lofty genius. He died in the reign of Valens" (*The Lives of Illustrious Men* 115 [*NPNF*² 3:382]).

71. On the Philokalia, see Kallistos of Diokleia, "The Spirituality of Philokalia," 6–24; Bingaman and Nassif, *Philokalia*.

72. McGuckin, *Orthodox Church*, 116.

73. E.g., *Confession of faith of Gennadios*, Patriarch of Constantinople (1455–56); *Confession of Dositheos*, Patriarch of Jerusalem, as ratified by the Synod of Jerusalem (1672).

74. *Bible, Church, Tradition*, 85.

75. On the theological debates surrounding the Council of Nicaea, see Behr, *The Nicene Faith*, vol. 2.

76. Stylianopoulos, "Biblical Authority in Eastern Orthodoxy," 1021.

77. *Bible, Church, Tradition*, 96.

78. "Orthodox Interpretation of Scripture," 71.

79. *Scripture in Tradition*, 21.

80. On the active meaning of *theopneustos*, "breathing," in 2 Tim 3:16, see Chapter 3.

81. *NPNF*² 6:32.
82. As Hanson, "Biblical Authority," 57, well notices: "The question of biblical authority as we face it today is in a sense a modern one. That is to say, it stems from the kinds of questions raised by the Enlightenment regarding the relation of biblical scholarship to the study of other writings of antiquity and the relation to the divine. Though in certain ways adumbrated by Renaissance scholarship, these questions were not urgent issues for the church fathers, for Medieval Scholars, or for the Reformers. For the theologians of all of these periods, Holy Scripture was God's Word, a gift of the Holy Spirit."
83. Chrysostom, *On Wealth and Poverty*, 85.
84. *ABD* 5:1021–23.
85. *Bible, Church, Tradition*, 28.
86. *Christian Tradition*, 1:55.
87. "Scripture and Tradition," 25.
88. For a detailed "decoding" of scriptures found in various components of the Holy Tradition, see Part II. Interpretation.
89. *NPNF*² 9:751–52.
90. See Part II. Interpretation.
91. Daniel H. Williams, *Tradition*, 17.
92. "For since all cannot read the Scriptures, some being hindered as to the knowledge of them by want of learning, and others by a want of leisure, in order that the soul may not perish from ignorance, we comprise the whole doctrine of the faith in a few lines. This summary I wish you both to commit to memory when I recite it, and to rehearse it with all diligence among yourselves, not writing it out on paper, but engraving it by the memory upon your heart, taking care while you rehearse it that no catechumen chance to overhear the things which have been delivered to you. I wish you also to keep this as a provision through the whole course of your life. . . . For the articles of the faith were not composed as seemed good to men; but the most important points collected out of all the Scripture make up one complete teaching of the faith. And just as the mustard seed in one small grain contains many branches, so also this faith has embraced in few words all the knowledge of godliness in the Old and New Testaments" (Cyril of Jerusalem, *Lecture* 5 12 [*NPNF*² 7:32]).
93. *NPNF*² 7:23.
94. Similarly, Socrates Scholasticus (b. about the end of fourth century c.e.) insists on the perfect harmony between church teachings and their scriptural matrix: "And if any one shall teach contrary to the sound and right faith of the Scriptures, affirming that there is or was a period or an age before the Son of God existed, let him be accursed. . . . For we truly and unreservedly believe and follow all things handed down to us from the sacred Scriptures by the prophets and apostles" (*Ecclesiastical History* 2.10 [*NPNF*² 2:40]). Basil of Caesarea (329–79 c.e.) articulates the same idea when he writes, "But we do not rest only on

the fact that such is the tradition of the fathers; for they too followed the sense of Scripture" (*On the Holy Spirit* 7.16 [*NPNF*² 8:10]).

95. Daniel H. Williams, *Tradition*, 63.

96. Ibid., 27.

97. *Bible, Church, Tradition*, 48.

98. See Pannenberg, *Systematic Theology*, 1:28–29.

99. *Bible, Church, Tradition*, 80.

100. The *Moscow Agreed Statement* was issued by the delegates of the Anglican-Orthodox Joint Doctrinal Commission that met in Moscow during July 26–August 2, 1976; see Ware and Davey, *Anglican-Orthodox Dialogue*, 83–85. A thorough analysis of this statement may be found in Ware, "Unity of Scripture," 231–45. According to Ware, the *Moscow Agreed Statement* "can be taken as the specifically Orthodox standpoint" on Scripture (234).

101. "Unity of Scripture and Tradition," 241.

102. Ibid., 242. Along the same line of thought, Staniloae, "Orthodox Conception of Tradition," 653–54, accentuates the continuity of tradition as Church's "lived experience": "Tradition in the Orthodox Church is not a sum of propositions learnt by heart, but a lived experience. . . . Tradition is a living reality, it is the uninterrupted life of the Church."

103. Staniloae wrote a seminal study on God's revelation as viewed in Eastern Orthodox Church, a mixture of words, acts, and symbols; see Staniloae, *Theology and the Church*, 109–154.

104. Ware, "Unity of Scripture," 234.

105. Ibid., 235.

106. *Scripture in Tradition*, 4.

107. "Unity of Scripture," 242.

108. *Biblical Exegesis*, 139.

109. *Bible, Theology, and Faith*, 6–7.

CHAPTER 5. DISCURSIVE

1. For a survey of bibliography and issues pertaining to patristic exegesis, the reader is directed to Kannengiesser, *Handbook of Patristic Exegesis*; Simonetti, *Biblical Interpretation*; Agouridis, "Church Fathers as Interpreters"; Daniélou, *From Shadows to Reality*.

2. See especially Chapters 6 and 7, where hermeneutical principles along with concrete examples of patristic exegesis may be detected at various levels of scriptural interpretation within the ecclesial context.

3. See Chapter 4.

4. See Chapter 3.

5. "Theoretical Hermeneutics," 95.

6. See Bruns, *Hermeneutics Ancient and Modern*.

7. Green, *Theology*, 1.

8. For an in-depth analysis of the key patristic hermeneutical works, see the seminal study of Torrance, *Divine Meaning*.

9. *Traditions of the Bible*, 14–19.

10. There are various ways to deal with the topic of the principles (assumptions, presuppositions) of patristic hermeneutics. For alternative orderings of these principles, the reader is directed to Breck, *Scripture in Tradition*, 33–44; see also Simonetti, *Biblical Interpretation*.

11. The word "exegesis" comes from Gk. *exēgēsis* "interpretation, exposition," verb *exēgeomai*, "to go first, to lead the way; to expound, interpret"; hence, an "exegete" is the one who leads the way in the area of interpretation.

12. On scriptural inerrancy in the patristic period, see Holmes, "Origen and the Inerrancy of Scripture," 221–31, and Dalton, "Inspiration and Inerrancy," 313–20. Kennengiesser, *Handbook of Patristic Exegesis*, 786, notes that, "Divine inspiration and inerrancy of scripture were intensely revered by John [Chrysostom]."

13. On the "rule of faith" and its hermeneutical import on scriptural interpretation, see Chapter 4.

14. Young, *Biblical Exegesis*, 21, 29.

15. See Zaharopoulos, "Theodore of Mopsuestia," 42–52; Hill, "St John Chrysostom's Teaching on Inspiration,'" 19–37; "Six Homilies on Isaiah 6," 307–22.

16. "Inspiration of the Scriptures," 39.

17. See, inter alia, Preus, *Inspiration of Scripture*; Lee, *Inspiration of Holy Scripture*; and Abraham, *Divine Inspiration*.

18. *Holy Scripture*, 32, 36.

19. *Bible, Church, Tradition*, 27.

20. Stylianopoulos, "Perspectives on Orthodox Biblical Interpretation," 329, remarks, "The theologians of the ancient Church, such as Origen, Athanasius, Gregory of Nyssa, John Chrysostom, and Cyril of Alexandria, confronted by repeated issues of interpretation, reflected more consciously on the human character of Scripture, which they explained as a form of divine condescension (*syngatabasis*) to human weakness, yet without compromising the authority and essential clarity of Scripture's divine message. . . . The parallel paradigm to biblical inspiration is the mystery of the incarnation."

21. On the centrality of scripture within the Church's unfolding life, see Chapter 4.

22. According to Daube, "Rabbinic Methods of Interpretation," 239–64, the seven rules (*middoth*) can be traced back to a Hellenistic usage.

23. Davies, "Judaism," 53.

24. See Grypeou and Spurling, *Exegetical Encounter*.

25. Kannengiesser, *Handbook of Patristic Exegesis*, 186.

26. Boys, "Biblical Interpretation," 56.

27. *Traditions of the Bible*, 20–22.

28. See McLay, *Use of the Septuagint*, where the author shows the great import of the Greek translation of Jewish Scripture on the text and theology of the New Testament.

29. As Juel, "Interpreting Israel's Scriptures," 286–88, well notices, the "use of Scripture" in the New Testament is a quite complex phenomenon including: explicit quotations, allusions, and "echoes of the Scriptures."

30. On this hermeneutical pattern and others, see Chapter 1.

31. Young, *Biblical Exegesis*, 286–88.

32. Ibid., 29 n. 1; cf. Gorday, *Principles of Patristic Exegesis*, 34–39.

33. According to Kennengiesser, *Handbook of Patristic Exegesis*, 213, "the terms history, literal sense, typology, allegory, *theoria*, and *anagoge* are the most commonly used with respect to the methods of interpretation by the Fathers."

34. Louth, *Discerning the Mystery*, 186; on medieval exegesis, see De Lubac, *Exégèse Médiévale*.

35. *NPNF*² 11:438.

36. Williamson, "Principles of Catholic Interpretation," 341–43.

37. *Sensus Plenior*, 92.

38. See Louth, "Typology," 727–29.

39. See Woollcombe, "Biblical Origins," 60–65; Guinot, "Typologie," 2:1–34.

40. *Biblical Exegesis*, 193, 201.

41. Interestingly, Gal 4:24, the only text in the New Testament where verb *allēgoreō* appears is not a good example of "allegory." The interpretation of the "two sons of Abraham" in Gal 4 proves to be a typology.

42. The word "typology" was coined by J. S. Semler, ca. 1770's. See Young, "Alexandrian and Antiochene Exegesis," 337.

43. *From Shadows to Reality.*

44. Inter alia, Lampe and Woollcombe, *Essays in Typology.*

45. "Alexandrian and Antiochene Exegesis," 337.

46. Ibid., 153.

47. *Handbook of Patristic Exegesis*, 229.

48. Daniélou, *From Shadows to Reality*, 12.

49. "Old Testament Canon," 309.

50. Young, *Biblical* Exegesis, 175, 342. Noteworthily, the term theoria was used by both schools of exegesis. The Alexandrines employed this term for allegory, while the Antiochenes used it with reference to a higher meaning but not detached from the letter. The very use of this term speaks against a clear-cut distinction between the two schools.

51. *Scripture in Tradition*, 11.

52. "Orthodox Principles," 91.

53. *Bible, Church, Tradition*, 28–36.

54. "Exegesis and Interpretation," 86.

55. Note Pseudo-Philo's (*Book of Biblical Antiquities* 10:7, 11:15) interpretation on the water of Meribah, "And it [the water] followed them in the wilderness forty years and went up to the mountains with them and went down into the plains." For a discussion of this *crux interpretum*, see Kugel, *Traditions of the Bible*, 620–21.

56. "Exegesis and Interpretation," 87.

57. Breck, "Orthodox Principles," 91.

58. *Face of Christ*, 43–44.

59. Rapp, "Old Testament Models," 178–80.

60. On the two "imitative modes" (i.e., Roman *exemplum* and Christian *typos*) and their use in the Byzantine society, see Goldfarb, "Transformation through Imitation."

61. Rapp, "Old Testament Models," 192.

62. More than any other emperor in the history of Byzantium, Heraklios was repeatedly associated with Old Testament figures. The twofold siege of Constantinople by Persians and Avars in 626 c.e. was diverted by the intervention of the Mother of God. Theodore Syncellus remarks that what Isaiah prophesied "by shadow and type" (*en skia kai typō*) about Jerusalem of his time was fulfilled in the time of Heraklios, "the David who is emperor in our times" (*tou David tou kath' hēmas basileuontos*). Surprisingly, Heraklios is described not as a new David but as the very biblical David; see Rapp, "Old Testament Models," 194.

63. On Porphyry's critique of Christian use of allegory as a biblical method of interpretation, see Sellew, "Achilles or Christ?" 84–85. One may mention that the history of allegorical interpretation began around sixth-fifth centuries b.c.e. with the efforts of Greek philosophers and grammarians to preserve the old texts by finding a meaning other than the literal one. By the first century c.e., allegorical interpretation reached its climax.

64. Porphyry in his lost work *Against Christians* notices, "Some, in their eagerness to find an explanation of the wickedness of the Jewish writings rather than give them up, had recourse to interpretations that are incompatible and do not harmonize with what has been written, offering not so much a defense of what was outlandish as commendation and praise of their own work" (Sellew, "Achilles or Christ?" 95).

65. *Sinai and Zion*, 4.

66. Pertaining to the differences between Talmudic and patristic methods of interpretation, see our discussion on Boyarin's research, in Chapter 4.

67. The early Christian use of this "proof-text" type of exegesis parallels the list of messianic proof-texts and the *pesher* to the Book of Habakkuk discovered at Qumran; see R. P. C. Hanson, "Biblical Exegesis," 412–13.

68. *ANF* 1:236.

69. Ibid., 1:179.

70. Young, *Biblical Exegesis*, 123–24; on Justin's Christology, see the seminal study of Trakatellis, *Pre-Existence of Christ in Justin Martyr*; on Justin's biblical interpretation, see Stylianopoulos, *Justin Martyr and the Mosaic Law*.

71. See Young, "Alexandrian and Antiochene Exegesis," 339.

72. "Theodoret's Commentary on Isaiah," 313.

73. Young, *Biblical Exegesis*, 80–81.

74. Ibid., 179.

75. Ibid., 164.

76. "Theodoret's Commentary on Isaiah," 323–24, 327, 339–40.

77. Ibid., 335–36.

78. See *Commentary on Psalms 1–51*.

79. Young, *Biblical Exegesis*, 175.

80. "'Spiritual Exegesis'," 343.

81. *Biblical Exegesis*, 169–70.

82. I have to confess that one of the reasons of this scriptural-patristic selection is my past personal research finalized in a commentary on Hosea with patristic annotations, *Long-Suffering Love*, at a time when the commentaries of already mentioned church fathers were not yet translated in English.

83. For a thorough discussion of textual and literary aspects of Hos 1–3 in light of patristic interpretations, see Pentiuc, *Long-Suffering Love*, 47–128.

84. On Theodoret of Cyrus's life and theological-biblical exegetical contribution, see Pásztori-Kupán, *Theodoret of Cyrus*.

85. Theodoret of Cyrus, *Commentaries on the Prophets*, 3:41.

86. Ibid., 3:40.

87. Ibid., 3:47.

88. Ibid., 3:46.

89. On Theodore's contribution as biblical exegete, see Simonetti, "Theodore of Mopsuestia," 799–828.

90. Ibid., 816.

91. Theodore of Mopsuestia, *Commentary on the Twelve Prophets*, 41.

92. Ibid., 51.

93. Ibid., 53.

94. Ibid.

95. See Russell, *Cyril of Alexandria*.

96. Cyril of Alexandria, *Commentary on the Twelve Prophets*, 1:39–40.

97. Ibid., 1:42–43.

98. Ibid.

99. Ibid.

100. Ibid.

101. Ibid., 1:90.

102. Ibid., 1:97.

103. Brock, *Luminous Eye*, 49.

CHAPTER 6. AURAL

1. "Biblical Authority Reconsidered," 77.
2. See Delling, *Worship in the New Testament.*
3. *The Shape of Liturgy,* 48.
4. See Johnson, "The Apostolic Tradition," 44.
5. *This Holy Place,* 32, 55.
6. On Torah-reading in the synagogue, see Schiffman, "Public Reading," 38–49; Aageson, "Early Jewish Lectionaries," 4:270–71; Perrot, "Reading of the Bible," 137–59; Schürer, *History,* 2:450–54.
7. Schiffman, "Public Reading," 45–46.
8. See Parsenios, *Departure and Consolation.*
9. Rouwhorst, "Early Christian Eucharist," 296.
10. Ibid., 304.
11. *ANF* 1:185.
12. Ibid., 7:421.
13. *Liturgy in Byzantium and Beyond,* 59.
14. See Dionysios the Pseudo-Areopagite, *The Ecclesiastical Hierarchy;* cf. PG 3:369–584.
15. See Maximos Confessor, *Selected Writings;* cf. PG 91:657–718.
16. See Germanos of Constantinople, *On the Divine Liturgy.*
17. See Auxentios and Thornton, "Three Byzantine Commentaries," 285–308.
18. See McClure and Feltoe, *The Pilgrimage of Etheria,* xlii–xliii.
19. Ibid., 76.
20. PG 31:1437.
21. "The Gospels are to be read on the Sabbath [Saturday], with the other Scriptures" (*The Canons of the Synod held at Laodicaea: Canon Sixteen* [*NPNF*² 14:130]).
22. Lamb, "Bible in the Liturgy," 568, 571.
23. The earliest witness is ms. *Sinai gr. 7* dated to the ninth century C.E. The critical edition of the *Prophetologion* was published by Engberg, Høeg, and Zuntz, *Prophetologium.* This critical edition is based on a thorough analysis of 71 mss. of the ninth through fourteenth centuries. Today there are 174 extant mss. of the Prophetologion.
24. The term *Paroimiarion,* used in churches and scholarly productions of Slavonic or Romanian origin, derives from Greek *paroimia,* "proverb, parable." Given the high frequency of scriptural lessons taken from the Book of Proverbs (LXX: *Paroimiai*), the Greek word *paroimia* came to designate any Old Testament reading.
25. Unlike the Byzantine Prophetologion containing only the Old Testament lessons and being lunar in orientation (i.e., centered on Pascha), the earlier Jerusalem lectionaries, solar in orientation (i.e., centered on Christmas / Epiphany) used to shelter both Old and New Testament lessons; see Alexeev, "Old Testament Lections," 96.

26. According to Miller, "Prophetologion," 55–56, the Prophetologion was the only "physical" Old Testament collection in Byzantine times. Nevertheless, it is known that Eusebius was commissioned by Constantine the Great to prepare fifty copies of the "Sacred Scriptures" of "portable size" to be used for the "instruction of the Church." This fact is recorded by two historians, Eusebius and Socrates Scholasticus; see Chapter 2.

27. Alexeev, "Old Testament Lections," 93 and n. 9.

28. Ibid., 92.

29. Byzantine hymnography is a synthesis involving three ancient liturgical centers, St. Sabbas Monastery in Palestine, the "Great Church" and the Studios Monastery in Constantinople, and the monastic community of Mount Athos, during a long period, between the end of the iconoclastic crisis (eighth-ninth century) and the beginning of the Hesychastic debate (fourteenth century). Some of the hymns were composed by famous hymnographers, such as Romanos Melodios (first half of the sixth century), Andrew of Crete (d. 740 C.E.) and John of Damascus (676–749 C.E.); see Bucur, "Exegesis of Biblical Theophanies," 92–112.

30. *NPNF*[2] 14:551.

31. *Orthodox Church*, 102.

32. McClure and Feltoe, *The Pilgrimage of Etheria*, 66; cf. xxxix, 51–52, 54, 64.

33. The liturgical texts in English are reproduced with slight alterations at lexical and orthographical levels according to *The Complete Menaion*.

34. See chapter 5.

35. Barrois, *Scripture Readings*, 11.

36. Ibid., 12.

37. The numbering of the Psalms in the present chapter as well as in the entire work follows the custom of the Septuagint while the KJV corresponding number is provided in the brackets. When the English translation is taken from the edition of Pietersma and Wright, it is noted NETS.

38. Hengel, *Septuagint*, 42, notices, "The frequency of Psalter manuscripts is no accident. In terms of frequency in citations in the early Christian literature up to Justin, the Psalms rival and even exceed Isaiah. With a view to use in worship, the Psalter as a 'Christian hymnbook' was probably the most important 'prophetic' document."

39. "Psalms of the Degrees" (Ps. 119[120]–133[134], i.e., the eighteenth *katisma*) represent a good example of lectio continua.

40. The Eastern Orthodox Psalter is divided up into twenty "sessions" (*kathismata*, from *kathēmai*, "to be seated, to sit") and each *kathisma* is divided into three "stations" (*staseis*, from *stasis*, "standing"). These kathismata are to be read during the daily Matins and Vespers throughout the week. Thus, Sunday: kathismata 2 and 3; Monday: 4, 5, 6; Tuesday: 7, 8, 9; Wednesday: 10, 11, 12; Thursday: 13, 14, 15; Friday: 19, 20, 18; and Saturday: 16, 17, 1.

41. Lash, "Biblical Interpretation in Worship," 37.

42. Mays, *Psalms*, 331.

43. Ibid., 336.

44. MT reads *liwyātān*, "Leviathan, sea monster"; cf. Ugaritic *ltn* (*lawtān*), "wreath animal."

45. *Scripture Readings*, 17.

46. During the "small entrance," the deacon or the priest exits the altar (sanctuary) holding the book of the gospel. Walking to the center of the nave, he raises the gospel by intoning "Wisdom. Arise!" and then reenters the altar. This ritual movement symbolizes the first public appearance of Christ, more precisely, the beginning of his teaching ministry.

47. Even though it does not use the term "footstool," the LXX of Ps 131(132):7 conveys a similar idea, obedience toward the place of God's presence: "We shall enter into his coverts; we shall do obeisance at the place where his feet stood." Note that MT reads *hădôm*, "footstool." One may mention that this Psalm is recited at the Pre-Sanctified Liturgy during the Great Lent. When the cantor reaches v. 7, the priest carries the presanctified gifts from upon the Holy Table to the place of preparation (i.e., *proskomidē*, "offering" table).

48. Theodoret of Cyrus, *Commentary on the Psalms*, 73–150, 141.

49. *NPNF*[1] 8:162.

50. *Scripture Readings*, 22.

51. *Theology of the Old Testament*, 75.

52. *NPNF*[2] 14:210.

53. Magdalino and Nelson, *The Old Testament in Byzantium*, 30.

54. Dix, *The Shape of the Liturgy*, 124.

55. The "Triodion" indicates the liturgical book and fasting period (also called Great Lent) leading to passion and resurrection of Christ. Between ninth and twelfth centuries, three Sundays were added to the initial seven weeks of Great Lent. Therefore, today, the Eastern Orthodox Lent numbers forty-eight days; see Schmemann, *Great Lent*. The readings for the weekdays of the Great Lent are taken exclusively from the Old Testament. For a complete table of Old Testament lessons prescribed for weekdays during the Great Lent, see Barrois, *Scripture Readings*, 70.

56. Constantelos, "Apocryphal / Deuterocanonical Books," xxviii, writes, "For the Orthodox in general, the Old Testament is propaideutic to (a preparation for) the New. . . . It is for this reason that no Old Testament lectionaries are found in the Divine Liturgy. With exception of psalmic verses in hymns of the Divine Liturgy, the Liturgy's lections are from the New Testament." Constantelos's post factum explanation does not make things right. The loss of Old Testament readings in the Byzantine liturgy is a tragic event. It is our responsibility as Church (people of God, hierarchy, and theologians) to request that the topic of reintroducing the Old Testament readings in the Sunday Liturgy be part of the agenda of the long projected and now seemingly imminent Pan-Orthodox Council.

57. *Scripture Readings*, 19.

58. This tripartite division of the Old Testament (Hebrew Bible) is attested as early as second century B.C.E., in the prologue of Sirach: "Law, Prophets and others" (*tou nomou, tōn prophētōn kai tōn allōn*); see Chapter 3.

59. MT *sullām*, "stepped ramp, flight of steps"; note the etymology of this word, probably an Aramaic form deriving from a root *s-l-l*, "to raise, pile up"; hence *sullām* may designate a raised structure, tower with steps (*ziggurat*—staged temple-tower).

60. MT reads *niṣṣāb ʿālāyw*, "he stood by / on it / him"; the masculine pronominal suffix *–āyw* may be rendered either "it" (i.e., ladder) or "him" (i.e., Jacob); hence MT's two reading possibilities: the Lord "stood" on or by the ladder, and above or by Jacob. By choosing *autēs* (feminine), LXX allows only one reading, the Lord "leaned on the ladder" (cf. *klimax* "ladder," a Gk. feminine noun).

61. *Genesis*, 243.

62. LXX's *ailam* is the Greek spelling of the Hebrew (MT) *ʿullām*, "porch."

63. *Ezekiel*, 440.

64. LXX (*harmozousa*, "in harmony with, suited to") depicts wisdom as suited to God's creative work, while MT (*ʾāmôn*, "craftsman"; cf. Akkadian *ummānu*, "workman") emphasizes the agency of wisdom in the creation scenario.

65. Perdue, *Proverbs*, 150.

66. Speaking of the divine nature of the Son, John Chrysostom uses the same term *apeiros*, "boundless, infinite": "If he [the Son] had a beginning from above, even though he were without end, yet he is not boundless (*apeiros*). Because boundless means to be boundless on both sides. As Paul made clear, 'Having neither beginning of days, nor end of life' [Heb 7:3]; by this expression showing that he is both without beginning and without end. . . . In one direction there is no end, in the other no beginning" (*In Joannem* 4.2 [PG 59:49, 25–32]).

67. Stefka Kancheva (personal communication, March 2013) suggests a nexus between the preparation of the tabernacle / Temple by Moses / Solomon for worship (mentioned in the Vespers lessons, Exod 40 and 1 Kgs 8) and the preparation of the Theotokos in the Temple for the day of Logos's incarnation, as attested in the following hymns: "Today the living temple of the great King enters into the temple, to be made ready for him as his divine dwelling" (Matins, after Ps 50[51]); "You temple and palace higher than the heavens, O all-pure one, you purely are consecrated in the temple of God, there to be prepared to be the divine dwelling and godly abode of his coming to us on earth" (Matins, First Canon, Ode One, troparion); "They that divinely begat you, O all-immaculate and pure Lady, offered you in the temple as a pure sacrifice; and you strangely dwelt in the innermost sanctuary of God, to be prepared beforehand as the dwelling of the Word" (Matins, Second Canon, Ode Eight, troparion).

68. Perhaps for *hē riza tou Iessai*, "the root of Jesse" (Isa 11:10); or alluding to Sir 47:22, *Dauid ex autou rizan*, "David, a root from him."

69. Phrantzoles, *Hosiou Ephraim tou Syrou erga*, 6:362, line 7; 364, line 7. Note Ephraem's moralizing explanation of the same episode centered on the word "ladder" (*klimax*): "Great is the repentance here on earth for it becomes a ladder on which the souls are going up, whereas through sin they are going down. It [repentance] refreshes the nature and restores the personal dignity" (*De paenitentia* [Ibid., 5:59 line 1]).

70. John Damascene, *On Holy Images*, 161–62. And a little bit further, in *Sermon III*, John of Damascus offers the same Mariological interpretation of the ladder, "Today the living ladder, through whom the Most High descended and was seen on earth, and conversed with men, was assumed into heaven by death" (Ibid., 202–203).

71. Sheridan, *Genesis 12–50*, 186.

72. Honscheid, *Didymus der Blinde*, 14:238.

73. Sheridan, *Genesis 12–50*, 188.

74. *Luke 1*, 86.

75. O'Connor, *The Holy Land*, 230, notices, "Many houses in the area are still built above or in front of caves, and perhaps we should envisage Joseph (then living with his parents) as taking his wife into such a back area in order to give birth away from the confusion of the living room; the cave part would have been used for stabling and storage."

76. *ANF* 1:237.

77. Ibid., 8:365.

78. Ibid., 4:418.

79. *NPNF*² 6:199.

80. Ibid., 1:531.

81. Speaking of Theodore of Mopsuestia's way of dealing with Ps 44(45), Zaharopoulos, *Theodore of Mopsuestia on the Bible*, 150, notices that "according to Theodore, it is a prophecy of Christ and his church. Consequently, we need not bewilder ourselves with fruitless attempts to identify the 'king' with an earthly monarch (Solomon or Hezekiah), and the 'queen' with a mortal princess, but we may at once see our Savior wedded to his bride, the church, in these adoring words of the psalm."

82. For a philological analysis of Ps 44(45)'s lexical peculiarities, see Dahood, *Psalms I:1–50*, 1:269–75.

83. Dahood, *Psalms I:1–50*, 1:273, proposes a different reading for v. 7(6)a by altering the Masoretic vocalization, *kisʾăkā*, "your throne" into *kissēʾᵃkā*, "(God) has enthroned you," a denominative Piel from *kissēʾ*, "throne." Craigie and Tate, *Psalms 1–50*, 336, follow Dahood's proposal underscoring that the latter's rendition, though not without difficulty, seems to be the most likely in the context.

84. In his study, "Translation of *ELOHIM*," 65–89, Harris reviews the modern scholarship on v. 7(6)a and lists a number of arguments supporting the text (MT, LXX) as it is with no alteration at all. By responding the major objection to this

textually conservative view, Harris shows that even though Ps 44(45) represents the climax of royal ideology in Israel, it does not deify the person of the king. The Israelite king was distinct from God. His 'divinity' was not intrinsic. He was "Yahweh's anointed" and based on this, the king was considered God's adopted son (Ps 2:7; 88[89]:27[26]; cf. 2 Sam 7:14). Harris explains the new and puzzling royal nomenclature in 44(45):7(6)a as due to the fact that through the power of the Spirit of Yahweh, the king shared with God same divine characteristics such as "glory and majesty" (vv. 4[3]–5[4]a; cf. Ps 95[96]:6). Moreover, the hyperbolic language should not come as a surprise because the king described here is of Davidic lineage. And, as 2 Sam 7:13, 16 states, God entered into an eternal relationship with Davidic dynasty. The exuberant style of Ps 44(45) is tamed by the twofold mention of "God" in the same verse, "God, your God anointed you." The presence of a second "God," remarks Harris, could be an indication of the psalmist's uneasiness with the use of "God" in v. 7(6)a with reference to the king's person. Another argument supporting the use of this appellation with regard to a king is the flexibility with which the biblical authors employ the term *ʾĕlōhîm*, "God": heavenly beings around God's throne (Ps 8:6 [LXX: *angelous*]; 96[97]:7; 137[138]:1), judges (Ps 81[82]:1, 6), Moses (Exod 7:1).

85. John Chrysostom, *Commentary on the Psalms*, 1:272. Unlike most of patristic commentators who explain Ps 44(45):7(6)–8(7) with reference to the eternal generation of the Son from the Father, Theodore of Mopsuestia suggests that these verses deal with the incarnate Christ in history. According to Pappas, "Theodore of Mopsuestia's Commentary on Ps 44 (LXX)," 71, Theodore's original interpretation is due to his exegetical method of postulating a single *prosōpon* (speaker) and *hypothesis* (subject matter) per narrative unity. In case of Ps 44(45), the speaker is David and the subject matter is the incarnate Christ in history.

86. Compare Sophronius's hymn with this fragment: "And she was in her sixth month; and, behold, Joseph came back from his building, and, entering into his house, he discovered that she was big with child. And he smote his face, and threw himself on the ground upon the sackcloth, and wept bitterly, saying: With what face shall I look upon the Lord my God? And what prayer shall I make about this maiden? Because I received her a virgin out of the temple of the Lord, and I have not watched over her. Who is it that has hunted me down? Who has done this evil thing in my house, and defiled the virgin? Has not the history of Adam been repeated in me? For just as Adam was in the hour of his singing praise, and the serpent came, and found Eve alone, and completely deceived her, so it has happened to me also" (*Protoevangelium of James* 13 [*ANF* 8:364]).

87. The term *parakoē* rendered here "disobedience" has the basic meaning "unwillingness to hear." Its use in this hymn hints at Adam's unwillingness to "hear" (observe) God's command pertaining to the trees of Eden.

88. The Septuagint reads the Hebrew word *gan*, "garden" as *paradeisos*, "garden, orchard, paradise," the Greek spelling of an Old Persian word (*pairi-daēza*) used first by Xenophon and meaning "enclosure," hence, "(royal) park" or "garden." The Persian word was also assimilated by the Hebrew lexicon under the spelling *pardēs*, "park" (Eccl 2:5) and orchard" (Song 4:13).

89. Septuagint reading *makarizō*, "I deem [him] happy," is due to the fact that the translator mistakenly interpreted the consonantal Hebrew form *'šwrnw* as deriving from the verbal root *'-š-r*, "to be happy," instead of the verbal root *š-w-r*, "to behold, to regard." The Masoretic vocalization *'ăšûrennû*, "I behold him" (verbal root *š-w-r*), is supported by the parallelism with the previous verbal root *r-'-h*, "to see."

90. The Essene community saw in the "star" the Levitical Messiah (CD 7:18: "The star is the interpreter [*dwrš*] of the Torah"). The *Testament of Levi* 18:3 speaks of the priestly Messiah as the one whose "star will rise in heaven as of a king."

91. Davies and Allison, *Gospel According to Saint Matthew*, 234.

92. The phrase "from a mountain" (v. 34), not found in MT but attested by LXX, Theodotion, and V, could be a reference to God given his association with various mountains (Ps 35[36]:7; 67[68]:17; Isa 14, 3; Ps 47[48]:3; Mic 4:1); see Siegman, "Stone," 369.

93. *Daniel*, 162.

94. Siegman, "Stone," 364–79.

95. PG 81:1301. For a copious list of patristic interpretations of Dan 2:44, see Pfandl, "Interpretations," 249–68.

96. For a different etymology of the Hebrew term *'almāh*, see Pentiuc, "A New Etymology," 129–36.

97. Blenkinsopp, *Isaiah 1–39*, 234.

98. On the extremely significant role played by Isa 7:14 in Christian theology and iconography, see Sawyer, *Fifth Gospel*.

99. *Scripture Readings*, 155.

100. MT reads *mərahepet*, "was hovering, moving back and forth"; the difference between LXX and MT is that in the latter version the Spirit's action is repetitive (Hithpa'el conjugation) while in LXX (*ephephereto*) the action is forceful, quick and punctual. Nonetheless, both versions portray the Spirit of God as if controlling the watery deep.

101. McCann, *Judges*, 66.

102. Constas, *Proclus of Constantinople*, 137, 150.

103. See chapter 7.

104. Baltzer, *Deutero-Isaiah*, 317.

105. *Scripture Readings*, 159.

106. Bray, *1–2 Corinthians*, 91.

107. PG 31:425B-C; see Daniélou, *The Bible and the Liturgy*, 89.

108. Daniélou, *The Bible and the Liturgy*, 21, notices: "Cyril of Jerusalem shows that the descent into the baptismal pool is as it were a descent into the waters of death which are the dwelling-place of the dragon of the sea, as Christ went down into the Jordan to crush the power of the dragon who was hidden there: 'The dragon Behemoth, according to Job,' writes Cyril, 'was in the waters, and was taking the Jordan into his gullet. But, as the heads of the dragon had to be crushed, Jesus, having descended into the waters, chained fast the strong one, so that we might gain the power to tread on scorpions and serpents. Life came so that henceforth a curb might be put on death, and so that all who have received salvation might say: O Death, where is your victory? For it is by Baptism that the sting of death is drawn. You go down into the waters, bearing your sins; but the invocation of grace, having marked your soul with its seal, will prevent your being devoured by the terrible dragon. Having gone down into the waters dead in sin, you come out brought to life in justice' (PG 33:441A)."

109. On the patristic theme of "divine deception," see Constas, "Last Temptation of Satan," 139–63.

110. The phrase *orthrō phananti*, "Shining Daybreak," is similar to the MT reading *hêlēl ben-šāḥar*, "The Shining One, son of Daybreak" (Isa 14:12); cf. LXX: *ho heōsphoros ho prōi anatellōn*, "the Morning Star who makes the morning rise"; Alexandrinus: *ololyzōn hyos orthrou*, "the bewailing son of the morning"; V: *Lucifer, fili aurorae*, "Lucifer (Morning Star) son of the Daybreak"; see Watts, *Isaiah 1–33*, 264.

111. In Hebrew the name of the place is *Marah*. Note the pun between *Marah* and *marîm*, "bitter" (verbal root *m-r-r*), referring to the water of Marah. The gemination of *r* in the Heb. root *m-r-r*, "to be bitter," is also detectable in the LXX reading *Merra*.

112. Does the story speak of a "tree" or a piece of "wood" taken from it? The Heb. word *'ēṣ* can mean either "tree" (so Tg. Neophyti, Tg. Pseudo-Jonathan) or "piece of wood." The same ambiguity obtains with the Gk. term used by LXX, *xylon*, "wood, tree." Based on parallelism with Ezek 47:1–12, one would lean toward reading "tree" here.

113. Propp, *Exodus 1–18*, 581.

114. Kugel, *Traditions of the Bible*, 614.

115. PG 52:839.

116. Kugel, *Traditions of the Bible*, 126.

117. Ware, *The Orthodox Church*, 199.

118. Constantelos, "Holy Scriptures," 78.

119. Taft, "Orthodox Liturgical Theology," 13.

120. Florovsky, *Bible, Church, Tradition*, 50.

121. Prokurat, "Orthodox Interpretation of Scripture," 98.

122. Rentel, "Byzantine and Slavic Orthodoxy," 278.

123. Costache, "Reading the Scriptures with Byzantine Eyes," 60.

CHAPTER 7. VISUAL

1. *NPNF*² 14:534.
2. *Synodikon* means "synodical decree." There is no critical edition of the *Synodikon* in English. See Gouilard, "Synodikon d'Orthodoxie," 1–316; a brief description may be found in Meyendorff, *Byzantine Theology*, 86–88.
3. Zenkovsky, *Medieval Russia's Epics*, 67.
4. On encountering God through senses, see Manoussakis, *God after Metaphysics*.
5. Ratzinger, "The Feeling of Things."
6. *The Life in Christ*, 90.
7. On the formative function of icons, see Vrame, *The Educating Icon*.
8. Louth, "Tradition and the Icon," 147, suggests that more recent popularity of Byzantine icons in the West parallels the rediscovery of "traditional" cultures (Asian, African, American): "The attraction these exert today could be interpreted in a variety of ways: a yearning for the exotic; the affluent West's nostalgia for lost certainties and simplicities; the denizens of a jaded, technological culture being fascinated by the naïve."
9. Jansen and Vrudny, *Visual Theology*, ix.
10. See Chase, "Kuntillet Ajrud," 63–67.
11. Note the third century C.E. Dura-Europos synagogue; see Kraeling, *Excavations of Dura-Europos*. According to Weitzmann and Kessler (*Frescoes of the Dura*), Dura synagogue's decorations may represent the missing link between a supposed Jewish tradition of manuscript illuminations and ancient Christian art.
12. Meyers, "Hasmoneans," 24–25. Similarly, "You shall not set up a figured stone in your land, to bow down to it, but a mosaic pavement of designs and forms you may set in the floor of your places of worship, so long as you do not do obeisance to it" (Tg. *Pseudo-Jonathan* on Lev 26:11); see Kessler, "Sacrifice of Isaac," 75.
13. See Milson, *Art and Architecture of the Synagogue*.
14. *Jewish Symbols*.
15. *Art and Judaism*.
16. According to Fine, "Iconography," 7:4343, in the new approach, "Jewish art is not merely a backdrop to Christian art but an equal."
17. See Magdalino and Nelson, *The Old Testament in Byzantium*, 20–21.
18. Mango, *The Homilies of Photius*, 293.
19. Ladner, "Concept of the Image," 1–34.
20. PG 44:137A; see Ladner, "Concept of the Image," 3.
21. Mercati, "Stephani Bostreni," 666, 668; see Ladner, "Concept of the Image," 15.
22. *On the Divine Images*, 72.
23. *Images of the Divine*, 25.
24. Fragments of Epiphanius's *Testament* are excerpted in Mango, *Art of the Byzantine Empire*.

25. Giakalis, *Images of the Divine*, 26.

26. *On Holy Images* 1.25; see John of Damascus, *Three Treatises*, 38.

27. Far from being over, the debate over the authenticity of the anti-iconic state-
    ments attributed to Epiphanius continues. For the current state of this debate,
    see Bigham, *Epiphanius of Salamis*. Personally, I think that placing Epiphanius
    in either camp—iconodules or iconophiles—seems to be anachronistic. Given
    his intricate theological profile, and some possible excesses in the area of the
    emerging icon worship, Epiphanius's dispassionate (rather than polemical) po-
    sition on images seems predictable, at the least. A good illustration of Epipha-
    nius's convoluted way of thinking is his view on biblical canon in relation to the
    Septuagint text. On the one hand, Epiphanius considers the Septuagint more
    accurate than the Hebrew text; on the other, he places two anaginōskomena
    writings (i.e., Wisdom of Solomon and Sirach) found only in Septuagint (his
    favorite text), at the very end of the Bible, right after the New Testament collec-
    tion—probably in order to flag the non-canonical status of these books. Yet
    Epiphanius's main works, *Panarion* and *On Measures and Weights*, containing
    such differing views on text and canon, have never been scrutinized or ques-
    tioned for their authenticity; see Chapters 2 and 3.

28. Brubaker, *Vision and Meaning*, 31 and n. 72.

29. Ibid., 32–33.

30. Louth, "Tradition and the Icon," 149.

31. Ibid.

32. Ouspensky, *Theology of the Icon*, 1:79–80.

33. "Tradition and the Icon," 148–49.

34. "Many of the sacred things which we have at our disposal do not need a prayer
    of sanctification, since their name says that they are all-sacred and full of
    grace. . . ." (*Nicaea II, Session 6*); see Sahas, *Icon and Logos*, 99.

35. John of Damascus, *On The Divine Images*, 21, 23.

36. *NPNF*² 8:28.

37. Theodore the Stoudite, *The Ordering of Holiness*, 59. For Theodore's theology of
    the icon, see, inter alia, Parry, "Theodore Studites," 164–83; and Theodore
    Damian, *Theological and Spiritual Dimensions*.

38. According to Cyprian, Melchizedek foreshadows Christ in terms of total self-
    offering: "Likewise, in the priest Melchizedek, we see the sacrament of the
    sacrifice of the Lord prefigured . . . Melchizedek portrayed a type of Christ. . . .
    For who is more a priest of the most high God than our Lord Jesus Christ, who
    offered sacrifice to God the Father and offered the very same thing that
    Melchizedek had offered, bread and wine, that is, actually, his body and blood?"
    (*Letter 63* 4 [Sheridan, *Genesis 12–50*, 26]).

39. In a Byzantine church, the *diakonikon*, situated on the south side of the sanctu-
    ary, is the room under the care of deacons where liturgical books, vestments,
    and vessels (e.g., chalice, paten) are kept. Opposite, on the north side, the

prothesis is the room where the offerings (i.e., bread and wine) are brought in preparation for the Eucharist.

40. Jensen, "Early Christian Images," 82, remarks, "The viewer could not help but draw direct lines from the images to the actions and realize at this place the past was being drawn into the present—the artistic representations on the walls mirroring the living human drama on the ground."

41. Ouspensky, *Theology of the Icon*, 1:8.

42. Germanos of Constantinople, *On the Divine Liturgy*, 57.

43. On *theosis*, see the seminal study of Russell, *The Doctrine of Deification.*

44. *Images of the Divine*, 5.

45. Roddy, "Mapping Boundaries of Meaning," 136.

46. See Cavarnos, "Byzantine Iconography," 91–105.

47. The Gk. term *Deēsis* ("Entreaty") refers to a well-attested Byzantine iconographic representation of the Theotokos and John the Baptist flanking Christ and interceding with him for the salvation of the faithful.

48. *On the Divine Images*, 31–32.

49. This was the opinion of the Council of Frankfurt in 794 c.e. At this council, the Westerners rejected the decisions of the Seventh Ecumenical Council at Nicaea in 787 c.e. by maintaining that icons were mere church decorations for didactic purposes; see Giakalis, *Images of the Divine*, 21.

50. *Frescoes of the Dura Synagogue.*

51. "Dura Europos Synagogue," 156–57. According to Jensen, "Images and Exegesis," 68, images are not simple interpretations of a textual or aural material but rather pointers showing the meaning of the entire story, or the meaning of one of its details.

52. The below synopsis of the main periods of the history of Byzantine sacred art follows closely the presentation found in Cormack's *Byzantine Art.*

53. Ibid., 40.

54. Ibid., 80.

55. On the use of Old Testament in liturgy, see chapter 6.

56. Magdalino and Nelson, *The Old Testament in Byzantium*, 30–31.

57. On Panselinos's school, see Hatziphotes, *Macedonian School.*

58. An example of "folklorization" obtains with St. Ilie (Elijah) Church, Suceava (Romania), built in 1488 and decorated with frescoes during the sixteenth century. A fresco shows prophet Elijah next to his disciple Elisha who ploughs with eight (cf. 1 Kings 19:19: twelve) yoke of oxen. The plow Elisha uses looks similar to the archaic Moldavian version of this agricultural implement.

59. Magdalino and Nelson, *The Old Testament in Byzantium*, 8.

60. For a complete list of illustrated psalters, see Dufrenne, *Tableaux synoptiques*; see also Weitzmann, "Byzantine Book Illumination," 1–60.

61. E.g., the Sinai icon of Virgin Kykkotissa; on the interpretive value of this icon and its abundant afterlife, see the comments below.

62. Annemarie Weyl Carr, "Painted Icons," 2:978–80

63. On the emergence and development of the Eastern Orthodox *iconostasis*, see Gerstel, *Thresholds of the Sacred.*

64. Cutler, "Mosaic," 2:1412–13

65. Wharton, "Fresco Technique," 2:805–806

66. Tkacz, "Commendatio animae," 1:488.

67. *Vision and Meaning*, 308–375.

68. Jensen, "Early Christian Images," 69, rightly notices, "A visual image, by contrast [to the verbal mode of expression], has an immediacy and concreteness."

69. Gračanica Monastery (today in Kosovo) is one of the most monumental churches of Serbian king Stefan Uroš Milutin Nemanji (1282–1321). The Gračanica church dedicated to the Dormition of the Theotokos was built in 1321. It represents the climax of Serbian medieval architecture following the Byzantine tradition. The form of the church is that of a double cross. The oldest frescoes were painted in 1321/2. The walls of the south *parekklēsion* (side chapel) are adorned with frescoes inspired from Old Testament scenes and episodes of Christ's and Theotokos's lives. The Gračanica frescoes reflect the luxurious style of the Palaeologan renaissance.

70. The reader is directed to Levenson, *Death and Resurrection*. In chapter 3 of his recent book, *Inheriting Abraham*, Levenson revisits Gen 22 as interpreted by each of the three Abrahamic religions, Judaism, Christianity, and Islam.

71. The term *Aqedah* (verbal root '-q-d [qal], "to bind together the legs of an animal for sacrifice," a *hapax*, Gen 22:9 [cf. LXX *sympodisas*]) is used in the second century C.E. Mishnah (*Tamid* 3:2–3:3, 7; 4:1) to designate the binding of the sacrificial lamb for Tamid ("perpetual") burnt offering brought every morning and evening at the Temple (Exod 29:38–42 and Num 28:1–8; cf. 2 Kgs 16:15; Ezek 46:13–15; Neh 10:34, and 2 Chr 13:11). According to Mishnah, the Tamid lamb had to be bound, fore- and hind legs (not tied) in remembrance of Isaac's binding.

72. As Levenson, *Death and Resurrection*, 142, well notes, "One paradox of the aqedah is that it is Abraham's willingness to give up Isaac that insures the fulfillment of the promise that depends on Isaac. The other paradox is this: though Abraham does not give up his son through sacrifice, he gives him up nonetheless-to the God who gave Isaac life, ordered him slaughtered, and finally grants him his exalted role in the divine plan."

73. Note though Levenson, *Inheriting Abraham*, 161–62, who thinks that there is a Christological message in the use of Aqedah in James 2.

74. Jensen, "Early Chirstian Images," 80.

75. "Sacrifice of Isaac," 77.

76. *Inheriting Abraham*, 99.

77. Jensen, "Offering of Isaac," 85–110. Nevertheless, earlier scholars, such as Van Woerden, "Iconography," 214–55, suggested that typological interpretation of

Isaac's sacrifice appeared much later in the fourth century, while the pre-Constantinian interpretation of Gen 22 was dominated by the crucifixion-deliverance theme.

78. "Image," 93–100. An example of image as meta-text may be found in the Khludov Psalter produced in Constantinople after the defeat of the iconoclasts in 843 c.e. Folio 67r of this psalter contains two images. In the upper level is Christ's crucifixion, with a man offering him a sponged soaked in vinegar and gall. This image is linked, based on relevant vocabulary, to Ps 68(69):22(21), "They gave me also gall for my food, and made me drink vinegar for my thirst." The image of crucifixion becomes a meta-text or a springboard for the actualizing image in the lower level, depicting an iconoclast whitewashing the icon of Christ. The inscription next to this image reads, "And they mixed water and lime on his face." The message conveyed by these two images is that profaning the icon of Christ is equal to crucifying the Lord.

79. Evangelatou, "Liturgy," 64–65, remarks that unlike patristic exegesis and liturgical use of the Psalms, relevant vocabulary "played a central role in the illustration of the ninth-century marginal psalters as a filter that limited the visualization of christological interpretations to those liturgical psalm verses that offered the most obvious and convincing allusions to Christ's life."

80. Walter, "Christological Themes," 271.

81. Anderson, "Date and Purpose," 60, dates Barberini Psalter between 1092 and 1118, most probably for 1095.

82. Note that in the ninth century Pantokrator Psalter (Mount Athos), the personified Hades holds Lazarus in a sarcophagus.

83. The Kiev Psalter or Spiridon Psalter, one of the most renowned East Slavic illuminated manuscripts, was written in 1397 by the Archdeacon Spiridon in Kiev. The over three hundred decorations, added later in Moscow, recapture the refined Byzantine style of the eleventh century marginal Psalters (i.e., dynamism of figures, vividness in chromatics, celestial aura by the copious use of gold). The fusion between image and text is indicated by thin red lines drawn between the image and the targeted Psalm passage. The Khludov Psalter employs an arrowlike sign to designate the linkage between image and text. The Kiev Psalter is kept today in the Public Library in St. Petersburg. According to Olga Popova, *Russian Illuminated Manuscripts*, the illustrator copied carefully most of decorations from a Byzantine art book of eleventh century.

84. Dölger, "Johannes 'von Euboia,'" 18–22, attributed this sermon to John of Euboea.

85. Walter, "Christological Themes," 275.

86. Ibid., 283.

87. Note also these hymns: "O divine might of your power, O Savior! Your voice has shattered the gates of Hades and the jaws of death. By the same might, free me from evil passions, as you delivered Lazarus, your friend, from four days in the

tomb" (Lazarus Saturday, Matins, Canon, Ode Five, *heirmos*); "Love led you to Lazarus at Bethany, O Master, though his body was already corrupt, you raised him up, for you are God. You have rescued him from the bonds of Hades" (Lazarus Saturday, Matins, Canon, Ode Six, heirmos); "You have confirmed my faith in your resurrection, O my Savior, even before it came to pass, by freeing Lazarus from Hades when he was four days dead" (Lazarus Saturday, Matins, Canon, Ode Nine, heirmos).

88. "Liturgy and the Illustration," 64.

89. The Khludov Psalter is one of the three ninth-century Byzantine psalters that survived the test of time. Produced in Constantinople shortly after the defeat of iconoclasm in 843, the Khludov Psalter contains only 169 folios. The illuminations were perhaps created before 843, many of them targeting the iconoclasts. Today, the Psalter is kept in the State Historical Museum in Moscow.

90. Luke 9:31 reports that Moses and Elijah conversed with Christ about "his departure (*exodon*) that he was about to accomplish in Jerusalem." According to the Byzantine writer Theophylactus, Archbishop of Ochrid (1088–1120), the conversation between Moses, Elijah, and Christ would have run this way. Moses would have said, "You are the one, whose passion I prefigured through the slaughtered lamb and the complete Pesach [Passover]," and Elijah, "I prefigured your resurrection by raising the widow's son" (*Enarratio in Matt.* 17.3; PG 123:328C); see Bovon, *Luke 1*, 380.

91. One may note that all three figures within the same mandorla is a rare feature of Byzantine iconography. A more customary depiction would have Moses and Elijah touching or slightly intersecting Christ's mandorla—something like in the portable icon of the Transfiguration painted by Theophanes the Greek in 1403 and kept in the Tretyakov Gallery, Moscow, where only Christ is circumscribed by a (circular) mandorla.

92. Among the ancient interpreters that related Ps 88(89) to Christ's transfiguration, one may list Origen (*Selecta in psalmos*, PG 12:1548D) and Eusebius (*Commentaria in psalmos*, PG 23:1092D); see Evangelatou, "Liturgy and the Illustration," 63 n. 73.

93. If one must choose between Hermon and Tabor, the former seems to be much closer to the description by the gospel accounts. Whereas Hermon is a true mountain (9,200 feet high), Tabor, though high as elevation in Galilee (4,100 feet), may hardly be labeled "(high) mountain." Moreover, the presence of a Roman camp on Tabor's summit at the time of the transfiguration, a camp fortified by Josephus Flavius in the second half of the first century (cf. *Jewish War*, 4.1, 18.), renders the detail that Jesus and his apostles went up to pray "privately" (*kat' idian*, cf. Matt 17:1) unrealizable.

94. *Holy Land*, 413.

95. The fourth-fifth century is considered the starting point for the East, and tenth century for the West, in the history of this festival. In 1456, Pope Callixtus III

decreed that the feast of the Transfiguration be observed on August 6 in remembrance of the Christian victory over the Turks at the siege of Belgrade. The siege was led by Janos Hunyadi in alliance with the Roman Catholic St. John of Capistrano and a young Romanian prince, the famous Vlad III the Impaler.

96. One may mention that the LXX verb *oryssō* matches the Hebrew roots *ḥ-p-r*, "to dig," *k-r-h* "to dig," and *ḥ-ṣ-b*, "to hew out." The MT reads *kā'ărî*, "as a lion." Based on Septuagint reading (supported by the Peshitta, Vulgate), the Hebrew consonantal form *k'ry* can be revocalized *kā'rê(y)*, infinitive absolute from *k-r-h* < *k-r-y*, "to dig," with an archaic *-y-* (cf. Gen 30:8; 49:11), hence the rendition of the emended MT, "piercing my hands and my feet." *Aleph* in the Hebrew consonantal form *k'ry* should be considered intrusive and not part of the verbal root (cf. Prov 24:7); see Dahood, *Psalms I*, 140; see also Pentiuc, *Jesus the Messiah*, 158–59.

97. PG 80:1017.

98. Fitzmyer, *Acts of the Apostles*, 516.

99. Attridge, *Hebrews*, 54.

100. Blaising and Hardin, *Psalms 1–50*, 14.

101. Ibid.

102. "The Art of Comparing in Byzantium," 88–103.

103. Walter, "'Latter-Day' Saints," 218.

104. In the Bristol Psalter (early eleventh century), f. 9, the members of the ungodly council (Ps 2:2), based on the inscription, are Herod, Pilate and the leaders of the Jews. In the London Psalter (dated 1066), f. 2, another image appended to that of the council depicts Christ before Annas and Caiaphas; see Walter, "Christological Themes," 286. Note that Theodoret of Cyrus, *Commentary on the Psalms, 1–72*, 52–53, interprets Ps 2:2 as referring to the Jewish leaders, including the Pharisees and high priest Caiaphas, who brought Christ to trial and crucifixion.

105. MT reads *tərō'ēm*, "you shall break them" (verbal root *r-'-'*); LXX's reading *poimaneis*, "you shall shepherd," presupposes a different Hebrew verbal root, *r-'-h*. The context of Ps 2:9 (i.e., a potter breaking his vessels with an iron rod) supports apparently the MT's reading; yet the LXX's reading is also possible.

106. Sheridan, *Genesis 12–50*, 63.

107. The Basilica di Santa Maria Maggiore was built in the fourth century C.E., and its mosaics depicting Old and New Testament scenes date to the fifth century.

108. One gets a similar impression looking at the fourth century painting of Abraham's hospitality preserved in Rome's Via Latina catacomb: the three men with no auras are depicted as if hovering over the ground.

109. Likewise, the targums see no difference in rank or honor among the three visitors. Here is how the Targum of Pseudo-Jonathan expands interpretatively the text of Gen 18:2: "And he [Abraham] lifted up his eyes and looked, and, behold,

three angels in the resemblance of men were standing before him; (angels) who had been sent from the necessity of three things; because it is not possible for a ministering angel to be sent for more than one purpose at a time; one, then, had come to make known to him that Sarah should bear a man-child; one had come to deliver Lot; and one to overthrow Sedom and Amorah. And when he saw them, he ran to meet them from the door of the tent, and bowed himself on the earth."

110. McKay, "Daniel's Vision," 139–61, especially 153–54.

111. See the whole discussion in Pentiuc, *Jesus the Messiah*, 52–56 and note 37.

112. Louth, "Tradition and the Icon," 150–51.

113. Established by king Stefan Dečanski in 1327, Visoki Dečani Monastery, was completed by Stefan Dusan in 1335. The wall painting was finalized in 1350. This major Serbian Orthodox monastery is situated in Metohija, few miles south from Peć.

114. Kugel, *Traditions of the Bible*, 146–47.

115. Ibid., 152–53.

116. Charles, *Pseudepigrapha of the Old Testament*, 2:139.

117. Abel as a martyr appears in the following liturgical hymn, "The God and Lord of all accepted Abel, who offered his gifts with a most noble soul; and when he was slain of old by a blood-stained hand, he brought him to the light as a divine Martyr" (Sunday of the Forefathers, Matins, Ode One, troparion).

118. Hess, "Abel," 1:9–10

119. Kugel, *Traditions of the Bible*, 151.

120. For Jewish and Christian interpretations of Cain and Abel story, see Springer, "Proof of Identification," 259–72.

121. The *aer* (Gk. *aēr*, "air; veil"), the largest of the three veils, is carried during the "great entrance" with the holy gifts as part of the Byzantine liturgy. When the gifts are placed on the altar table, the *aer* is used to cover both the paten and the chalice. The *aer* symbolizes the shroud in which the body of Christ was wrapped prior to being laid in the tomb.

122. Ševčenko, "Virgin's Lament Revisited," 261–62; "Art and Liturgy," 130–31.

123. Mentioned for the first time in fourth-sixth century c.e. papyri, the *maphorion*, covering the head and the shoulders, was a distinguishing piece of vestment worn by noble women. The blue, brown or purple *maphorion* became the traditional "veil" of the Virgin Mary in Byzantine iconography; see Ševčenko and Kazhdan, "Maphorion," 2:1294.

124. The inscriptions on the scrolls are reproduced from Mouriki, "Icons," 385 n. 27.

125. Ibid.

126. On the Sinai icon of Virgin Kykkotissa, see Mouriki, "Icons," 105, 385 nn. 26–28; Annemarie Weyl Carr, "Presentation," 239–48; "'Virgin Veiled by God'," 215–27.

127. Ševčenko, "Virgin Eleousa," 3:2171.

128. See Mouriki, "Icons," 105, 385 n. 28.

129. Staro Nagoričino (today part of Republic of Macedonia) is the site of St. George Monastery built by king Stefan Uroš II Milutin in 1313. The church was constructed on the foundations of an eleventh century basilica. The shape of the church is a combination of the original three-aisle design and a cross-in-square structure. The marble iconostasis containing fresco paintings is original. Characteristic of this church fresco program is the thematic variety and didactic character of the scenes; see Babić, "Staro Nagoričino," 3:1943–44.

130. Some scholars identify Manuel Panselinos with Michael (Astrapas) but there is no concrete evidence to support such identification; see Cutler, "Panselinos, Manuel," 3:1572.

131. Cutler, "Michael (Astrapas) and Eutychios," 2:1368.

132. See Taft and Carr, "Dormition," 1:651–53.

133. "Borne from the ends of the earth as it were upon a cloud, the company of the apostles was gathered in Sion to minister to you, O Virgin, the swift cloud whence the Most High God shone forth as the Sun of Righteousness upon those in darkness and shadow" (Dormition, Matins, Ode Five, troparion).

134. "Your Dormition is now glorified by dominions, powers, principalities and thrones, authorities, cherubim and the dread seraphim; the earthborn are filled with joy, adorned with your divine glory and majesty; and kings worship, falling down with all the angels and archangels, and they sing: Maiden Full of Grace, rejoice you, with you is the Lord our God, who abundantly grants his great mercy to the world through you" (Dormition, Great Vespers, troparion).

135. Note the basic meaning of the Greek word *kibōtos*, "box, chest," hence, "ark" (of Noah). The "ark" associated with David in this fresco may reflect a verbal-visual pun between "box" and "ark." David's ark as Noah's typifies the Church.

136. A theotokion reads, "Moses was astonished seeing that singularly marvelous spectacle, the bush and the flame prefiguring the strange and uncorrupted intertwining, even God come forth of a Virgin Mother, whom he saw in the flesh after the passage of many years" (September 4, The Holy God-seer Moses the Prophet and His Brother Aaron, Matins, Ode One).

137. The alternative translation of the introducing phrase (or the title of this hymn) is "Prophets of old. . . ."

138. Stathis, *Morphes kai Morphes*, 382–83.

Bibliography

Aageson, James W. "Early Jewish Lectionaries." In *ABD*, 4:270–71.

Abraham, William J. *The Divine Inspiration of Holy Scripture.* New York: Oxford University Press, 1981.

Aghiorgoussis, Maximos. "Towards the Great and Holy Council: The First Pre-synodal Pan-Orthodox Conference in Geneva." *GOTR* 21 (1976): 423–28.

Agouridis, Savas. "The Church Fathers as Interpreters of Holy Scripture." *Resonance* 8 (1975): 19–42.

Alexeev, Anatoly A. "The Old Testament Lections in Orthodox Worship." In *Das Alte Testament als christliche Bibel in orthodoxer und westlicher Sicht*, edited by Ivan Z. Dimitrov, James D. G. Dunn, Ulrich Luz, and Karl-Wilhelm Niebuhr. Wissenschaftliche Untersuchungen zum Neuen Testament 174. Tübingen: Mohr Siebeck, 2004, 91–117.

Anderson, Jeffrey C. "The Date and Purpose of the Barberini Psalter." *Cahiers archéologiques* 31 (1983): 35–68.

Attridge, Harold W. "The Gospel of Truth as an Exoteric Text." In *Nag Hammadi, Gnosticism, and Early Christianity*, edited by C. W. Hedrick and R. Hodgson, 239–55. Peabody, MA: Hendrickson, 1986.

———. *The Epistle to the Hebrews: A Commentary on the Epistle to the Hebrews.* Hermeneia. Philadelphia: Fortress, 1989.

Auxentios Hieromank, and James Thornton. "Three Byzantine Commentaries on the Divine Liturgy: A Comparative Treatment." *GOTR* 32:3 (1987): 285–308.

Babić, Gordana. "Staro Nagoričino." In *ODB*, 3:1943–44.

Baltzer, Klaus. *Deutero-Isaiah: A Commentary on Isaiah 40–55.* Hermeneia. Minneapolis: Fortress, 2001.

Barrois, Georges A. *The Face of Christ in the Old Testament.* Crestwood, NY: St. Vladimir's Seminary Press, 1974.

———. *Scripture Readings in Orthodox Worship.* Crestwood, NY: St. Vladimir's Seminary Press, 1977.

Barthélemy, Dominique. *Les devanciers d'Aquila: première publication intégrale du texte des fragments du dodécaprophéton trouvés dans le desert de Juda, précédée d'une etude sur les traductions et recensions grecques de la Bible réalisées au premier siècle de notre ère sous l'influence du rabbinat palestinien.* Vetus Testamentum Supplement 10. Leiden: Brill, 1963.

———. "Qui est Symmaque?" *CBQ* 36 (1974): 451–65.

———, ed. *Critique textuelle de l'Ancien Testament.* Orbis biblicus et orientalis 50/1–3. Göttingen: Vandenhoeck and Ruprecht, 1982–92.

Baumstark, Anton. "Die Zitate des Mt.-Ev. aus dem Zwölfprophetenbuch." *Biblica* 37 (1956): 296–313.

Behr, John. "Scripture, the Gospel, and Orthodoxy." *SVTQ* 43 (1999) 223–48.

———. *The Nicene Faith: Formation of Christian Theology.* 2 vols. Crestwood, NY: St. Vladimir's Seminary Press, 2001, 2004.

———. *Irenaeus of Lyons: Identifying Christianity.* Oxford: Oxford University Press, 2013.

Benoit, Pierre. "L'inspiration des Septante d'après les Pères." In *L'homme devant Dieu. Mélanges offerts au père Henri de Lubac,* edited by J. Guillet et al. 3 vols. 1:169–87. Theologie 56–58. Paris: Aubier, 1963.

Betz, Hans Dieter. *Galatians: A Commentary on Paul's Letter to the Churches in Galatia.* Hermeneia. Philadelphia: Fortress, 1979.

Bigham, Steven. *Epiphanius of Salamis, Doctor of Iconoclasm? Deconstruction of a Myth.* Rollinsford, NH: Orthodox Research Institute, 2008.

Bingaman, Brock, and Bradley Nassif, eds. *The Philokalia: A Classic Text of Orthodox Spirituality.* New York: Oxford University Press, 2012.

Blackman, Edwin Cyril. *Marcion and His Influence.* London: SPCK, 1948.

Blaising, Craig A., and Carmen S. Hardin, eds. *Psalms 1–50.* Ancient Christian Commentary on Scripture Old Testament 7. Downers Grove, IL: InterVarsity, 2008.

Blenkinsopp, Joseph. *The Pentateuch: An Introduction to the First Five Books of the Bible.* The Anchor Bible Reference Library. New York: Doubleday, 1992.

———. *Isaiah 1–39: A New Translation with Introduction and Commentary.* The Anchor Yale Bible. New Haven: Yale University Press, 2000.

Bogaert. Pierre-Maurice. "La *vetus latina* de Jérémie: texte très court, témoin de la plus ancienne Septante et d'une forme plus ancienne de l'hébreu (Jer 39 et 52)." In *The Earliest Text of the Hebrew Bible: The Relationship Between the Masoretic Text and the Hebrew Base of the Septuagint Reconsidered,* edited by Adrian Schenker. Society of Biblical Literature Septuagint and Cognate Studies 52. Atlanta: Scholars Press, 2003, 51–82.

Bovon, François. *Luke 1: A Commentary on the Gospel of Luke 1:1–9:50.* Hermeneia. Minneapolis: Fortress, 2002.

Boyarin, Daniel. "The Gospel of *Memra*: Jewish Binitarianism and the Prologue of John." *HTR* 94:3 (2001): 243–84.

——. *Border Lines: The Partition of Judaeo-Christianity.* Philadelphia: University of Philadelphia Press, 2004.

——. "Talmud and 'Fathers of the Church.' Theologies and the Making of Books." In *The Early Christian Book,* edited by William E. Klingshim and Linda Safran, Washington, DC: The Catholic University of America Press, 2007, 69–85.

——. "Rethinking Jewish Christianity: An Argument for Dismantling a Dubious Category (to which is Appended a Correction of my Border Lines)." *JQR* 99:1 (Winter 2009): 7–36.

Boys, Mary C. "Biblical Interpretation." In *A Dictionary of Jewish-Christians Relations,* edited by Edward Kessler and Neil Wenborn, 56–57. Cambridge: Cambridge University Press, 2005.

Bratcher, Robert G., ed. *Old Testament Quotations in the New Testament.* New York: United Bible Societies, 1987.

Bray, G. L., ed. *Romans.* Ancient Christian Commentary on Scripture New Testament 6. Downers Grove, IL: InterVarsity, 1998.

——, ed. *1–2 Corinthians.* Ancient Christian Commentary on Scripture New Testament 7. Downers Grove, IL: InterVarsity, 1999.

Breck, John. "Exegesis and Interpretation: Orthodox Reflections on the 'Hermeneutic Problem.'" *SVTQ* 27:2 (1983): 75–92.

——. "Orthodox Principles of Biblical Interpretation." *SVTQ* 40:1–2 (1996): 77–93.

——. *Scripture in Tradition: The Bible and Its Interpretation in the Orthodox Church.* Crestwood, NY: St. Vladimir's Seminary Press, 2001.

Brock, Sebastian P. "The Phenomenon of the Septuagint." *OtSt* 17 (1972): 11–36.

——. "Translating the Old Testament." In *It Is Written: Scripture Citing Scripture. Essays in Honour of Barnabas Lindars, SSF,* edited by D. A. Carson and Hugh Godfrey Maturin Williamson. Cambridge: Cambridge University Press, 1988, 87–98.

——. *The Luminous Eye: The Spiritual World Vision of Saint Ephrem.* Kalamazoo, MI: Cistercian Press, 1992.

Brown, Raymond E. *The Sensus Plenior of Sacred Scripture.* Baltimore: St. Mary's University Press, 1955.

Brubaker, Leslie. *Vision and Meaning in Ninth-Century Byzantium: Image as Exegesis in the Homilies of Gregory of Nazianzus.* Cambridge Studies in Palaeography and Codicology. Cambridge: Cambridge University Press, 2001.

——. "Image, Meta-Text and Text in Byzantium." In *Herméneutique du texte d'histoire: orientation, interpretation et questions nouvelles,* edited by S. Sato. Tokyo: Nagoya University, 2009, 83–100.

Bruce, F. F. *The Canon of Scripture.* Downers Grove, IL: InterVarsity Press, 1988.

Brueggemann, Walter. *Genesis.* Interpretation. Atlanta: John Knox Press, 1982.

——. *Theology of the Old Testament: Testimony, Dispute, Advocacy.* Minneapolis: Fortress, 1997.

Bruns, Gerald L. *Hermeneutics Ancient and Modern.* Yale Studies in Hermeneutics. New Haven: Yale University Press, 1995.

Bucur, Bogdan G. "Exegesis of Biblical Theophanies in Byzantine Hymnography: Rewritten Bible?" *Theological Studies* 68 (2007): 92–112.

Burke, David G. "The Bible Societies and the Deuterocanon as Scripture." *United Bible Societies Bulletin* 182–83 (1997): 223–40.

Burrus, Virginia. *"Begotten, Not Made": Concerning Manhood in Late Antiquity.* Stanford: Stanford University Press, 2000.

Carleton, J. "Jewish Christianity." In *Cambridge History of Judaism. Volume 3: The Early Roman Period,* edited by William Horburury, W. D. Davies, and John Sturdy. Cambridge: Cambridge University Press, 2008, 731–76.

Carr , Annemarie Weyl. "Painted Icons." In *ODB*, 2:978–80.

——. "The Presentation of an Icon at Mount Sinai." *Deltion tês Christianikês Archaiologikês Etaireias* 4/17 (1993–94): 239–48.

——. "The 'Virgin Veiled by God': The Presentation of an Icon on Cyprus." In *Reading Medieval Images: The Art Historian and the Object,* edited by Elizabeth Sears and Thelma K. Thomas. Ann Arbor, MI: University of Michigan Press, 2002, 215–27.

Carr, David M. *Writing on the Tablet of the Heart: Origins of Scripture and Literature.* New York: Oxford University Press, 2005.

Cavarnos, Constantine. "Byzantine Iconography." *Theologia* 1–2 (1972): 91–105.

Ceriani, Antonio Maria, ed. *Monumenta Sacra et Profana ex Codicibum Praesertim Bibliothecae Ambrosianae* 7. Milan: Biblioteca Ambrosiana, 1874.

——, ed. *Translatio syra pescitto Veteris Testamenti: ex codice Ambrosiano sec. fere VI, photolithographice edita.* Milan: Biblioteca Ambrosiana, 1876–81.

Charles, R. H. ed., *Pseudepigrapha of the Old Testament: The Pseudepigrapha.* Bellingham, WA: Apocryphile Press, 2004.

Charlesworth, James H. "What Has the Old Testament to Do with the New?" In *The Old and New Testaments: Their Relationship and the Intertestamental Literature.* edited by James H. Charlesworth and Walter P. Weaver, Faith and Scholarship Colloquies. Valley Forge, PA: Trinity Press International, 1993, 39–87.

Chase, Debra A. "A Note on an Inscription from Kuntillet Ajrud." *BASOR* 245 (Spring, 1982): 63–67.

Childs, Brevard S. *Introduction to the Old Testament as Scripture.* Philadelphia: Fortress, 1979.

——. *Biblical Theology of the Old and New Testaments: Theological Reflection on the Christian Bible.* Minneapolis: Fortress, 1993.

——. "Retrospective Reading of the Old Testament Prophets." *ZAW* 108 (1996): 362–77.

Clabeaux, John J. "Marcion." In *ABD*, 4:514–16.

Clark, William R., ed. and trans. *A History of the Councils of the Church: From the Original Documents by Charles Joseph Hefele.* 2 vols. Edinburgh: T. and T. Clark, 1876.

Collins, John J. *Daniel: A Commentary on the Book of Daniel.* Hermeneia. Minneapolis: Fortress, 1993.

Congar, Yves. *Jalons pour une théologie du laïcat.* Paris: Éditions du Cerf, 1953.

Constantelos, Demetrios J. "The Holy Scriptures in Greek Orthodox Worship." *GOTR* 12 (1966): 7–83.

———. "The Apocryphal / Deuterocanonical Books: An Orthodox View." In *The Parallel Apocrypha*, edited by John R. Kohlenberger III, xxvii–xxx. New York: Oxford University Press, 1997.

Constas, Nicholas P. "'To Sleep, Perchance to Dream': The Middle State of Souls in Patristic Literature." *Dumbarton Oaks Papers* 55 (2001): 91–124.

———. *Proclus of Constantinople and the Cult of the Virgin in Late Antiquity: Homilies 1–5. Texts and Translations.* Vigiliae Christianae Supplements 66. Leiden: Brill, 2003.

———. "The Last Temptation of Satan: Divine Deception in Greek Patristic Interpretations of the Passion Narrative." *HTR* 97:2 (2004): 139–63.

Cook, John Granger. *The Interpretation of the New Testament in Greco-Roman Paganism.* Studies und Texte zu Antike und Christentum 3. Tübingen: Mohr Siebeck, 1999.

Cormack, Robin. *Byzantine Art.* New York: Oxford University Press, 2000.

Costache, Doru. "Reading the Scriptures with Byzantine Eyes: The Hermeneutical Significance of St. Andrew of Crete's Great Canon." *Phronema* 23 (2008): 51–66.

Craigie, Peter C., and Marvine E. Tate. *Psalms 1–50.* Word Biblical Commentary 19. Nashville, TN: Thomas Nelson, 2004.

Cross, Frank Moore. *The Ancient Library of Qumran and Modern Biblical Studies.* Grand Rapids, MI: Baker, 1961.

Cullmann, Oscar. "The Tradition." In *Studies in Early Christianity. Volume 3. The Bible in the Early Church*, edited by Everett Ferguson. New York: Garland, 1993, 109–49.

Cutler, Anthony. "Michael (Astrapas) and Eutychios." In *ODB*, 2:1368.

———. "Mosaic." In *ODB*, 2:1412–13.

———. "Panselinos, Manuel." In *ODB*, 3:1572.

Cyril of Alexandria. *Commentary on the Twelve Prophets.* vol. 1. Translated by Robert Charles Hill. The Fathers of the Church: A New Translation. Patristic Series 115; Washington, DC: The Catholic University of America Press, 2007.

Dahood, Mitchell. *Psalms I:1–50: Introduction, Translation, and Notes.* The Anchor Yale Bible. New Haven: Yale University Press, 2008.

Dalton, W. J. "St. Jerome on the Inspiration and Inerrancy of Scriptures." *ACR* 33 (1956): 103–116.

Damaskinos of Tranoupolis. "Towards the Great and Holy Council." *GOTR* 24 (1979): 99–116.

Damian, Theodore. *Theological and Spiritual Dimensions of Icons According to St. Theodore of Studion.* Texts and Studies in Religion 94. Lewiston, NY: Edwin Mellen Press, 2002.

Daniélou, Jean. *The Bible and the Liturgy*. University of Notre Dame Liturgical Studies 3. Notre Dame, IN: University of Notre Dame Press, 1956.

————. *From Shadows to Reality: Studies in the Biblical Typology of the Fathers*. London: Burns and Oates, 1960.

Daube, David. "Rabbinic Methods of Interpretation and Hellenistic Rhetoric." *HUCA* 22 (1949): 239–64.

Davies, Philip R. "Judaism and the Hebrew Scriptures." In *The Blackwell Companion to Judaism*, edited by Jacob Neusner and Alan J. Avery-Peck. Oxford: Blackwell, 2000. 1:31–44.

Davies, W. D., and D. C. Allison. *A Critical and Exegetical Commentary on the Gospel According to Saint Matthew*. London: T. and T. Clark, 2004.

Dean, James Elmer, ed. *Epiphanius' Treatise on Weights and Measures: The Syriac Version*. Studies in Ancient Oriental Civilizations 11. Chicago: The University of Chicago Press, 1935.

De Boer, Pieter Arie Hendrik, and M. J. Mulder, eds. *The Old Testament in Syriac according to the Peshitta Version*. Leiden, Brill: 1966.

De Lange, Nicholas. "A Thousand Years of Hebrew in Byzantium." In *Hebrew Study from Ezra to Ben-Yehuda*, edited by William Horbury. Edinburgh: T. & T. Clark, 1999, 147–61.

De Lubac, Henri-Marie. *Éxégése Médiévale: les quatre sens de l'écriture*. 4 vols. Paris: Aubier, 1959–64. English translation: De Lubac, Henri-Marie. *Medieval Exegesis*. Translated by M. Sebanc. Grand Rapids, MI: Eerdmans, 1998.

Delling, G. *Worship in the New Testament*. Translated by P. Scott. Philadelphia: Westminster/London: Darton, Longman, and Todd, 1962.

Dibelius, M., and H. Conzelmann, *The Pastoral Epistles*. Hermeneia. Philadelphia: Fortress, 1972.

Diodore of Tarsus. *Commentary on Psalms 1–51*. Translated by Robert Charles Hill. Writings from the Greco-Roman World 9. Atlanta: Society of Biblical Literature, 2005.

Dionysios the Pseudo-Areopagite. *The Ecclesiastical Hierarchy*. Translated by Thomas L. Campbell. New York: University Press of America, 1981.

Dirksen, P. B., and M. J. Mulder, eds. *The Peshitta: Its Early Text and History. Papers read at the Peshitta Symposium held at Leiden 30–31 August 1985*. Monographs of the Peshitta Institute 4. Leiden: Brill, 1988.

"*Divino Afflante Spiritu*. Encyclical of Pope Pius XII on Promoting Biblical Studies, Commemorating the Fiftieth Anniversary of *Providentissimus Deus*, September 30, 1943." In *The Papal Encyclicals: 1939–1958*, edited by Claudia Carlen. Wilmington, NC: McGrath, 1981, 65–79.

Dix, Gregory. *The Shape of the Liturgy*. London: Dacre Press, 1945.

Dobschütz, Ernst von, ed. *Das Decretum Gelasianum de libris recipiendis et non recipiendis*. Leipzig: J. C. Hinrichs, 1912.

Dölger, Franz. "Johannes 'von Euboia', Anhang Die Predigt des Johannes 'von Euboia' auf die Erweckung des Lazaros." *Analecta Bollandiana*, 68 (1950): 3–26.

Dufrenne, Suzy. *Tableaux synoptiques de 15 psautiers marginaux médiévaux à illustrations intégrales issues du texte*. Paris: Association des amis des études archéologiques byzantines slaves, 1978.

Duncker, Peter G. "The Canon of the Old Testament at the Council of Trent." *CBQ* 15(1953): 277–99.

Dungan, David L. *Constantine's Bible: Politics and the Making of the New Testament*. Minneapolis: Fortress, 2007.

Edwards, Mark J., trans. and ed. *Optatus: Against the Donatists*. Liverpool: Liverpool University Press, 1997.

———. *Galatians, Ephesians, Philippians*. Ancient Christian Commentary on Scripture New Testament 8. Downers Grove, IL: InterVarsity, 1999.

Elliott, C. J. "Hebrew Learning Among the Fathers." In *A Dictionary of Christian Biography, Literature, Sects and Doctrines: being a Continuation of "The Dictionary of the Bible,"* edited by W. Smith and H. Wace. London, 1880, 2:841–72.

Ellis, Edward Earle. *The Old Testament in Early Christianity: Canon and Interpretation in the Light of Modern Research*. Wissenschaftliche Untersuchungen Zum Neuen Testament 54. Tübingen: Mohr Siebeck, 1991.

Evangelatou, Maria. "Liturgy and the Illustration of the Ninth-Century Marginal Psalters." *Dumbarton Oaks Papers* 63 (2009): 65–116.

Feinberg, John S., ed. *Continuity and Discontinuity: Perspectives on the Relationship Between the Old and New Testaments. Essays in Honor of S. Lewis Johnson, Jr.* Westchester, IL: Crossway, 1988.

Fine, Steven. *This Holy Place: On the Sanctity of the Synagogue During the Greco-Roman Period. Christianity and Judaism in Antiquity*. Notre Dame, IN: University of Notre Dame Press, 1998.

———. *Art and Judaism During the Greco-Roman Period: Toward a New "Jewish Archaeology."* Cambridge: Cambridge University Press, 2005.

———. "Iconography: Jewish Iconography [Further Considerations]." In *Encyclopedia of Religion*, edited by Lindsay Jones, 7:4341–44. Farmington Hills, MI: Thomson Gale, 2005.

Fitzmyer, Joseph A. *The Acts of the Apostles: A New Translation with Introduction and Commentary*. The Anchor Yale Bible. New Haven: Yale University Press, 2008.

Florovsky, Georges. *Bible, Church, Tradition: An Eastern Orthodox View. Volume One in the Collected Works of Georges Florovsky*. Belmont, MA: Nordland, 1972.

———. *The Ways of Russian Theology*. 2 vols. Belmont, MA: Nordland, 1979.

Friedmann, Meir. *Onkelos und Akylas*. Jahresbericht der israelitisch-theologischen Lehranstalt in Wien für das Schuljahr 3. Vienna: Verlag der israelitisch-theologischen Lehranstalt, 1896.

Gamble, Harry Y. "Marcion and the 'Canon'." In *Cambridge History of Christianity. vol. 1: Origins to Constantine,* edited by Margaret M. Mitchell and Frances M. Young. Cambridge: Cambridge University Press, 2008, 195–213.

Germanos of Constantinople. *On the Divine Liturgy.* Translated by Paul Meyendorff. Crestwood, NY: St. Vladimir's Seminary Press, 1984.

Gerstel, Sharon E. J., ed. *Thresholds of the Sacred: Architectural, Art Historical, Liturgical, and Theological Perspectives on Religious Screens, East and West.* Dumbarton Oaks Studies. Washington, DC: Dumbarton Oaks Research Library and Collection, 2007.

Giakalis, Ambrosios. *Images of the Divine: The Theology of Icons at the Seventh Ecumenical Council.* Studies in the History of Christian Traditions. Leiden: Brill, 2005.

Gilbert, Maurice. "Textes exclus, textes inclus: les enjeux." In *L'autorité de l'Écriture,* edited by Jean-Michel Poffet. Paris: Éditions du Cerf, 2002, 51–70.

Ginsburg, Christian David. *The Massorah Compiled from Manuscripts, Alphabetically and Lexically Arranged.* 4 vols. London, 1880–1905.

——. *Introduction of the Massoretical-Critical Edition of the Hebrew Bible.* London: Trinitarian Bible Society, 1897.

Glessmer, Uwe. "Liste der biblischen Texte aus Qumran." *RQ* 16 (1993): 153–92.

Goldfarb, Elizabeth Bisbee. "Transformation through Imitation: Biblical Figures as Moral Exempla in the Post-Classical World." PhD diss., University of California, Los Angeles, 2005.

Goodenough, Erwin R. *Jewish Symbols in the Greco-Roman Period.* 13 vols. New York: Pantheon Books, 1953–68.

Gorday, Peter. *Principles of Patristic Exegesis. Romans 9–11 in Origen, John Chrysostom and Augustine.* New York: Edwin Mellen Press, 1983.

Goshen-Gottstein, Moshe H. "The Aleppo-Codex and the Rise of the Massoretic Bible Text." *BA* 42:3 (Summer 1979): 145–63.

Gouilard, Jean. "Le Synodikon d'Orthodoxie: Édition et commentaire." *Travaux et Mémoires* 2 (1967): 1–316.

Grabbe, Lester L. "Aquila's Translation and Rabbinic Exegesis." *JJS* 33(1982): 527–36.

Gray, Patrick T. R. "'The Select Fathers': Canonizing the Patristic Past." *Studia Patristica* 23 (1989): 21–36.

Green, Garrett. *Theology, Hermeneutics, and Imagination: The Crisis of Interpretation at the End of Modernity.* Cambridge: Cambridge University Press, 2000.

Greenspoon, Leonard Jay. "The Use and Abuse of the Term 'LXX' and Related Terminology in Recent Scholarship." *BIOSCS* 20 (1987): 21–29.

Grypeou, Emmanouela, and Helen Spurling, eds. *The Exegetical Encounter between Jews and Christian in Late Antiquity.* Jewish and Christian Perspectives 18. Leiden: Brill, 2009.

Guinot, Jean-Noël. "La typologie comme technique herméneutique." In *Figures de l'Ancien Testament chez les Pères*, edited by Pierre Maraval. Cahiers de Biblia Patristica 2. Strasbourg: Centre d'Analyse et de Documentation Patristique, 1989, 1–34.

Hagner, Donald A. *Matthew 1–13*. Word Biblical Commentary 33A; Dallas: Word Books, 1993.

Hanhart, Robert. "Die Bedeutung der Septuaginta-Forschung für die Theologie." In *Drei Studien zum Judentum*, edited by Robert Hanhart. Theologische Existenz Heute NF 140. München, 1967, 38–64.

Hansen, Morgens Herman. *Polis: An Introduction to the Ancient Greek City-State.* New York: Oxford University Press, 2006.

Hanson, Paul D. "Biblical Authority Reconsidered." *Horizons in Biblical Theology* 11/1 (January 1989): 57–79.

Hanson, R. P. C. "Biblical Exegesis in the Early Church." In *The Cambridge History of the Bible. Volume 1. From the Beginnings to Jerome*, edited by P. R. Ackroyd and C. F. Evans. Cambridge: Cambridge University Press, 1970, 412–53.

Harl, Marguerite. "Traduire la Septante en Français: Pourquoi et Comment?" In *La Langue de Japhet: Quinze Études sur la Septante et le Grec des Chrétiens*, edited by Marguerite Harl. Paris: Éditions du Cerf, 1992, 33–42.

Harris, Murray J. "The Translation of *ELOHIM* in Psalm 45:7–8" *Tyndale Bulletin* 35 (1984): 65–89.

Hatziphotes, M. *The Macedonian School, the School of Panselenos (1290–1320).* Athens: The National Foundation for Youth, 1995.

Hayes, John H., ed. *Dictionary of Biblical Interpretation.* 2 vols. New York: Abingdon, 1999.

Heine, Ronald E. *Reading the Old Testament with the Ancient Church: Exploring the Formation of Early Christian Thought.* Evangelical Ressourcement: Ancient Sources for the Church's Future. Grand Rapids, MI: Baker Academic, 2007.

Henderson, Ian H. "Didache and Orality." *JBL* 111 (1992): 283–306.

Hengel, Martin. *The Septuagint as Christian Scripture: Its Prehistory and the Problem of Its Canon.* Grand Rapids, MI: Baker Academic, 2004.

Heschel, Abraham Joshua. *The Sabbath: Its Meaning for Modern Man.* New York: Farrar, Straus and Giroux, 1951, reprinted 2005.

Hess, Richard S. "Abel." In *ADB*, 1:9–10.

Hill, Robert Charles. "St John Chrysostom's Teaching on Inspiration in 'Six Homilies on Isaiah.'" *Vigiliae Christianae* 22 (1968): 19–37.

——. "St. John Chrysostom as Biblical Commentator: Six Homilies on Isaiah 6." *SVTQ* 47:3–4 (2003): 307–322.

Hofer, Andrew. "Who is God in the Old Testament? Retrieving Aquinas after Rahner's Answer." *International Journal of Systematic Theology* 14:4 (2012): 439–58.

Holmes, Michael W. "Origen and the Inerrancy of Scripture." *JETS* 24:3 (September 1981): 221–31.

———. ed. *The Apostolic Fathers: Greek Texts and English Translations*. Grand Rapids, MI: Baker Academic, 1999.

Honscheid, J., trans. and ed. *Didymus der Blinde. De trinitate, Buch 1*. Beiträge zur klassischen Philologie 44. Meisenheim am Glan: Hain, 1975.

Imp. Justiniani PP. A Novellae quae vocantur sive Constitutiones quae extra codicem supersunt ordine chronologico digestae, edited by Karl Eduard Zachariae von Lingenthal, II. Bibliotheca scriptorum Graecorum et Romanorum Teubneriana. Leipzig: Teubner, 1881.

Jansen, Robin M., and Kimberly J. Vrudny. *Visual Theology: Forming and Transforming the Community through the Arts*. Collegeville, MN: Liturgical Press, 2009.

Jedin, Hubert. *A History of the Council of Trent*. Translated by Ernest Graf. 2 vols. London: Thomas Nelson, 1957–61.

Jellicoe, Sidney. *Septuagint and Modern Study*. Winona Lake, IN: Eisenbrauns, 1989.

Jensen, Robin M. "The Offering of Isaac in Jewish and Christian Tradition." *Biblical Interpretation* 2 (1994): 85–110.

———. "The Dura Europos Synagogue, Early-Christian Art, and Religious Life in Dura Europos." In *Jews, Christians, and Polytheists in the Ancient Synagogue: Cultural Interaction during the Greek-Roman Period*, edited by Steven Fine. Baltimore Studies in the History of Judaism. New York: Routledge, 1999, 174–89.

———. "Early Christian Images and Exegesis." In *Picturing the Bible: The Earliest Christian Art*, edited Jeffrey Spier. New Haven: Yale University Press, 2007, 65–85.

Jerome: Biblia Sacra iuxta Vulgatam versionem, ed. Bonifatius Fischer. Stuttgart: Deutsche Bibelgesellschaft, 1983.

Jewett, Robert. *Romans: A Commentary*. Hermeneia. Minneapolis: Fortress, 2007.

Jobes, Karen H., and Moisés Silva. *Invitation to the Septuagint*. Grand Rapids, MI: Baker, 2000.

John Chrysostom. *Old Testament Homilies. vol. 3: Homilies on the Obscurity of the Old Testament and Homilies on Psalms*. Translated by Robert Charles Hill. Brookline, MA: Holy Cross Orthodox Press, 2003.

John of Damascus. *On the Divine Images: Three Apologies against Those who Attack the Divine Images*. Translated by D. Anderson. Crestwood, NY: St. Vladimir's Seminary Press, 1980.

———. *On Holy Images, Followed by Three Sermons on the Assumption*. Translated by Mary H. Allies. London: Thomas Baker, 1898.

———. *Three Treatises on the Divine Images*. Translation and Introduction by Andrew Louth. Crestwood, NY: St. Vladimir's Seminary Press, 2003.

Johnson, Maxwell E. "The Apostolic Tradition." In *The Oxford History of Christian Worship*, edited by Geoffrey Wainwright and Karen B. Westerfield Tucker. New York: Oxford University Press, 2006, 32–75.

Juel, Donald H. "Interpreting Israel's Scriptures in the New Testament." In *A History of Biblical Interpretation. vol. 1. The Ancient Period*, edited by Alan J. Hauser and Duane F. Watson. Grand Rapids, MI: Eerdmans, 2003, 283–303.

Kahle, Paul E., ed. *The Cairo Geniza*. Oxford: Blackwell, 1959.

Kallistos of Diokleia. "The Spirituality of Philokalia." *Sobornost* 13/1 (1991): 6–24.

Kaminsky, Joel S. *Corporate Responsibility in the Hebrew Bible*. Sheffield: Sheffield Academic Press, 1995.

Kelly, John Norman Davidson. *Early Christian Creeds*. London: Longman, 1972.

Kessler, Edward. "The Sacrifice of Isaac (the *Akedah*) in Christian and Jewish Tradition: Artistic Representations." In *Borders, Boundaries and the Bible*, edited by Martin O'Kane. Sheffield: Sheffield Academic Press, 2002, 74–98.

Klijn, Albertus Frederik Johannes, trans. and ed. "Baruch (Syriac Apocalypse of Baruch)." In *The Old Testament Pseudepigrapha. vol. 1: Apocalyptic Literature and Testaments*, edited James H. Charlesworth. New York: Doubleday, 1983, 615–52.

——, and G. J. Reinink, eds. *Patristic Evidence for Jewish-Christian Sects*. Leiden: Brill, 1973.

Konstantinou, Miltiadis. "Old Testament Canon and Text in the Greek-Speaking Orthodox Church." In *Text, Theology and Translation: Essays in Honor of Jan DeWard*, edited by S. Crisp and M. M. Jinbachian. London: United Bible Societies, 2004, 89–107.

Kraeling, C. H. *The Excavations of Dura-Europos: The Synagogue*. New Haven: Yale University Press, 1956.

Kugel, James L. *Traditions of the Bible: A Guide to the Bible As It Was at the Start of the Common Era*. Cambridge: Harvard University Press, 1998.

La Bible grecque d'Alexandrie. Traduction et annotation des livres de la Septante sous la direction de Marguerite Harl, Gilles Dorival et Olivier Munnich. Paris: Éditions du Cerf, 1986–.

Ladner, Gerhardt B. "The Concept of the Image in the Greek Fathers and the Byzantine Iconoclastic Controversy." *Dumbarton Oaks Papers* 7 (1953): 1–34.

Lamb, J. A. "The Place of the Bible in the Liturgy." In *The Cambridge History of the Bible. Volume 1. From the Beginnings to Jerome*, edited by P. R. Ackroyd and C. F. Evans. Cambridge: Cambridge University Press, 1970, 563–86.

Lamsa, George M. *The Holy Bible from Ancient Eastern Manuscripts Containing the Old and New Testaments Translated from the Peshitta, The Authorized Bible of the Church of the East*. Nashville: Holman Bible Publishers, 1957.

Lash, Ephrem. "Biblical Interpretation in Worship." In *The Cambridge Companion to Orthodox Christian Theology*, edited by Mary B. Cunningham and Elizabeth Theokritoff. Cambridge: Cambridge University Press, 2008, 35–48.

Lee, William. *The Inspiration of Holy Scripture: Its Nature and Proof. Eight Discourses Preached Before the University of Dublin*. New York: Robert Carter and Brothers, 1857.

Levenson, Jon D. *Sinai and Zion: An Entry into the Jewish Bible.* New York: Harper-Collins, 1985.

———. *The Death and Resurrection of the Beloved Son: The Transformation of Child Sacrifice in Judaism and Christianity.* New Haven: Yale University Press, 1993.

———. *The Hebrew Bible, the Old Testament and the Historical Criticism: Jews and Christians in Biblical Studies.* Louisville, KY: Westminster John Knox, 1993.

———. "Interpreting the Bible: Three Views." *First Things* 45 (August-September 1994): 42–44.

———. "Can Roman Catholicism Validate Jewish Biblical Interpretation?" *Studies in Christian-Jewish Relations* 1:1/19 (2005–6): 170–85.

———. *Inheriting Abraham: The Legacy of the Patriarch in Judaism, Christianity, and Islam.* Library of Jewish Ideas. Princeton and Oxford: Princeton University Press, 2012.

Levering, Matthew. *Jewish-Christian Dialogue and the Life of Wisdom: Engagements with the Theology of David Novak.* London: Continuum, 2010.

Levine, Amy-Jill, and Marc Z. Brettler, eds. *Jewish Annotated New Testament.* New York: Oxford University Press, 2011.

Lewis, Jack P. "Jamnia Revisited." In *The Canon Debate*, edited by Lee Martin McDonald and James A. Sanders. Peabody, MA: Hendrickson, 2002, 146–62.

Lienhard, Joseph T. *The Bible, the Church, and Authority: The Canon of the Christian Bible in History and Theology.* Collegeville, MN: Liturgical Press, 1995.

Lieu, Judith M. *Christian Identity in the Jewish and Graeco-Roman World.* New York: Oxford University Press, 2004.

Lim, Timothy. "The Defilement of the Hands as a Principle Determining the Holiness of Scriptures." *JTS* 61:2 (October 2010): 501–515.

Lossky, Vladimir. "Tradition and Traditions." In *In the Image and Likeness of God*, edited by J. H. Erickson and T. E. Bird, 141–68. Crestwood, NY: St. Vladimir's Seminary Press, 1974.

Louth, Andrew. *Discerning the Mystery: An Essay on the Nature of Theology.* New York: Oxford University Press, 1990.

———. "Typology." In *The Oxford Companion to Christian Thought*, edited by Adrian Hastings, Alistair Mason, and Hugh Pyper. New York: Oxford University Press, 2000, 727–29.

———. "Tradition and the Icon." *The Way* 44:4 (October 2005): 147–59.

———. "Inspiration of the Scriptures." *Sobornost* 31:1 (2009): 29–44.

Magdalino, Paul, and Robert Nelson, eds. *The Old Testament in Byzantium.* Dumbarton Oaks Byzantine Symposia and Colloquia. Washington, DC: Dumbarton Oaks Research Library and Collection, 2010.

Maguire, Henri. "The Art of Comparing in Byzantium." *The Art Bulletin* 70:1 (March 1988): 88–103.

Mango, Cyril, trans. and ed. *The Homilies of Photius.* Cambridge: Harvard University Press, 1958.

———. *The Art of the Byzantine Empire 312–1453: Sources and Documents*. The Medieval Academy Reprints for Teaching 16. Toronto: University of Toronto Press and the Medieval Academy of America, 1986.

Manoussakis, John Panteleimon. *God after Metaphysics: A Theological Aesthetic*. Indiana Series in Philosophy and Religion. Bloomington: Indiana University Press, 2007.

Marcos, Natalio Fernández. *The Septuagint in Context: Introduction to the Greek Versions of the Bible*. Translated by Wilfred G. E. Watson. Leiden: Brill, 2000.

Marcus, Joel. "Jewish Christianity." In *Cambridge History of Christianity. vol. 1: Origins to Constantine*, edited by Margaret M. Mitchell and Frances M. Young. Cambridge: Cambridge University Press, 2008, 87–102.

Martens, Peter W. *Origen and Scripture: The Contours of the Exegetical Life*. Oxford Early Christian Studies. Oxford: Oxford University Press, 2012.

Maximos Confessor. *Selected Writings*. Translated by George C. Berthold. New York: Paulist, 1985.

Maximos of Simonopetra. *The Art of Seeing: Paradox and Perception in Orthodox Iconography*. Brookline, MA: Holy Cross Orthodox Press, forthcoming.

Mays, James Luther. *Psalms*. Interpretation. Louisville, KY: Westminster John Knox Press, 1994.

McCann, J. Clinton. *Judges*. Interpretation. Louisville, KY: Westminster John Knox Press, 2002.

McClure, M. L., and C. L. Feltoe, trans. *The Pilgrimage of Etheria*. London: SPCK, 1919.

McDonald, James I. H. *Kerygma and Didache: The Articulation and Structure of the Earliest Christian Message*. Society for New Testament Studies. Monograph Series 37. Cambridge: Cambridge University Press, 1980.

McDonald, Lee Martin, and James A. Sanders, eds. *The Canon Debate*. Paebody, MA: Hendrickson, 2002.

McGuckin, John A. "*Recent Biblical Hermeneutics in Patristic Perspective: The Tradition of Orthodoxy*." In *Sacred Text and Interpretation: Perspectives in Orthodox Biblical Studies. Papers in Honor of Professor Savas Agourides*, edited by Theodore G. Stylianopoulos. Brookline, MA: Holy Cross Orthodox Press, 2006, 293–324.

———. *The Orthodox Church: An Introduction to its History, Doctrine, and Spiritual Culture*. Hoboken, NJ: Blackwell, 2008.

McKay, Gretchen Kreahling. "The Eastern Christian Exegetical Tradition of Daniel's Vision of the Ancient of Days." *Journal of Early Christian Studies* 7:1 (1999): 139–61.

McLay, R. Timothy. *The Use of the Septuagint in New Testament Research*. Grand Rapids, MI: Eerdmans, 2003.

Meade, David G. *Pseudonymity and Canon: An Investigation into the Relationship of Authorship and Authority in Jewish and Early Christian Tradition*. Grand Rapids, MI: Eerdmans, 1986.

Menken, Maarten J. J. *Matthew's Bible: The Old Testament Text of the Evangelist.* Bibliotheca Ephemeridum Theologicarum Lovaniensium 173. Louvain: Peeters, 2004.

Mercati, J. M. "Stephani Bostreni nova de sacris imaginibus fragmenta e libro deperdito *kata Ioudaiôn.*" *Theologische Quartalschrift* 77 (1895): 663–68.

Metal, Zelig. *The Samaritan Version of the Pentateuch in Jewish Sources.* Tel Aviv, 1979.

Metzger, Bruce Manning. "The Lucianic Recension of the Greek Bible." In *Chapters in the History of the New Testament Textual Criticism,* edited by Bruce Manning Metzger. New Testament Tools and Studies 4. Leiden: Brill, 1963, 1–41.

———, and Michael D. Coogan, eds. *The Oxford Companion to the Bible.* New York: Oxford University Press, 1993.

Meyendorff, John. *Byzantine Theology: Historical Trends and Doctrinal Themes.* New York: Fordham University Press, 1979.

Meyers, Eric M. "Were the Hasmoneans Really Aniconic?" *Images* 1:1 (2007): 24–25.

Miller, James. "The Prophetologion: The Old Testament of Byzantine Christianity?" In *The Old Testament in Byzantium,* edited by Paul Magdalino and Robert Nelson. Washington, DC: Dumbarton Oaks Research Library and Collection, 2010, 55–76.

Milson, David. *Art and Architecture of the Synagogue in Late Antique Palestine: In the Shadow of the Church.* Ancient Judaism and Early Christianity 65. Leiden: Brill, 2007.

Moberly. R. W. L. *The Bible, Theology, and Faith: A Study of Abraham and Jesus.* Cambridge: Cambridge University Press, 2004.

Monceaux, Paul. *Le manichéen Faustus de Milève: Restitution de ses Capitula.* Mémoires de l'Institut National de France. Académie des Inscriptions et Belles-Lettres 43. Paris, 1933.

Mourant John A., and William J. Collinge, trans. *Saint Augustine: Four Anti-Pelagian Writings.* The Fathers of the Church 86. Washington, DC: Catholic University of America Press, 1992.

Mouriki, Doula. "Icons from the 12th to the 15th Century." In *Sinai: Treasures of the Monastery of Saint Catherine,* edited by Konstantinos A. Manafis, Athens: Ekdotike Athenon, 1990, 102–124.

Mowinckel, Sigmund. *The Old Testament as Word of God.* New York: Abingdon, 1959.

Moyise, Steve. *The Old Testament in the New.* The Clark Approaches to Biblical Studies. New York: T. and T. Clark, 2004.

Müller, Mogens. *The First Bible of the Church: A Plea for the Septuagint.* JSOT Supplement Series 206. Copenhagen International Seminar 1. Sheffield: Sheffield Academic Press, 1996.

Murray, Robert. "Tradition and Sacred Texts." *International Journal of Systematic Theology* 6:1 (January 2004): 4–20.

Nassif, Bradley. "'Spiritual Exegesis' in the School of Antioch." In *New Perspectives on Historical Theology: Essays in Memory of John Meyendorff,* edited by Bradley Nassif. Grand Rapids, MI: Eerdmans, 1996, 343–77.

Negrov, Alexander I. *Biblical Interpretation in the Russian Orthodox Church: A Historical and Hermeneutical Perspective.* Tübingen: Mohr Siebeck, 2008.

Nicholas Cabasilas. *The Life in Christ.* Translated by Carmino J. De Catanzaro. Crestwood, NY: St. Vladimir's Seminary Press, 1974.

Nicodemus the Hagiorite, and Agapius the Monk. *The Rudder (Pedalion) of the Metaphorical Ship of the One Holy Catholic and Apostolic Church of the Orthodox Christians, or All the Sacred and Divine Canons.* Translated by Denver Cummings. Chicago: Orthodox Christian Educational Society, 1957.

O'Connor, Jerome M. *The Holy Land: An Oxford Archaeological Guide From Earliest Times to 1700.* Oxford Archaeological Guides. Oxford: Oxford University Press, 2008.

Oikonomos, Constantine. *Four Books on the LXX Interpretation of the Old Holy Scripture.* [In Greek.] Athens: P. B. Melahoure & F. Karamnine, 1844–49.

Oikonomos, Elias. "The Hebrew Language and the Greek Fathers." [In Greek.] *Bulletin of Biblical Studies* 13 NS (January-June 1994): 29–47.

Old Testament Greek (LXX) Text Codex Vaticanus, edited by Alan E. Brooke, Norman McLean, and Henry St. John Thackeray. Known as Thackeray's "Larger Cambridge Septuagint." Cambridge, 1906–1940.

Ouspensky, Leonid. *Theology of the Icon.* 2 vols. Crestwood, NY: St. Vladimir's Seminary Press, 1992.

Painchaud, Louis. "The Use of Scripture in Gnostic Literature." *Journal of Early Christian Studies* 4:2 (Summer 1996): 129–46.

Pannenberg, Wolfhart. *Systematic Theology.* Translated by Geoffrey W. Bromiley. 2 vols. Grand Rapids, MI: Eerdmans, 1991–94.

Pappas, Harry S. "Theodore of Mopsuestia's Commentary on Ps 44 (LXX): A Study of Exegesis and Christology." In *Sacred Text and Interpretation: Perspectives in Orthodox Biblical Studies,* edited by Theodore G. Stylianopoulos. Brookline, MA: Holy Cross Orthodox Press, 2006, 55–79.

Parkes, James. *The Conflict of the Church and the Synagogue: A Study in the Origins of Antisemitism.* Philadelphia: Jewish Publication Society, 1974.

Parry, K. "Theodore Studites and the Patriarch Nicephoros on Image-Making as a Christian Imperative." *Byzantion* 59 (1989): 164–83.

Parsenios, George. *Departure and Consolation: The Johannine Farewell Discourses in Light of Greco-Roman Literature.* Novum Testamentum Supplement 117. Leiden: Brill, 2005.

Pásztori-Kupán, István. *Theodoret of Cyrus.* The Early Church Fathers-University of Durham. New York: Routledge, 2006.

Pelikan, Jaroslav. *The Christian Tradition: A History of the Development of Doctrine.* Vol. 1, *The Emergence of the Catholic Tradition (100–600).* Chicago: University of Chicago Press, 1971.

——. *The Christian Tradition. Volume 2.* The Spirit of Eastern Christendom (600–1700). Chicago: University of Chicago Press, 1974.

Pentiuc, Eugen J. *Long-Suffering Love: A Commentary on Hosea with Patristic Annotations.* Brookline, MA: Holy Cross Orthodox Press, 2002. Reprinted 2005, 2008.

——. *Jesus the Messiah in the Hebrew Bible.* New York: Paulist, 2005.

——. "The Word *'almah* in Isaiah 7:14: A New Etymology." In *Bible et Terre Sainte. Mélanges Marcel Beaudry,* edited by José Enrique Aguilar Chiu et al. New York: Peter Lang Press, 2008, 129–36.

Perdue, Leo G. *Proverbs.* Interpretation. Louisville, KY: Westminster John Knox Press, 2000.

Perrot, Charles. "The Reading of the Bible in the Ancient Synagogue." In *Mikra: Text, Translation, Reading and Interpretation of the Hebrew Bible in Ancient Judaism and Early Christianity,* edited by M. J. Mulder. Minneapolis: Fortress, 1990, 137–59.

Pfandl, Gerhard. "Interpretations of the Kingdom of God in Daniel 2:44." *Andrews University Seminary Studies* 34:2 (Autumn 1996): 249–68.

Phayer, Michael. *The Catholic Church and the Holocaust, 1930–1965.* Bloomington, IN: Indiana University Press, 2000.

Phrantzoles, K. G. *Hosiou Ephraim tou Syrou erga.* In Greek. Thessalonica: To Perivoli tis Panagias, 1995.

Pietersma, Albert, and Benjamin G. Wright, eds. *A New English Translation of the Septuagint.* New York: Oxford University Press, 2007.

Poirier, John C. "Judaism, Christianity and the Hebrew Bible." *Journal of Ecumenical Studies* 43:4 (Fall 2008): 525–36.

Pontifical Biblical Commission. "The Interpretation of the Bible in the Church." *Origins* 23/29 (January 6, 1994): 498–528.

Popova, Olga. *Russian Illuminated Manuscripts.* Translated by K. Cook, V. Ivanov, and L. Sorokina. London: Thames and Hudson, 1984.

Porter, Stanley E., ed. *Hearing the Old Testament in the New Testament.* McMaster New Testament Studies. Grand Rapids, MI: Eerdmans, 2006.

Preus, Robert D. *The Inspiration of Scripture: A Study of the Seventeenth Century Lutheran Dogmaticians.* Edinburgh: Oliver and Boyd, 1955.

Prokurat, Michael. "Orthodox Interpretation of Scripture." In *The Bible in the Churches: How Various Christians Interpret the Scriptures,* edited by Kenneth Hagen. Milwaukee: Marquette University Press, 1994, 59–97.

Prophetologium, ed. Høeg, Carsten, Günter Zuntz, and S. Engberg. vol. 1: Monumenta Musicae Byzantinae: Lectionaria. Copenhagen: Munksgaard, 1939–81.

Propp, W. H. *Exodus 1–18: A New Translation with Introduction and Commentary.* The Anchor Yale Bible. New Haven: Yale University Press, 2008.

Rahlfs, Albert, ed. *Septuaginta, id est Vetus Testamentum Graece iuxta LXX interpretes.* 2 vols. Stuttgart, 1935.

Rajak, Tessa. *Translation and Survival: The Greek Bible of the Ancient Jewish Diaspora.* Oxford: Oxford University Press, 2009.

Rapp, Claudia. "Old Testament Models for Emperors in Early Byzantium." In *The Old Testament in Byzantium*, edited by Paul Magdalino and Robert Nelson. Washington, DC: Dumbarton Oaks Research Library and Collection, 2010, 175–98.

Ratzinger, Joseph. "The Feeling of Things, the Contemplation of Beauty." 2002 Message to Communion and Liberation. Rome, May 2, 2005, http://www.zenit.org/article-12907?l=english.

Ryan, Stephen D. "The Ancient Versions of Judith and the Place of the Septuagint in the Catholic Church." In *A Pious Seductress: Studies in the Book of Judith*, edited by Geza Xeravits. Deuterocanonical and Cognate Literature Studies 14. Berlin and New York: De Gruyter 2012, 1–21.

———. "The Word of God and the Textual Pluriformity of the Old Testament." Washington, DC: Dominican House of Studies, 2011.

Rentel, Alexander. "Byzantine and Slavic Orthodoxy." In *The Oxford History of Christian Worship*, edited by Geoffrey Wainwright and Karen B. Westerfield Tucker/ New York: Oxford University Press, 2006, 254–306.

Ruether, Rosemary Radford. *Faith and Fratricide: The Theological Roots of Anti-Semitism.* Eugene, OR: Wipf & Stock Publishers, 1996.

Robinson, Henry Wheeler. *Corporate Personality in Ancient Israel.* Edinburgh: T. and T. Clark, 1981.

Roddy, Nicolae. "And the Blue Became Red and Dwelt Among Us: Mapping Boundaries of Meaning in Eastern Orthodox Iconography." *Journal of Religion and Society Supplement* 8 (2012): 133–44.

Rogerson, J. W. "History of Interpretation." In *ABD*, 3:424–33.

Rouwhorst, Gerard. "The Roots of the Early Christian Eucharist: Jewish Blessings or Hellenistic Symposia." In *Jewish and Christian Liturgy and Worship: New Insights into Its History and Interaction*, edited by Albert Gerhards and Clemens Leonhard. Jewish and Christian Perspectives Series 15. Leiden: Brill, 2007, 295–308.

Russell, Norman. *Cyril of Alexandria.* The Early Church Fathers. University of Durham. New York: Routledge, 2000.

———. *The Doctrine of Deification in the Greek Patristic Tradition.* Oxford Early Christian Studies. Oxford: Oxford University Press, 2006.

Sadaqa, Avraham, and Ratson Sadaqa, eds. *Jewish and Samaritan Version of the Pentateuch—With Particular Stress on the Differences between Both Texts.* Tel Aviv: A. and R. Sadaqa, 1964.

Sahas, Daniel J. *Icon and Logos. The Sources of Eighth-Century Iconoclasm.* Toronto: University of Toronto Press, 1986.

Salvesen, Alison. *Symmachus in the Pentateuch.* JSS Monograph 15. Manchester: University of Manchester Press, 1991.

Sawyer, J. F. A. *The Fifth Gospel: Isaiah in the History of Christianity.* Cambridge: Cambridge University Press, 1996.

Scanlin, Harold P. "The Old Testament Canon in the Orthodox Churches." In *New Perspectives on Historical Theology: Essays in Memory of John Meyendorff,* edited by Bradley Nassif. Grand Rapids, MI: Eerdmans, 1996, 300–312.

Schäfer, Peter. "Die sogenannte Synode von Jabne. Zur Trennung von Juden und Christen im ersten/zweiten Jh. n. Chr." *Judaica* 31 (1975): 54–64.

Schenker, Adrian. *The Earliest Text of the Hebrew Bible: The Relationship Between the Masoretic Text and the Hebrew Base of the Septuagint Reconsidered.* Society of Biblical Literature Septuagint and Cognate Studies 52. Atlanta: Scholars Press, 2003.

——. "Septuaginta und christliche Bibel." *Theologische Revue* 91 (1995): 459–64.

——. "L'Ecriture sainte subsiste en plusieurs forms canoniques simultanées." In *L'interpretazione della Bibbia nella Chiesa. Atti del Simposio promosso dalla Congregazione per la Dottrina della Fede,* Rome, September 1999. Atti e Documenti 11. Città del Vaticano: Libreria Editrice Vaticana, 2001, 178–86.

Schiffman, Lawrence H. "The Early History of Public Reading of the Torah." In *Jews, Christians, and Polytheists in the Ancient Synagogue: Cultural Interaction during the Greco-Roman Period,* edited by Steven Fine. Baltimore Studies in the History of Judaism. New York: Routledge, 1999, 38–49.

Schmemann, Alexander. *Great Lent: Journey to Pascha.* Crestwood, NY: St. Vladimir's Seminary Press, 1974.

Scott, S. P., trans. and ed. *Corpus Juris Civilis: The Civil Law.* 17 vols. Cincinnati: The Central Trust Company, 1932.

Sellew, Philip. "Achilles or Christ? Porphyry and Didymus in Debate over Allegorical Interpretation." *HTR* 82:1 (January 1989): 79–100.

Septuaginta. Vetus Testamentum Graecum Auctoritate Academiae Scientiarum Gottingensis editum. 24 vols. Göttingen: Vandenhoeck & Ruprecht, 1931–2006.

Sperber, Alexander, ed. *The Bible in Aramaic Based on Old Manuscripts and Printed Texts.* 4 vols. Leiden: Brill 1959–68.

Ševčenko, Nancy P. "Virgin Eleousa." In *ODB,* 3:2171.

——. "Art and Liturgy in the Later Byzantine Empire." In *The Cambridge History of Christianity. Volume 5. Eastern Christianity,* edited by Michael Angold. Cambridge: Cambridge University Press, 2006, 127–53.

——. "The Service of the Virgin's Lament Revisited." In *The Cult of the Mother of God in Byzantium. Text and Images,* edited by Leslie Brubaker and Mary B. Cunningham. Birmingham Byzantine and Ottoman Studies. Aldershot: Ashgate, 2011, 247–62.

——, and Alexander Kazhdan. "Maphorion." In *ODB,* 2:1294.

Sheridan, Mark. *Genesis 12–50.* Ancient Christian Commentary on Scripture Old Testament 2. Downers Grove, IL: InterVarsity, 2002.

Shutt, R. J. H. "Letter of Aristeas." In *The Old Testament Pseudepigrapha*, edited by James H. Charlesworth. 2 vols. New York: Doubleday, 1985, 2:7–34.

Siegman, Edward F. "The Stone Hewn from the Mountain (Daniel 2)." *CBQ* 18 (1956): 364–79.

Simonetti, Manlio. *Biblical Interpretation in the Early Church: An Historical Introduction to Patristic Exegesis*. Edinburgh: T. and T. Clark, 1994.

——, ed. *Matthew 1–13*. Ancient Christian Commentary on Scripture New Testament 1a. Downers Grove, IL: InterVarsity, 2002.

——. "Theodore of Mopsuestia." In *Handbook of Patristic Exegesis. The Bible in Ancient Christianity*, edited by Charles Kannengiesser. Leiden: Brill, 2006, 799–828.

Soulen, R. Kendall. *The God of Israel and Christian Theology*. Minneapolis: Fortress, 1996.

Springer, A. J. "Proof of Identification: Patristic and Rabbinic Exegesis of the Cain and Abel Narrative." In *Papers Presented at the Fourteenth International Conference on Patristic Studies Held in Oxford 2003. Historica, Biblica, Ascetica et Hagiographica*, edited by F. Young, M. Edwards, and P. Parvis. Louvain: Peeters, 2006, 259–72.

Staniloae, Dumitru. "The Orthodox Conception of Tradition and the Development of Doctrine." *Sobornost* 5:9 (1969): 625–62.

——. *Theology and the Church*. Crestwood, NY: St. Vladimir's Seminary Press, 1997.

Stathis, Gregorios. *Morphes kai Morphes tēs Psaltikēs Technēs, ētoi Melopoiia-Morphologia tēs Byzantinēs Mousikēs, Idryma Byzantinēs Mousikologias, Latreiolo-gēmata 5*. In Greek. Athens, 2011.

Stendahl, Krister. "Qumran and Supersessionism—and the Road not Taken." *The Princeton Seminary Bulletin* 19:2 (July 1998): 134–42.

St. Ephrem the Syrian. *Selected Prose Works*. Translated by Edward G. Matthews, Kathleen McVey, and Joseph P. Amar. The Fathers of the Church. Washington, DC: The Catholic University of America Press, 1994.

St. John Chrysostom. *On Wealth and Poverty*. Popular Patristic Series. Crestwood, NY: St. Vladimir's Seminary Press, 1999.

Stone, Michael Edward. *Fourth Ezra: A Commentary on the Book of Fourth Ezra*. Hermeneia. Minneapolis: Fortress, 1990.

Stuhlhofer, Franz. *Der Gebrauch der Bibel von Jesus bis Eusebius: Eine statistische Untersuchung zur Kanongeschichte*. Monographien und Studienbücher 335. Wuppertal: Brockhaus, 1988.

Stylianopoulos, Theodore G. *Justin Martyr and the Mosaic Law*. Society of Biblical Literature Dissertation Series 20. Missoula, MT: Scholars Press, 1975.

——. "Biblical Authority in Eastern Orthodoxy." In *Anchor Bible Dictionary*, edited by Daniel Noel Freedman. New York: Doubleday, 1992, 5:1021–23.

——. *The New Testament: An Orthodox Perspective. Volume One: Scripture, Tradition, Hermeneutics*. Brookline, MA: Holy Cross Orthodox Press, 2002.

——. "Perspectives in Orthodox Biblical Interpretation." *GOTR* 47: 1–4 (2002): 327–38.

——. "Scripture and Tradition in the Church." In *The Cambridge Companion to Orthodox Christian Theology*, edited by Mary M. Cunningham and Elizabeth Theokritoff. Cambridge: Cambridge University Press, 2009, 21–34.

——. "The Making of the New Testament." Holy Cross Greek Orthodox School of Theology, Brookline, MA, 2012.

Sundberg, Albert C. Jr. *The Old Testament of the Early Church*. HTS 20. Cambridge: Harvard University Press, 1964.

Swete, Henri Barclay. *An Introduction to the Old Testament in Greek*. Cambridge: Cambridge University Press, 1914. Reprint Peabody, MA: Hendrickson, 1989.

Taft, Robert F. *Liturgy in Byzantium and Beyond*. Aldershot: Variorum, 1995.

——. "Orthodox Liturgical Theology and Georges Florovsky's Return to the Fathers: Alexander Schmemann, St. Symeon of Thessalonika, or Both?" *GOTR* 53: 1–4 (2008): 1–29.

——, and Annemarie Weyl Carr. "Dormition." In *The Oxford Dictionary of Byzantium*, edited by Alexander P. Kazdhan, 1:651–53. New York: Oxford University Press, 1991.

Tantlevskij, Igor R. "Ebionites." In *Encyclopedia of the Dead Sea Scrolls*, edited by Lawrence H. Schiffman and James C. VanderKam. New York: Oxford University Press, 2000, 1:225–26.

Tkacz, Brown Catherine. "Commendatio animae." In *ODB*, 1:488.

The Acts and Decrees of the Synod of Jerusalem Sometimes Called The Council of Bethlehem Holden Under Dositheus, Patriarch of Jerusalem in 1672. Translated from Greek and with notes by J. N. W. B. Robertson. London: Thomas Baker, 1899.

The Ante-Nicene Fathers. Edited by Alexander Roberts and James Donaldson. 1885–87. 10 vols. Reprinted Peabody, MA: Hendrickson, 1994.

The Complete Menaion. Translated from Greek. 12 vols. Brookline, MA: The Holy Transfiguration Monastery, 2005.

The Nicene and Post-Nicene Fathers. Edited by Philip Schaff et al. 2 series. 1987–94. 14 vols. Reprinted Peabody, MA: Hendrickson, 1994.

The Proof of the Gospel being the Demonstratio Evangelica of Eusebius of Caesarea. Translated by W. J. Ferrar. Translations of Christian Literature. Series I. Greek Texts. London: SPCK, 1920.

Theodore of Mopsuestia. *Commentary on the Twelve Prophets*. Translated by Robert Charles Hill. The Fathers of the Church. Washington, DC: The Catholic University of America Press, 1984.

Theodore the Stoudite. *The Ordering of Holiness*. Translated by Roman Cholij. Oxford Theological Monographs. Oxford: Oxford University Press, 2009.

Theodoret of Cyrus. *Commentary on the Psalms, 1–72*. Translated by Robert Charles Hill. The Fathers of the Church. Washington, DC: The Catholic University of America Press, 2000.

——. *Commentary on the Psalms, 73–150*. Translated by Robert Charles Hill. The Fathers of the Church. Washington, DC: The Catholic University of America Press, 2001.

Thiselton, Anthony. "Biblical Studies and Theoretical Hermeneutics." In *The Cambridge Companion to Biblical Interpretation*, edited by John Barton, 95–113. Cambridge Companions to Religion. Cambridge: Cambridge University Press, 1998.

Thomassen, Einar. *The Spiritual Seed: The Church of the Valentinians*. Nag Hammadi and Manichaean Studies. Leiden: Brill, 2005.

Torrance, Thomas F. *Divine Meaning: Studies in Patristic Hermeneutics*. Edinburgh: T. and T. Clark, 1995.

Tov, Emanuel. "Lucian and Proto-Lucian: Toward a New Solution of the Problem." *RB* (1972): 101–113.

——. "The Nature of the Large-Scale Differences between the LXX and MT S T V, Compared with Similar Evidence in Other Sources." In *The Earliest Text of the Hebrew Bible: The Relationship Between the Masoretic Text and the Hebrew Base of the Septuagint Reconsidered*, edited by Adrian Schenker. Society of Biblical Literature Septuagint and Cognate Studies 52. Atlanta: Scholars Press, 2003, 121–44.

——. *Textual Criticism of the Hebrew Bible*. Leiden: Brill, 2005.

——. *Hebrew Bible, Greek Bible, and Qumran: Collected Essays*. Texts and Studies in Ancient Judaism 121. Tübingen: Mohr Siebeck, 2008.

——. "The Septuagint between Judaism and Christianity." In *Die Septuaginta und das frühe Christentum: The Septuagint and Christian Origin*, edited by Thomas S. Caulley and Hermann Lichtenberger. Tübingen: Mohr Siebeck, 2011, 3–25.

——, R. A. Kraft, and P. J. Parsons, eds. *The Greek Minor Prophets Scroll from Nahal Hever (8HevXIIgr): The Seyial Collection I*. Discoveries in the Judaean Desert 8. Oxford: Clarendon, 1990.

Trakatellis, Demetrios C. *The Pre-Existence of Christ in Justin Martyr: An Exegetical Study with Reference to the Humiliation and Exaltation Christology*. Harvard Theological Review Series. Harvard Dissertations in Religion 6. Missoula, MT: Scholars Press, 1976.

——. "Theodoret's Commentary on Isaiah: A Synthesis of Exegetical Traditions." In *New Perspectives on Historical Theology: Essays in Memory of John Meyendorff*, edited by Bradley Nassif. Grand Rapids, MI: Eerdmans, 1996, 313–42.

Ulrich, Eugene. "The Notion and Definition of Canon." In *The Canon Debate*, edited by Lee Martin McDonald and James A. Sanders. Peabody, MA: Hendrickson, 2002, 21–35.

Van Buren, Paul Matthews. *According to the Scriptures: The Origins of the Gospel and of the Church's Old Testament*. Grand Rapids, MI: Eerdmans, 1998.

Van Woerden, I. "The Iconography of the Sacrifice of Abraham." *Vigiliae Christianae* 15 (1961): 214–55.

Vassiliadis, Petros. "Orthodoxy and Ecumenism." In *Eucharist and Witness. Orthodox Perspectives on the Unity and Mission of the Church*, edited by WCC, 7–27. Geneva: World Council of Churches Publications/Brookline, MA: Holy Cross Orthodox Press, 1998.

———. "Canon and Authority of Scripture: An Orthodox Hermeneutical Perspective." In *Das Alte Testament als christliche Bibel in orthodoxer und westlicher Sicht*, edited by Ivan Z. Dimitrov, James D. G. Dunn, Ulrich Luz, and Karl-Wilhelm Niebuhr. Wissenschaftliche Untersuchungen zum Neuen Testament 174. Tübingen: Mohr Siebeck, 2004, 259–76.

Venard, Olivier-Thomas. "'La Bible en ses traditions,' the New Project of Ecole biblique et archéologique française de Jerusalem Presented as a 'Fourth Generation' Enterprise." *Nova et Vetera* 4 (2006): 142–58.

Von Compenhausen, Hans. *The Formation of the Christian Bible*. Philadelphia: Fortress. 1972.

Vrame, Anton C. *The Educating Icon: Teaching Wisdom and Holiness in the Orthodox Way*. Brookline, MA: Holy Cross Orthodox Press, 1999.

Walter, Christopher. "Christological Themes in the Byzantine Marginal Psalters from the Ninth to the Eleventh Century." *Revue des études byzantines* 44 (1986): 269–88.

———. "'Latter-Day' Saints and the Image of Christ in the Ninth-Century Byzantine Marginal Psalters." *Revue des études byzantines*, 45 (1987): 205–222.

Ware, Kallistos (Timothy). *The Orthodox Church*. Baltimore, MD: Penguin Books, 1963.

———. "Toward the Great Council?" *Eastern Churches Review* 4 (1972): 162–68.

———. "The Unity of Scripture and Tradition; An Orthodox Approach." In *What Is It That the Scripture Says? Essays in Biblical Interpretation, Translation and Reception. In Honor of Henry Wansbrough OSB*, edited by Philip McCosker. New York: T. and T. Clark, 2007, 231–45.

———, and Colin Davey, eds. *Anglican-Orthodox Dialogue: The Moscow Statement Agreed by the Anglican-Orthodox Joint Doctrinal Commission, 1976*. London: SPCK, 1977.

Watts, J. D. W. *Isaiah 1–33*. Word Biblical Commentary 24. Nashville, TN: Thomas Nelson, 1985.

Weitzmann, Kurt. "The Study of Byzantine Book Illumination: Past, Present, and Future." In *The Place of Book Illumination in Byzantine Art*, edited by Kurt Weitzmann, William C. Loerke, Ernst Kitzinger, and Hugo Buchthal. Princeton: Princeton University Press, 1975, 1–60.

———, and Herbert L. Kessler. *The Frescoes of the Dura Synagogue and Christian Art*. Washington, DC: Dumbarton Oaks Research Library and Collection, 1990.

Wendland, Paul. *Aristae Epistula. Ad Philocratem Epistula cum ceteris de origine versionis 70 interpretum testimoniis*. Leipzig: Teubner, 1900.

Wharton, Annabel Jane. "Fresco Technique." In *ODB*, 2:805–806.

Whiston, William, trans. *The Works of Josepus*. Complete and Unbridged. Peabody, MA: Hendrickson, 1987.

Wilken, Robert Louis. *Church's Bible*. Grand Rapids, MI: Eerdmans, 2003.

Williams, Daniel H. *Tradition, Scripture, and Interpretation: A Sourcebook of the Ancient Church*. Grand Rapids, MI: Baker Academic, 2006.

Williams, Frank, trans. *The Panarion of Epiphanius of Salamis: Book 1 (Sects 1–46)*. Nag Hammadi and Manichaean Studies 63. Leiden: Brill, 2009.

Williams, Jacqueline. *Biblical Interpretation in the Gnostic Gospel of Truth from Nag Hammadi*. SBL Dissertation Series 79. Atlanta: Scholars Press, 1988.

Williamson, Peter S. "Principles of Catholic Interpretation." *CBQ* 65 (2003): 327–49.

Wilson, Robert McL. "The Gnostics and the Old Testament." In *Proceedings of the International Colloquium on Gnosticism. Stockholm, August 20–25, 1973*, edited by G. Widengren. Stockholm: Almqvist and Wiksell, 1977, 164–68.

Wintermute, Orval S. "A Study of Gnostic Exegesis of the Old Testament." In *The Use of the Old Testament in the New and Other Essays. Studies in Honor of William F. Stinespring*, edited by J. M. Efird. Durham, NC: Duke University Press, 1972, 241–70.

Woollcombe, K. J. "The Biblical Origins and Patristic Development of Typology." In *Essays on Typology*, edited by G. W. H. Lampe and K. J. Woollcombe. Studies in Biblical Theology 22. London: SCM, 1957, 39–75.

Woude, Adam S. van der. "Pluriformity and Uniformity: Reflections on the Transmission of the Text of the Old Testament." In *Sacred History and Sacred Texts in Early Judaism: A Symposium in Honour of A.S. van der Woude*, edited by J. N. Bremmer and F. Garcia Martinez. Contributions to Biblical Exegesis and Theology 5. Kampen: Kok Pharos, 1992, 151–69.

Würthwein, Ernst. *The Text of the Old Testament: An Introduction to the Biblia Hebraica*. Translated by Erroll F. Rhodes. Grand Rapids, MI: Eerdmans, 1995.

Yonge, Charles Duke, trans. *The Works of Philo*. Complete and Unabridged. Peabody, MA: Hendrickson, 1993.

Young, Frances M. *Biblical Exegesis and the Formation of Christian Culture*. Cambridge: Cambridge University Press, 1997.

——. "Alexandrian and Antiochene Exegesis." In *History of Biblical Interpretation. vol. 1. The Ancient Period*, edited by A. J. Hauser and D. F. Watson. Grand Rapids, MI: Eerdmans, 2003, 334–54.

——. "Prelude: Jesus Christ, Foundation of Christianity." In *Cambridge History of Christianity. Volume 1: Origins to Constantine*, edited by Margaret M. Mitchell and Frances M. Young. Cambridge: Cambridge University Press, 2008, 1–34.

Zaharopoulos, Dimitri Z. "Theodore of Mopsuestia: Views on Prophetic Inspiration." *GOTR* 23: 1 (1978): 42–52.

——. *Theodore of Mopsuestia on the Bible: A Study of His Old Testament Exegesis.* *Theological Inquiries.* New York: Paulist, 1989.

Zenkovsky, S. A., ed. *Medieval Russia's Epics, Chronicles, and Tales.* New York: New American Library, 1974.

Zimmerli, Walther. *Ezekiel: A Commentary on the Book of the Prophet Ezekiel. vol. 2.* Translated by James D. Martin. Hermeneia. Philadelphia: Fortress, 1983.

Zizioulas, John D. *Being as Communion.* Contemporary Greek Theologians 4. Crestwood, NY: St. Vladimir's Seminary Press, 1985.

Index

CPSIA information can be obtained at www.ICGtesting.com
Printed in the USA
BVOW02s0400160914

366976BV00001B/2/P